This volume contains two major papers prepared for the Bank of England's Tercentenary Symposium in June 1994. The first, by Professors Capie and Goodhart and Dr Schnadt, provides an authoritative and comprehensive account of the evolution of central banking in the major economies, tracing the development of both the monetary and financial stability concerns of central banks; explaining their institutional characteristics; and introducing some of the strands in academic thinking. It includes individual sections on the evolution and constitutional positions of thirty-one central banks from around the world, which will make it a valuable reference work in its own right. The second paper, by Professor Fischer, explores the major policy dilemmas now facing central bankers: the extent to which there is a short-term trade-off between inflation and growth; the choice of inflation targets; and the choice of operating procedures. Important contributions by leading central bankers from around the world, and the related Per Jacobsen lecture by Professor Lamfalussy, are also included in the volume, which will be essential reading for anyone interested in central banking or in the conduct of monetary policy.

The Future of Central Banking

The Future of Central Banking

The Tercentenary Symposium of the Bank of England

Forrest Capie
Charles Goodhart
Stanley Fischer
Norbert Schnadt

CAMBRIDGE
UNIVERSITY PRESS

Published by the Press Syndicate of the University of Cambridge
The Pitt Building, Trumpington Street, Cambridge CB2 1RP
40 West 20th Street, New York, NY 10011–4211, USA
10 Stamford Road, Oakleigh, Melbourne 3166, Australia

First published 1994

Printed in Great Britain at the University Press, Cambridge

A catalogue record for this book is available from the British Library

Library of Congress cataloguing in publication data applied for

ISBN 0 521 496 349 hardback

CE

Contents

Figures

Tables

Foreword

This volume records one of the major events staged to mark the Tercentenary of the Bank of England – a Symposium on the Future of Central Banking, held at the Barbican Centre on 9 June 1994, and involving more than 130 Governors or former Governors from central banks around the world. It was, as the Prime Minister put it in his speech of welcome, 'the largest gathering of central bankers ever to meet completely free of the restraining influence of finance ministers'.

On the previous day, most of those present at the Symposium had sat in the Barbican Hall, listening to Alexandre Lamfalussy, President of the European Monetary Institute, giving his Per Jacobbson lecture on 'Central Banking in Transition'. This set the scene very usefully for our discussions at the Symposium, and although not strictly part of our proceedings, Professor Lamfalussy's lecture is included in this volume.

For the Symposium itself, the Bank had commissioned two major papers, one from Professor Charles Goodhart, of the London School of Economics, on 'The Development of Central Banking'; and another from Professor Stanley Fischer, then at MIT but more recently Deputy Managing Director of the IMF, on 'Modern Central Banking'. Our original thought had been to study central banking through time and then cross-sectionally, but in practice both authors deviated rather helpfully from their briefs. Charles Goodhart, in particular, together with his co-authors Forrest Capie and Norbert Schnadt, produced a major reference work comparing the origins and objectives of thirty-two central banks around the world. This is to be found in the appendices to his paper.

The discussants in each session – Alan Greenspan, Jean-Claude Trichet, Yasushi Mieno, Donald Brash, Josef Tosovsky and Miguel Mancera – all succeeded both in illuminating the issues raised by the authors and in giving fascinating insights into their own domestic priorities.

Both papers engendered a lively debate, covering the intermediate objectives of policy, the area of central bank autonomy, and in particular the ways in which monetary policy decisions could be explained and justified to the public at large. This latter debate was prompted by the Prime Minister's suggestion, at the end of his speech, that the Symposium look at ways in which the 'consensus for stability' – shared by all the central bankers present – could be reinforced and deepened, 'so that it is shared by all – not only those who take monetary decisions, but by those who are affected by them'. One aspect of this debate, very topical in the UK, was the question of disclosure of monetary policy deliberations through, for example, the publication of minutes.

Some of the most interesting contributions came from the representatives of emerging countries, and from those in transition to a market economy, where the consensus for stability was often growing in a harsher climate. Their experience was plainly relevant to the pace at which central banks sought to restore monetary stability after an inflationary period or shock.

The final session, involving four legendary former central bank Governors, was entitled 'The philosophy of central banking' and proved one of the most enjoyable and instructive. New readers might prefer to start there, for the discussion neatly encapsulated the themes of the day, set them in an historical context, and above all cut through the detail and made central banking sound as simple as in reality it should be.

Those interested in central bankers as a class will see from the panel sessions that we speak as well as write in paragraphs! But I commend this book to all with an interest in monetary and political economics; and I would like to thank all those who contributed to the immense success of the Symposium.

EDDIE GEORGE, GOVERNOR OF THE BANK OF ENGLAND
September 1994

1 The development of central banking

Forrest Capie, Charles Goodhart, Norbert Schnadt[1]

1.1 Introduction

On the occasion of the 300th anniversary of the Bank of England there is a natural tendency to look back at the historical record of central banks, to examine their development to the present time, and, more daringly, to speculate about their future. Although it is hard to depart from a chronologically ordered narrative (particularly since two of the authors are economic historians), we have tried to structure our paper by concentrating on the key functions undertaken by the central bank.

The main objective of central banks, over the centuries, has been the maintenance of the (internal and external) value of the currency, and we, therefore, turn in section 1.2 to an historical account of central bank macroeconomic policy. While the maintenance of the value of the currency has, historically, almost always been achieved via the same instrument, varying the central bank's discount rate, this objective has not always meant the same thing. Under the classical gold standard the objective was cast in terms of metal convertibility: that is, the value of central bank notes was expressed in terms of their metal (gold) 'content', which central banks attempted to maintain at stated levels over time. The purchasing power of currency relative to goods in general (i.e. to a price index) was thus only indirectly an objective of central banks, with gold acting as the true nominal anchor. With the gradual erosion of the gold standard throughout the first half of the twentieth century, and its replacement everywhere by a pure fiat

[1] We should like to thank the Bank of England for the opportunity to prepare this paper, and Mervyn King in particular for encouragement and support. Naturally, the views expressed in this paper are those of the authors and not necessarily those of the Bank of England.

We are heavily indebted to the many central bank officials who provided valuable research material and references used in the compilation of the appendices, as well as useful comments. Furthermore, Pablo Martin Acena, Michael Bordo, Kevin Dowd, Milton Friedman, Charles Kindleberger, David Laidler, Dieter Lindenlaub, Morris Perlman, Alain Plessis, Leslie Pressnell, Angela Redish, Jaime Reis, Richard Sylla, Gianni Toniolo, Eugene White, Geoffrey Wood and Dieter Ziegler all provided comments and/or suggestions for which we are very grateful. The authors, however, are responsible for any errors. Finally, research assistance by Devaiah Ballachandra, Olga Christodoulaki and Niral Maru is gratefully acknowledged.

standard, the objective of central bank policy has now been recast in terms of price stability. The value of central bank notes has come to be understood as the inverse of the price level, the price of a particular bundle of goods, and monetary authorities try to achieve (often implicit) price level or inflation targets.

To argue, therefore, that price stability has always been the main aim of central banks, is not strictly true. Recent academic interest in a so-called 'new monetary economics' (see Cowen and Kroszner 1994), which emphasises the regulatory underpinnings of monetary regimes, has uncovered a long line of economists who have criticised the conventional gold standard for failing to stabilise the price level. They include Jevons who favoured supplementing gold with indexation (as did Marshall), and both Marshall and Edgeworth who advocated symetallism. Walras inclined to bimetallism, while Francis Walker was a convinced bimetallist. Wicksell favoured managed paper money on an international basis. Laidler argues convincingly that all the good monetary economists of the late nineteenth century thought that something better than the gold standard could be achieved, and that the defenders of the gold standard were a lesser breed – such as Price and Giffen (Laidler 1991). Irving Fisher proposed in 1911 to replace the gold standard by a 'compensated dollar' standard under which the gold-currency price would be varied to offset fluctuations in the price level. It is noteworthy that Fisher's proposal was, in part, motivated by developments in 'the calculation of an official index number of prices' (1912, p. 498). Whilst it is not our intention to examine this or any other specific proposal, we mention it here to reinforce the point that the policy objective of the early central banks was not, and was not perceived as, the preservation of price stability in the modern sense. In the absence of fluctuations in the value of gold relative to goods, however, the maintenance of a fixed parity between currency and gold clearly amounted to the same thing. Moreover, comparisons between the classical gold standard period (1873–1913) and subsequent monetary regimes (see Bordo 1993) indicate that, whilst none of them actually delivered price stability, the former system clearly outperformed all others in this respect.

There has been an inherent tension throughout the history of central banks between their desire for maintaining the value of their currency and their function as banker to the (central) government. Central banks have almost invariably been established by an Act of government (e.g. a government charter), and have been designated as banker to the government. Governments have a natural preference for cheap finance from their own bank, and, particularly when the existence of the state is threatened, notably by war, they have both the power and the incentive to force the central bank to give priority to their immediate needs. We discuss the shifting relationships between the central bank and its government in section 1.3.

Besides the government, the other main clients of the central bank have been the commercial banks. As described in section 1.2, prior to the latter part of the nineteenth century, central banks were generally expected to carry out a commercial banking function; in some cases, in the European countries when they were first established, they offered the only sources of commercial banking services in that country (e.g. Scandinavia), and for a longer period they were often the most important and largest commercial bank in their country. Consequently the early relationships between central banks and commercial banks were often ones of business rivalry and competition. This adversarial relationship was resolved around the early twentieth century in most cases, with a few exceptions (e.g. Australia), by a largely uncodified concordat, whereby, in return for the central bank's withdrawal from commercial banking, the commercial banks voluntarily accepted the central bank's leadership – even by such informal mechanisms as the Governor's eyebrows. We chart the changing pattern of this relationship, including the expanding function of central banks as regulators and supervisors of the banking system in section 1.4.

Institutions and their functions do not develop in a vacuum. They are profoundly influenced by the development of ideas, theories and perceptions about their proper role. In section 1.5 we look at two of the main intellectual currents which have influenced the path of central banking, with a natural emphasis, given our background, on the analysis and arguments of Anglo-Saxon economists. Indeed, our Anglo-Saxon affinities may have coloured our selection of examples, references and arguments throughout. Fortunately for our purposes, two main themes in these debates occur regularly, although in somewhat different guises, throughout our history. The first of these battles is that between the proponents of rules and the adherents of discretion; this controversy has erupted in two main periods of intellectual ferment, initially in the first half of the nineteenth century, pitting Bullionists against Anti-bullionists and Currency against the Banking Schools, and then later in the second half of the twentieth century, with Monetarists versus Keynesians.

The second of these debates is, perhaps, even more fundamental, since it raises the question of whether the very existence of a central bank is either necessary or desirable. The 'free banking' school has argued that it is not. Again, this issue has had several differing aspects over the course of history. The debate goes back to that between the Cartalists, who argued that the issue and control of money was a natural and central aspect of sovereignty, and the Metallists, who argued that the value of money depended on its (convertibility into a given) metallic content. In so far as the State pre-empts this issue by establishing legal tender fiat money it will need an institution to manage the value of that money, which institution will be, de facto, a central bank.

But even should the monetary system revert to being one in which commercial bank liabilities are convertible into some good, or asset, of inherent, real value – as Metallists would advocate – there still remains a second issue, which is whether a fractional-reserve banking system, of the kind that we have had, would, or would not be, inherently stable in the absence of a central bank to direct and protect it.

In other words, would a 'free banking' system exhibit stability without a central bank? This, of course, goes to the heart of the question of whether a central bank is necessary and desirable. Some may think that we should have put such a fundamental question at the start, rather than at the end, of this paper, but we have two reasons for our ordering. First, our aim has been to concentrate on the positive aspects of what central banks actually have done over the course of the last two hundred years, rather than the more normative, and less historical, issue of whether they are a 'good thing'. Second, one of us did try specifically to cover this subject in an earlier book (Goodhart 1988).

Perhaps, however, the main contribution will not be the text but the Appendices (below, pp. 113–231) which bring together the historical details of the major central banks within a common framework. We hope that these will prove a definitive, and easily accessible, source of comparable, factual data on the history of central banks around the world.

1.2   The macro-policy objectives of central banks

1.2.1   Developments in Europe (1668–1873)

The earlier-established central banks were founded as special commercial banks, rather than as the non-profit-maximising, public-sector institutions into which they developed much later. They were, however, in each case special, because they received a charter from government, were made the government's (main) banker and in several cases received certain (monopolistic) privileges, especially with respect to note issue.[2] In some countries, notably in Sweden, Norway, Finland, Denmark, the Netherlands and Austro-Hungary, it was hardly necessary to provide them with special monopolistic privileges, because the government's chartered bank was effectively the only commercial bank in existence when first founded. One

---

[2] Examples include the Bank of England, Banque de France (in part), Reichsbank, Banque Nationale de Belgique and Banco de España.

of the incentives for establishing banks in these countries was to encourage the provision of commercial banking services, where otherwise there would have been none.

Another incentive, particularly among those central banks founded around the time of the end of the Napoleonic Wars, e.g. those of Austria-Hungary, Norway, Denmark, and the Second Bank of the United States, was that the State had generated very high inflation through the 'excessive' issue of government paper currency, to meet its wartime expenditures, described in Denmark by the splendid term 'Statsbankerot' (State bankruptcy). The establishment of a somewhat independent, commercial banking institution, whose note issue was to be convertible into specie, either through legal restrictions on issue (e.g. Norges Bank, Reichsbank, Danmarks Nationalbank) or through the exercise of discretion by the Bank's directors (e.g. Banque de France, Nederlandsche Bank, Austrian National Bank), was perceived as a means of restoring monetary stability. The founding of the Iberian central banks in the middle of the nineteenth century had a similar genesis.

Defining central banking is problematic. In one sense we recognise it when we see it. The Bank of England was established in 1694, but at that time there was no concept of central banking. Something close to a modern conception had emerged by the end of the eighteenth century and Henry Thornton (1802) probably regarded the Bank as the central bank in a modern sense of the term, albeit recognising some deficiencies in its behaviour. But there are others who would prefer to date it from 1844 or at least see the 1844 Act as an important landmark. For example, White (1984) considers the Act to have bolstered the Bank of England's monopoly privileges in note issue and enhanced its status as an incipient central bank. For others still it would have to wait until the 1870s when the Bank accepted its function as a lender of last resort (we return to this issue in section 1.4).

Table 1.1 provides a chronology of central banking institutions, established prior to the twentieth century, that shows their original date of founding and also the decade within which we identify it as becoming a central bank in the modern sense of the term.[3] What the table shows is that there were just a handful of institutions prior to the 1820s and that none was a central bank. By the beginning of the twentieth century there were eighteen institutions and all of them were central banks. Thereafter the concept was so thoroughly established and the institutions so widely desired that many independent countries established their own central banks, although there are still some cases where some other quasi-commercial

---

[3] This definition is functional, identifying a central bank as (i) the government's bank, (ii) the monopoly note issuer and (iii) the lender of the last resort.

Table 1.1. *Central banking institutions before 1900**

Bank	Founded	Monopoly note issue	Lender of last resort (decade)
Sverige Riksbank	1668	1897	1890
Bank of England	1694	1844	1870
Banque de France	1800	1848	1880
Bank of Finland	1811	1886	1890
Nederlandsche Bank	1814	1863	1870
Austrian National Bank	1816	1816	1870
Norges Bank	1816	1818	1890
Danmarks Nationalbank	1818	1818	1880
Banco de Portugal	1846	1888	1870
Belgian National Bank	1850	1850	1850
Banco de España	1874	1874	1910
Reichsbank	1876	1876	1880
Bank of Japan	1882	1883	1880
Banca D'Italia	1893	1926	1880

* The table excludes central banking institutions of the Netherlands Antilles (est.1828), Indonesia (1828), Bulgaria (1879), Romania (1880) and Serbia (1883).
Sources: Appendix B

Table 1.2. *The number of central banks 1900–1990*

Decade	Number of central banks
1900	18
1910	20
1920	23
1930	34
1940	41
1950	59
1960	80
1970	108
1980	137
1990	161

Source: Pringle and Mahate (1993)

institution carried out the function before the full blown version came into being (e.g. India, Australia). Table 1.2 shows that, by 1950, there were 59 central banks and that this number had nearly trebled to 161 by 1990. With the world moving in the way that it is, the numbers are likely to go on growing.

The basis of (fractional-reserve) commercial banking is the maintenance of convertibility of bank liabilities, predominantly bank notes in the early stages of banking, into base money, then specie, gold and silver. The problem with maintaining a high reserve ratio, pro tanto a 100 per cent reserve ratio, as in 'narrow-bank' schemes (Litan 1987), is that doing so is comparatively unprofitable. There is always a temptation for private bankers to increase both return and risk by reducing their reserve ratio, often by covert means; an early example of this is found in Sweden in the seventeenth century, see (Flux 1911 and Goodhart 1988). The circumstances of the (government-authorised) establishment of these special commercial banks may be seen as reinforcing their owners' and managers' commitment to the maintenance of convertibility. Their favoured position as monopoly note-issuer provided them with a sufficient return to make them congenitally risk averse (Bagehot 1873), while the investment of their comparatively large capital into fixed-interest government stock gave them an incentive to seek price stability (Santoni 1984).

It was, indeed, this investment of the bank's capital into government bonds that provided much of the incentive to governments to found these banks in the first place. Such banks could offer a (temporary) haven for additional government debt finance that should also be non-inflationary, so long as the bank met its convertibility obligations. Whereas such additional debt finance was inherently transitional, while the initial capital was invested in such stock, the existence of such a large and powerful debt holder could be expected to widen and deepen the market for such debt, and the periodic need for these banks to renew their charters would give the government opportunities for extracting further rents. Such debt finance motives played a considerable part in the establishment of the Bank of England (Clapham 1944), both the first two Banks of the United States (Timberlake 1993), the Banque de France (Wilson 1957) and the Iberian central banks (Hamilton 1945 and 1946).

Inflation, like other taxes, especially taxes whose incidence is inherently uncertain, is unpopular, and governments will have an incentive to prevent it. But they have other priorities as well, perhaps the strongest of which is self-preservation. War was, and has remained, the main factor driving government expenditures. Given the temporary nature of wars, which are often expected to last for less time than actually occurs, as in 1914–18, it is both rational and politically expedient to meet such expenditures by deficit finance. In view of the limited scope of the government debt market (though the ratio of the national debt to GDP in the UK in 1815 exceeded 200 per cent), it was almost inevitable that the government would turn to their own special chartered bank for financial assistance. Moreover, the government is, almost always, a large net debtor, especially during, and after, a major war. Consequently, as in the case of the Banque de France and the Prussian Bank (see Appendix B), the government also imposed maximum interest rates.

The obligation to provide finance, at restricted interest rates, to their own governments at times of crisis conflicted with, and overrode, the central banks' commitment to the maintenance of specie convertibility. Since the erosion of their specie reserves, and their inability to maintain convertibility, was clearly associated with wartime disturbances, even when the precise responsibility of money-financed government deficit expenditures was less clearly remarked, central banks, in such instances, had a powerful case for pressing their government to relieve them of the convertibility obligation. This was done, and monetary order maintained, by making the notes of the central bank effectively legal tender, cours forcé. The Napoleonic Wars induced the greatest number of such suspensions of convertibility, prior to 1914, but some countries which were so unfortunate as to fight a series of wars, such as Austria (later Austro-Hungary), also suffered a series of such suspensions. Table 1.3 shows periods of suspensions, and related wars between 1797 and 1914.

Legal tender status is sometimes now regarded as imparting strength to a central bank's note issue. It was not perceived as such in the nineteenth century. A strong central bank did not need legal tender status for its notes, because they were as good as gold, or silver. Nevertheless granting legal tender status to the notes of the central bank did bolster its primacy among other commercial banks, since their notes were not given similar status (e.g. France in 1848; see Smith 1936). Thus, suspension of convertibility reinforced the tendency for the other commercial banks to hold central bank liabilities, notes and deposits, as their main reserves, rather than holding their own stocks of specie in coin or bar (see Edgeworth 1888, Wicksell 1898, Fetter 1965, Laidler 1991).

Even where the central banks had initially been the sole commercial bank operating in the country, as in much of Scandinavia, a variety of other banks, savings banks, other commercial banks, were founded during this period. In all those European countries, the central bank had to coexist with other private banks. The proper form of the relationship between them, and especially of the relationship between the note issues of the central bank and of the other private commercial banks, forms one of the main themes of section 1.4, and also of the analytical and academic debates on central banking in section 1.5, and further discussion of these issues is deferred to these later Sections.

The same issue, of the nature of the relationship between the central bank and the other private banks, was, of course, present in the USA as well, both in the Suffolk system (see Selgin 1988) and with both the first

Table 1.3. *Wars and suspensions of convertibility*

Year	War	Suspension of convertibility
1793–1815	Napoleonic Wars	England: 1797–1821 France: 1805 and 1813
1848	Revolutions in France, Germany and Austria	France: 1848–1850 Austria: 1848–1858
1859	Austro-Sardinian War	Austria: 1859–1866
1861–1865	American Civil War	US: 1862–1879
1866	Prusso-Austrian War	Austria: continuation of suspension from 1866 Italy: 1866–1883
1870–1871	Franco-Prussian War	France: 1870–1874
1914	World War I	Most countries, except Japan (1917) and South Africa

Source: Kindleberger (1993) and Appendix B.

two Banks of the United States. The United States' experience was particular in that the private/central bank nexus, and conflict, was overlain with the conflict over Federal versus States' rights. This issue helped to bring about the demise of both Banks of the United States (see Timberlake 1993 and Calomiris 1992), to defer the establishment of the Federal Reserve System until 1913, and to lead to a (federal) structure for the Fed that caused damaging uncertainty about the relative powers and functions of the Banks and the Board in the 1920s (Eichengreen 1992a). This US experience was diametrically opposite to that in most of Continental Europe (and Russia). There the role of the central bank in helping, through monetary means, to reinforce national unity and identity was generally seen as one of its positive and important functions. The unification and standardisation of the currency, and the establishment of nation-wide payment systems and clearing-houses, were regarded as important and valuable steps not only for their own sake, but also as a highly important aspect of nation building. This was especially so in Germany and Italy, but similar considerations applied in other Continental European countries (less so in the United Kingdom, where the special circumstances of Scotland and Ireland constrained the geographical ambit of the Bank of England).

Amidst the recent dissolution of Yugoslavia and the former Soviet Union, at the same time as the move towards Monetary Union in Western Europe, it is important to recall the strength of the links between currency and monetary unity on the one hand and political unity on the other (Goodhart 1995a). This has been so throughout our historical period.

1.2.2   Consolidation under the gold standard (1873–1914)

The year 1873 represents a natural dividing line for a history of central banking for three main reasons. First, it marks the beginning of the period when the gold standard formally became established as the main exchange rate regime for much of the industrialised world. Under the second coinage Act, Germany formally adopted the gold standard, accompanied by the Netherlands and several Scandinavian States, as shown in table 1.4. Secondly, it was also a year of crisis in many countries, and marked the beginning of a long deflation that lasted until the mid-1890s.

Thirdly, Walter Bagehot published *Lombard Street* in that same year. Although most connoisseurs reckon Henry Thornton's treatise on 'An Enquiry into the Paper Credit of Great Britain', 1802, to be a more profound study of monetary issues, *Lombard Street* had an enduring influence on the practice of central banking. It was a textbook on how central bankers should react to fluctuations and drains, both internal into domestic coinage and external, in their gold reserves, and in particular how they should respond should such drains be associated with the onset of banking panics. In particular, Bagehot proposes that the central bank should attempt, in the long-term interests of the financial system as a whole, to prevent contagious panic and to maintain systemic stability: the central bank should not be concerned with short-run profit maximisation. It is interesting that Bagehot's main opponent at the time, Hankey, a Director of the Bank of England, applied an explicit moral hazard argument to object to such implicit insurance of the banking system.[4]

Be that as it may, the gold standard ushered in an era, 1873–1914, during which the macro-policy functions of central banking in the major industrialised countries were relatively straightforward, and when their operations were quite simple and generally successfully executed. There was a single, overriding objective, to maintain the convertibility of the currency into gold, and this discipline maintained both the internal and external value of the currency. Although fluctuations in gold production led to some comparatively minor fluctuations in world price levels, by comparison with later price movements, this was generally tolerable (see the charts at the end of this section). We noted above that many leading economists of the day were expressing dissatisfaction with the gold standard. And it may be that in the absence of the cyanide process and the extensive gold discoveries of the 1890s the standard would not have lasted. But in most of the developed world the maintenance of the gold standard was widely accepted as the

---

[4] It is, perhaps, a pity that none of the free banking proponents has yet sought to re-establish Hankey's reputation.

Table 1.4. *The transition to the gold standard*

Year	Country
1871[a]	Germany (mint ceases to purchase silver)
1872	Holland (minting of silver suspended).
1873	Germany, Denmark, Norway, Sweden (formally adopt gold)
	US (silver demonetised)
1876	Spain (silver coinage suspended)[b]
1878	Belgium, Italy, France, Switzerland (formally suspend silver coinage)
1879	Austro-Hungary (silver coinage suspended)

[a] Britain was already on a gold standard by 1870, and had been since 1816.
[b] Spain suspended gold convertibility in 1883.
Source: Gallarotti (1993).

proper basis for a stable, well-functioning, *laissez-faire*, financial system. Only in the more peripheral, primary producing regions of the global market, such as Argentina (Ford 1962) or the western states of the USA (Friedman and Schwartz 1963), was it opposed by broad interest groups and political parties (Eichengreen 1992b, chapter 2). For the most part the nature of the monetary regime, and the objectives of the central bank, ceased during these years to be a serious political issue; this gave the central bank freedom to pursue this agreed single objective without much governmental interference, or oversight, even in those central banks where the Governor was a political appointee. Such independence was, of course, greatly enhanced by the fact that during this period there were few serious wars. Such imperial/colonial wars as did occur (e.g. Boer war, Spanish/American war) were generally fairly easily financed; so central banks did not need to facilitate government deficit finance.

Central banks had a variety of instruments for achieving their objective. By far the most important was their ability to control the level of nominal short-term interest rates, described further below. The need to vary interest rates was, however, less pressing the more that gold flows could be absorbed by accepting large variations in gold reserves. To do the latter successfully required a large average stock of gold reserves. So there was a well-known trade-off between having more volatile short-term interest rates and maintaining a larger gold reserve, with the UK at one end of this spectrum and France at the other (and Germany in the middle). A comparison of the volatility of short-term interest rates at two periodicities, one month and one year, for the UK and the USA is given in table 1.5. The ranking of relative volatilities for the shorter periodicity is particularly marked, with rates in the UK almost twice as volatile as those of the US between 1870 and

Table 1.5. *The volatility* of short-term nominal interest rates*

	Country		Volatility		
		1870–1914	1919–1939	1946–1971	1972–1991
UK	Monthly	.312	.189	.023	.040
	Annual	.262	.406	.327	.222
US	Monthly	.189	.192	.061	.053
	Annual	.569	.361	.303	.295

* Volatility is calculated here and in table 1.6 as the *standard deviation of logged first differences.*
Source: see Appendix.

Table 1.6. *The volatility of long-term nominal interest rates*

	Country		Volatility		
		1870–1914	1919–1939	1946–1971	1972–1991
UK	Monthly	.013	.029	.087	.086
	Annual	.026	.108	.075	.114
US	Monthly	.013	.024	.022	.165
	Annual	.070	.064	.075	.115

Source: see Appendix.

1914. After this period, volatility in rates converged and, at least for the shorter periodicity, have become less over time. Table 1.6 gives a companion exercise for long-term rates. It is clear that expectations of future short rates must have been mean reverting, since long rates exhibit an awesome stability in the years 1870–1914 relative either to short rates, or to long rates in subsequent periods.

Besides intervention and interest rate adjustments, there were a number of other minor infractions of the pure working of the gold standard which some central banks (notably the Banque de France) would adopt as a further protection for their Gold Reserves (Bloomfield 1959; Bordo and Schwartz 1984). By the end of the period there were also a very few recorded cases of central banks lending gold amongst themselves to help stabilise interest rates in the international monetary system (see Eichengreen 1992b, chapter 2). One such loan, when the Banque de France discounted bills for the Bank of England, was recorded as early as July 1839 (Fetter 1965), but such cooperation was, perhaps, just beginning to develop more systematically at the very end of this period. Our judgement, however, is that such secondary mechanisms, including such incipient central bank co-operation, played a relatively minor role in the overall scheme (though not perhaps at a few specific instances, e.g. in 1907).

In order to avoid having to absorb gold flows directly onto the reserves, the central bank needed to vary interest rates as its main instrument.[5] That meant that the essential operational requirement for central banks was to be able to make their interest rate, which they wanted to establish in the short-term money market, the effective rate, from which all other money market rates derived. In those cases where the commercial banks were regular borrowers of reserves from their central bank, this was no problem, and commercial bank and money market rates adjusted naturally to the rate at which the central bank would make marginal reserves available.

In other countries, notably the UK, there was quite a lot of concern whether, and how, the central bank could force market rates into line with Bank Rate (see Appendix A, and Sayers 1936). The problem was that the commercial banks, now comparatively large joint stock banks, were not usually (especially between 1850 and 1914) indebted to the Bank of England, and also, partially, that there was some continuing hangover of commercial rivalry. Hence these banks were far from willing to accept Bank leadership in rate setting in a passive fashion. The Bank responded to this challenge in three ways. First it developed prototype forms of open market operations, notably repos in Consols (see Appendix A), to bring about changes in the reserve base of the commercial banks; second, it fostered the growth of discount houses and the discount market as a mechanism and market for bringing about adjustments to the reserve base without having to go head-to-head with the larger and often – in these years – adversarial commercial banks; third, it took steps to withdraw from commercial business and rivalry with the commercial banks (see Clapham 1944), a process slowed by its organisation as a private sector body with a need to make profits to satisfy its shareholders. This was eventually effected in part by transforming the dividend into a constant payment, unrelated to current profits, so that the shareholders became transformed, in practice, into bond holders.

---

[5] Given the need to maintain convertibility under the gold standard, a banking system without a central bank, as in the National Banking System in the USA (1863–1913), would also incur interest rate adjustments in response to gold flows. Wherein lay the difference? The profit maximisation incentives of a system without a central bank would mean that reserve fluctuations perceived as temporary (e.g. owing to seasonal fluctuation) could not be absorbed, but would cause greater, short-term seasonal interest rate volatility (Miron 1986). By the same token, although self-interest caused Clearing Houses to respond to banking panics after a fashion (Timberlake 1984), panics and crises were managed, and avoided, more effectively – during these years at least – by countries with central banks than by those without them.

In some European countries (e.g. France and Italy), commercial rivalry did exist as central banks were encouraged to conduct commercial business from their inception. In other European countries (e.g. The Netherlands since 1888) the central bank transferred its excess profit to the state, not to private shareholders.

The experience of central banks in Continental Europe was leading to a consolidation of one kind of practice of how a central bank should be established and run. When the Japanese sent envoys to Europe to consider best practice, prior to the establishment of the Bank of Japan in 1882, they chose the Banque Nationale de Belgique as role model. When the US Congress set up the National Monetary Commission in 1908 (it presented its reports in 1910 and 1911) to examine existing central banking structures, there appears to have been more enthusiasm for the German, than for the English model. Meanwhile where the specialised government banks had remained largely commercial and competitive, such as the Banco de España and the Sverige Riksbank for example, they were now transformed into a standard central bank (e.g. the renewal of the charter of the Banco de España in 1874, and the passing of the Sverige Riksbank Act of 1897, gave each of these banks the monopoly note issue and consolidated their central banking functions). One exception to this trend was Australia, where the banking crash of 1893 persuaded the Labor Party that what was needed was a state bank to compete with the trading banks, as well as controlling them (see Giblin 1951 and Schedvin 1992).

Part of the background to Bagehot's book, and a reason for writing it, was the perceived (mis)handling by the Bank of the Overend Gurney crash in 1866.[6] Although Overend Gurney had been badly and speculatively managed, and was insolvent, there was still some suspicion that the Bank refused to help because of the animosity that had long obtained between the two institutions, as much as a judgement that the firm was too insolvent to assist. Moreover, the Bank has been accused of being slow to quell the panic that then ensued by liberal loans to other (solvent) financial institutions caught up in the panic. But the 1844 Act was again suspended and another step taken on the road to full acceptance of lender of last resort responsibility.

Although Bagehot, in *The Economist* in the 1860s and in *Lombard Street* (1873) may have convinced the Bank how to act, there was no public commitment by the Bank that it would do so. The relatively calm economic conditions of the late nineteenth century may have been brought about in part by the Bank's behaviour (see Ogden 1988). In Europe there had been a

---

[6] Frank Fetter was writing a monograph on this at the time of his death. This was in a nearly-finished state, but has never been published and may even now be lost.

number of bank rescues and Lender of Last Resort operations by Continental central banks. Examples are Austria-Hungary (stock market crash, 1873), Portugal (banking crisis, 1876), and France (stock market crash, 1882). As shown in table 1.1, if we treat the 1870s as the decade when the Bank of England clearly accepted its role as Lender of Last Resort, then it probably led most Continental practice.

Be that as it may, by 1913 a common, standardised role for the central bank had become generally adopted among all the main industrialised countries. Its main functions and operational techniques were generally accepted, with little political controversy – with the continuing partial exception of the USA. Its main objective was to maintain convertibility of the currency into gold, the gold standard; its main control instrument was to vary interest rates to that end; it made its interest rate effective by discounting bills and, increasingly, by open-market operations. It operated independently from government. It had become the bankers' bank, a role enhanced by withdrawing from commercial rivalry. On occasions it might help to rescue financial institutions, but on an *ad hoc*, co-operative basis without general commitment and without accepting any formal regulatory or supervisory role.

1.2.3 The (mis)management of disturbances (1914–45)

The outbreak of war in August 1914 came as an unforeseen shock to financial markets (Kindleberger 1993; Seabourne 1986).[7] The financial institutions in the countries now suddenly at war held large amounts of claims on residents in hostile countries, which would not be paid and whose market value was, to say the least, problematical, whereas their liabilities owed to such residents could not, at this initial stage, be written down. Consequently many of the key financial institutions, notably those in the City of London, were technically insolvent when assets and liabilities were valued on a mark-to-market basis. Even the most vociferous advocates of non-intervention and *laissez faire* 'free banking' would hardly have persisted with a 'hands-off' policy here. In practice, however, the Bank of England has been severely blamed for being dilatory and uncertain both in recognising the need for direct intervention to maintain systemic stability and in organising it, though the commercial banks had behaved even more crassly (see Sayers 1976).[8]

---

[7] Panic began on the Viennese stock market on 25 July, and by 31 July all major stock markets were closed. Paris remained open, but settlement was deferred for one month (Kindleberger 1993).

[8] De Cecco (1974, chapter 7) suggests that the crisis was intensified by attempts by the main parties involved (e.g. the Bank, the Treasury, the main joint stock banks and the accepting

The crisis in London was comparatively short-lived. Following the assassination of the heir to the Austro-Hungarian throne in June, war between Austria and Serbia was inevitable and was declared on 28 July. In the second half of July fears of a European war grew and anticipations of that provoked the financial crisis. The crisis broke quickly and with considerable ferocity in the last week of July. Intense efforts by all the interested parties brought about a resolution by the end of the first week in August, though there were repercussions that lasted a long time.

With war a probability in late July, selling speeded up on the Stock Exchange, exchange-rates became more volatile, and foreigners were unable to make remittances to the London acceptance houses. On 28 July banks in London began calling in loans they had made to the stock market. Difficulties led to the Stock Exchange closing on 31 July – the first time that had happened since its foundation in 1773. Bank Rate, which had been eased up from 3 to 4 per cent on 31 July, was raised to 8 per cent on 1 August and then to 10 per cent on 2 August. There was a three-day bank holiday, and a moratorium placed on bills of exchange. Britain declared war on Germany on 5 August. A variety of measures was introduced to deal with different but related problems. On 7 August the banks reopened with Bank Rate down to 5 per cent.

The root cause of the crisis was a failure of remittance. London was a massive creditor to most of the rest of the world, including Germany. London brokers were squeezed in late July when foreign stock exchanges were closing, moratoria were being declared, and debts became irrecoverable at least for the foreseeable future. The London banks had lent money to the brokers 'on the margin'. That is, they had called for securities as collateral for the loans to an amount 10 per cent to 20 per cent greater in value than the loan. When security prices began to fall that margin was eroded and the banks began to call in the loans. The brokers sold securities in order to repay the loans but in the process drove security prices down further. These banks have been criticised for calling in loans to brokers; though some have argued that it was foreign banks in London that were most culpable.

The variety of responses made were: the suspension of the 1844 Act (this occurred, legally, on 1 August, but served no useful purpose); the suspension of specie payments; a general moratorium; the issue of Treasury Notes of £1 and 10/- denomination. On 3 August there was a partial moratorium on bills of exchange and that enabled the acceptance houses to postpone, for one month, payment of all bills accepted before 3 August. The bill market

houses) to use the event to protect and, if possible, to increase their own power and influence, but this position is extreme, and in places unwarranted.

needed reviving and the Bank of England was authorised to discount any bill that had been accepted before 4 August. The Bank also made the generous offer that it would lend sufficient funds to meet bills at 2 per cent above Bank Rate.

After the moratoria the authorities had to take over the bad debts of the bills and acceptances that were unlikely to be recovered from the various parties in the hostile countries, and from others whose circumstances were irrevocably altered by the war. The extent of this and the means whereby the costs were absorbed have never been accurately assessed. The essence of the response to the crisis was an injection of base money on a huge scale – entirely appropriate to the needs of the time. What was needed in order to allay the panic was the provision of sufficient cash or at least the promise of it.

Similar actions were pursued by many countries – stock exchanges closed, moratoria, monetary expansion. However, central banks were able to move quite smoothly from their normal peace-time mode (maintaining the gold standard) to their wartime, crisis-functional form. In this latter mode, priority is given to financing government deficits, helping to pay for the war.[9] Gold was withdrawn from circulation, and centralised in order to meet a current account deficit; it was replaced by inconvertible, legal-tender paper money (the liability either of the government or of the central bank). As the gold (and foreign exchange) reserves became progressively exhausted, the authorities mobilised residents' holdings of foreign (portfolio) assets, either to sell directly or to pledge as collateral against loans; exchange controls were progressively imposed; and the exchange rate depreciated, either in a managed, or unmanaged way, depending on circumstances and the financial acuity of the authorities.

Not only was the onset of World War I unforeseen, but so was its terrible scale and duration (Sayers 1976). Partly in consequence the authorities were much slower, than in World War II, to restrain other inessential expenditures (public and private), to raise taxes and to place direct ceilings on domestic credit. With inflation soon rising, nominal interest rates rose (see the charts at the end of this section). With huge deficits financed at quite high interest rates, the debt/income ratio also ballooned. Despite massive debt sales, the money stock and prices shot up. The European belligerents, with increasing physical constraints on their supply of exports and price inelastic demands for war material, sought to hold their nominal exchange rates pegged relative to the US dollar during the war so that their real exchange rates appreciated (see the charts at the end of this section).

[9] France and Germany, for example, had already legislated, in 1911 and 1890 respectively, for the automatic extension of credit by their central banks to the government in the event of a war (Kindleberger 1993).

The Bolshevik Revolution in October 1917 frightened the authorities in the West. So, even after the war itself ceased, there was considerable concern to prevent conditions developing that might foment social unrest and revolution. Nevertheless, the immediate economic response in most Western countries, excluding the defeated central European powers, was a restocking, inventory boom, which gave yet further impetus to inflation. This soon terminated as immediate needs were met, government defence expenditures cut, and interest rates raised. The resulting cyclical deflation (in 1920/21) was steep and severe, but quite short. One feature of this deflation was that wages and prices exhibited considerable downwards flexibility, considerably more so than later in the inter-war period (see Dimsdale 1981). Quite what caused such a difference in wage/price rigidity over time is unclear.

Abstracting from the immediate, sharp, post-war cycle, the monetary authorities in each country had to review the objectives of monetary macro-policy, and to decide what the role of the central bank should become, in the light of the economic devastation caused by the war. The answer in the UK, epitomised in the Cunliffe Committee Report (1919), was to try to return, as fully as possible, to the status quo ante. In view of previous history and the intellectual background of those in power, this proposal was surely almost inevitable. What is, perhaps, more surprising is that there was so little discussion about the exchange rate at which sterling should be repegged to gold. In view of the fact that many other Continental European countries would be forced to adopt a different exchange rate (against gold), and given the disruption in price relativities between the UK, the USA and gold, one might have expected more discussion whether £1 should equal $4.86 or 113 grams of fine gold (£3.17.10½ per standard ounce). As Sayers (1976, p. 118) notes, 'it does emphasize the identification of the gold standard with the particular parity'. But, to use current terminology, it was feared that the discretionary choice of a different exchange rate would threaten the credibility of the external commitment (see Eichengreen 1992b, pp.153–4 and 163). Even the patently necessary adjustment for those Continental European powers, which had suffered much greater inflation than the UK, was strongly opposed by them in principle for several years, e.g. at the Genoa Conference (Eichengreen 1992b, p. 158). Another suggestion that has been made is that some in the UK expected prices in the USA to rise significantly in the 1920s in response to the wartime influx of gold there, as would be in line with the standard rules of the gold standard game (Eichengreen 1992b, p. 165; Sayers 1976, p. 127).

One major problem of this period was that the exigencies of war finance had concentrated so much of the world's monetary gold stock in the USA (Glasner 1989; Eichengreen 1992b). Yet, as seen from the chart at the end of this section, the US also suffered from inflation. There is an inherent asymmetry of response to reserve flows; countries losing reserves can be forced to deflate, but countries gaining reserves can sterilise almost without limit. In view of their prior experience of wartime inflation, it would have been too much to expect the Fed consciously to expand the money stock and to inflate, just to ease the predicament of other countries and to resolve problems of reverting to the gold standard. Moreover, the US had kept the dollar price of gold constant, despite the sharp increase in the dollar price of other goods between 1914 and 1920. With the US money supply growing at rates of nearly 20 per cent over the same period, this had two detrimental consequences. First, the sharp fall in the relative price of gold reduced the flow supply of additional monetary gold (Eichengreen 1992b, pp. 198–202). Second, despite the massive gold inflows into the US, the increase in the money supply meant that, at certain crucial times, the Fed's minimum required gold reserve ratio bit, e.g. in 1920 and 1933, forcing tighter monetary policies at just the wrong moments (Eichengreen 1992b, chapter 4, and chapter 7, pp. 194–5).

Such tight monetary policies in the USA imparted a deflationary tendency elsewhere, as other countries, notably the UK, sought to build up and/or to defend their depleted gold reserves. Moreover, the Fed no longer had a clear objective by which to steer. It had been established in 1914 for the purpose of providing 'an elastic currency' consistent with the gold standard. Now in the 1920s that was mostly an ineffective external constraint. The Fed was forced into discretionary management, looking at domestic activity, and asset price and goods price inflation, on the one hand, while Benjamin Strong reminded them of the international need for lower interest rates on the other (Friedman and Schwartz 1963). It was, therefore, faced with circumstances for which it had not been previously prepared, during the early stages of its existence while the relative decision-making powers of the Board and the Reserve Banks were still being established (Eichengreen 1992a).

If the asymmetry and general insufficiency of gold holding was one major problem, the other was the extreme political and economic weakness of Central and Eastern Europe in the aftermath of Versailles. The break-up of the former Austro-Hungarian Empire led to the establishment of States that were initially hardly financially viable (including Austria itself), at a juncture both of severe post-war disruption and of continuing Communist threat. Similar problems in Germany were exacerbated by reparations. Under these circumstances government deficits increased, and were monetised, leading to hyperinflation. In view of the obvious link between the monetisation of such deficits and hyperinflation, the Allied governments imposed considerable pressure to make the central banks in these countries statutorily independent of their own governments (Dornbusch 1992; Garber and Spencer 1994). While this did help to bring about monetary stabilisation, e.g. in Czechoslovakia and Austria, it is worth recalling, given the current interest in central bank independence, that the central banks in Germany (and Austro-Hungary) that presided over their national hyper-inflations were notionally 'independent' (Eschweiler and Bordo 1993). There are, perhaps, two main lessons from this. Firstly, central banks, whatever their statutory relationship with government, are unlikely to deviate far from the domestic political consensus about appropriate action. Secondly, monetary stability is impossible in the absence of fiscal stability.

In time, however, control over government expenditures, and their monetisation, was achieved (e.g. in Germany, through the Rentenmark), at least sufficiently to allow Montagu Norman, and the Bank of England, to try to encourage their central bank colleagues in these countries to return to the gold standard, a much desired normalisation (Sayers 1976). But their financial position remained fragile, and, when the 1929 downturn and stockmarket crash occurred in the USA, the banking systems in Austria, Germany and Hungary buckled soon after in 1931.

Quite why the 1929/33 downturn was so virulent remains a contentious issue. The experience of 1988–1992 should, however, remind us that central banks have often found it difficult to know how to respond to sharp asset price fluctuations, which are not closely mirrored in goods' price inflation. The time path of equity and goods' prices in the USA in 1927–31 and in Japan in 1988–92 have some similarity (see diagrams in *The Economist*'s *100 Years of Economics Statistics*). Again in both these episodes the growth rate of bank lending and of (broad) money collapsed (see the chart at the end of this section). A crucial difference is that in the USA the authorities allowed waves of bank failures, and further monetary contraction to occur, whereas in Japan the authorities have, fortunately, managed to preserve and protect their banks from the ravages of asset deflation.

Be that as it may, the collapse of trade, resulting from the Great Depression exacerbated by the rise in protectionism (e.g. the notorious Hawley-Smoot tariffs), and the increasing political unpopularity of unemployment and high interest rates, broke the already fragile attempt to restore a fixed exchange-rate gold standard. The UK, followed by most of the British Empire, floated in September 1931. Roosevelt took the US off gold in April 1933, and then raised the dollar price of gold later that year, as part of his domestic policy to arrest the decline in (producer) prices. The French, despite a valiant but doomed attempt to maintain the gold value of the franc, were forced off in September 1936. Despite attempts, such as the Tripartite Agreement that accompanied the French devaluation, to restore some order into the international monetary system, it effectively broke up into somewhat autarchic trading areas, separated by discriminatory tariff barriers (e.g. the British Imperial Preference System). Dr Schacht of Germany was particularly adept at manipulating such arrangements.

During the inter-war period, monetary management was unsuccessful. Although output levels between 1921 (following post-war adjustment) and 1939 in those countries which avoided the post-war hyperinflations (e.g. the UK and the USA) had, on average, grown by some 2.5 per cent per annum, this period coincided with the worst depression and highest unemployment ever seen in the capitalist world, and the collapse of the world trading and financial system. Interest rates in most countries, especially real rates, were much more volatile than in 1873–1913, as was monetary growth. The economic calamities befalling Germany have often been held to be partly responsible for Hitler's political success. The apparent failures of the free market system led, more generally, to cries for state intervention and control in order to manage and to improve the economy. Keynes believed that his policies for government management of the economy were not intended to subvert the market economy, but to protect it from much more far-reaching Socialist alternatives.

Although many of the disturbances and calamities of the inter-war period may be ascribed to the failures of the monetary authorities, and central banks in particular (e.g. Friedman and Schwartz 1963; Eichengreen 1992b], this did not slow the dissemination of nascent central banks to independent nation states. In particular, the Bank of England exhibited almost mission-ary fervour in helping to establish central banks in its own image in the Dominions (see Sayers 1936); Sir Otto Niemeyer was indefatigable. Similarly American experts, especially E.W. Kemmerer, were spreading the gospel of central banking in Latin America. Indeed, the intensity of the economic and monetary disturbances in this period appeared to make it more necessary to have a central bank to assuage the effect of such outside disturbances on the domestic economy. For example, in Canada the com-mercial banks had operated successfully without a central bank for over a century; it was the onset of the Depression that shifted the political and economic consensus about the need for such (see Bordo and Redish 1987). By the same token, the shift in views during this period towards the need for greater state management of the economy, in banking as elsewhere, encour-aged the establishment of central banks as public sector bodies (e.g. Aus-tralia, see Schedvin 1992). Such state management of the monetary system was taken to its extreme in the USSR, where the commercial banks were re-absorbed back into the central bank to form a mono-bank, whose credit allocation was not determined by commercial considerations but by the Plan.

The collapse of the international monetary order in the early 1930s left central banks without an external objective. The fragility of the economy, and the weakness of prices, also indicated little need to maintain domestic constraint, though precautionary concerns about the potential dangers of surplus liquidity played a role in the US cyclical downturn in 1936–37 (Friedman and Schwartz 1963). Consequently, central banks, under prompting from governments, applied themselves to the task of getting nominal interest rates both short and long (e.g. the UK Conversion offer of 1932; see Capie, Mills and Wood 1986) as low as was thought decent, and consistent with maintaining the existing structure of the financial system (see Sayers 1976, pp. 536–44, on the discount house problem). It is doubtful whether much of this shift in policy was due to Keynes' influence; the publication of the General Theory in 1936 followed, rather than led, the policy change, but it was consonant with it, and provided an intellectual justification for 'managed money.'

Falling nominal interest rates played a part in the recovery from the Great Depression; housing construction was an important leading sector in the UK (Dimsdale 1981; Broadberry 1986). In the UK prices rose in the 1930s, and hence perceived real interest rates stayed low. Strong recovery followed in Britain and after 1933 in the US and some other countries (e.g. Sweden). After the mid-1930s re-armament expenditures rose and their scale began to produce inflationary pressures. The Directorate of the Reichsbank wrote a letter, warning of the potential inflationary effect, to Hitler: they were nearly all immediately sacked (see Marsh 1992, chapter 4). In most other countries, full employment did not come till after the outbreak of war. This once again shifted the priorities of monetary management. However, the increased enthusiasm for direct state intervention and control, combined with an assessment of the errors of wartime finance in 1914–18 (e.g. too few controls, too high interest rates, too much inflation), meant that the 1939–45 war would be managed by controls (exchange controls, credit controls, price controls, rationing), while interest rates would be held low, to reduce the burden of debt finance (Sayers 1976; Capie and Wood 1986). During the war, central banks became subservient organs of the central government. In those few cases, where they had remained formally within the private sector, their status was generally brought into line with current reality by nationalisation during, or shortly after, the war (see table 1.7). Even the Fed, which maintained its particular part private/ part public status, fell increasingly under Treasury domination.

1.2.4   Post-war success: Keynes and/or Bretton Woods? (1945–1971)

The asymmetries in the aftermath of World War II were even greater than in 1918. Physical capital in the USA had been augmented during the war; it

Table 1.7. *The nationalisation[a] of central banks*

Year	Central bank
1936	Danmarks Nationalbank
	Reserve Bank of New Zealand
1938	Bank of Canada
1945	Banque de France
1946	Bank of England
1948	Nederlandsche Bank
	Banque Nationale de Belgique[b]
1949	Norges Bank
	Reserve Bank of India

[a] Nationalisation here refers to the state ownership of 100 per cent of the share capital of the central bank.
[b] In the case of Belgium the ownership share of the state in the Banque Nationale was only 51 per cent.
Source: Appendix B

was the world's dominant economic power, and it held virtually all the world's gold. By comparison, Japan and Europe had been devastated, and the latter was now split by the Iron Curtain. But this time the earlier failures and mistakes were avoided, partly as a result of farsighted American leadership.

The immediate problems of post-war recovery, within a world where the US was often the only source of scarce capital goods, were alleviated by Marshall Aid, and the dollars thus made available were efficiently economised, and used to promote inter-European trading, by the establishment of the European Payments Union (EPU) (Kaplan and Schleiminger 1989; Eichengreen 1994). The underlying framework for the post-war international monetary system had been decided in, primarily US–UK, discussions and negotiations in 1943/44, the Bretton Woods system. Besides setting up the international institutions, IMF, the World Bank, and (with complications en route) GATT, it was agreed that the exchange rate system would be pegged, but adjustable. In theory each currency would peg to gold; in practice the US was such a dominant hegemon that every other currency pegged to the US dollar and the US separately kept the link of the dollar to gold. Although Keynes had feared that the system would be too deflationary (no doubt influenced by the UK's continuing structural weakness), and had argued for the more expansionary 'bancor' system, with the benefit of hindsight it appears that this system provided a successful compromise between the external discipline of the peg, and the ultimate freedom and flexibility to adjust exchange rates, if caught in a 'fundamental' disequilibrium. Or at least it would work successfully so long as the US, the hegemon, managed to combine economic growth with price stability.

Nevertheless, recovery in Europe and Japan was initially hindered by the dollar shortage. Despite fears about its continuation (MacDougall 1957), this turned out to be brief. With so much of their economy dislocated by the War, the exchange rates that initially seemed appropriate for Germany and Japan soon turned out, once recovery was under way, to be supercompetitive. Meanwhile, the USA, in contrast to the inter-war years, took the brunt of the task of defending the West from the Communist threat. The resulting defence expenditures, both abroad in Korea and Vietnam and domestically, not only kept the US (and world) economy at full employment, but gave Germany and Japan a further comparative advantage.

Meanwhile, France and the UK were both embroiled in the retreat from Empire, which involved them in continuous, difficult and expensive rearguard actions (Vietnam and Algeria; Malaya, Cyprus, Aden, Kenya, etc.; Suez). Whereas both were losing an Empire, only France found an alternative role in Europe. The UK ended the World War with the albatross of the sterling balances around its neck. As John Fforde (1992) described, the UK was rebuffed in its hopes for much more generous assistance from the USA, unwilling to take really radical action (such as the ROBOT plan in 1952 to float and freeze the sterling balances), and thereby forced into a series of second-best and unsatisfactory compromises. The UK, and in the earlier part of this period, France, became the congenitally weaker members of the system (see Pressnell 1986).

As noted earlier, the war had brought full employment. Many feared that this might not last after the war, and everyone was determined that the inter-war disaster of persistent high unemployment should not recur. In order to prevent this, demand was to be managed, generally along Keynesian lines. Monetary management was to be a co-ordinated part of such overall demand management, often regarded as a somewhat subsidiary part, since the interest elasticity of demand for goods (the IS curve) was thought to be rather low, while the interest elasticity of the demand for money (the LM curve) was felt to be comparatively higher (see the Radcliffe Report 1959). The objectives of central banks were extended to include high employment, and growth, as well as maintaining the value of the currency. In practice, the central bank became a junior branch of the Treasury. Demand management, comprising fiscal, monetary and incomes policies, was to be co-ordinated. But, because of lags, and uncertain and supposedly weak effects of monetary policy, interest rates were to be held as low as might be consistent with external balance, in the immediate post-war era, 1945–50, and the economy was to be adjusted primarily through fiscal changes. In so far as monetary policy was to be used, this would be done through changes in direct controls.

That was the idea in theory, and in political rhetoric, at least in those countries (e.g. Australia and UK) where Keynesian policies held sway. It is doubtful whether the system worked that way in practice. Whereas Treasury officials and Ministers believed that they were adjusting fiscal policies in order to achieve the desired level of demand, with the optimum trade-off between unemployment and inflation (along the short-run Phillips curve), in reality they did not have the knowledge or the timing skills to do so (Dow 1964). What 'really' happened was that each country's external position, vis-à-vis its Bretton Woods peg, determined whether it would be forced to tighten monetary and fiscal policies, or to relax them (Bordo and Eichengreen 1993).

This latter was not, of course, true for the US, which did not have an external constraint. The US was one of the first countries to give up direct intervention, credit controls, incomes policies, etc. – all wartime controls. Given the problems of the balance of power between the Executive and the Legislature in the USA, and the delays that that entails, the conduct of fiscal policy as an instrument of demand management is problematical at best. With the Fed being somewhat independent of both the President and Congress, and never entirely sold on Keynesian theory either, neither the objectives, nor the operational effects, of monetary policy during the 1950s are entirely clear, though the Fed did seek to vary interest rates countercyclically. Perhaps the relatively smooth and successful functioning of the US economy, prior to the late 1950s, should be seen more as a natural self-equilibration of the economy rather than the result of conscious demand management? If so, the gulf between economic theory and rhetoric, which was then primarily Keynesian, and reality, whereby the world economic system was largely self-steering within the international Bretton Woods framework, was unusually large at this juncture.

As noted earlier, monetary policy during World War II was primarily undertaken via direct credit controls, while interest rates were held low and constant. This reliance on direct credit controls continued in the immediate post-war period; variations in controls on bank lending, on new capital issues, on hire-purchase terms were the main operational tools, often supported in the case of the banking system with controls over interest rates and over their minimum holdings of (liquid) government debt and reserve ratios. Whether these latter were to be seen as prudential, or macro-policy, instruments was rarely clear, even to those who enforced them.

Within a few years of the end of the war, a trend set in, away from such direct controls, and back to market-related mechanisms of monetary management, especially to the use of (short-term) interest rate adjustment. This was, of course, part of a much more general recovery of confidence in the workings of a capitalist market economy, and growing associated doubts about the ability and wisdom of state planning, even within the more relaxed framework of the French indicative Plans, which were so admired by the Labour Party in the 1960s, and formed the model for the UK's abortive National Plan (HMSO, Cmnd 2764, 1965).

Within the context of the financial system, direct lending controls increasingly led to disintermediation, as fringe institutions, outside the ambit of the controls, were given artificial impetus (external disintermediation was, however, effectively constrained by exchange controls). The central core of commercial banks was being turned into a declining public utility, wherein the main function of bankers was to say 'no' to aspiring borrowers with varying degrees of decisiveness. Both commercial and central bankers became increasingly unhappy with this, since it was making the financial system distorted and inefficient. It proved difficult to persuade HM Treasury in the UK to abandon these direct controls, partly because they, and Ministers, tended to discount claims that their own application of controls could lead to inefficiency, partly because they were always worried (with good reason as shown in 1971–73) that any relaxation would unloose an unmeasurable, but potentially huge, flood of pent-up demand. Despite such rear-guard action from (more left-wing) politicians and Treasury bureaucrats in Britain, in virtually all Western countries there was a slow, but steady, continuing trend from controls to market mechanisms.

The withdrawal by central banks from direct intervention for macro-policy purposes was, perhaps, further facilitated by the lack of a need to intervene on prudential and systemic stability grounds. Economic cycles, apart from the Korean War boom, were mild. Both goods and asset prices trended upwards, but slowly and quite steadily. Although more freely used over time, nominal, and real, interest rates did not fluctuate much, either over short (one-month) or long (one-year) periodicities (see tables 1.5 and 1.6). Partly because of the continuing constraints on their operational freedom, partly because the economic framework was so stable and benign, partly because of conservatism engendered by the memory of the inter-war disasters, there were virtually no bank failures during this period. Such supervision over the banking system as was carried out by the Bank of England during this period was undertaken by one senior official, the Principal of the Discount Office, on a part-time basis!

It had become accepted, during the inter-war period, that any self-respecting independent country should have its own central bank and its own currency. As the Colonial period receded, more and more countries became independent. Many of these countries, especially in Africa, had previously operated on a Currency Board basis (Newlyn and Rowan 1954). These had linked the Colony to the currency and the capital market of the (Imperial) home country. While this system had helped to maintain price stability, there had been little attempt by the Colonial rulers to build up an indigenous financial system, and the extent of reserves held against the local currency was often felt to be excessive for developing countries. Consequently, these Boards were transformed into full-scale central banks on, or shortly after, independence. The number of central banks, as shown in table 1.2 in section 1.2 grew even faster.

What brought this successful era to an end? Once again, the disruptive catalyst was war, the Vietnam War. The pursuit by President Johnson of his ambitious domestic objectives, 'The Great Society', while simultaneously pursuing the war, both guns and butter, put additional strain on the US economy, on inflation in the USA, and on the Bretton Woods system. Moreover the Bretton Woods system made it difficult for the US to adjust its exchange rate relative to its main competitors, and many in the USA felt that it was, therefore, putting their tradable goods industries at a competitive disadvantage. Germany objected to importing inflation; the alternative of revaluing was not acceptable, because German exchange rates were not out of line with its (European) competitors; the problem was perceived as being in the USA, not in Germany. General de Gaulle objected to (what he described as) financing the Vietnam War, and along with Prof. Rueff wanted to give gold a more central role as an effective discipline on the USA. By contrast the British wanted to avoid the effects of the Bretton Woods discipline on themselves in perpetrating 'stop-go' policies and low growth.

So, for a variety of reasons, many of the main national participants became disenchanted with the Bretton Woods system towards the end of the 1960s. At much the same time academic opinion was moving strongly in favour of freely flexible exchange rates, and this too was influential. Meanwhile, despite the maintenance of exchange controls in many countries, capital flows were increasing in scale, relative to available foreign exchange reserves. Once serious doubt was cast on the continued maintenance of the parities, speculative attack could force their abandonment.

For all these reasons, the political consensus and willingness to maintain the prior international monetary order eroded. Once that happened the shocks of the late 1960s and early 1970s broke the system.

1.2.5   The inflationary upsurge and the monetary counter-reaction (1971–1994)

The end of section 1.1 noted the drastic increase in turbulence in external monetary affairs in 1971–1973 – which culminated in the breakdown of the Bretton Woods system and the onset of generalised floating. This was associated with an accompanying increase in domestic monetary disorder, with the direction of causality running in both directions. The extent of volatility in monetary (and also real) variables, such as monetary growth, interest rates, equity prices, exchange rates over the five year period, 1971–76, has rarely been matched in any other period (except perhaps 1928–33 or 1978–83). Although wars and revolutions (the Arab-Israeli 'Yom Kippur' war in 1973; the overthrow of the Shah in 1979) played some considerable role (just how important is a question which cannot be answered here), it was, nevertheless, still a relatively peaceful period.

The main domestic problem was that people's concern about the future impact of expected inflation had slowly been gathering strength. Previously inflation had been perceived as a phenomenon connected with the financing of wars and revolutions, after which were resolved proper monetary order with a stationary price level would be restored. But the experience of the post-war years, itself founded on a reaction to the disastrous unemployment of the Great Depression of 1929–33 in the US, was that the politicians would (successfully) strive to use demand management, including monetary policy measures, to maintain employment at such a high level that prices would tend to rise year by year. In due course, perhaps during the 1950s, people came to expect that, and to factor that into their wage/price nego-tiations. With an unchanged pressure of demand (desired level of employ-ment), that would lead inflation to accelerate, and people began, in some cases, to anticipate that too, by the end of the 1960s. The collapse of the Bretton Woods system removed, in a number of countries outside the US, one of the remaining constraints on the accommodation of inflation.

The authorities were caught between (politically unpopular) disinflation (as under the British Labour Party 1968–70) to hold back inflation and maintain external balance, and expansion (as under the British Conservative Party 1971–74) which seemed now to exhaust itself in higher inflation quite soon, with less effect on output. The short-run trade-off between employ-ment and inflation along the Phillips curve had dramatically worsened. Not surprisingly, perhaps, politicians in several countries (Nixon and Heath) turned to incomes policies in the attempt artificially to flatten the Phillips curve. Such attempts (after some initial success) soon failed; indeed, the gratuitous inclusion of a wage indexation clause in UK incomes policies in 1972 drastically worsened the wage-price spiral in the UK in the aftermath of the 1973 Oil Shock.

Stagflation had arrived. Friedman (1968) and Phelps (1968) had already warned us how a sloping short-run Phillips curve (promising an output/inflation trade-off) would transmute, once expectations began to adjust, into a vertical (or even a backwards-bending) Phillips curve. There was no longer-term trade-off. Even so, expansion (contraction) now would have some immediate benefits (costs) (given the current state of expectations), whereas the effects of future counteracting contraction (expansion) could be discounted. Not only, however, would it take people (governments) with a fairly high discount rate to make any such short-term expansion worthwhile, but also (as was developed in the subsequent time inconsistency literature), other people would soon come to recognise the short-term pressures on government (e.g. the political business cycle of Nordhaus 1975), and adjust their inflationary expectations accordingly.

There, therefore, seemed no sensible alternative but to focus demand management (monetary policy) on the attainment of price stability, while leaving other policies (labour market policies, supply side policies, fiscal policies) to aim to lower the Natural Rate of Unemployment. Quite why there has been such a massive failure to achieve this latter objective over the last two decades, and whether this reflects mistaken analysis, adverse shocks or incorrect policies, is outside the remit of this paper. While there was some discussion of the correct dynamic path for the attainment of price stability, gradualism versus shock therapy ('cold turkey'), there was no real disagreement from then on of the primary objective of monetary policy, price stability (though there was an undercurrent of discussion on how this might best be measured).

There was, in contrast, considerable debate and analysis on the operational means, whereby the monetary authorities might achieve this objective. In the past, central banks had operated by varying interest rates in a discretionary and counter-cyclical manner, with exchange rates usually as their main intermediate target. Now exchange rates were flexible, and domestic inflation, and varying expectations thereof, were making the discretionary choice of interest rates more problematical. Moreover, central bankers could see, more clearly and directly than most, the political pressures that often caused interest rates to be varied (upwards) 'too little too late'. It was just at this same time that economists in country after country (e.g. Goldfeld 1973 for the US, and Laidler 1965 for the UK) were coming forward with their econometric studies to demonstrate that national demand for money functions were stable functions of a small set of variables. Hence velocity was predictable; and by setting targets for monetary growth, the authorities should be able to control nominal incomes in the short run and inflation in the longer run. Even in those cases where the prior econometric fit soon worsened, such as £M3 in the UK between 1971–73 and the case of the 'missing money' in the USA (see Goldfeld 1976), this did not dampen enthusiasm for targetry. Thus, in the UK the explosion in £M3 (out of line with past income levels, etc.), presaged a future surge in inflation, and was therefore held to warrant even greater faith in such targets.

These factors led central banks into the era of monetary targetry, begin-

Table 1.8. *The adoption of formal monetary targeting*

Country	Date
Germany	1974
USA	
Switzerland	1975
Canada	
UK	1976

Source: Griffiths and Wood (1981).

ning with the West German adoption of a target for central bank money in 1974; the dates of the adoption of such targetry by other countries is given in the table above.

Although there was some remission of inflation in most countries during the 1975/76 downturn, the use of such targetry did not prove effective in dampening inflation during the remainder of the 1970s, nor in bringing about positive real interest rates (West Germany and Switzerland being partial exceptions).

There were several explanations for this. The conversion of some governments (the Carter Democrats in USA; the Callaghan Labour Government in the UK; the Trudeau Liberals in Canada), to these new policies was skin-deep. Central banks were perplexed at how to respond to overshoots. To claw back monetary growth to the previous targeted path seemed too draconian; after all bygones are bygones. But the widely-adopted alternative of 'base-drift' was lax, both in spirit and in effect. Finally, central banks sought to achieve their monetary targets by varying interest rates to that end. Monetarists claimed that they did not have either the information, the skill or the incentives to do so; instead they pressed for the authorities to control the (seasonally adjusted) monetary base directly and allow interest rates to be freely determined in the market. This final debate continued unresolved throughout the era of targetry, until it was overtaken by the effective collapse of the predictability of velocity in the mid 1980s (Goodhart 1989 and 1995b).

Inflation worsened with the second oil shock in 1979, though not necessarily just as a result of this shock. Concern about monetary stability increased. The year 1979 proved to be a policy watershed. On 6 October 1979 Paul Volcker introduced his new operating technique of controlling non-borrowed reserves. While it was soon appreciated that this was not (and could not be, given the lagged reserve accounting system) a full blooded monetary base control system, it shifted the scenery in such a way as to allow the Fed to raise short-term interest rates dramatically. Earlier in June 1979 the Conservatives under Thatcher were elected, and they shortly thereafter (in 1980) re-emphasised, and extended into the Medium Term, their commitment to a Financial Strategy of holding to a monetary target.

In practice, monetary growth remained highly unstable in both countries, and short-term monetary targets were comprehensively missed in both countries, and medium-term ones as well in the UK. As a technical exercise it was hardly a success. Nevertheless the resolution of Volcker (and Reagan) in the USA, and Thatcher (with Howe and Lawson at the UK Treasury and Richardson at the Bank), together with their willingness to live with high and volatile interest rates (and high and volatile exchange rates in UK) did break the momentum of inflationary expectations. It broke much else besides. The accompanying downturn in 1980–82 was severe, and was followed by a sizeable reduction in the UK's manufacturing capacity. It caused a fearful crisis among primary producers world-wide, especially over-borrowed LDC countries in Latin America, which threatened for some time to feed back into financial fragility among Western banks.

This threat was carefully averted by the main central banks working in concert with the IMF, though whether the policies adopted were as beneficial to the borrowing countries as they were to the banking systems of the industrialised countries is another question. This crisis accompanied the abandonment of targetry. The domestic objective, a sharp deflation to break inflationary expectations, had been achieved despite (technical) failures to meet the numerical targets. Velocity was proving to be unpredictable. This was largely attributed to the innovations (e.g. interest-bearing chequable deposits), brought about by the circumstances (high and variable inflation and interest rates), by information technology, and by associated de-regulation (driven by both national and global competition for financial markets). It was not clear then, or now, when such innovations might slow-up and a new equilibrium financial structure emerge; consequently it was not sure then, or now, when stable (econometric) relationships might return. Although some monetarists still press claims for the continued reliability of a variety of aggregates, their credibility has been damaged. Apart from some continued attention in Germany, and in the European Monetary Institute, explicit monetary targetry was generally abandoned in the mid-1980s and has not returned.

Initially such targets were hardly missed. The downturn of 1981–82 was followed by one of the longest sustained stretches of steady growth on record, 1983–1989, combined with quite low inflation (in comparison with the 1970s). As in the 1920s in the USA, such success generated (unfounded) optimism in its unlimited extension. Such confidence, in future growing asset prices, helped to spark off asset price bubbles, first in equity prices, which broke spectacularly in October 1987, and then more generally in real estate, commercial property and housing prices in 1988–89. Such asset (housing) price increases raised wealth and increased consumption expenditures. Eventually the resulting fast (broad) monetary growth and rising expenditures fed through into higher consumer goods prices. This induced the monetary authorities, somewhat belatedly, to tighten in order to check the boom. By now the asset price bubble had been in full swing for some time, and the counter-cyclical policy measures broke the asset price bubble. The resulting collapse in asset prices, coming on top of the cyclical downturn, put extreme financial pressure both on wide sectors of bank borrowers (e.g. property developers, construction companies) and on their bankers in many areas, e.g. Japan, Victoria in Australia, the Coasts in the USA, the Nordic countries, to a lesser extent the UK. Bank lending collapsed, though how much owing to a decline in demand as contrasted with a cut-back in supply, is uncertain; broad money growth plummeted, and bad debts and failures soared. Bank failure rates, acknowledged or hidden, rose to levels last seen in the Depression of 1929–33.

With the recovery, albeit hesitant, established in the USA and UK, despite continuing problems in Japan and Continental Europe, a rather difficult corner has, probably, now been turned (1994). Although continental Europe, apart from Scandinavia, did not suffer as severely from the asset price bubble and bust, the asymmetric shock of German reunification, impacting on its partners in the ERM, both extended their boom at the end of the 1980s and now also the slump of the early 1990s.

Reference to the ERM provides a marker for shifting from a review of the domestic macro-objectives of monetary policy back to external monetary considerations. As noted earlier, academics had been hopeful that the switch to floating exchange rates would allow the exchange rate to adjust smoothly to movements in relative economic fundamentals, especially to relative price levels (thereby maintaining purchasing power parity in the medium term), instead of the large, occasional, discrete jumps in rates at a time of parity readjustment as under the Bretton Woods system. That hope was not fulfilled. Real exchange rates were even more variable under floating rates. It was, and remains, hard to relate exchange rate changes (except perhaps over very long periodicities, e.g. twenty years or so), to movements in economic fundamentals.

Hence the experience of floating rates not only disappointed prior academic hopes, but the volatility and the major misalignments that eventuated further disturbed economic policy-making, both nationally and internationally. During this period there has been a history of attempts to mitigate such external disturbances through a variety of schemes for international policy co-ordination of a more or less formal kind.

The shocks to the external monetary order in 1971–73 forced the demise of the first attempt at European Monetary Union, as set out in the Werner Report (1970). Nevertheless, the major European countries tried to limit the range of permissible exchange rate fluctuation amongst themselves under the Smithsonian Agreement of December 1971 via 'the snake in the tunnel'. The UK was forced out (in June 1972) after a minor speculative attack, and when France, too, had to float, it became little more than a residual Germanic grouping. The subsequent volatility of exchange rates between members of the European Community caused severe difficulties for the operation of the Common Agricultural Policy (CAP), and was seen as a serious obstacle for the achievement of greater political and economic unity in the EC more generally (Giavazzi and Giovannini 1989). Consequently a bilateral French/German political initiative (between D'Estaing and Schmidt) in 1978/79 led to the establishment of the Exchange Rate Mechanism of the European Monetary System. This became the most successful of the various attempts during these years to restore (regional) external monetary order. By the end of the 1980s it had evolved into a system of German leadership, with the other members of the ERM pegging to the Dm as their main counter-inflationary precommitment. So successful had it become that, by the early 1990s, not only were all the members renouncing exchange controls (Greece remaining outside the ERM), but also a progressive hardening of the ERM was seen as the route into EMU. Even this hard-won successful credibility was not, however, sufficient to withstand the shocks in the early 1990s, notably German reunification.

The European Community provided both a framework and a rationale for policy co-ordination among its members, and the objective of achieving German-level inflation provided a common objective. There was no such framework, or rationale, among the G3, USA, Germany and Japan, let alone wider G groupings. Nevertheless, following a period of neglect of the exchange rate by the US Treasury (1980–84), the misalignment of the US$ appeared so large, and so destabilising, that by 1985 the new Secretary of the Treasury (Baker) inaugurated a series of understandings among Finance Ministers about appropriate ranges for the main exchange rates (Funabashi 1988). Such understandings, with more or less commitment and fuzzy edges, have continued sporadically subsequently. How much difference such understandings, or such changes in (co-ordinated) foreign exchange intervention, or more rarely in interest rates, that they evoked, made to the historical course of exchange rates is an uncertain and unknowable counter-factual: the markets and most observers tend to be unimpressed and sceptical.

So, currently, at the end of this historical journey, the international monetary system remains as disordered as at any intervening time, and the way forward unclear. A pure float has been found, for reasons still unknown, to have been much more volatile than either expected or wished; the ERM has been battered, and the road to EMU remains uncertain; wider international exchange rate co-ordination is modest both in scope and objective and in actual achievement.

1.2.6   And now?

The most profound event of these last few years has been the collapse of Communism. Within the former Communist countries, the transition to a market economy has been much more difficult than initially hoped. This has been so no less in the monetary sphere than elsewhere, and extreme monetary disturbances, notably hyperinflation, have occurred in several countries (e.g. Ukraine), and are only being narrowly avoided in others (e.g. Russia).

Price deregulation, and other factors in the transition, cut off the cash flow to central government from the large State Owned Enterprises (SOEs), upon which those governments had previously relied for fiscal balance. Amidst the worsening inflation and falling output it was hard for central governments to obtain alternative sources of tax revenue, or cut their expenditures, sufficiently to restore fiscal balance. So, with the debt market in its infancy, the deficit was monetised. Meanwhile a sizeable proportion of the SOEs was loss-making. Because they were large employers, and provided most of the local social services, they could not be easily shut (or privatised). Consequently loans from the (often closely connected) so-called commercial banks to such SOEs were largely disguised fiscal subsidies, and such loans were often bad (i.e. non-performing) from the start. Under such circumstances, and with no history of credit assessment or its market allocation, credit control remained more often direct, by imposed quantitative limit (often immediately offset by an explosion of inter-enterprise 'trade credit'), rather than by market interest rate mechanisms. Given the (political) interest in keeping the SOEs going, it has been hard to control credit expansion, whether directly or otherwise. With the deficits of both governments and SOEs being regularly monetised, hyperinflation becomes an immediate concern. While the more advanced members among the former Communist countries (e.g. Poland, Hungary, the Czech Republic, the Baltic States) are successfully overcoming this nexus of monetary problems, most of the remaining countries are not. Even in China, which has been so comparatively successful in other ways, the problem of monetary control remains.

What effect the collapse of Communism will have on the rest of the world, and its associated monetary relationships remains quite uncertain. One possibility is that the end of the main bilateral, USSR/Communist versus Western/Capitalist, divide may lead to a splitting of the world into regional, trading, groupings, e.g. the Americas, Asia and the European Union (EU). If so, a consequential question is what are the implications for the internal monetary relationships of such regional groupings. Here there is an interesting division of views between the EU, where some internal monetary order is frequently perceived as a necessary complement, perhaps even a prerequisite, for the successful continuation of the Single Market, and NAFTA where there has been no call, nor consideration, for any side-agreement on monetary inter-relationships to support the free trade area. Is this because one, or other, group (the European or North Americans) is wrong? Or are the assumptions on which the two groups are working different? Thus the EU may fear that, unless prevented, member States may use monetary policy and exchange rate adjustment to obtain an (unfair) competitive advantage. By contrast, the North Americans may assume that, whatever else determines monetary policy in their three countries, a desire to manipulate competitive trading advantage is not among them. Can both assumptions be correct in their own regional circumstances?

Within their own regions, the leading countries, the hegemons, are, now that demand-for-money functions have become so unreliable, apart perhaps from Germany, carrying out an essentially discretionary policy, aimed in the very short-run at stabilising the growth rate of nominal incomes and in the somewhat longer-run (a few years forward) at achieving and maintaining price stability. In the last few years discussion and debate has switched from operational techniques (e.g. interest rate control versus monetary base control: rules versus discretion) towards concern with structure, incentives and accountability, in short to most of the issues that come together under the heading of central bank independence.

In the meantime, central bankers have been left, largely unchallenged now by monetarist critics, to use their single main instrument, i.e. the control over short-term interest rates, in the light of their own discretion for the, generally agreed, objective of achieving medium-term price stability. The main operational problem is that interest rate changes affect the economy (and monetary expansion) with a considerable, and varying lag. Consequently central bankers need to vary interest rates in response to deviations of the uncertain future rate of inflation (from the desired, say, 0 to 2 per cent rate), rather than react to current data. This means that the forecasts of future price inflation, say 1½ to 2 years hence, now play a central role in the conduct of monetary policy (e.g. the Bank of England quarterly forecast).

Especially given the uncertainty of such forecasts (see Brunner and Meltzer 1993, Lecture 4), there remains considerable room for political, and other interest group, pressures to be applied to central banks, usually to defer interest rate increases at (politically) inconvenient moments. The 'time inconsistency' literature suggests that it has been the incentive structure (on central banks) rather than technical/operational limitations that has hindered the attainment of price stability.

It is in this context that the campaign for central bank independence has developed, particularly in Europe where such independence is not only statutorily required for the ECB, but also for all national central bank members of the ESCB (Maastricht Treaty 1992). In this approach the central bank is to be statutorily mandated to give primacy to the achievement of price stability, and provided with freedom (from any government constraint) and autonomy to vary short-term interest rates to that end. Subsidiary questions of democratic accountability, appropriate other functions (e.g. prudential supervision) and management structure have been handled variously in the differing current models of independent central banks (e.g. Bundesbank and ECB model, as compared with the RBNZ model, see for example the CEPR Roll Committee Report 1993).

Besides the theoretical arguments for central bank independence, the case for it has been strengthened by the empirical evidence that, in recent decades, the more independent central banks have presided over lower inflation but had largely similar growth/employment outcomes compared with their more dependent colleagues (Alesina and Summers 1993).

The counter-claim has been made (Posen 1993) that there is little evidence that more independent central banks can directly lower the unemployment cost of lowering inflation (the sacrifice ratio). Rather, more independent central banks are established where there is, in any case, a dominating political constituency for low inflation. While this may well be so, an independent central bank by its own actions, words and reputation can help to extend and to sustain that constituency.

This latter view, that the establishment of an independent central bank will largely succeed, or fail, depending on its 'political' skills in holding together a low inflation constituency, implies that the passage of Acts to grant such independence will be much less of a panacea than its, more credulous (academic) advocates would hope. A danger in this context is that 'independence' may get oversold as the solution to the ills of the monetary system, just as monetary targeting, exchange rate floating, and so many prior economic nostrums were often given exaggerated credence in some quarters, to their own subsequent detriment.

It is, perhaps, inevitable that there will be some degree of hype in the promotion of new ideas, in order for them to overcome the barrier of inertia. Fortunately, it is hardly necessary to remind central bankers of the merits of a cautious scepticism. This will stand them in good stead during the next 300 years.

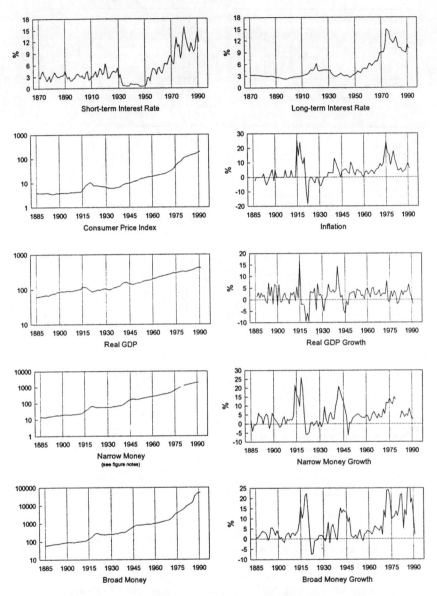

1.1 Britain. All series up to 1980 taken from *The Economist* (1989), except: interest rates, taken from Homer and Sylla (1991); and narrow and broad money, taken from Capie and Webber (1985). All series are updated from International Monetary Fund (1992), International Financial Statistics Yearbook, Washington. This last point applies to all figures 1.1–1.10.

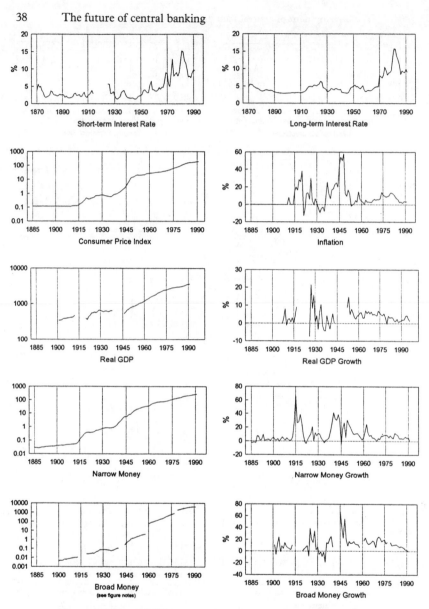

Figure 1.2 France. All series up to 1980 taken from *The Economist* (1989), except: interest rates, taken from Homer and Sylla (1991); narrow and broad money supply (currency and bank deposits) and real GDP, taken from Mitchell (1970). Breaks in time series during the two world wars are due to missing data. Breaks in time series during the 1980s are due to the start of a new, redefined series. The break in broad money series (1958–9) is due to the redefinition of the franc.

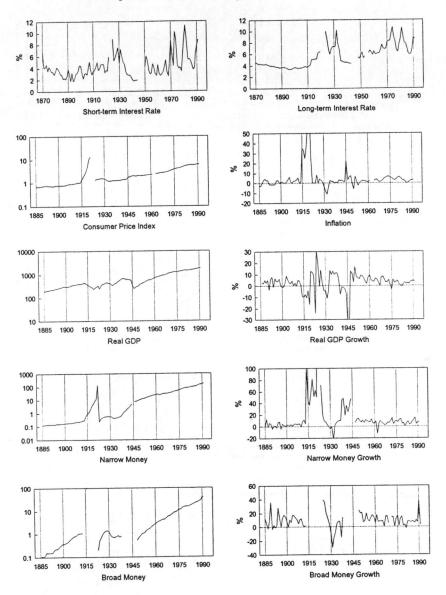

Figure 1.3 Germany. All series up to 1980 taken from *The Economist* (1989), except: interest rates, taken from Homer and Sylla (1991); narrow and broad money supply (currency and bank deposits), taken from Mitchell (1970). Breaks in time series during the two world wars are due to missing data.

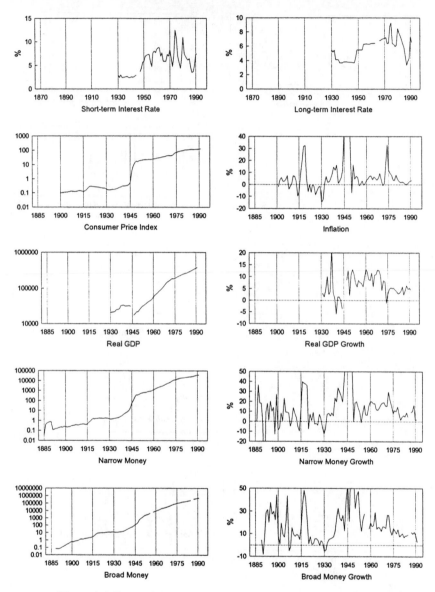

Figure 1.4 Japan. All series up to 1980 taken from *The Economist* (1989), except: narrow and broad money (currency and bank deposits), taken from Japanese Statistical Association (1987). Breaks in time series are due to missing data.

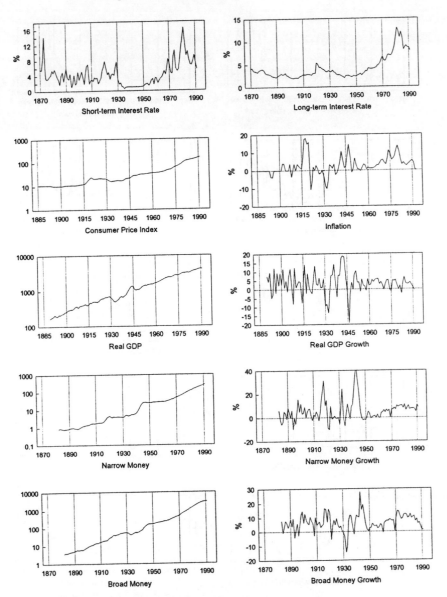

Figure 1.5 USA. All series up to 1980 taken from *The Economist* (1989), except: narrow and broad money, taken from Friedman and Schwartz (1970). Breaks in time series are due to missing data.

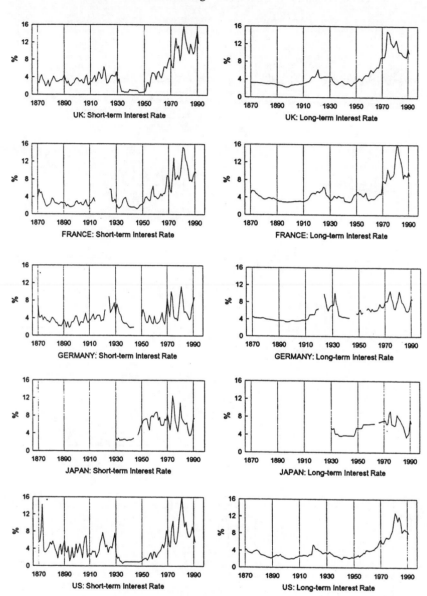

Figure 1.6 Interest rates: short-term and long-term. Breaks in time series are due to missing data.

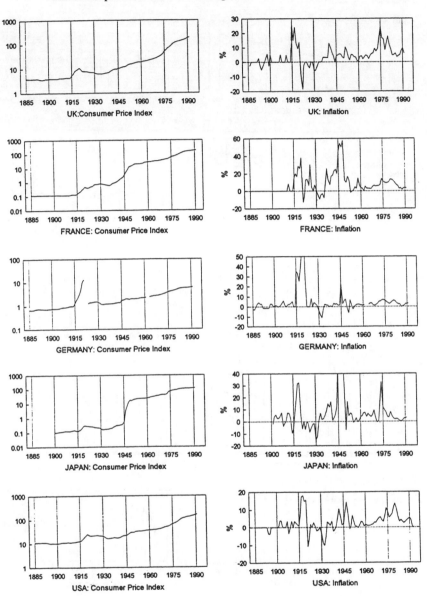

Figure 1.7 Price levels (log) and inflation rates. Breaks in time series are due to missing data.

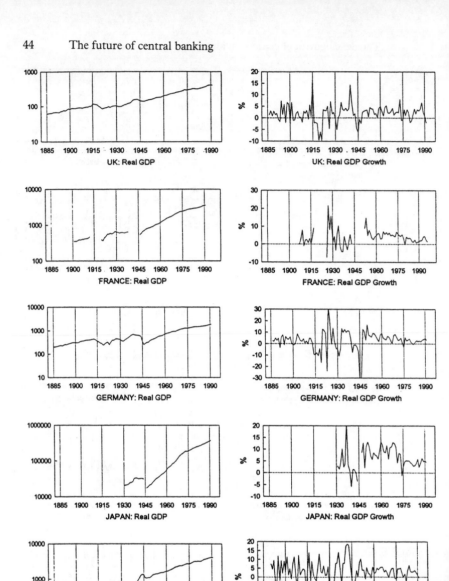

Figure 1.8 Real GDP: levels (log) and growth rates. Breaks in time series are due to missing data.

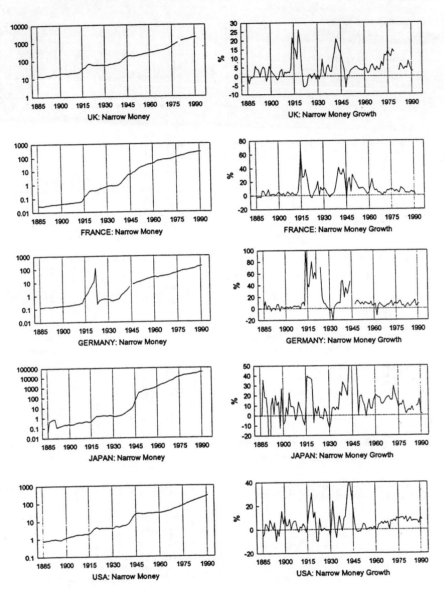

Figure 1.9 Narrow money: levels (log) and growth rates. Breaks in time series are due to missing data.

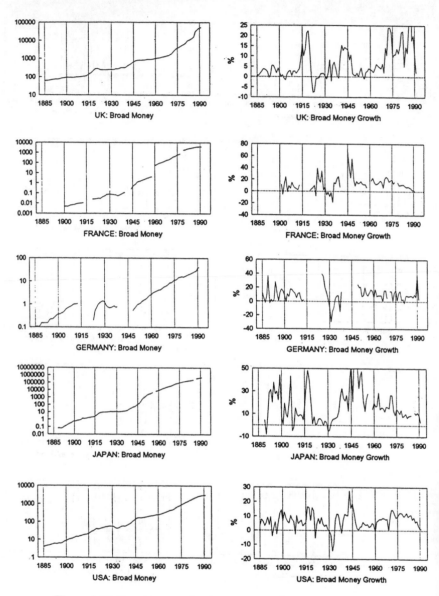

Figure 1.10 Broad money: levels (log) and growth rates. Breaks in time series are due to missing data.

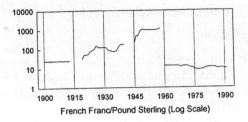

French Franc/Pound Sterling (Log Scale)

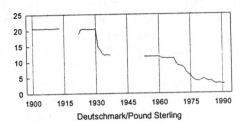

Deutschmark/Pound Sterling

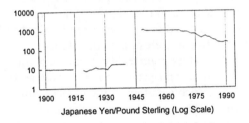

Japanese Yen/Pound Sterling (Log Scale)

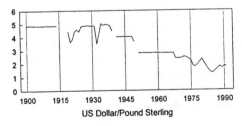

US Dollar/Pound Sterling

Figure 1.11 Exchange rates (against £ sterling). Breaks in time series are due to missing data.

1.3   The relations between central banks and governments

1.3.1   Introduction

In this section we explore the nature of central bank/government relations, and what has influenced these at different times. At base the issue considered here is the question of the extent of closeness (or distance) between the respective parties.

The current concern over central bank independence, as noted in the previous section, has already spawned a large literature, a benefit of which has been to draw attention to how difficult it is to define, let alone measure, independence (see, for example, Cukierman 1992 and Eijffinger and Schaling 1993). A variety of indicators of degrees of independence has been devised but their use is fraught with difficulty. Our concern extends beyond a definition of independence to an attempt to examine the factors and considerations that have helped to shape the ebb and flow in the closeness of the relationship between central banks and governments. It is difficult to reduce this to a common single denominator. Should we look for one? The historian in the economic historian is perhaps more comfortable with the uniqueness of events and happy to explain each change as the product of a number of factors specific to that change. The economist in the economic historian is always tempted to look for generalisations and we are succumbing to that temptation in spite of the difficulties.

A pattern of alternating regimes is not uncommon in economic history. For example, free trade and protection, and fixed and floating exchange-rates, have followed such a pattern in the modern world economy. In very general terms the explanation seems to be that there arises a dissatisfaction with current economic performance and the perceived role that the prevailing regime has in that performance and that brings about the desire for change.[10]

In a recent study of the related topic of alternating regimes of fixed and floating exchange-rates Eichengreen (1994) examined a number of hypotheses that considered the role of: international economic leadership, international co-operation, intellectual consensus, underlying macro-stability, fixed rates as an anti-inflationary rule, and domestic distributional politics. He concluded that any explanation that was based on any single one of these

---

[10] The nineteenth-century triumph of free trade over protection was the adoption of a policy that was followed by the most successful economy of the time – Britain. The re-emergence of trade liberalisation after World War II was a consequence of the failure of the alternative protectionist policies adopted in the years between 1880 and 1914 (much of that widely seen at the time as depression years) and extended in the inter-war years when international trade suffered its greatest collapse ever.

was inadequate. In any case several of them are rather nebulous (see Bordo and Capie 1993 on some of the difficulties in identifying the reasons for changes in monetary regimes).

When we turn to changing fashions in relation to monetary policy, there are perhaps three important elements to the explanation. First, are the underlying political conditions. Secondly, within that we identify some short-term factors that trigger change. And thirdly, there is a difference according to the simplicity or complexity of the task confronting the central bank.

In very broad terms, the period from the origins of central banking at the beginning of the nineteenth century through to the First World War is the period when *laissez-faire* emerged, dominated, and then faded. That was a period when the state tended to keep its distance, particularly in trade and monetary matters. The belief that the gold standard, the prevailing international monetary system, provided a largely automatic means of adjustment, was important to this philosophy. A considerable degree of independence therefore obtained, particularly in so far as it related to the central bank assisting in the smooth working of the gold standard. The period from the First World War to the 1970s has in contrast been the age of the state, of economic management, of socialism. It was in this period that there was a move to greater government control, and of more dependent central banks. This era is probably over now and we may be entering another of relative economic freedom.

The second area of explanation lay in the immediate proximate cause or trigger for change. Within the very broad underlying political conditions set out above there have been some factors, not always exogenous, which have provoked a change. War, or a similar type of crisis, is the most obvious. The state has always been tempted to gain control over resources; the revenue motive has never been far away. In times of crisis such as war there is an obvious incentive to ensure greater control over resources, and independence is likely to suffer and even disappear. Other triggers have been: the acquisition of sovereignty by former colonial countries, leading to more dependent institutions; rapid inflation leading in due course to greater independence, because of the perceived responsibility of the monetary financing of governments for such inflation, as in Germany; and deflation leading to less independence, as greater government intervention becomes desired. In this respect our judgement differs from that of Cukierman (1992), perhaps because we take a much longer horizon.

The third element in the story concerns the simplicity or complexity of the central bank's task. When the role of the central bank was relatively simple, when there was for example a single objective (especially if that was a technical one, as in the maintenance of convertibility under the gold standard when what was required was the adjustment of interest rates), there was more likelihood of independence. At the other extreme, with the advent of Keynesian economics a range of possibilities was opened up. What weakens or perhaps destroys independence is this complexity in the range of choices.

Although there are serious difficulties in dealing with the question of independence, and our aim is to broaden this particular discussion, it is useful to provide at least a working definition of independence. The one we prefer is: the right[11] to change the key operational instrument without consultation or challenge from government. This instrument has, in practice, almost always been a central short-term money market rate, often the discount rate. While the majority of academics do not believe that this is necessarily so (in many cases proposing that central banks instead focus on the control of the monetary base), almost all central bankers do. So, in practice, interest rates are the key. It might be expected that the ownership of central banks plays an important part in their ability freely to determine interest rates (i.e. act independently). The forthcoming discussion in section 1.3.3 indicates that, in the event, this has not been so. This is clearly relevant to the current discussions of central bank independence, which are reviewed below in section 1.3.4.

Defining independence in the way that we have, or indeed in any other that is operationally useful, does not at a stroke remove the difficulties. It is still not possible to read the extent of independence from the statutes. This is made more difficult by the fact that these statutes were invariably modified frequently (to take just one example, New Zealand since World War II provides a good illustration; see Hawke 1973). Furthermore, the question of interest rates is seldom dealt with explicitly. And even if interest rate policy was stated explicitly it does not follow that it always or even normally prevailed. Categorisation still requires a fairly intimate knowledge of the structure, organisation, and the working practices of the institution, to say nothing of the personalities in both the central bank and the government.

1.3.2   The historical pattern of the relationship

The history of this relationship is a story of ebb and flow in the closeness between central banks and governments. First some reminder of what that broad pattern was. Although some institutions were founded before the

---

[11] The need to change the key instrument, the interest rate, may be largely predetermined by the objectives of the monetary authorities, for example by the desire to maintain the gold standard or a pegged exchange rate. But the question of who decides exactly when, and by how much, to pull the interest rate trigger still remains.

nineteenth century there were no real central banks before about 1800 (unless a case is made for the Bank of England – something we come back to). For those institutions founded in the nineteenth century and gradually emerging as central banks in the course of the century there was relative independence. These banks increasingly, particularly as the century wore on, acquired the responsibility of maintaining convertibility of the currency under the gold standard. It was in this period that central banking as we understand it today can be said to have emerged. The philosophy of *laissez-faire* dominated much of the century and under its influence the state's role was a diminished one. It was natural therefore that such banks enjoyed a greater latitude than at other times. (Obviously there are some differences in the timing of this in different countries but as a broad generalisation it holds.) The First World War brought that to an end; and while after the war there was a desire to return to independence and some movement towards that, that was damaged first by the great depression and the perceived role of banking in that, and then further by the Second World War, and then more lastingly by the rise of the managed economy. Only in recent years has that trend begun to be reversed.

We hinted in the previous paragraph that there may be a case to be made for the Bank of England being considered as a central bank from as early as the Napoleonic Wars. By 1790 the Bank dominated the monetary system and held the reserves of that system. There are examples of the Bank acting (in this, more limited, sense) as a lender of last resort in the eighteenth century (see Lovell 1957). Freed from the obligation to convert its notes after 1797 it was accused, by those who went under the name of bullionists, of being responsible for the falling exchange rate – a consequence of its over issue of notes. The Bank rejected the idea that it had the power to influence the price level, or indeed that it had public responsibilities. But the case was clearly developing that the Bank was something other than a private profit maximising institution. It had many of the characteristics of a modern central bank. And it was being urged by people such as Henry Thornton to behave in keeping with that.

Even for nineteenth-century England, however, the situation is far from straightforward. The 1844 Act helped, but the exact nature of the relationship continued to be debated. In the financial crises of 1847, 1857, and 1866 there was a need for the government to intervene or for the Bank to consult the government. In the first case suspension of the Act was allowed and in the latter two suspension actually took place. Fetter (1965, p. 281) summed up a lengthy discussion in the following fashion:

Officially the Bank made no suggestion to the Government, and officially the Government did nothing beyond letting the Bank know it was free to break the law if it felt this necessary to carry out its public responsibilities. What went on in the clubs, at the country estates, at the meetings of old Etonians, Oxonians, and Cantabrigians, and possibly at the Political Economy Club, was another matter. The important thing was that somehow or other the Government and the Bank worked things out reasonably well.

This leaves the issue open. At other points Fetter talks about the 'fiction' of Bank of England independence in the nineteenth century.

It would be misleading to imply that independence was widespread elsewhere, even in the age of liberalism when it was seen as desirable. There was less independence in practice in some countries. The Banque de France had been subjected to considerable control from its birth in 1800 until the mid nineteenth century. But with the increasing liberalism that followed, things were expected to change. Even so, the historian of the Banque de France, Alain Plessis wrote:

it is surprising to note, in a so-called liberal period, just how much the Banque de France, a private undertaking which was fiercely proud of what it thought of as its independence, was subject to frequent intervention amounting to constant control, on the part of the Ministry of Finance in particular and the public authorities in general. (quoted in Bouvier 1988)

However, if we apply our definition of independence – control of interest rates – then there was surely a good measure of independence, or freedom of action in the operation of monetary policy in France, and in other countries too in the nineteenth century. Central European experience was somewhat different and undoubtedly owes something to the fact that the age of economic liberalism arrived there much later and barely had time to emerge and flourish before the end of the nineteenth century. Intervention was always more popular there.

The story that is usually told of much of Continental Europe derives from the work of Gerschenkron (1962). The original hypothesis was that since European countries had come to industrialisation relatively late (in varying degrees) they needed to take actions that were not needed in Britain. It was this that gave rise to the universal bank, and for a greater role for the state. The more backward the country the greater was the need for intervention. The thesis has been under some challenge in recent years particularly with respect to the contribution of the universal bank, but it is still useful as an explanation for the extent of intervention (see Teichova 1992).

When the gold standard was disrupted and in effect abandoned at the outbreak of the First World War, and as governments sought greater control over resources, price levels soared almost everywhere. The nature of the relationship between the state and the central banks was sharpened. Irrespective of the degree of independence, either statutory or in practice, that obtained, at times of crisis of this kind the state enforces its authority.

When the First World War broke out there was then a stern test of Bank independence. In England the Prime Minister (Asquith) invited the Governor of the Bank (Cunliffe) to make a written promise: 'that during the war the Bank must in all things act on the directions of the Chancellor of the Exchequer (McKenna) and must not take any action likely to affect credit without prior consultation with the Chancellor' (Sayers 1976, pp. 99–107). Cunliffe in a demonstration of independence refused to sign, and the Committee of Treasury gave its support when it agreed, 'that it was impossible for the Bank to renounce its functions' (p. 105). But after a month Cunliffe gave an undertaking to work with the Chancellor. The same sort of thing was happening all around the world. The Federal Reserve, designed as an independent institution just before the war, lost that independence almost immediately when the US entered the war. Then, having regained it after the war, it lost it again at the outbreak of the Second World War.

At the end of the First World War there was a widespread desire to return to the world of normality and stability, that is to the years before 1914. That was of course impossible. Too much had changed. But 'business as usual' and 'back to 1914' were popular slogans. The desire was seen in monetary matters too. A return to the gold standard was immediately pursued. Further, in the aftermath of the war and its inflationary experience there was widespread acceptance of the dangers inherent in political interference, and equally widespread desire to bring about central bank independence. At the Brussels Conference in 1920 a resolution was passed stating: 'Banks and especially banks of issue should be freed from political pressure and should be conducted solely on the lines of prudent finance' (Resolution III, Commission on Currency and Exchange). The years till the Great Depression were characterised by this pursuit of independence as a result of the price experience of the years 1914–20, and reinforced by the hyperinflations of the early 1920s. It was a cardinal feature of the reconstruction schemes of the League of Nations. It was also true separately of Latin America.

Using our definition of independence, that of freedom to alter interest rates, the Bank of England seems to have returned to its independent status after the First World War. Indeed a principal complaint against the Bank at the time was that Montagu Norman as Governor had the power to change the discount rate without consulting anyone either inside the Bank or outside the Bank (Pollard 1970). From the depression years onwards there was a greater desire on the part of government to influence interest rates. The war loan conversion of 1932 is an example of one attempt, to quote Kaldor (1986, p. xx), 'which brought down the whole structure of long-term interest rates'. Whether or not that is true is not the point at issue here. It demonstrates the role the Treasury wished to play in influencing interest rates. The fact that Bank Rate remained unchanged at 2 per cent from

1932–1939 is possibly indicative of the growing influence of government. If it remains difficult to sort the issue out for the Bank of England, how much more so is it for many other banks whose histories have not been researched so intensively and about which we know a great deal less.

It may be thought that if governments almost invariably set up central banks then their relationship with them, at least at the time of origin, must have been close. That is not necessarily the case. In some periods, as noted, the call was for independence and even though the central bank was the creation of the state it may nevertheless have been set up to operate at arm's length, and perhaps later, not much later in some cases, have been brought under tighter control. For example in the early inter-war years when independence was highly prized the central banks in New Zealand, Canada and Greece were set up explicitly as independent institutions even if their independence lasted only a short time.

At the end of the interwar period Plumptre (1940, p. 23) wrote, 'One of the primary tenets of accepted central banking thought has been the importance of keeping central banks politically independent'. As we have seen such a view had been weakening for some years. The great depression of 1929–33 was regarded in many countries as a consequence of central and commercial bank failings. Reform was seen as urgently required. One aspect of this was the removal of independence. Independence was desirable in the 1920s but had lost appeal by the 1930s.

Thus Plumptre's view was effectively obsolete by the middle decades of the twentieth century, as confidence in liberal capitalism weakened. Three factors were primarily responsible. Perhaps the most important was the world-wide drift to socialism and intervention. The second was the rise of Keynesian economics. The third, more or less coincident with the second, was the Second World War and its aftermath. There was also a generally improved price performance in these years (1939–51) – certainly compared with 1914–20/23. Governments were therefore encouraged to return to interventionist policies. Nationalisation of central banks was common as governments everywhere took a closer interest in monetary policy (a striking example was the Netherlands and others can be found in table 1.7 in section 1.2).

Indeed it went much further, for monetary policy was conceived in a wholly different way. To quote the Radcliffe Committee Report (1959, para. 767): 'More than that, monetary policy, as we have conceived it, cannot be envisaged as a form of economic strategy which pursues its own independent objectives. It is a part of a country's economic policy as a whole and must be planned as such.'

Further, in the 1940s, 1950s, and 1960s there was a great extension of national political independence. The birth of new states and acquisition of sovereignty by former colonies resulted in the emergence of governments who sought control over their own affairs. Governments established central banks or took over or converted existing institutions (such as currency boards). Thus the period from the Second World War until around 1970 was another period of great growth in central banking but on this occasion the desired and pursued relationship was of relative closeness – dependence – unlike the earlier inter-war years, and for most of the nineteenth century.

The inflationary experience of the two decades that followed – roughly the late 1960s to the late 1980s – when the world for the first time ever, in a generally peaceful period, adopted fiat money, brought home again the clear relationship between expansionary monetary policy and inflation. The view developed that where central banks were less susceptible to government pressure they delivered lower inflation. The desire was then for more independence and currently the desire is being turned into realisation.

1.3.3   Who owns the central bank?

Tables 1.9 and 1.10 indicate that formal ownership, and therefore rights to the residual profits of the central bank, are likely either to be in the hands of the government, or to be shared between the government and other share-holders (often other banks), with the majority stake usually being in the hands of the government. Even where the government is not a majority shareholder, however, dividends are subject to a maximum, with any residual surplus being paid to the government.

In so far as the public sector (the government) owns and controls the central bank, either by itself or jointly with the commercial banks, it is also likely to take to itself the power to appoint the main officials, the governors and directors. The modes of appointment are depicted in table 1.11.

People in power normally appoint others to centres of power with whom they are comfortable. Hence, the appointment power is, of itself, likely to make the central bank subservient to the wishes of government. On the other hand, the senior officials of the central bank have a specialised technical job to undertake. They need to be respected in the financial community, and to have the ability to absorb, to assess and to impart specialised monetary information and analysis. They need a reputation for sound, independent judgement, even, perhaps especially, when they are formally subservient to the dictates of the government in the conduct of macro-monetary policy.

In order to foster their independence of judgement, and their technical reputation, central bank senior officials are often appointed for quite lengthy tenures, shown in table 1.12 below. As Cukierman (1992, chapter 19) records, however, the formal tenure is in some countries (e.g. Argentina)

Table 1.9. *The ownership of central banks*

State	Mixed (% of government holding)	Private
Argentina	Austria (50%)	South Africa
Australia	Belgium (50%)	Switzerland[c]
Canada	Chile (50%)	USA[d]
Denmark[a]	Greece (10%)	
France	Japan (55%)	
Finland	Mexico (51%)	
Germany	Turkey (25%)	
Ireland	Italy[b]	
India		
Netherlands		
New Zealand		
Norway		
Spain		
Sweden		
UK		

[a] The National Bank of Denmark is not strictly owned by the government, but has the status of a self-governing institution whose profits accrue to the government.
[b] The Banca d'Italia is not a joint stock company but is incorporated under public law, and can only be owned by other public companies.
[c] The Swiss National bank is owned jointly by the cantons (63 per cent) and private shareholders.
[d] The Federal Reserve is owned by the member banks of the System.
Source: Aufricht (1961, 1967) and Appendix B.

considerably longer than the actual tenure where there is an (unwritten) convention that senior bank officials submit their resignations whenever there is a change of either government or, even, of Finance Ministers within a Government.

Another safeguard for the reputation, and technical expertise, of central banks is that governments most often appoint existing experts with a track-record of proven ability, rather than their fellow politicians to the field. The background of most Governors and directors lies in banking, either central or commercial, or closely adjunct fields, such as journalists, lawyers, economists or accountants specialising in money and banking.

Besides their suitability for senior appointment in terms of personal expertise and capacity, there is also the question of whether appointments to the Board should be entirely on a personal basis, or should ensure a wide representation from differing major sectors (e.g. banks, industry, Unions, possibly even academic). Table 1.13 below shows the requirements on the composition of central bank boards. In general, the kind of checks and

Table 1.10. *Distribution of central bank profits*

Country	Maximum dividend?	Residual profits (after dividends and reserve provisions)
Austria	10%[a]	Government
Belgium[b]	6%	Government[c]
Chile	No dividend	Government
Greece	12%	Government[d]
Italy	6%	Government[d]
Japan	5%	Government
Mexico	6%	Government
South Africa	10%	Government
Switzerland	6%	Cantons first receive 80 centimes per capita. Residual then divided between government ($\frac{1}{3}$) and cantons ($\frac{2}{3}$)
Turkey	6%	Government[cd]
USA	6%	Government

[a] After the government has taken 33 per cent of net profits.
[b] Article 20 of the Organic Law of the Banque Nationale states that the net earnings of the Banque 'which are in excess of 3 per cent of the difference between the average amount of [its] assets and liabilities are assigned to the state'.
[c] The personnel of the central bank may receive some of the residual profits.
[d] An additional dividend may be paid out of residual profits.
Source: Appendix B.

Table 1.11. *Modes of appointment of central bank governing board*

Governor appointed by . . . (on proposal of . . .)			Directors appointed by . . .	
Government	Directors	Crown	Government	Other (specify)
Australia	Canada	Belgium	Australia	Belgium
Austria	Italy	(government)	Austria	(crown)
Chile	Mexico	Denmark	Canada	Germany
Finland	Sweden	(government)	Chile	(parliament)
(directors)		Netherlands	Denmark	Norway
France		(directors)	Finland	(parliament)
Germany		Norway	France	Mexico
(directors)		(government)	India	(government/
India		Spain	Japan	shareholders)
Ireland		(government)	Spain	South Africa
Japan		UK	UK	(shareholders)
New Zealand		(government)	US	Sweden
South Africa				(parliament)
Switzerland				Switzerland
US				(parliament/ shareholders)

Source: Aufricht (1961, 1967), Fair (1980) and Appendix B.

Table 1.12. *Tenure of central bank officials*

Country	Governor[a]	Directors (executive)
Australia	7	5
Austria	5	5
Belgium	5	6 (3)
Canada	7	3
Chile	5	10
Denmark	unlimited	5[b]
Finland	unlimited	(unlimited)
France	unlimited[c]	4 (unlimited)
Germany	8	6
Greece	4	8
India	5	3
Ireland	7	4
Italy	unlimited	5
Japan	5	4
Mexico	unlimited	4
Netherlands	7	2
New Zealand	5	5
Norway	unlimited	5
Portugal	5	6
South Africa	5	4
Spain	unlimited	3
Sweden	unlimited	3 (unlimited)
Switzerland	6	3
UK	5	4
US	4	14

[a] In all cases the appointment of Governor is renewable.
[b] 1 year for those elected by the Council of Representatives.
[c] In practice limited to 5–7 years.
Source: Aufricht (1961, 1967), Fair (1980), Skånland (1984) and Appendix B.

balances needed for the successful operation of a federal country carries over to the constitution of its central bank, and the composition of central bank boards in federal countries is more likely to be 'representative' than in a unitary country.

Not only does the composition of the Board of Directors vary between countries, but so also does their power. In some countries, especially the more unitary countries, the Governor assumes ultimate personal responsibility for the acts of his/her central bank, and the Board has an essentially advisory role. In others, especially in the more federal countries, major macro-monetary decisions (e.g. on interest rate changes) are taken by way of

Table 1.13. *Requirements on the composition of central bank boards*

Country	Requirements
Australia	Directors selected for eminence in academic, agricultural or business activity.
Austria	At least one representative of banking, industry, trade and small business, agriculture, salaried employees, and labour respectively.
Canada	Directors selected from 'diversified occupations'.
Chile	3 representatives in the area of economy, 1 representative of the President of the Republic.
Denmark	8 Directors with a seat in Parliament, 1 economist and 1 lawyer.
Greece	At least 5 representatives of industry, commerce and agriculture.
Ireland	2 representatives of banking and 1–2 civil servants.
Italy	Minimum regional representation.
Japan	2 government representatives (without voting rights) who represent the Economic Planning Agency and Ministry of Finance, and 4 appointed members with knowledge of the business of the large city banks, regional banks, commerce and industry, and agriculture respectively.
Norway	Composition of Board determined by political balance in Parliament.
Sweden	Composition of Board determined by political balance in Parliament.
Switzerland	Minimum representation of geographical regions and economic sectors.
USA	No more than one Director from any Federal Reserve District

Sources: Aufricht (1967), Fair (1980), Skånland (1984), Appendix.

a formal vote in the Board, and the Chairman (President) can be outvoted (though this will rarely happen in practice; a Chairman who is frequently outvoted will lose stature and consider resignation).

The personal responsibility of Governors in certain unitary countries both emphasises the hierarchy of power and decision-making in those banks, and also makes the locus of responsibility and accountability transparent. But it also exposes the Governor in such cases to personal (political) pressures that can be more easily deflected when responsibility belongs to a Board. For example, the, sometimes personalised, attacks on the policies of the Deutsche Bundesbank that were directed at Dr H. Schlesinger at various international meetings in 1992 and 1993 could be more easily met by reminding his interlocutors that the policies were those of the Direktorium in Frankfurt, not his alone and personally.

Given that any transition from a subservient to an independent central bank is likely to place it much more squarely in the political limelight, there is an argument for shifting the locus of power somewhat from the single hands of the Governor to the Bank's Board, commensurately. The Act to give the Banque de France independence appears to move in this direction.

1.3.4   The politics of central bank independence

The maintenance of price stability involves the application of deflationary policies in the face of an expansionary impulse.[12] As McChesney Martin said, 'it is the role of the central banker to take away the punch bowl, just when the party is getting going'. Such deflationary actions will have particularly adverse effects on certain sectors of the economy, notably debtors, primary producers,[13] those who have invested in the expectation of future growth, and inflation, and the economically weak. By contrast, the beneficiaries are the creditors, the conservative, the economically stronger, and, to some extent, manufacturing interests, who have both a comparatively greater need of longer-term stability and certainty (in order to plan efficiently for the investment and use of product-specific capital), while being able to protect themselves somewhat better from short-term fluctuations (than primary producers). Poor, small-scale, indebted farmers are likely to be most opposed to central banks; the rich retired, with large holdings of financial assets, are likely to be the most supportive, especially if there remain recent memories of the ravages of (hyper)inflation on savings.

This line-up of natural opponents and supporters for central banks would suggest that political parties of the left would be more suspicious of, and antagonistic to, central banks than the parties of the right. This has frequently been so, but the connections (between political parties and central banks), are complicated by the fact that central banks have also been an instrument for government intervention in the working of the financial system. The more subservient the central bank to government direction, and the greater the desire of government to control the working of the financial system directly, rather than by market mechanisms, the more the left-wing party will support, and the right attack the central bank. The extreme example was the use of central banks as monobanks in the Communist system, but Australian central bank history (Schedvin 1992) reflects these influences.

---

[12] It also, of course, implies the reverse, i.e. introducing expansionary policies in the face of deflationary shocks. Such policies would seem less likely to be controversial. Yet it is arguable that several of central banks' worst mistakes have occurred as a result of hesitations in reacting to deflation, with the Great Depression in the USA, 1929–33, being the main, but not the only example. It may be that periods of severe deflation have been less common than continuing inflationary pressures. Hence central bankers have had less practice in coping with such problems. In order to stand firm against such inflation, they seek to engender a reputation for toughness, and this may militate against an appropriate expansionary reaction to deflationary shocks.

[13] With relatively inelastic demand and supply functions, and flexibly adjusting prices, the real incomes of primary producers tend to vary in an exaggerated way in response to shifts in monetary conditions. While over the long run they too benefit from price stability, they tend

Since the support of left-wing parties for central banks has often been conditioned on them acting as an agent of government, one would expect that they would be usually more opposed to constitutional measures to give the central bank more independence and autonomy. Even in this respect, however, current game theory would suggest that, since financial markets are more suspicious of left-wing governments, such prospective governments might have more to gain by allocating the control of inflation to an independent agency (predicated on the assumption that left-wing governments now expect to work with, rather than to suppress, free financial markets). South Africa may, perhaps, be a current example.

The central bank is a natural monopoly within a fiat money regime. As emphasised many times in the discussion of the transition to EMU, there can only be one locus for the determination of monetary policy in a given currency area. Consequently a central bank acts, and has often done so consciously, as a centralising, unifying institution in that currency area. The political overlap between the nation state on the one hand, and an associated national currency and central bank, is extremely strong, much stronger for example than the economic relationship between 'optimal currency areas', whose empirical delineation remains obscure, and separate actual currency areas (see Goodhart 1995a). Consequently there will be strong political support for the establishment of a (single) central bank in an area from those who want political unification within those same boundaries, and opposition from those who want less centralisation, more regional autonomy. Examples are numerous, but in the present context the fact that we are celebrating the anniversary of the Bank of England, rather than the Bank of the United Kingdom, can be partially ascribed to continuing tenderness about separatist tendencies in the other parts of the Union.

Thus, the establishment of a central bank within a federal country, for that country as a whole, has typically followed the achievement of a political consensus that there should be a relatively strong, central, Federal constitution and government (e.g. Germany, USA, Switzerland, Australia, etc.). Where that consensus was, or became weak (USA before the Civil War; the former USSR), a single central bank for the whole area has been fragile. The Maastricht Treaty proposals for EMU and the ECB imply a temporal reversal of the previously normal historical ordering of political and monetary unification. This has led many to doubt the viability of the programme.

On the other hand, once a Federal Constitution and government has become established, the central bank inaugurated within that country may well stand a better chance of having some considerable independence (from

to blame the severe short-run costs of deflation on the monetary system and on the central bank that runs it.

the Executive) and autonomy of action. The careful division of powers, between state and federal authorities, and the checks and balances that are often consciously written into a Federal Constitution, make it easier in those countries to accept the idea of a separation of power (and the allocation of certain powers under certain specified conditions to agencies outside the direct control of the Federal Executive), than in a unitary nation. It has been argued that independent central banks would only be suited to countries with federal constitutions, and would not be acceptable in a unitary country where all economic responsibility flowed through to the national government.

This argument can be overstated. When the essential interests (the survival) of the Federal State are at risk, the State will commandeer whatever levers of powers it feels necessary. All central banks will become subservient during war. By contrast, when there is general agreement that the central bank should aim at a single, simple, achievable and clearly defined objective, and when its actions to that end can be easily monitored, then it is possible to treat the central bank as an independent technician, operating within a well-defined framework. This was the case, for example, under the gold standard. There was then no significant difference between the roles and functions of central banks according to whether it operated in a Federal or a Unitary country. If a new consensus is developing that central banks should be allocated a primary, single responsibility for price stability, then such prior distinction as did exist between Federal and Unitary countries may again disappear. Several of the countries that have established, or are inaugurating, independent central banks in the last five years (e.g. Chile, France, New Zealand) are more unitary than Federal.

1.3.5   Summing up

In summary the principal factors influencing government/central bank relations over almost two centuries have been the prevailing political conditions (essentially peace/war), the dominant political/economic philosophy of the time, and the exchange-rate regimes. Thus in the nineteenth century, peace, *laissez-faire*, and the gold standard and stable prices encouraged the appearance of independence and sometimes allowed a considerable measure of independence. After what has been called, 'the end of the intermission in mercantilism' that arrived with the First World War things changed. Crises provoke government intervention. But the experience of inflation and the return to peace of a kind saw independence enjoy a brief return. Greater changes came in the new dirigiste environment after World War II. In the current climate where market solutions have been in the ascendancy and intervention falling out of favour, and following more inflation, the pendulum has swung again. Thus, as in much of economic life, there has been an alternating pattern, in this case of relative dependence and independence. And it is worth emphasising that, whatever was on the statute book, personalities had a powerful part to play in practice.

1.4 The relations between central banks and commercial banks

1.4.1 Introduction

According to an authoritative source from the 1920s, 'The very idea of a central bank presupposes that the commercial banks will deposit their cash resources, other than till money, with it, and that a system will be established under which the commercial banks will not counter the credit policy of the central bank by any actions on their part' (Kisch and Elkin, 1932, p. 106). And, according to one recent view (Congdon 1981), this was a perfectly sensible and natural evolutionary process. For just as individuals choose to place their deposits in banks, so banks place their own deposits in a safe bank and ultimately they find their way to the safest of all banks, the government's bank.

Further, Kisch and Elkin argued that, since the central bank must on occasions enforce a credit policy unwelcome to merchants and commercial banks, it should not have private customers. (For a recent view on this, see Goodhart 1988.) This was broadly the English tradition, but as we shall see there were different traditions in America and Europe; and other parts of the world picked upon yet different traditions. In this section we describe the nature of central bank/commercial bank relations and on how and why they evolved as they did.

The character of this particular relationship is governed by the nature of the product. Banks in fractional reserve systems take deposits and make loans and by doing so increase the stock of money. Similarly, when they fail or take steps to reduce their assets, they reduce the stock of money, and in the face of wage and price stickiness that has a deleterious impact on real output. The danger of one bank failure leading to others failing increases the danger of a major collapse in the stock of money and hence a severe recession in the real economy.

Avoiding financial instability and the dangers it carries has been both an evolutionary process and the conscious application of some specific measures. An example of the former is the evolution of the banking system itself into a stable structure – a well diversified and branched system. A good example of one of the earliest such systems is that of Scotland in the eighteenth century. It was a well branched system that was virtually unregulated and it proved to be robustly stable. There were, however, some other factors involved such as unlimited liability, the absence of any limitation on note issue, and access to the London money market. At the other end of the spectrum lies the suggestion of the 100 per cent reserve rule. But that removes the main purpose of the modern bank.

Some way short of that extreme position there is scope for action by the central bank or by the banks themselves. For example, since the central bank has a crucial interest in, indeed an over-riding objective is, financial stability (upon which economic stability is predicated) it may come to the rescue of the system by lender of last resort means. If this is the case the central bank may be inclined to argue that in order to avoid, or at least to minimise, the need for rescue it should lay down some guidelines for commercial bank behaviour and monitor their behaviour. In other words it should supervise and, if necessary, regulate the system. These then are the key microeconomic functions of central banks: the lender of last resort, and frequently in association with that goes supervision, and regulation.

We consider first the emergence of the last resort function and then examine the supervisory and regulatory functions as they evolved in different systems. What we find is that regulation and the accompanying supervision is almost always (perhaps always) the consequence of crisis, and that such regulation is invariably carried out in haste. As a result it is less good than it might have been, had it been more considered. It also frequently outlasts its usefulness.

1.4.2   Peace, liberalism and 'laissez-faire' (1815–1914)

When we came to address the history of the evolution of central banks into their role as Lenders of Last Resort, we encountered a problem. How exactly should one define this role, in particular for the purpose of giving an historical date to the moment when the central bank assumed it? Any commercial bank may, from time to time, extend additional loans to clients who are temporarily illiquid, or even may be by some accounting standards insolvent. They may do so, even when the present expected return from the new loan itself is zero or negative, if the wider effects, e.g. on their own reputation for commitment to clients, or the knock-on effects of the failure of the first client on other customers, should warrant it. By the same token, a nascent central bank may 'rescue' some client, correspondent bank, just as a commercial bank may support a business customer. But we would not want to describe such occasional, and *ad hoc*, exercises as involving a conscious assumption of a systematic LOLR function. Otherwise, for example, we would have to date the Bank of England as filling this role from a very early date, probably in the eighteenth century (Lovell 1957).

On the other hand no central bank would want to pre-commit itself to giving special support to any individual bank which was running into liquidity problems. Especially with the development of efficient, broad interbank and other short-term money markets, a bank liquidity problem that is not caused by some technical problem (e.g. computer failure) is likely itself to be a reflection of some deeper (market) suspicions about solvency. Consequently, an unqualified pre-commitment to provide last resort assistance would involve too much moral hazard.

Our view is that the assumption by a central bank of the role of LOLR can be dated as occurring at the moment when it accepts a responsibility for the stability of the banking system as a whole, which should override any (residual) concern with its own private profitability. Thus, we would argue that it is the intellectual basis, and reasoning, of central bankers for providing such support, rather than the individual act of rescue itself, that determines whether the central bank had become a LOLR in fact. But while rescues can be clearly dated, shifts in mental perceptions are harder to date. As Fetter (1965) shows, the Bank of England's Court remained divided and uncertain over this issue at least until after the publication of Lombard Street; and we have less insight into the appropriate date in other countries with early founded central banks – by about 1900, however, this function was widely accepted as a core function of any newly established central bank.[14]

We have much the same problem with our account of when central banks came to use open market operations (see Appendix A). The early central banks were often the largest, or sole (special) commercial bank in the country. By extending, or reducing, their own loans and discounts they found themselves able to influence market rates of interest and external gold flows. And they used this power to that end. Nevertheless it is dubious whether we should regard this as showing that these central bankers had a full understanding and command of open market operations. As the commercial banks in England increased in size relative to the Bank of England in the middle of the nineteenth century, the Bank often found that market rates fell away from its announced discount rate (Bank rate), and worried how to make Bank rate effective. Sayers (1936) records in some detail how the Bank began to develop its understanding of how to use open market operations in this period in order to maintain day-to-day control over short-term interest rates under all (market) conditions. Again our knowledge of similar learning processes among other early founded central banks is deficient.

---

[14] The lender of last resort is sometimes used to mean the bailout of individual institutions. Our definition rejects that. However, in the Appendices we have left the claims for lender of last resort action as given by the bank's themselves, or their histories.

England   The first use of the term Lender of Last Resort was by Francis Baring at the end of the eighteenth century, writing on the Bank of England (Baring 1797). As already noted, the function can be defined in different ways, and agreement on what is ideal will be hard to find. One view stresses that lender of last resort action should be limited to market operations that provide liquidity to the system as a whole. A contrasting view argues that support for an individual institution should be allowed in view of (i) the difficulty of distinguishing between insolvency and illiquidity, (ii) the need for speed of action and (iii) the likelihood that the event of (large) bank failures may itself shift the demand functions for liquidity in ways that may be difficult to predict.

The historical literature on the subject is fuzzy. Even Bagehot (1873) seems a little uncertain over his prescription. On the one hand, he places a stress on the market as a whole, but there is nevertheless reference to the danger that may arise if any individual large joint stock bank got into difficulties. (These latter were a relatively recent feature of the system when Bagehot was writing.) There is further ambivalence, in that while there is the suggestion that insolvent institutions should not be rescued, nevertheless speed of action in a panic is critical. Therefore the Bank may have had to act before it was possible to make a thorough assessment of solvency.

The particular system that evolved in England was one where the Bank was initially at some distance from the commercial banks. Considerable animosity had developed between the two as a consequence of two factors. The first was the privileged monopoly position the Bank had held from 1694 until the early nineteenth century. The second was the believed abuse of that monopoly position in the Napoleonic Wars where the Bank was accused of over-issue for the sake of its own profits. That animosity encouraged the emergence of the buffer that discount brokers provided. Later these brokers developed their own capital base and portfolios and they continued to provide a buffer between the central bank and the commercial banks. What this allowed was a certain anonymity. If a bank was running into difficulty it could obtain cash by taking its bills to the discount market. The discount house would in turn obtain the cash from the Bank. By this means the Bank need never know where the bills came from and this anonymity allowed it to supply liquidity to the market in time of pressure without taking any interest in an individual institution. This marks English experience out as being quite different from all other countries. The Bank could deal in an anonymous fashion with the market rather than individuals.

That is one strand in the particular development in England. It should however not be overdone. By different means the Bank has, across two centuries, come to the rescue in one way or another of individual banks from George Peabody and Co in the 1850s, to William Deacons in the 1920s, and

Johnson Matthey in the 1980s. On other occasions it was instrumental in organising the rescue of one or more banks in difficulties as in the case of Barings in the 1890s, and of a group of smaller (fringe) banks in the early 1970s. There were other occasions, of course, when it allowed banks to fail, one of the best known being that of the City of Glasgow Bank in 1878 and more recently the Bank of Credit and Commerce International (BCCI). On both these latter occasions there was talk of malpractice.

It is probably fair to say, however, that the most widely held view of the lender of last resort function is that it should allow for the rescue of individual institutions. This approach carries with it the risk of moral hazard. When the function is interpreted in this way, it has led to the central bank taking a closer interest in the behaviour of individual banks. In England, perhaps by virtue of the relative distance between the two parties, self-regulation was encouraged, with only a minimum of oversight from the monetary authority.

The example of England is one where, throughout the financial system, groups of individual institutions were encouraged to attend to their own affairs. The banks did this through the Committee of the London Clearing Banks. British banking was 'self-regulated' until the very recent past when a number of statutory regulations have been imposed. Though once again this should not be overstated. Much has been made of the informal control the Bank exercised and how this was made easier with just a small number of banks' chairmen for the governor to use his eyebrows on.

USA This contrasts most starkly with the US where a regulatory system was in place long before there was a central bank. The North American tradition has thus been quite different and it in turn has been adopted in parts of South America. Prior to the establishment of national banks during the Civil War in the 1860s, American banks were governed by the laws of individual states. In the north they had tended to favour unit banks while in the south the charters invariably encouraged branching. Calomiris (1992, pp. 66–7) writes, 'From the beginning, banks in the south operated branches and banks in the north did not but there was little clamor in the north to allow or prohibit branching'. The 1837 panic is generally seen as a landmark. Many banks failed and a demand for new banks developed. In the north free banking was a major response whereas in the south they continued to rely on chartering. 'During the panics of 1837 and 1839 branch banking enabled southern banks to weather the storm of the credit crunch ... remarkably well compared to their counterparts in the north' (Calomiris 1992, p. 26).

The explanation for the north/south differences is not easy to pin down. Some of the explanation may be found in the nature of production in the south and in the less democratic tradition that obtained there. Links were needed between the tobacco and cotton plantations and the distribution network through to the ports. The plantation owners had considerable influence in the state and a disproportionately large say in organisational matters. Added to this, it is also likely that the Scottish influence was important. Scots were prominent in the south in tobacco growing and trade from the eighteenth century. And they undoubtedly contributed to the structure of the institutions there.

After the Civil War, the National Banking Act of 1864, and the collapse of the south, the Comptroller of the Currency restricted branching by the national banks. Currency in the form of National bank notes could be issued only to the extent that Union Government bonds were held – leading, it was widely claimed, to an inelastic money supply, a consequence of which was an intensification of the severity and frequency of the financial crises of the second half of the nineteenth century (Sprague 1910).

There were also regulations on capital and reserve requirements. The only form of bank co-operation left was the clearing house (Timberlake 1978), an institution that had spread to most of the major cities. Nevertheless, there was no national organisation to co-ordinate clearing across the country. The US suffered a series of banking crises between 1870 and 1913 in some large part as a result of these regulations. Further, since the unit system at the end of the nineteenth century was ill-equipped to finance large scale industry, new methods of corporate finance developed and these in turn damaged bank profitability.

The main point to make here though is that it was primarily the frequent banking panics (themselves in part the consequence of particular regulations) that prompted the investigations that led to the formation of the Federal Reserve System (National Monetary Commission, 1908–1911). As a consequence the Federal Reserve's charter was drawn up with special reference to the central bank's position as the bankers' bank. Furthermore, the central bank as the overseer responsible for the system was seen as being entitled to support from the banks in the system. Thus member banks were required to keep minimum balances with the Reserve bank. In this way a strong two-way relationship was established between the Federal Reserve and the commercial banks.

The same was true of Chile and also of some other South American countries and, interestingly, of South Africa which followed the American rather than the British model in this respect. Such statutory balances were part of the scheme for the control of the system. In a recent paper Schwartz (1992) has argued for an extension of a more anonymous system for the provision of lender of last resort assistance to the United States. She argues that the discount window of the Federal Reserve has been abused, and that it has been used to prop up poorly run institutions. The alternative strategy that she favours is that the window should be closed and that open market operations should be adhered to, to supply the whole system with the right amount of cash. But how would the central bank know what was the 'right' amount of cash should panic conditions develop following the failure of a large bank, or banks?

Europe   Europe was different in that the relationship between the central bank and the commercial banks was freer. It was established by negotiation and so provided greater flexibility. The circumstances in Europe were, of course, in the main quite different from England and both North and South America. European countries had come to industriali-sation later than England, and the view developed there that they required assistance in the catching up process. Financial institutions and particularly banks were regarded as being of vital importance in the finance of industry and so the large universal bank emerged, one that had close connections with large-scale industry. This essentially Austro-German model was also found in many other European countries. These countries had therefore comparatively small numbers of commercial banks. And that affected their relationship with the central bank.

Furthermore, some European central banks had charters that did not distinguish between the business done with the commercial banks and that done with other customers. Both the Banque de France and the Reichsbank seemed to fall into this group. And the Banque de France had an extensive branch network and close relationships with industrial customers, as did the Nederlandsche Bank and the Banca D'Italia. This is clearly in danger of violating one of Goodhart's laws:

It was the metamorphosis from their [central banks] involvement in commercial banking, as a competitive, profit-maximising bank among many, to a non-competi-tive non-profit-maximising role that marked the true emergence, and development of proper central banking. (1988, p. 7)

Plessis has shown recently (1994), for example, that the Banque de France in the second half of the nineteenth century was in fierce competition with the three major deposit banks, Credit Lyonnais, Société Générale, and Comptoir d'Escompte. By the 1880s not only was this a threat to the Bank's profits, but it 'cast doubt on its ability to influence the price of money in the short term, since adjusting the discount rate was only really effective when the commercial banks needed to make use of the Banque de France at some time' (p. 5). The Bank's response was to pursue more vigorously its lending to industry. This may have been the sensible course for a profit maximiser but by behaving like any other commercial bank the Bank had, in the words of Plessis, 'great difficulty in achieving recognition as a central bank'. The picture is confused because there was assistance given to other institutions at some times. For example, the Banque de France on some occasions rescued individuals and institutions – for instance the Comptoir d'Escompte in 1889 – and at other times did not. Notable examples of the latter were the Credit Mobilier in 1868, and Union General in 1882.

The case of the Prussian State bank and its successor the Reichsbank is more difficult to be clear about. While Kisch and Elkin (1932) claimed that the Reichsbank was involved with industry, Ziegler (1993) argues it was not. He maintains that the universal banking system and the needs of the Provincial banking system meant that both the Prussian Bank and later the Reichsbank had to stand ready to meet the liquidity needs of the German banks and therefore did not compete with them. However, Bopp (1953, p. 38) quotes a President of the Reichsbank in 1880: 'the Reichsbank should not look for business but neither should it decline a proper opportunity to invest in safe, bankable paper'. As discussed in Appendix A, this attitude led the Reichsbank to introduce a system of preferential discount rates between 1880 and 1896, basically to compete with the other banks in its discount business.

The Nederlandsche Bank remained a significant commercial lender throughout the late nineteenth century, and by 1900 still accounted for half of all bank loans to the industrial sector. Thereafter, the Bank's commercial activities steadily declined, and by 1920 the Bank had lost vitually all of its customers except the commercial banks. The experience of the Banca d'Italia, founded much later (1893), is similar. Although the Bank had a virtual monopoly of the note issue from that date (it issued 80 per cent of government authorised notes) it was a private bank that could compete for the largest industrial loans, and in the First World War it provided large scale finance to industry. It was not until 1936 that it became a public institution and discontinued its private business (see Frattiani and Spinelli 1995, forthcoming).

1.4.3   Wars, depressions and the State (1914–1971)

For England this period can be divided into two. The first runs from World War I to 1939; the second from then until 1971, when Competition and Credit Control was introduced, which marks the start of our final period, 1971 to date. A highly cartelised banking system had emerged after the First World War which, together with the mature operation of the Bank of England as a lender of last resort, produced considerable financial (and economic) stability. And at least until the Second World War it is not clear that there were any great costs in terms of efficiency. For the years from

1939 to the early 1970s there were considerable constraints on bank lending and/or other measures of control which, increasingly, resulted in inefficiencies in the sector developing; and the costs involved became harder to ignore or to defend. This was one of the reasons for the introduction of Competition and Credit Control then. The succeeding two decades, to which we shall revert in section 1.4.4 below, were characterised both by increasing competition, and in the UK by the imposition of statutory regulation on the banking system, as financial cartels and with them self-regulation were eroded by outside competition.

In the United States, the 1920s were prosperous though there were problems for agriculture and for the banks most closely associated with that sector. However, the great depression of 1929–33 was possibly the worst in recorded history, and the financial collapse that accompanied it was on a scale seldom if ever witnessed before or since. One-third of all banks failed. The conventional wisdom on the explanation for these events is that it was a failure of monetary policy and of the institutions. The collapse of the banks came about as a result of the failure of the Fed, and because of limits on bank branching which led to weaker and undiversified (unit) banks.

It is something of a paradox that, for all the US being seen as the apotheosis of free market capitalism, regulation has always loomed larger there. One current school of thought would argue that it was the defective structure of the system, itself partly a product of regulation, that exacerbated the effects of the ineptitude of the Federal Reserve. The diagnosis of the causes of the great depression at the time, however, led to further regulation (the Glass-Steagall Act that separated commercial and investment banking) and to the provision of deposit insurance. The system prospered for some long period after that, but, whereas Friedman and Schwartz (1963) gave credit for that relative success to the deposit insurance scheme, Schwartz (1992) now argues that it was rather price stability that allowed the banks to be stable. When price stability faded in the 1970s and 1980s banking failures reappeared. Fresh calls for regulation were heard (Pierce 1991).

European experience was different. The trend to universal banking in the nineteenth century was not without its problems, and when at the end of the 1920s some of the large banks' recent problems were being revealed, the state was obliged to bail them out and reform many of the largest and set in place fresh regulation.

This was particularly true of Italy. Italy was a relatively late industrial developer and imported the German model of universal banking. However, mixed banking did not prove successful and the transition to commercial banking took place between the late 1890s and the 1920s. The Banca d'Italia came into being in 1926, was the sole bank of issue and then in 1936 it stopped transacting commercial business and formally became the commercial banks' bank. From that point on but even more so after 1947, it had a supervisory role and considerable authority to direct the banks and to specify the use of various balance sheet ratios.

We noted above that Germany was the source of the 'Universal' model, and that in the nineteenth century the Reichsbank had offered some competition to the big banks. It continued to do so after the First World War but by the inter-war years the extent of its direct commercial business was limited by the high quality requirements imposed on the bills it discounted. After 1945, however, complete separation from the commercial system was seen as desirable. The authority of the central bank was believed to be enhanced the further it was removed from competition with the other banks. The Bundesbank and its immediate predecessor the Bank deutscher Länder had no commercial business. They could fix minimum reserve requirements and issue guiding principles, but had no supervisory powers. In Austria following the decoupling from the Reichsbank, an agreement was struck between the National Bank and the Austrian Banking Association for both quantitative and qualitative credit controls, and some highly specific regulation was instituted.

Elsewhere in Europe there were variations on these themes. Central banks that before World War II had been relatively independent and with no formal or informal responsibility for the banking system, found themselves the subject of state control after 1945 with varying degrees of supervisory responsibility for the system. In the Netherlands the Bank was nationalised, and the 1948 Act obliged it to supervise the system. Next door in Belgium there was a highly concentrated banking system; regulation was administered by the Banking Commission. The Commission could ask the central bank to investigate a commercial bank. Similarly in France where the Banque de France had been heavily engaged in commercial business in the nineteenth century, after the 1920s this was greatly diminished and after 1945 disappeared. It was after 1948 that it became more heavily involved in the regulation of the banking system, a system that was subjected increasingly to greater control.

Other countries in other regions have followed different paths. Some have pursued the English/British model. Central banking in the British Commonwealth came after 1920 in common with many other war babies around the world. And as Plumptre (1940) put it, 'war babies are more often the product of impulse than reflection'. Encouragement came from the League of Nations, often through its international conferences, the newly established BIS, and the growing belief that maturity could not be claimed without such a bank. It is true that various arguments were advanced and discussed and some opposition (mostly from the commercial banks) was encountered. In the Dominions at least there was a desire for greater monetary control and when there were various schemes for monetary intervention in the air, the central bank was seen as a relatively conservative reform – especially if it was based on the English model. But a harmonious relationship between the central bank and the commercial banks was often very slow to develop (as indeed it had been in England in the second half of the nineteenth century). Supervision and regulation were not part of the early experience. Again in common with many other forms of state intervention they came in the more collectivist years after 1939.

Although there was often some initial rivalry between the central bank and commercial banks, particularly when the former maintained some private client business, both tended to become increasingly restive at the degree of state intervention and direction in the post-World War II period. Central banks remembered that they were primarily specialised banks, and not just a bureaucratic offshoot of the Ministry of Finance. It irked them, almost as much as commercial banks, that the latter were then often transformed into public utilities (Schedvin 1992) told to whom to provide credit (or not to), and at what interest rates. With the central bank being perceived to support the commercial banks' aim for more freedom and flexibility in discussions with the Treasury, relationships between the central banks and the banks improved.

Indeed one of the few arguments that has now been largely resolved in this field would seem to be that of the appropriate relationship between the central bank and the commercial banks. Although central banks in the nineteenth century often started as commercial banks, and in the twentieth century were often split from the dominant commercial bank to form a separate entity (e.g. India, Brazil, Iran), it has now become entirely accepted that the controlling, and often the supervising, body (i.e. the central bank), should not simultaneously be in competition with the commercial banks that it controls and supervises. The dangers of conflict of interest, actual or suspected, outweigh any advantages in the extra information, training, career structure or scope that may accrue to the central bank (see Schedvin 1992, chapter 9) from undertaking a joint central/ commercial role.

By much the same token the desire to maximise (short-term) profits might conflict with the central bank's objectives to maintain monetary stability. If it is to offset inflationary (deflationary) pressures, it should take restrictive (expansionary) open market operations, reducing (expanding) the size of its balance sheet just when interest rates are usually already high (low), and when most commercial banks are on the other tack. So, besides being non-competitive, the central bank needs to be non-profit-maximising. If it is to be non-profit-maximising the central bank cannot be owned by, or beholden to, private-sector share-holders whose objective is to maximise the present value of the expected residual stream of profits. Nor would it seem appropriate for a central bank to be primarily owned by the banks that it is set up to manage, the more so the more supervisory functions that it undertakes. Again conflicts of interest would arise, and capture of the regulator by the regulated would become even more likely.

1.4.4   Competition and bank control (1971–1994)

It may appear, superficially, a paradox that the trend towards greater competition among banks, and between banks and other financial intermediaries, during these last two decades should have gone hand-in-hand with the introduction of greater statutory legislation on bank regulation. Moreover, the nature and form of regulation has changed, from its earlier emphasis on asset ratios, reserve and liquidity ratios imposed, and adjusted, by the central bank, in some countries without much statutory basis, on purely domestic grounds; and has shifted now towards concentration on capital adequacy ratios applied on an international basis, following cross-country deliberation under the aegis of the BIS or the EU, but applied domestically by statutory authority.

The resolution of this paradox is that, prior to the 1970s, the banking industry in most countries was heavily cartelised. It was both oligopolistic, and regimented in its activities by the authorities. On both counts, risk was limited, and, while profits were also somewhat constrained by official regulations, the banks were usually able to make representations about their needs for sufficient profitability to maintain an adequate capital base. In this context the banking system in most countries was inherently stable, and the members of the cartelised financial and banking clubs could be left to undertake self-regulation with the lightest of supervisory oversight by the authorities. As mentioned earlier, until 1973 such supervision as the Bank of England undertook, primarily on the discount and acceptance houses, was the responsibility of a single senior official! Moreover, it was not entirely clear to those who manipulated the asset ratios then widely applied, e.g. the liquidity ratios, whether these were primarily to be used for prudential, for operational or for seigniorage purposes; sometimes (changes in) these ratios were justified on one ground, sometimes on another, without outstanding clarity of thought or exposition.

The main exception to the cartelisation of the banking system, prior to the 1970s, was the USA. But here the continuation of a system of myriad, often small unit, banks was not so much due to the forces of free competition, but to the continuing populist fear of an eastern money trust, and the consequent imposition and retention of regulations that served to prevent amalgamations, to restrict competition and to preserve fragile unit banks. Many of these regulations (e.g. the prohibition of interest payments on demand deposits) had the same kind of effect on the profitability and riskiness of the banking system in the USA that was achieved by the regimented cartelisation of the oligopolistic club of banks in most other countries.

Such regimentation, and external official intervention and direction, led to increasing frictions, as the national economies expanded and as confidence in a free market system revived. Initially, after 1945, the commercial banks were able to deal with some of the most acute of such frictional pressures by asset management. Banks in many countries found themselves, after World War II, in a disequilibrium condition with an excess of holdings of government bills and bonds, and an insufficiency of loans to the private sector. Whenever interest rate controls on deposits, or other measures to restrict monetary growth, in order to limit inflation (central bankers have always retained a strain of monetarism), conflicted with the demand of clients for credit, the banks were able to allow their excess stock of government debt to run off.

By the middle of the 1960s in the USA, and shortly thereafter in the UK, that safety valve was used up, and banks then turned to liability management. With ever improving and cheapening information technology, such liability management became largely undertaken in the rapidly emerging wholesale, international euromarkets, centred in London because it combined a high reputation for stability and an efficient infrastructure with the fewest burdensome constraints and regulations on such wholesale business. Such international wholesale euro-markets, continuously developing from the euro-money and euro-bond markets into more exotic derivative markets, e.g. for futures and swaps, have been both largely unregulated and also mostly free either from serious scandal or the source or venue of financial crisis or panic. Some may regard this as further evidence that regulation itself is more often the cause, than the cure, for financial panics and difficulties. But it is also the case that such wholesale financial markets, e.g. the foreign exchange market, are dominated by professionals who can expect to deal with each other repeatedly. So the maintenance of a good reputation is crucial, and information asymmetries are minimised. Moreover, when trouble does arrive, in the shape of a failure of a large player, e.g. Continental Illinois, the monetary authorities have stepped in to prevent systemic risk and market seizure (the failure of the tin market in autumn 1985 was an exception here, and this was largely owing to the extreme political complexity of the problem, rather than to any pure *laissez-faire* attitude among the protagonists).

From the euromarkets, it was then but a small step to the development of cross-border banking, with large national banks following their own multi-national firms abroad, and at the same time trying to pick up (some of) the business of large companies head-quartered in the countries in which they were establishing branches and subsidiaries. By the 1970s, wholesale banking business, with large corporate clients, of all kinds was becoming much more competitive as cross-border banking was breaking down the defences of the domestic cartel. Even where regulations still prevented the entry of foreign banks, the large corporate clients could move some of their financial business, exchange controls permitting, to the international markets.

Such cross-border international bank competition did not, as a generality, extend to retail markets. But even in these latter the limitations, regulations and controls on commercial banks made them vulnerable to encroachment from a variety of fringe financial intermediaries not subject to similar burdens. Such competition, both in banks' wholesale and retail markets, undermined their oligopolistic 'club', and with it the banks' willingness and ability to maintain self-regulation, which had allowed the central bank to maintain its hands-off stance. Financial markets and institutions, and the countries in which they were situated, which could hitherto be treated as segregated and separated for prudential purposes, were no longer so.

Under such competitive pressures, those financial institutions and markets which continued to be regimented by the authorities, and subject to burdensome controls, would increasingly lose out to competitors, not so constrained. Thus there was continuing pressure for deregulation in the 1970s and early 1980s. But such deregulation, as Competition and Credit Control (Bank of England 1971), or the greater freedom allowed to S&Ls in the USA to diversify, led to structural changes that faced the central bank, and the monetary authorities generally, with new and unforeseen problems, in the operation of both monetary and prudential policies.

A good example of this latter was the difficulty confronting the Bank of England how to analyse and to contend with the upsurge in bank lending and liability management, involving some large but inevitably uncertain amount of 'round-tripping', in the competitive frenzy for new business unleashed by the banks in the aftermath of Competition and Credit Control during 1972/73. The erosion, and collapse, of the old interventionist regime at the start of the 1970s, particularly perhaps the demise of the Bretton Woods system, played a role, though how important a role we cannot and do not judge here, in the emergence of the financial disturbances, the high and volatile inflation – and the (initial) failures of the central banks and their governments to find an adequate response to such problems – in the 1970s and to a lesser extent in the 1980s.

The high and volatile inflation of the 1970s, and early 1980s, led inevitably to high, and volatile, nominal interest rates. These latter made the comparative handicap of the existing regulatory constraints on banks (and mortgage lending institutions) in the guise of interest rate controls, or reserve and liquidity ratios, much more severe in effect. While this had some influence in restraining banks', and therefore monetary, expansion during inflationary periods, and was therefore welcomed in some cases and countries, in those countries where competition and the substitution of business between those caught by such controls, and those free of them, was more pronounced, the main effect was disintermediation and disaffection among the banks. This led to calls to get rid of such direct controls on interest rates (e.g. Regulation Q), and to lower and harmonised asset ratios, on grounds of equity and a level playing field; and by the 1980s most of the panoply of pre-1970 regulation, involving direct controls, or guidance, over bank lending, interest rate controls and asset ratios, had either been swept away, or was being phased out, at least in most industrialised countries.

The removal of such controls did, presumably, help somewhat to restore bank profitability, but the increasing intensity of competition between banks for wholesale business, and between banks and other financial inter-mediaries for retail business led to pressure on bank margins and bank profitability. Moreover, the more disturbed financial conditions of the 1970s and early 1980s, especially 1972–75 and 1979–82, made it harder for both banks and their customers to foretell the likely direction of future events. In such circumstances bad debts mounted. The most famous, and widespread, instance was the LDC crisis, breaking in 1982; but there was a somewhat similar re-run with the property boom and bust, involving banks in Scandinavia, Japan, US, Australia and UK (in declining order of serious-ness) in 1989–92.

Such bad debts directly led to a diminution of capital, and to a decline in the strength and credit rating of the banks involved. Bank intermediation arises, in part, because the bank, being better known and better capitalised than the bank customer, can borrow on significantly better terms than the client can on her own. By the mid-1980s at least, any such bank advantage vis a vis the bank's previous large corporate customers was becoming lost. Large corporates were turning directly to capital markets (though banks could still hope for fee income to facilitate their clients' introduction to such markets). Such bank loans to large corporates had previously represented a sizeable, and relatively safe, though low margin, proportion of bank loans. After their loss banks were left with a somewhat riskier portfolio of loans to the private sector with a higher ratio of property-related lending.

Competition was driving down profits, and bad debts adversely affected capital and credit ratings. During the 1970s and early 1980s, the risk/return trade-off was worsening, and bank capital ratios, e.g. in the USA, were declining. The demise of the protected cartel, the increase in competition, and the impairment of capital also meant that moral hazard, i.e. the tendency to 'bet the bank' and go for broke in the expectation that someone else, notably the central bank, might pick up the pieces if the bet failed, increased perceptibly. Where these circumstances were reinforced by 100 per cent deposit insurance, moral hazard increased dramatically; the prime example being, of course, the S&Ls in the USA.

This syndrome faced central banks, and associated regulatory agencies, with new problems, problems which had really not been in evidence before the 1970s and which seemed to worsen almost throughout this latest period. They had neither the wish, nor in the context probably the ability, to restrain the competition which was driving down bank profitability.[15] So if the risk/return trade-off was to be improved, it would have to be by reducing the worsened riskiness of banks, especially the risks to depositors, to regulatory agencies and to the taxpayer at large.

The route that has been chosen is, of course, to require higher capital ratios from banks in relation to their assessed risks. But competition, at least in wholesale financial markets, is now international, and the imposition of tougher capital requirements by one country's authorities in isolation would involve a comparative competitive disadvantage on the banks over whom that regulatory authority had jurisdiction. This was the incentive for central banks, and other bank regulators, to attempt to translate such regulation, and the adoption of common, international (capital adequacy) requirements onto an international, multilateral plane via, in particular, the BIS Committee dealing with such matters, though the need for the European Community to harmonize financial regulation throughout the EU has provided a second forum for such initiatives.

This has not been an easy exercise. Differences in commercial laws, in accounting practices, in the customary practices and activities of banks between the major countries involved has meant that the achievement of a level playing field can not be exact or complete. This will continue to generate some friction. It is probably even harder to measure risk, particularly on an *ex ante* basis, in a manner that is generally accepted as both reasonably simple and accurate. There are, for example, so many forms of risk, credit risk, interest rate risk, liquidity risk, foreign exchange risk, etc. In a world where covariances are not unity, and hedging practices are not

---

[15] Some commentators, however, have suggested that the sharply upwards sloping yield curve in the USA in recent years was, at least in part, an intentional and brilliantly engineered ploy by the Fed to enhance American bank profitability. While we cannot comment on the validity of this suggestion, we doubt whether it is a means that can be widely or frequently used for such a purpose, if that was indeed the intended purpose.

only possible but practicable, risks should clearly not be calculated just on an additive basis, but more sophisticated measures will often be controversial, complex and beyond the capacity of smaller banks to operate.

Nevertheless there are dangers that this exercise will distort banking business into areas where the risk/return trade-off has been, artificially, influenced by the regulatory authorities. Moreover, the general increase in the need for bank capital is perceived as burdensome (though the extent that it actually is so remains a subject of academic debate), and is quite likely to involve a widening of required margins on (less-favoured) business. There is a perception that the traditional business of banking, at least in those countries with advanced, efficient, and transparent competitive capital markets, is under threat and in potential decline. Another aspect of this same syndrome is that non-bank institutions are moving into core banking business, e.g. mutual fund banking in the USA, and banks are trying to diversify into other areas. The dividing lines between the functional roles of financial institutions are becoming fuzzier.

Under these circumstances bank regulators, including notably central banks, are under increasing pressure to reassess which institutions and functions they should regulate and supervise; and what exactly are the principles involved. As noted earlier in this section, bank regulation has largely evolved so far as an accretion of *ad hoc* responses to particular crises. In the growing flux of structural change, such an approach becomes increasingly unsatisfactory.

Perhaps the main principle to which central banks adhere is the need to prevent a contagious, systemic crisis within the monetary and banking system (George 1994). Such a crisis is most likely to be triggered by the failure of a large bank with manifold connections with other banks. But any (implicitly) guaranteed support of such large banks leads to the 'too large to fail' condition. But this would lead in turn either to inequity between large and small banks, or to an (implicit) guarantee for all banks, with a consequence of much worsened moral hazard. Is a (partial) answer to be found in the Structured Early Intervention and Resolution proposals in the USA (Benston 1993), whereby even very large banks can be placed under external constraint and reorganisation before their capital becomes so impaired that they pose a threat to the taxpayer?

Central bank regulatory officials have needed to be resolute and resilient in character during these last two decades. Even so, they have often felt harassed. The many problems of establishing the appropriate regulatory and supervisory structure for the financial system, and the banks within it, have not been fully resolved at the close of our history.

To conclude, the relationships between central bank and commercial banks have passed through three main phases during our historical period. The first involved a shift from a competitive, and even adversarial, relationship, towards the acceptance by the central bank of its (Lender of Last Resort) responsibility for the health of the banking system as a whole. In the second period the central bank was able to maintain this role with a very limited hands-on direct regulatory or supervisory function (except during the inter-war crisis), because of the cartelised, protected, club nature of the banking (financial) system, which fostered self-regulation. Competition, enhanced by information technology, and driven on by financial and inflation instability and de-regulation, undermined that system, and has led to a sharp worsening in the risk-return profile of banks in many countries in the last two decades. Central banks are still struggling with the question of how to respond to that. This has led to the emergence of many difficult problems, many of which remain to be resolved in any fully satisfactory fashion.

1.5   Central banks: perceptions and ideas

1.5.1   Introduction

The switch to Keynesian principles of 'managed money' after World War II, the adoption of floating exchange rates and then monetary targets in the 1970s, and now the enthusiasm for central bank independence, all have owed much of their force to the power of academic ideas whose time had arrived. Almost by definition we cannot predict the future course of ideas (though the dissonance between the concept of the natural rate of unemployment and the experience of actually shifting long-term average rates of unemployment in Europe would seem to cry out for an explanation).

While many of these ideas seem to spring freshly out of their particular historical context, there are a couple of intellectual debates that have continued to echo, though continuously revived and discussed in the current setting of their times, mutatis mutandis, through the history of central banking. The first of these concerns rules versus discretion. The second combines the question of whether the issue and control of money is, or ought to be, an aspect of sovereign power, i.e. Cartalists versus Metallists, with the question of whether a fractional banking system would be inherently stable on its own, or needs outside direction and protection. This now goes under the general heading of the 'free banking' debate, and raises broad issues of whether a central bank is either necessary or desirable for a modern economy.

We turn now to these two issues.

1.5.2   Rules versus discretion

The most famous, and best known, intellectual arguments in the history of central banking have related to operational techniques, rather than to organisation or objectives. As noted above, in section 1.4.4, the main organisational issues have been largely settled. Throughout central bank history, it has been generally accepted that their main (peace-time) objective should be the stability of the currency. There were a couple of decades, after World War II, when the deflationary experience of the inter-war period, Keynesian analysis, and the emerging concept of the downward sloping Phillips curve combined to suggest that monetary policy should be subsumed under demand management more generally for the achievement of a desired level of unemployment. But this period passed. The experience of stagflation in the 1970s, and the analytical argument that a downward-sloping short-run Phillips curve transmutes, as expectations adjust, into a vertical, or even an upwards-sloping long-run Phillips curve, then restored price stability to its former position as the central bank's main (peace-time) priority.

Such a medium-term general objective (price stability), however, leaves open a great deal of flexibility about the choice of immediate, specific, short-term objectives, for example the use of intermediate targets, the choice of the exchange rate, nominal incomes, inflation or the price level as ultimate targets, and about the selection of operational mechanisms to achieve both the short- and medium-run targets. The main intellectual debates have occurred primarily about such operational mechanisms, particularly following historical periods when the central bank was adjudged to have failed to achieve the accepted medium-term objective of price stability.

The two chief occasions of academic/intellectual ferment were the British monetary debates, primarily between the Bullionists and Anti-Bullionists and between the Currency and the Banking Schools in the first half of the nineteenth century, and the Monetarist/Keynesian debates between about 1960 and 1985. The circumstances, conduct and outcome of these two debates are uncannily similar, as discussed below.

Both debates arose out of the perceived failings of the system to achieve the desired objective, currency stability. Thus, the currency debates in the 1800s initially grew out of discussions and analysis of the causes and effects of the suspension of convertibility in the UK (1797–1821) and its association with contemporary inflation, though this was further spiced by analysis of the determinants of monetary disturbances in the 1820s and 1830s (see Fetter 1965). Similarly the monetarist/Keynesian debate arose out of increasing concern with the endemic, and steadily worsening, medium-term inflationary experience in most developed countries in the 1960s and 1970s.

In both cases the Currency/Monetarist School advocates emphasised the essentially monetary causes of the prior inflation, whereas the Banking/ Keynesian school pointed to non-monetary supply-side shocks (harvest failures, oil shocks, labour wage-push, etc). In both cases, the argument has generally been settled in favour of the Currency/Monetarist position.

Since the cause of the failure was assessed in both cases (by the Currency/ Monetarist school), as arising from a failure of monetary management, an excessive rate of growth of the relevant aggregates (bank notes in the nineteenth century, some preferred monetary aggregate (M) in the twentieth century), the obvious answer for them was to introduce appropriate controls (rules) on such monetary growth. But if such Currency/Monetarist arguments for tighter monetary control would be generally accepted, why not leave the achievement of monetary control to the discretion of the central bank?

In both these episodes, however, central banks, notably the Bank of England, were often repositories of supporters of the opposing (Banking/ Keynesian) schools of thought, perhaps naturally so since people are always likely to blame failures on factors beyond their own control. So, the Currency/Monetarist theorists tended to be suspicious and dismissive about either the capacity or the willingness of central bankers to carry out their own preferred programme, a Monetarist example being Friedman (1982 and 1984). Ricardo's comment, reported by Fetter (1965, p. 94), was that 'the House [of Commons] did not withdraw its confidence from the Bank from any doubt of its wealth or integrity, but from a conviction of its total ignorance of political economy', a thrust that was greeted with 'hear, hear, and a laugh'. Monetarists and Currency School proponents tended to think that their programme would only be carried out, by the central bankers, if the latter were firmly tied down by clear, transparent, statutory rules.

Besides this somewhat *ad hominem* argument, there was also a concern whether the (incentive) structure within the system, unless tied down by formal rules, would encourage, or enable, the central bank to deliver monetary control. This was even clearer in the earlier debates. Note issue was not the monopoly of the Bank of England, but was then undertaken by the country banks as well. The country banks would expand (contract) note issue during a boom (slump). Even in so far as the Bank of England could control aggregate, overall monetary conditions by offsetting the (pro-cyclical) note issue fluctuations elsewhere in the country, its own profit-maximising concern as the major commercial bank would tend to make it also act pro-cyclically. Rather, however, than change the (incentive) structure of the Bank of England, the Currency School's attempted solution was to make note-issue centralised, rule-determined and quasi-automatic, leaving the Banking Department to act, so it was then intended, as any other freely competitive bank. Both Ricardo, in his proposed Plan for the Establishment of a National Bank (reproduced in Capie 1993) and Sir Robert Peel (see Fetter 1965, p. 183), would have preferred, in logic, a separate government-run currency board, but felt that this was, in practice, too radical a step to gain general acceptance.

By the twentieth century, the commercial incentive for inappropriate note issue by the central bank had gone. But it has been replaced, so it is now argued (probably to an exaggerated extent), by a political incentive. Tight money and increased interest rates are unpopular. Everyone wishes for approval; so, even left to themselves central bankers are likely to delay unduly necessary restrictive measures, and the resulting inflation could also make them slow to respond to deflation, a syndrome much worsened and complicated, of course, by the long and variable lags in the system. But this condition might be seriously worsened by politicians seeking short-term popularity in advance of an election (the political business cycle, Nordhaus 1975). Rhetoric about commitment would be nullified by time-inconsistency. The first solution, once again, was to try to tie the central bank and the monetary authorities down to clear, simple rules for monetary expansion, such as Friedman's (1960) constant growth rate rule.

In both episodes the *ad hominem* aspects of the debate were enhanced by the fact that a key leader of the Currency/Monetarist school was the leading economist of his day (Ricardo/Friedman), though Ricardo died in 1823, before the Currency School became fully established in the 1830s. In each case he tended to attract to his side many of the leading younger theorists, for example McCulloch, Nassau Senior and Torrens. The analytical economic arguments presented by this School were not always, at least initially, appreciated by the opponents among the Banking/Keynesian Schools, such as Tooke, Fullarton and Blair.

Be that as it may, the Currency/Monetarist school in both instances won the intellectual battle about how to reform the monetary system, no doubt aided by the fact that the current Prime Minister, Peel in the 1840s, Thatcher in the 1980s, was in each case of their persuasion. Peel's Bank of England Act, 1844, faithfully reproduced the main proposals of the Currency School; central banks in all major industrialised countries adopted some form of intermediate monetary target during the 1970s, and these were reinforced in several major countries. (e.g. UK with the 1980 Medium Term Financial Strategy, USA in 1979) by the end of the decade.

Yet in both cases the Currency/Monetarist School lost the war. The rules, which had been so carefully worked out, depended for their efficacy on an underlying, implicit assumption that the structure of the monetary system would remain unchanged. But the very introduction of these new rules helped to change that structure. This is particularly clear in the nineteenth century. The restriction on note issue led the commercial banks to place more emphasis on marketing their chequable deposit accounts, as the Banking School had warned.

In the 1980s the new set of policies, bringing with them high and variable nominal interest rates in a context of deregulation and enhanced competition, led to the introduction of new interest-bearing forms of chequable deposits that helped to undermine the prior predictability of velocity and of the demand-for-money functions. The break-down of these prior regularities was, perhaps, even quicker and more complete in the 1980s than in the mid 1800s, but had been less well foreshadowed in the debate. This was partly because such prior regularities had appeared to be 'robustly' and 'significantly' established by the novel and arcane science of econometrics. Mere mortals could hardly be expected to challenge Chow tests and the like! Although there was some subsequent intra-academic reconsideration of the validity of some of these claims, it was Lucas (1976) who demonstrated that prior 'structural' equations are unlikely to remain stable after a new regime has been established, so that predicting the way that the new system may work is fraught with danger.

Not only did the monetary structure alter in a way unpredicted by the Currency/Monetary theorists, but also the central bank failed to adapt its own behaviour as the theorists had intended. Since the Currency School believed that, with the note issue firmly tethered, major monetary disturbances would be avoided, they felt that the Banking Department could then act freely as a commercial bank, unconstrained by concerns about systemic stability and the public good. Fetter (1965, p. 169) reports 'an idea that for the next twenty years was basic to the Currency School case: the need for using discretion would never arise if the Bank Directors had not previously misguidedly used their discretion in ignoring their declining reserves, thus creating a crisis which could be cured only by a further use of discretion'. The analogy to recent criticism of central banks is apparent.

Monetary disturbances were not, however, then averted; the Bank Act had to be temporarily rescinded three times between 1844 and 1873. As earlier noted, 1873 marked the publication of *Lombard Street*, wherein Bagehot argued that the centralisation of banking reserves with the Bank of England, which had in effect been taken further by the 1844 Bank Act, made it more rather than less essential for the Bank of England to act as a central bank for the public good to preserve systemic stability. The proposed separation of function, which lay behind the division of the Bank into Issue and Banking Departments, soon ceased to hold. Nevertheless, that same division has continued unchanged both in Statute and in statistics, hardly an aid to transparency or clarity of understanding.

In the recent period, the monetary authorities accepted the arguments for introducing intermediate monetary targets, but they were not prepared to accept the monetarists' proposals for attaining such targets. Monetarists claimed that the correct way to do so was via monetary base control. The central bank should estimate the likely future money multiplier (linking the monetary base with the chosen M aggregate), and then vary the high-powered monetary base (H) to achieve the desired level of M.

Central bankers believed that such a mechanism would be inconsistent with existing banking structures, that its introduction would cause more violent interest rate instability and might well not deliver greater M control, since the regime change might make the multiplier less predictable (Goodhart 1995b). They also tended to argue that, with their existing techniques of varying interest rates, they could, so long as fiscal policy was also reasonably restrained, control monetary growth over the relevant target period (i.e. over periodicities of twelve months or more), if not in the shorter run (see the Green Paper on Monetary Control 1980).

In practice, experience of achieving these targets was mixed at best, and monetarists claimed that their policies had not been properly or seriously attempted. These operational debates became quite inflamed in the early 1980s. They were not resolved, and there was little meeting of minds. What happened, instead, in most of the relevant countries, was the breakdown in the predictability of velocity. That meant that it became impossible to select a generally acceptable intermediate monetary target. But without an objective for M, there was no point left in monetary base control, though the movement in high powered money (H) could remain of itself a useful information variable.

What more general lessons, if any, can we infer from observing the analytical similarities of these two episodes? One possible lesson is that economists are good at explaining to central bankers the causes, and consequences, of the latter's past failures, but much less good at designing ways of improving the system. Their proposed 'rules' tend to be conditioned – to a far greater extent than realised – on implicit assumptions about market structures and infrastructures. Given the continuing rapid pace of the evolution of such structures, central banks will rightly aim to retain their discretionary flexibility.

1.5.3   Free banking

Whereas some (Socialist) countries abolished commercial banks, relying only on a single central mono-bank, and others have operated primarily with foreign-based commercial banks, virtually every country that has established a separate national currency has also set up a central bank, or at a minimum a monetary authority (Hong Kong, Singapore) that carries out several of the functions of a central bank. Even when the currency of a country is linked to that of a larger (more central) country through some currency board arrangement (e.g. African countries under Colonial rule, Hong Kong since 1983, Argentina since 1991 and Estonia since 1992; see Newlyn and Rowan 1954; Walters and Hanke 1992; and Hanke, Jonung and Schuler 1993), considerations both of national pride and seigniorage revenue lead to a separate national currency and central bank/monetary authority. The establishment and existence of a central bank would appear to have become an appurtenance of national monetary autonomy. As such, the basic functions, role and importance of central banks within the financial system appear, at the moment, without serious political and constitutional challenge.

The value, and validity, of its role has, however, remained under irregularly recurring academic attack, not only from those who would constrain and limit central banking functions to carrying-out certain simple rules of operation (as described above), but also from those who query whether a central bank is either necessary or beneficial for the operation of a country's monetary system. The alternative is usually described as 'free banking', i.e. free of the presence and interventions of a central bank. Once again, similar arguments have recurred periodically for much of our historical period.

Indeed, the latest revival of academic interest and advocacy for free banking has taken place within the context of reassessments of the history of monetary thought and of the actual experience of historical 'free' banking systems. The seminal books that started the latest revival were by White (1984) and Hayek (1976), and sparked off a considerable literature reassessing historical episodes of free banking, e.g. in Scotland, Canada, USA and elsewhere (see Capie and Wood 1991; and Dowd 1992), as well as more theoretical contributions by Selgin (1988) and Glasner (1989).

Such free banking proposals have, as already noted, remained in recent years a somewhat fringe, academic exercise without much support from practitioners. Nevertheless such ideas have, over the years, been advanced by several of the most serious academic students of central banking. Bagehot would have preferred a free banking system to that established by the Bank of England Act, and Vera Smith's (1936) book, The Rationale of Central Banking, is simultaneously one of the major studies of central banking and a sustained plea for the resumption of Free Banking.

In the nineteenth-century British monetary debate, the Free Banking School did, however, have some considerable support from practitioners. In particular, the Scottish banks wished to protect their autonomy from any encroachment on their (note-issuing) powers by the UK Parliament or the Bank of England. Some (country) bankers in England (see White 1984, p. 68) also argued in favour of a freely independent system, with each bank guarding its own reserves, rather than one in which note issue and reserve management would be progressively centralised under the Bank of England, either under rules (Currency School) or discretion (Banking School).

Yet, once central banks had ceased to compete with the commercial banks and their main functions (of achieving price and systemic stability), had become well established, very little residual generic opposition to, or resentment of, central banks persisted within the commercial banking, or financial, system more widely. This is not to suggest that all individual central bank actions are invariably well received by the commercial banking fraternity. But how often, if ever, have leading commercial bankers called in recent years for the root-and-branch abolition of central banks, as academics are from time to time wont to do? Indeed, the opposite is common. Much of the support for the actions of central banks, and for the extension of their autonomy (in the field of macro monetary management, much less uncritically so in the field of prudential supervision), has come from the financial community in general, and commercial banks in particular.

This continuing support by financial practitioners for the exercise of central banking has been important. It is somewhat more speculative to hazard why central bankers have enjoyed it. In part, it will be because commercial bankers welcome central bank services in allowing the economisation of systemic (non-interest bearing) reserves (see Edgeworth 1888; Fetter 1965; Goodfriend 1990; and Laidler 1992), in offering a safety-net and hence enabling economies in individual bank capital requirements, in providing leadership in joint exercises (e.g. to establish new and improved payments and settlements systems). In part, it may be due to inertia (practitioners prefer incremental changes to well-known structures, rather than radical jumps in the dark). The more cynical commentators would, no doubt, suggest that commercial banks generally approve the operations of central bankers, because they have 'captured' them to serve their own interests. The theory of capture is often, however, little more than an exaggeration of the fact that controllers and controlled, supervisors and the supervised, have to establish a modus vivendi. Our view is that the evidence indicates that this latter has been usually done well in the central/commercial banking field.

Although the academic case against central banks, and for free banking, has failed, so far, to gather much practitioner support, should the current enthusiasm for central bank independence, discussed in section 1.1.6 prove a disappointment, in terms of successful re-establishment of price stability, then it is possible, though far from certain, that the cause of 'free banking' would obtain renewed support. The two main functions of a central bank are the maintenance and achievement of price and systemic stability. The free banking claim is that the existence of a central bank is necessary for neither, and may be inimical to both. The arguments why central banks may, in practice, cause, rather than cure, inflation have already been rehearsed, e.g. in the previous Part, and are based on the suggestion that they are prone to become the manipulable instrument of government, who have a (time inconsistency) incentive to generate surprise inflation (e.g. Barro and Gordon 1983; Cukierman 1992).

Instead of relying on a central bank to achieve price stability, free bankers would place their trust in the commitment of individual commercial bankers to maintain the convertibility of their liabilities (notes and deposits) into an asset or a basket of assets of real value, e.g. gold, wheat, government bills and bonds, standardised labour time, etc. (see Hall 1982; Glasner 1989; and Sumner 1990). In so far as interest could not, technically or legally, be paid on their note liabilities, banks might compete in seeking to offer convertibility into the most convenient/highest quality external asset (see Dowd 1989). In so far as interest could be paid, a quasi-equilibrium would exist when the interest differential just offset the differential expected rates of appreciation (against some general basket) of the reserve assets chosen by any pair of banks (see Klein 1974).

Such a (free banking) system would lead to extra transactions costs, some additional use of real assets as bank reserves, and other, possibly minor, inefficiencies (e.g. connected with multiple note issue). More important, the guarantee of the real value of the moneys (price stability) depends on the convertibility commitment being honoured at all times and on all occasions. This is problematic.

Advocates of free banking place much reliance on the law of reflux whereby a note issuing bank will lose/gain reserves at the clearing if it expands faster/slower than other competing note issuing banks. While this is relatively uncontroversial, it leaves the question of the behaviour of the system as a whole indeterminate. Moreover, an individual competing bank can offset any reserve losses from faster expansion by bidding more aggressively for funds by raising deposit interest rates. An insufficiently capitalised bank would have an incentive to adopt a riskier portfolio, and finance it in this way, because much of any resulting loss would fall on the depositors, or their insurance fund.

Some advocates of free-banking argue that, given the demand for bank loans and the supply of funds to banks, there will be a single, determinate, unique, profit-maximising equilibrium for the scale of intermediation through banks (see Selgin 1988; and Sechrest 1993). They believe that, left alone to compete freely, the banking system would be stable. This is contentious. Others believe that, in a world of limited and asymmetric information, herd-type behaviour patterns, etc., fractional reserve banking is inherently liable to runs and crises, endangering the convertibility commitment and giving rise to risks of systemic instability. The historical record certainly demonstrates that these risks have been present, but even that view has been challenged (Dowd 1992).

Such banking crises have been destabilising and have caused considerable public loss (Sprague 1910 and Kindleberger 1993). A common response of the public has been to call for government measures and intervention both to alleviate the loss and to prevent it happening again; hence the need for banking regulations and supervision, whether by the central bank or some associated regulatory body, the role of the central bank as Lender of Last Resort, deposit insurance, etc.

There have been a variety of responses by advocates of free banking to this argument that the susceptibility of the present, fractional reserve banking system to runs and contagious panics, i.e. systemic instability, requires a central bank to provide systemic protection. The first is, as we have seen, just to deny that in a free, competitive system such crises and potential instability would occur (see, for example, Selgin 1988). The second is to argue that the apparent inability to set appropriate prices on either the central bank implicit safety net or on an explicit 100 per cent deposit insurance scheme leads to a moral hazard risk that can make the potential crises worse rather than better, and that this risk can at best only be mitigated by intrusive regulation of banks that will lead to further distortion and misallocation of resources (see, for example, Dowd 1989). Not only has the S&L debacle in the USA been blamed in part on such moral hazard, but also some economists have argued that commercial banks would not have lent so much, so freely to LDCs prior to 1982 if they had not been relying on an implicit safety net and future bail-out from the monetary authorities.

The third line of argument has been that free banking could lessen its potential susceptibility to runs and panics by the adoption of certain mechanisms or (self-regulatory) controls. While this may lessen the pure *laissez-faire* nature of the proposed free system, they may nevertheless, according to its advocates, be preferable to a more comprehensive central Bank/regulatory framework. One such mechanism is the 'option clause', suggested by Dowd (1988), whereby banks can suspend their convertibility commitment temporarily on payment of a high interest rate. Again, a clearing house is an essential ingredient of any free banking system, and such clearing houses can organize limited rescue and controlled suspension arrangements, as under the National Banking System in the USA (Sprague 1910 and Timberlake 1993); though the experience of crises under that system was clearly not felt to be acceptable. Another approach is to require customer protection in the form of collateral (e.g. government bonds) against note issue, and capital against total liabilities, though such measures often tend to approximate to those that a central bank might itself introduce. A more recent proposal in this genre is the 'narrow bank' model advocated by Litan (1987). If an intermediary is restricted to holding completely safe assets, such as money market mutual funds, or the value of its liabilities adjusts automatically with the value of its assets, as with other mutual funds (unit trusts), then there would seem little need for any external body to need to guarantee the systemic stability of that part of the financial system. This, of course, begs the question of which intermediaries would continue to make risky loans, how those intermediaries would be funded, and supported in the face of a major withdrawal of funds.

A fourth line of argument has been to deny either the likelihood of contagion in a properly established banking system, or that there are any sizeable externalities, social losses in excess of internalised private losses, in the case of banking failures, or at least that such externalities are no greater in banking than in other industries. George Benston, for example, appears sympathetic to the first of these arguments. He views the US banking system, with its limitations on diversification, either geographical or functional, as almost uniquely badly designed (Benston 1990). With a better structured branch-banking, universal banking system, with mark-to-market accounting and a structured early intervention and resolution (SEIR) system based on stepped capital adequacy requirements, the need for direct central bank, or other administrative, regulation and direct support (LOLR) could be much reduced (Benston 1993). While there is little doubt that improvements to the regulatory system can be envisaged, whether any of them could be so fool-proof as to allow for a totally hands-off role in this respect for the central bank also remains contentious.

The second part of such arguments, that bank failures do not entail serious externalities, or no more serious than closures of mines or factories, appears to us somewhat implausible. But it has been vigorously advanced in recent years by Kaufman (1988, 1990 and 1994).

To summarise, the main case against free banking is that the balance of evidence, historically, shows that it leads to systemic instability, though this assessment of history is contentious and rebutted by its academic advocates. This question leads on, more or less directly, to the issue of whether some degree of (external) bank regulation is necessary and, if so, whether it is appropriately done by a central bank. In this latter respect a variety of critics of current banking regulation tends to join forces with free bank proponents to deny that bank supervision is a necessary or desirable function for central banks to undertake.

Even if the more root and branch attack of free bankers on the existence of central banks should remain, as we guess most likely, an academic diversion, the appropriate function of central banks in ensuring systemic stability in the payments systems, the banking system or the wider financial system is likely to remain a lively field for discussion, debate and experimentation.

1.6   Conclusion

If the fundamental, evolutionary criterion of success is that an organisation should reproduce and multiply over the world, and successfully mutate to meet the emerging challenges of time, then central banks have been conspicuously successful. Their existence is treated as a crucial aspect of political sovereignty. When a new nation state seeks to establish itself, the foundation of an independent central bank will be an early item on the agenda, slightly below the design of the flag, but above the establishment of a national airline.

Moreover, central banks (and bankers) are, in general, respected and admired, considerably more so than the rest of the political apparatus. When much of the political system has been questioned in Italy, it was the Banca d'Italia that was without taint, and its governor, Ciampi, that was asked to be Prime Minister. Central bankers are, perhaps, seen as having more in common with the judiciary, than with politicians or commercial bankers; and are perceived as both technically expert, above the fray of self-seeking, and a necessary agent (of democratic government) for imposing order on a potentially unruly financial system. In terms of the general esteem in which institutions are held, central banks would again appear to be successful now, probably more so than in the middle of the century, when it was widely held that they should be made subservient to the central government.

Yet, if we should judge an institution by the effect of its actions, the recent record has been mixed. Price stability has not been achieved. From the 1960s onwards, but particularly in the 1970s, there was the worst episode of endemic inflation that has occurred during periods of peace and political stability – without much excuse in the form of exogenous events such as gold discoveries. While current opinion attributes more of the blame to politicans than to central banks for that, the trend to central bank independence will put the latter on their mettle. Moreover, in so far as there has been success in reining back inflation in recent years, this has gone hand in hand, in Europe at least, with rising average unemployment to levels that have mirrored the 1930s in proportionate extent, if not in equivalent distress or potential political unrest. This is hardly an indication of the 'credibility' of monetary policy, which was supposed to act in the opposite direction, to lower the sacrifice ratio.

Besides their macro objective of price stability, central banks have a micro objective of maintaining financial stability, especially in the core areas of the payment system and the commercial banks who operate it. In the last few years, the number and size of banking institutions who have failed, and have had to be bailed out by the authorities, have risen to levels last seen in the 1930s. While there have been recent episodes in which the authorities have been conspicuously successful in averting systemic financial failure, e.g. the LDC debt problem in 1982 and the 1987 stock market collapse, their handling of the property bubble and bust, 1988–93, has not been so sure. Recent developments have thrown up difficult micro-level problems, such as the universalisation and globalisation of financial institutions, the danger of moral hazard, the 'too big to fail' syndrome, with which central banks have been struggling, not always successfully, to find answers.

That same globalisation has led to a massive expansion of international capital flows and foreign exchange dealing. In the face of this, the authorities in general, and central banks in particular, have seemed increasingly incapable of maintaining a stable international exchange rate regime. Floating exchange rates have behaved poorly, and pegged exchange rates have been blown asunder. Where do we go now from this?

So, looking at the record of domestic price stability, financial market stability, or international monetary order, the recent record is at best spotty. Despite their institutional success, central banks cannot afford to be complacent. There is much to learn, and much room for improvement.

REFERENCES

Acres, W. M. (1931) *The Bank of England from Within.* Oxford University Press.

Aguirre Carrillo, E. (1991) *La Genesis de la Banca Central.* Banco de la República: Bogotá.

Akyüz, Y. (1989) 'Financial system and policies in Turkey in the 1980s', Discussion Paper No. 25, United Nations Conference on Trade and Development.

Alesina, A. and L. Summers (1993) 'Central bank independence and macroeconomic performance', *Journal of Money, Credit and Banking*, 24, 2.

Almaula, N. I. (1960) *Operations of the Reserve Bank of India 1935–54.* Asia Publishing House: London.

Almeida, J. R. N (1992) 'Essays on Brazilian monetary polices and history, 1945–1988'. Unpublished MPhil thesis. The George Washington University.

Andréadès, A. (1909) *A History of the Bank of England.* PS King and Sons: London.

Arnaudo, A. (1987) *Cincuenta Anos de Politica Financiera Argentina, 1934–1983.* El Ateneo: Buenos Aires.

Arndt, E. H. D. (1928) *Banking and Currency Development in South Africa 1652–1927.* Juta & Co: Cape Town.

Auburn, H. W. (1966) *Comparitive Banking.* 3rd edition. Waterlow and Sons: Dunstable.

Aufricht, H. (1961) *Central Banking Legislation: A Collection of Central Bank, Monetary and Banking Laws.* International Monetary Fund: Washington D.C.

Aufricht, H. (1967) Central banking Legislation: A Collection of Central Bank, Monetary and Banking Laws. Volume II: Europe. International Monetary Fund: Washington D.C.

Austrian National Bank (1991) *Striking a Balance: 175 Years of Austrian Central Banking.* Vienna.

Bachmeyer, O. (1960) *Die Geschichte der Österreichischen Währungspolitik.* (The History of Austrian Monetary and Exchange Rate Policy). Vienna.

Bagchi, A. M. (1987) *The Evolution of the State Bank of India 1806–1876.* Oxford University Press: Bombay.

Bagehot, W. (1973) Lombard Street. 14th edition. Kegan, Paul: London.

Bagehot, W. (1866) 'What a panic is and how it might be avoided', *The Economist*, 12 May.

Banco Central de Chile (1990) *Constitutional Organic Act of the Central Bank of Chile.*

Banco Central de Chile (1988) 'Banco Central de Chile'. Official Publication.

Banco Central de Venezuela (1992) *The Law of the Central Bank of Venezuela.* Caracas.

Banco de España (1970) *El Banco de España: Una Historia Economica.* (The Bank of Spain: An Economic History). Madrid.

Banco de España (1982) *El Banco de España: Dos Siglos de Historia 1782–1982.* (The Bank of Spain: Two Centuries of History 1782–1982). Madrid

Banco de España (1983) (Compiled by G. Perez de Armiñan) *Legislacion Bancaria Española.* (Spanish Banking Legislation). 6th edition. Madrid.

Banco de la República (1990) *El Banco de la República: Antecedentes, Evolución y Estructura.* Bogotá.

Banco de la República (1991) *LXVIII Informe anual del Gerente a la Junta Directiva.*

Banco de la República (1994) *Kemmerer y el Banco de la República: Diarios y Documentos.* Bogotá.

Banco de la República Oriental del Uruguay (1964) *Carta Organica.* Montevideo.

Bang, P. and J. P. Holter (1991) *Norges Bank 175 År.* (Norges Bank 175 Years). Norges Bank: Oslo.

Bank of Canada (1990) *Bank of Canada Act.* February.

Bank of England (1971) 'Competition and credit control', *Bank of England Quarterly Bulletin*, 11, 2, June.

Bank of Finland (1984) *Currency Acts and Regulations for the Bank of Finland.* Helsinki.

Bank of Finland (1992) *The Bank of Finland.* Helsinki.

Bank of Finland (1991) 'Financial markets in Finland', *Bank of Finland Monthly Bulletin*, Special Bulletin.

Bank of Greece (1928) *Annual Report.* Athens.

Bank of Greece (1975) *Statutes.* 6th edition. Athens

Bank of Japan (1964) *The Bank of Japan: Its Function and Organisation.* Economic Research Department. Tokyo.

Bank of Japan (1982) *Nippon Ginko Hyakunenshi.* (Centennial History of the Bank of Japan). Tokyo.

Bank of Portugal (1990) *Organic Law.*

Bank for International Settlements (1963) 'Banca d'Italia', in *Eight European Central Banks.* Allen and Unwin: London

Bank for International Settlements (1963) 'Banque de France', in *Eight European Central Banks*. BIS: Basle.

Bank for International Settlements (1963) 'Banque Nationale de Belgique', in *Eight European Central Banks*. Allen and Unwin: London.

Bank for International Settlements (1963) 'Sverige Riksbank', in *Eight European Central Banks*. BIS: Basle.

Bank for International Settlements (1963) 'Schweizerische Nationalbank', in *Eight European Central Banks*. Allen and Unwin: London.

Bank for International Settlements (1963) 'Bank of England', in *Eight European Central Banks*. BIS: Basle.

Bank for International Settlements (1964) 'Nederlandsche Bank', in *Eight European Central Banks*. BIS: Basle.

Banque de France (1992) *The Banque de France: History, Organisation, Role*. Direction de la Communication, Paris.

Baring, F. (1797; reproduced in 1993) 'Observations on the establishment of the Bank of England and on the paper circulation of the country', in F. Capie (ed.) *A History of Banking*. Pickering and Chatto: London.

Barker, H. A. F. (1952) *The Principles and Practice of Banking in South Africa*. Juta and Co: Johannesburg.

Barro, R. J. and D. B. Gordon (1983) 'A positive theory of monetary policy in a natural rate model', *Journal of Political Economy*, 91, 4.

Barrow, G. L. (1975) *The Emergence of the Irish Banking System, 1820–1845*. Gill and MacMillan: Dublin.

Batten, D. S., Blackwell, M. P., Kim, I., Nocera, S. E. and Y. Ozeki (1990) 'The conduct of monetary policy in the major industrial countries: instruments and operating procedures', IMF Occasional Paper, July.

Baumgartner, W. (1971) *La Banque de France*. Historia: Paris.

Beckhart, B. J. (1972) *Federal Reserve System*. Columbia University Press: New York.

Belongia, M. T. (1991) *Monetary Policy on the 75th Anniversary of the Federal Reserve System. Proceedings of the 14th Annual Conference of the Federal Reserve Bank of St Louis*. Kluwer: Boston.

Benston, G. J. (1990) 'US banking in an increasingly integrated and competitive world economy', *Journal of Financial Services Research*, 4, December.

Benston, G. J. (1993) 'Safety nets and moral hazard in banking', paper delivered to the Bank of Japan Conference in Tokyo on 'Financial Stability in a Changing Environment', October.

Bett, V. M. (1957) *Central Banking in Mexico*. University of Michigan: Ann Arbor.

Bigo, R. (1927) *La Caissse d'Escompte (1776–1973) et les Origines de la Banque de France*. Presses de Universitaire de France: Paris.

Bloomfield, A. I. (1959) *Monetary Policy Under the International Gold Standard*. Federal Reserve Bank of New York: New York.

Board of Governors of the Federal Reserve System and the United States Treasury Department (1963) *The Federal Reserve and the Treasury: Answers to Questions from the Commission on Money and Credit*. Prentice Hall: Englewood Cliffs.

Bodenhorn, H. (1992) 'Free banking in Ireland', in K. Dowd (ed.) *The Experience of Free Banking*. Routledge: London.

Bopp, K. R. (1944) 'Central banking at the crossroads', *American Economic Review*, 34, March.

Bopp, K. R. (1953) *Reichsbank Operations 1876–1914*. University of Pennsylvania.

Bordo, M. D. (1990) 'The lender of last resort: alternative views and historical evidence', *Federal Reserve Bank of Richmond Economic Quarterly*, 76, 1.

Bordo, M. D. (1993) 'The gold standard, Bretton Woods and other monetary regimes: an historical appraisal', *NBER* Working paper Series, No. 4310.

Bordo, M. D. and F. Capie (1993) *Monetary Regimes in Transition*. Cambridge University Press: Cambridge.

Bordo, M. D. and B. Eichengreen (1993) *A Retrospective on the Bretton Woods System*. National Bureau of Economic Research/Chicago University Press: Cambridge, MA.

Bordo, M. D. and Redish, A. (1987) 'Why did the Bank of Canada emerge in 1935?' *Journal of Economic History*, June.

Bordo, M. D. and A. J. Schwartz (1984) *A Retrospective on the Classical Gold Standard, 1821–1931*. Chicago University Press: Chicago.

Bouvier, J. (1988) 'The Banque de France and the State from 1850 until the present day,' in G. Toniolo (ed.) *Central Banks' Independence in Historical Perspective*. Walter de Gruyter: Berlin.

Bowman, W. D. (1937) *The Story of the Bank of England: From its Foundation in 1694 until the Present Day*. Herbert Jenkins: London.

Brash, D. T. (1993) 'Reconciling central bank independence with political accountability – the New Zealand experience', Address to the European Policy Forum, June.

Broadberry, S. N. (1986) *The British Economy between the Wars: A Macroeconomic Survey*. Blackwell: Oxford.

Brown, E. C. (1990) 'Episodes in the public debt history of the United States', in Dornbusch, R. and M. Draghi (eds.) *Public Debt Managment: Theory and History*. Cambridge University Press: Cambridge.

Brunner, K. and A. Meltzer (1993) *Money and the Economy: Issues in Monetary Analysis*. Cambridge University Press: Cambridge.

Bundesverband des Privaten Bankgewerbes (1957) *Relations between the Central Banks and Commercial Banks*. Lectures delivered at the Tenth International Banking Summer School, Garmisch-Partenkirchen, September.

Burns, A. F. (1985) *Reflections of an Economic Policymaker: Speeches and Congressional Statements 1969–1978*. American Enterprise Trust for Public Policy Research: Washington D.C.

Butlin, S. J. (1983) 'Australian central banking, 1945–59', *Australian Economic History Review*, 23, 2.

Butlin, S. J. (1986) *The Australian Monetary System 1851–1914*. Ambassador Press: Sydney.

Calomiris, C. W. (1992) 'Regulation, industrial structure, instability in US banking', in Klausner and L. White (eds.) *Structure and Change in Banking*. New York University Press: New York.

Cameron, R. (1963) 'Belgium 1800–1875', in R. Cameron (ed.) *Banking in the Early Stages of Industrialisation*, Oxford University Press: Oxford.

Cameron, R. (1967a) *Banking in the Early Stages of Industrialisation: A Study in Comparative Economic History*. Oxford University Press: Oxford.

Cameron, R. (1967b) 'France 1800–1870', in R. Cameron *Banking in the Early Stages of Industrialisation*. Oxford University Press: Oxford.

Cameron, R. (ed.) (1972) *Banking and Economic Development: Some Lessons of History*. Oxford University Press: Oxford.

Cameron, R. and V. I. Bovykin (1991) *International Banking 1870–1914*. Oxford University Press: Oxford.

Campbell Committee of Inquiry into the Australian Monetary System (1981) *Final Report*. Australian Government Publishing Service: Canberra.

Capie, F. (1993) *A History of Banking*. Pickering and Chatto: London.

Capie, F., Mills, T. and G. Wood (1986) 'Was the war loan conversion a success?' *Applied Economics*.

Capie, F. and A. Webber (1985) *A Monetary History of the United Kingdom*. Allen and Unwin: London.

Capie, F. and G. Wood (1986) *Financial Crises and the World Banking System*. Macmillan: London.

Capie, F. and G. Wood (1991) *Unregulated Banking: Chaos or Order?* Macmillan: London.

Carrillo, E. A. (1991) *La Genesis de la Banca Central Banco de la Republica*. Bogotá.

Central Bank of Ireland (1992) 'Summary material relating to the role, functions, structure and independence of the Central Bank of Ireland', Manuscript, Monetary Policy Division, March.

Central Bank of Ireland (1992) *Annual Report*. Dublin.

Chapham, R. A. (1968) *Decision Making: A Case Study of the Decision to Raise the Bank Rate in September 1957*. Routledge and Kegan Paul: London.

Chlepner, B. S. (1943) *Belgian Banking and Banking Theory*. The Brookings Institution: Washington D.C.

Ciampi, C. A. (1987) 'The functions of the central bank in today's economy', in P. Ciocca (ed.) *Money and the Economy: Central Bankers' Views*. St Martin's Press: New York.

Clapham, J. H. (1944) *The Bank of England: A History*. (Official History of the Bank of England). Cambridge University Press: Cambridge.

Clark, L. E. (1935) *Central Banking under the Federal Reserve System*. Macmillan: New York.

Clay, H. (1957) *Lord Norman*. Macmillan: London.

Clayton, G. (1962a) 'Portugal', in R. S. Sayers (ed.) *Banking in Western Europe*. Clarendon Press: Oxford.

Clayton, G. (1962b) 'Sweden', in R. S. Sayers (ed.) *Banking in Western Europe*. Clarendon Press: Oxford.

Clayton, G. (1962c) 'Denmark', in R. S. Sayers (ed.) *Banking in Western Europe*. Clarendon: Oxford.

Clifford, A. J. (1965) *The Independence of the Federal Reserve System*. University of Pennsylvania Press: Philadelphia.

Collins, M. (1993) *Central Banking in History*. Elgar Reference Collection: London.

Conant, C. A. (1909) *A History of Modern Banks of Issue*. G. P. Putnam's Sons: London

Congdon, T. (1981) 'Is the provision of a sound currency a necessary function of the state?', *National Westminster Quarterly Review*, August.

Copland, D. B. (1929) 'The banking system of Australia', in Willis, H. P. and B. H. Beckhart (eds.) *Foreign Banking Systems*. Sir Isaac Pitman and Sons: London.

Cowen, T. and R. Kroszner (1994) *Explorations in the New Monetary Economics*. Basil Blackwell: London.

Crazut, R. J. (1990) *El Banco Central de Venezuela: Notas sobre su Historia y Evolución, 1940–1990*. 4th edition. Banco Central de Venezuela: Caracas.

Cukierman, A. (1992) *Central Bank Strategy, Credibility and Independence*. MIT Press: Cambridge MA.

Cunliffe Report (1919) *Committee on Currency and Foreign Exchanges After the War*. First Interim Report. Cmnd 9182. HMSO: London.

Danmarks Nationalbank (1991) *Central Bank Responsibilities and Tasks*, Copenhagen.

Danmarks Nationalbank (1983) *The New Building*. Copenhagen.

Dawe, S. (1993) 'Reserve Bank of New Zealand Act 1989', Unpublished manuscript.

De Cecco, M. (1974) *Money and Empire*. Basil Blackwell: Oxford.

De Kock, G. (1954) *A History of the South African Reserve Bank 1920–52*. J. L. Van Schaik: Pretoria.

De Kock, M. H. (1954) Central Banking. 3rd edition. Staples Press: London.

De Kock Commission (1985) *Final Report of the Commission of Inquiry into the Monetary System and Monetary Policy in South Africa*.

De Nederlandsche Bank (1964) *De Bank 1814–1964*. (Jubilee Issue on the Occasion of the 150th Anniversary of the Netherlands Bank). Amsterdam.

De Nederlandsche Bank (1968) *De Instrumenten van de Monetaire Politiek in Nederland*. (The instruments of monetary policy in the Netherlands). Amsterdam.

De Nederlandsche Bank (1991) *Bank Act 1948 and Articles of Association*. Amsterdam.

Delivanis, D. and W. C. Cleveland (1950) *Greek Monetary Developments 1939–1948*. Indiana University Publications, Social Science Series No. 6.

den Dunnen, E. and S. de Wilde (1992) 'Instruments of money and foreign exchange market policy in the Netherlands', NIBE Serie Bank- en Effectenbedrijf, 31.

Deutsche Bundesbank (1988) *30 Jahre Deutsche Bundesbank: Die Entstehung des Bundesbankgesetzes vom 26 Juli 1957*. (30 Years of the Deutsche Bundesbank: Origins of the Bundesbank Statute of 26 July 1957). Frankfurt-on-Main.

Deutsche Bundesbank (1985) 'Recent developments with respect to the Bundesbank's securities repurchase agreements', *Monthly Report of the Deutsche Bundesbank*, No. 10, October.

Deutsche Bundesbank (1989) 'The Deutsche Bundesbank: its monetary policy instruments and functions'. 3rd edition. Deutsche Bundesbank Special Series, No. 7.

Deutsche Bundesbank (ed.) (1976) *Währung und Wirstschaft in Deutschland 1876–1975*. (Money and the Economy in Germany 1876–1975). Fritz Knapp: Frankfurt-on-Main.

Deutsche Bundesbank (1983) 'The Bundesbank's transactions in securities under repurchase agreements', *Monthly Report of the Deutsche Bundesbank*, No. 5, May.

Deutsche Bundesbank (1989) *The Deutsche Bundesbank: Its Monetary Policy Instruments and Functions*. 3rd Edition, Deutsche Bundesbank Special Series No. 7.

Diaz-Alejandro, C. F. (1970) *Essays on the Economic History of the Argentine Republic*.

Díaz-Alejandro, C. F. (1976) *Foreign Trade Regimes and Economic Development: Colombia*. National Bureau of Economic Research: New York.

Dick, T. J. O. and J. E. Floyd (1993) 'Canada and the gold standard 1871–1914: a durable monetary regime', in Bordo, M. and F. Capie (eds.) *Monetary Regimes in Transition*. Cambridge University Press: Cambridge.

Difrieri, J. (1967) *Moneda y Bancos en la Republica Argentina*. Abeledo-Perrot: Buenos Aires.

Dillen, J. G. van (ed.) (1964) *History of the Principal Public Banks*.

Dimsdale, N. H. (1981) 'British monetary policy and the exchange rate 1920–38', *Oxford Economic Papers*, Supplement, 33.

Dodwell, D. W. (1934) *Treasuries and Central Banks*. P. S. King and Sons: London.

Doherty, J. (1993) 'The evolution of central banking in Ireland', in Central Bank of Ireland, Annual Report 1992, Summer.

Dornbusch, R. (1992) 'Monetary problems of post-Communism – lessons from the end of the Austro-Hungarian empire', Weltwirtschaftliches Archiv, 128.

Dow, J. C. R. (1964) *The Management of the British Economy 1945–60*. Cambridge University Press: Cambridge.

Dowd, K. (1988) 'Option clauses and the stability of a laissez-faire monetary system', *Journal of Financial Services Research*, 1, December.

Dowd, K. (1989) *The State and the Monetary System*. St Martin's Press: New York.

Dowd, K. (1992) *The Experience of Free Banking*. Routledge: London.

Downes, P. and R. Vaez-Zadeh (eds.) *The Evolving Role of Central Banks*. Central Banking Department, International Monetary Fund, Washington.

Drake, P. W. (1989) *The Money Doctor in the Andes: The Kemmerer Missions 1923–1933*. Duke University Press: London.

Du Plessis, E. (1980) 'Structure and operation of the Reserve Bank and its relationship to the Government', *Modern Business Law*, July.

Economist, The (1991) *One Hundred Years of Economic Statistics*. London.

Edgeworth, F. Y. (1888) 'The mathematical theory of banking', *Journal of the Royal Statistical Society*, 51.

Eichengreen, B. (1992a) 'Designing a central bank for Europe: a cautionary tale from the early years of the Federal Reserve System', in Canzoneri, M. B., Grilli, V. and P. R. Masson (eds.) *Establishing a Central Bank: Issues in Europe and Lessons from the US*. Cambridge University Press: Cambridge.

Eichengreen, B. (1992b) *Golden Fetters: The Gold Standard and the Great Depression, 1919–1939*. Oxford University Press: Oxford.

Eichengreen, B. (1994) 'The endogeneity of exchange rate regimes', in Reis, J. and P. Martin-Acena (eds.) *International Monetary Arrangements in Historical Perspective*. Macmillan: London.

Eijffinger, S. and E. Schaling (1993) 'Central bank independence in twelve industrial countries', *Banca Nazionale del Lavoro Quarterly Review*, 184, March.

Eizenga, W. (1990) 'The Banque de France and monetary policy', *SUERF Papers on Monetary Policy and Financial Systems*, No. 8.

Eizenga, W. (1991) 'The Bank of England and monetary policy', *SUERF Papers on Monetary Policy and Financial Systems*, No. 10.

Eizenga, W. (1993) 'The Banca d'Italia and monetary policy', *SUERF Papers on Monetary Policy and Financial Systems*, No. 15.

Eizenga, W. (1994) 'The National Bank of Belgium and monetary policy', SUERF Papers on Monetary Policy and Financial Systems, No. 17.

Eschweiler, B. and M. D. Bordo (1993) 'Rules, discretion and central bank independence: the German experience 1880–1989', *National Bureau of Economic Research*, Working Paper, No. 4547.

Escobar, J. B. (1992) *Jurisprudencia del Máximo Tribunal de la República Relacionada con el Banco Central de Venezuela, 1940–1990*. Volumes I and II. Banco Central de Venezuela: Caracas.

Eulambio, M. S. (1924) *The National Bank of Greece: A History of the Financial and Economic Evolution of Greece*. S.C. Vlastos: Athens

Fair, D. E. (1980) 'Relationships between central banks and governments in the determination of monetary policy'. *Sociéte Universitaire Européenne de Recherches Financières*, Paper No. 31A.

Falkena, H. B. (1989) *The Mechanics of the South African Financial System*. Macmillan: London.

Feavearyear, A. E. (1963) *The Pound Sterling: A History of English Money*. 2nd edition, revised by E. V. Morgan. Clarendon: Oxford.

Fengler, H. (1992) *Geschichte der deutschen Notenbanken vor Einführung der Mark-Währung*. Regenstauf.

Fetter, F. W. (1965) *The Development of British Monetary Orthodoxy*. Harvard University Press: Cambridge, MA.

Fforde, J. (1992) *The Bank of England and Public Policy 1941–1958*. (Official History of the Bank of England). Cambridge University Press: Cambridge.

Fforde, J. S. (1954) *The Federal Reserve System 1945–1949*. Clarendon: Oxford.

Finch, M. H. J. (1981) *A Political Economy of Uruguay since 1870*. Macmillan: London

Fisher, I. (1912a) *The Purchasing Power of Money*. Macmillan: New York.

Fisher, I. (1912b) 'A more stable gold standard', *Economic Journal*, 22, 88.

Flink, S. (1930) *The German Reichsbank and Economic Germany*. Harper and Brothers: London.

Flux, A. W. (1911) 'The Swedish banking system', Senate Document No. 586 in *Banking in Sweden and Switzerland*, National Monetary Commission, Vol. XVII. Washington DC: Government Printing Office.

Ford, A. G. (1962) *The Gold Standard 1880–1914: Britain and Argentina*. Clarendon Press: Oxford.

Francke, H. and M. Hudson (1984) *Banking and Finance in West Germany*. Croom Helm: London.

Fraser, B. (1991) 'Some observations on the role of the Reserve bank', Speech at Annual General Meeting of CEDA, Sydney, November.

Fraser, B. (1993) 'Reserve Bank independence and all that', *Reserve Bank of Australia Bulletin*, December.

Frattiani, M. and F. Spinelli (forthcoming 1995) *A Monetary History of Italy*. Cambridge University Press: Cambridge.

Friedman, M. (1960) *A Program for Monetary Stability*. Fordham University Press: New York.

Friedman, M. (1968) 'The role of monetary policy', *American Economic Review*, 58, 1.

Friedman, M. (1982) 'Monetary theory: policy and practice', *Journal of Money, Credit and Banking*, 14, 1.

Friedman, M. (1984) 'Lessons from the 1979–82 monetary policy experiment', *American Economic Review*, 74, 2.

Friedman, M. and A. J. Schwartz (1963) *A Monetary History of the United States, 1867–1960.* Princeton University Press: Princeton.

Fry, M. J. and M. R. Farhi (1979) *Money and Banking in Turkey.* Bo aziçi University Publications: Istanbul.

Funabashi, Y. (1988) *Managing the Dollar: From the Plaza to the Louvre.* Washington D.C.: Institute for International Economics.

Gaarden, A. van der (1964) 'The Netherlands Bank – 150 years old', *Amsterdamsche Bank Quarterly Review,* No. 144, June.

Gallarotti, G. M. (1993) 'The scramble for gold: monetary regime transformation in the 1870s', in Bordo, M. and F. Capie (eds.) *Monetary Regimes in Transition.* Cambridge University Press: Cambridge.

Garber, P. and M. Spencer (1994) 'The dissolution of the Austro-Hungarian empire: lessons for currency reform', *Essays in International Finance No. 191,* Department of Economics, Princeton University, February.

Geddes, P. (1987) *Inside the Bank of England.* Boxtree: London.

George, E. A. J. (1992) 'The pursuit of financial stability', *Bank of England Quarterly Bulletin,* 34, 1.

Gershenkron, A. (1962) *Economic Backwardness in Historical Perspective.* Harvard University Press: Cambridge MA.

Giavazzi, F. and A. Giovannini (1989) *Limiting Exchange Rate Flexibility.* MIT Press: Cambridge MA.

Giblin, L. F. (1951) *The Growth of a Central Bank: The Development of the Commonwealth Bank of Australia 1924–1945.* Melbourne University Press: Melbourne.

Giuseppi, J. (1966) *The Bank of England: A History from its Foundation in 1694.* Evans Brothers Limited: London.

Glasner, D. (1989) *Free Banking and Monetary Reform.* Cambridge University Press: Cambridge.

Glindemann, P. (1929) 'The banking system of Denmark', in Willis, H. P. and B. H. Beckhart (eds.) *Foreign Banking Systems.* Sir Isaac Pitman and Sons: London.

Goldfeld, S. M. (1973) 'The demand for money revisited', *Brookings Papers on Economic Activity,* 3.

Goldfeld, S. M. (1976) 'The case of the missing money', *Brookings Papers on Economic Activity,* 3.

Goldsmith, R. (1966) *The Financial Development of Mexico.* Development Centre of the OECD: Paris.

Gollan, R. (1968) *The Commonwealth Bank of Australia: Origins and Early History.* Australian National University Press: Canberra.

Goodfriend, M. (1990) 'Money, credit, banking and payment system policy', in Humphrey, D. B. (ed.) *The US Payment System: Efficiency, Risk and the Role of the Federal Reserve.* Kluwer: London.

Goodfriend, M. and W. Whelpley (1986) 'Federal funds', in Cook, T. Q. and T. D. Rowe (eds.) *Instruments of the Money Market.* Federal Reserve Bank of Richmond.

Goodhart, C. (1988) *The Evolution of Central Banks.* MIT Press: Cambridge: MA.

Goodhart, C. (1989) 'The conduct of monetary policy', *Economic Journal,* 99, 396.

Goodhart, C. (1995a) 'The political economy of European Monetary Union', forthcoming in P. B. Kenen (ed.) *Understanding Interdependence: The Macroeconomics of the Open Economy.* Princeton University Press: Princeton.

Goodhart, C. (1994b) 'Money supply control: base or interest rates', forthcoming in Hoover, K. and S. Sheffrin (eds.) *Monetarism and the Methodology of Economics*. Edward Elager: Cheltenham, Glos.

Goodman, J. B. (1992) *Monetary Sovereignty: The Politics of Central Banking in Western Europe*. Cornell University Press: London.

Gorton, G. (1984) 'Private clearinghouses and the origins of central banking', *Federal Reserve Bank of Philadelphia Business Review*, January–March.

Griffiths, B. and G. E. Wood (eds.) (1981) *Monetary Targets*. Macmillan: London.

Gupta. O. P. (1934) *Central Banking in India*. Hindustan Times Press: Delhi.

Halikias, D. J. (1978) *Money and Credit in a Developing Economy: The Greek Case*. New York University Press.

Hall, F. G. (1949) *The Bank of Ireland 1783–1946*. Hodges, Figgis and Co: Dublin.

Hall, R. E. (1982) 'Explorations in the gold standard and related policies for stabilising the dollar', in Hall, R. E. (ed.) *Inflation*. University of Chicago Press: Chicago.

Hamilton, E. J. (1945) 'The foundation of the Bank of Spain', *Journal of Political Economy*, 53.

Hamilton, E. J. (1946) 'The first twenty years of the Bank of Spain', *Journal of Political Economy*, 54.

Handsen, S. (1954) 'The Danish banking system', *Bankers' Magazine*, December.

Hanke, S. H., Jonung, L. and K. Schuler (1993) *Russian Currency and Finance: A Currency Board Approach to Reform*. Routledge: London.

Hankey, T. (1876) 'Banking in connection with the currency and the Bank of England', reproduced in Collins, M. (1993) *Central Banking in History*. Elgar Reference Collection: London.

Hasan, K. S. and L. N. Blythe (1973) *Banking in India*. Macdonald and Evans: Plymouth.

Hawke, G. R. (1973) *Between Governments and Banks: A History of the Reserve Bank of New Zealand*. A. R. Shearer: Wellington.

Hawtrey, R. G. (1932) *The Art of Central Banking*. Longmans, Green and Co.: London.

Hayek, F. A. (1976) *The Denationalisation of Money*. Institute for Economic Affairs: London.

Hennessey, E. (1992) *A Domestic History of the Bank of England 1930–1960*. Cambridge University Press: Cambridge.

Hirschmann, A. O. (1963) *Journeys Toward Progress: Studies of Policymaking in Latin America*. The Twentieth Century Fund: New York.

Hoffmann, M. (1987) *Die Geschichte des Schweizerfrankens*. (The History of the the Swiss Franc). Zurich.

Hoffmann, M. (1992) *Geld-, Währungs- und Bankenschichte der Schweiz*. (The History of Swiss Money, Exchange Rates and Banking). Zurich.

Hoffmeyer, E. (1960) 'Structural changes on the money and capital markets', English Summary of a Study by the Author. Copenhagen.

Holtfrerich, K. L. (1988) 'Relations between monetary authorities and governmental institutions: the case of Germany from the 19th century to the present', in G. Toniolo (ed.) *Central Banks' Independence in Historical Perspective*. Walter de Gruyter: New York.

Holtfrerich, K. L. (1989) 'The monetary unification process in 19th century

Germany: relevance and lessons for Europe today', in M. de Cecco and A. Giovannini (eds.) *A European Central Bank? Perspectives on Monetary Unification after Ten Years of the EMS*. Cambridge University Press.

Homer, S. and R. Sylla (1991) *A History of Interest Rates*. Rutgers University Press: London.

Hörgren, L. and A. Westman-Mårtensson (1991) 'Swedish monetary policy: institutions, targets and instruments', *Arbetsrapport*, No. 2, May. Sverige Riksbank: Stockholm.

Howitt, P. (1993) 'Canada', in Fratianni, M. U. and D. Salvatore (eds.) *Monetary Policy in Developed Economies*. Greenwood Press: London.

Hueyo, A. (1958) *El Banco Central: Aspectos Fundamentales y Antecedentes de su Implantación en la Republica Argentina*. Francisco A. Colombo: Buenos Aires.

Hurst, J. W. (1983) *A Legal History of Money in the United States 1774–1970*. University of Nebraska Press: Lincoln.

Iengar, H. V. R. (1962) 'Central banks and governments', speech delivered under the joint auspices of the Democratic Group of Indian Merchants' Chamber, the Commerce Graduates Association and the Progressive Group, Bombay, January.

Issawi, C. (1980) *The Economic History of Turkey 1800–1914*. University of Chicago Press: Chicago.

Ja, L. K. (1985) 'Redefining the role of RBI and the government', *Commerce*, 7 September.

James, H. (1985) *The Reichsbank and Public Finance in Germany 1924–1933*. Fritz Knapp Verlag: Frankfurt.

Jamieson, A. B. (1957) *Chartered Banking in Canada*. Ryerson Press: Toronto.

Johnson, G. G. (1939) *The Treasury and Monetary Policies 1933–38*. Harvard University Press: Cambridge, MA.

Johnston, R. A. (1989) 'The Reserve Bank's role in economic management', *Reserve Bank of Australia Economic Bulletin*, May.

Jong, A. M. de (1929) 'The banking system of Holland', in Willis, H. P. and B. H. Beckhart (eds.) *Foreign Banking Systems*. Sir Isaac Pitman and Sons: London.

Jong, A. M. de (1934) 'The origin and foundation of the Netherlands Bank', in J. G. Van Dillen (ed.) *History of the Principal Public Banks*, Martinus Nijhoff: The Hague.

Jong, A. M. de (1967) *Geschiedenis van de Nederlandsche Bank*. (History of the Netherlands Bank, in two volumes, 1814–1864 (I) and 1865–1914 (II). De Nederlandsche Bank: Amsterdam.

Jonung, L. (1993) 'The rise and fall of credit controls: the case of Sweden 1939–89', in Bordo, M. D. and F. Capie (eds.) *Monetary Regimes in Transition*. Cambridge University Press: Cambridge.

Joslin, D. (1963) *A Century of Banking in Latin America*. Oxford University Press: Oxford.

Kaldor, N. (1985) *The Scourge of Monetarism*. 2nd edition. Oxford University Press: Oxford.

Kamitz, R. (1949) 'Die Österreichische Geld- und Währungspolitik von 1848 bis 1948' ('Austrian monetary and exchange rate policy from 1848 to 1948') in H. Mayer (ed.) *Hundert Jahre Österreichische Wirtschaftsentwicklung 1848–1948*. Vienna.

Kaplan, J. J. and G. Schleiminger (1989) *The European Payments Union: Financial Diplomacy in the 1950s*. Clarendon: Oxford.

Kasman, B. (1992) 'A comparison of monetary policy operating procedures in six industrial countries', *Federal Reserve Bank of New York Quarterly Review*, Summer.

Kauch, P. (1950) *La Banque Nationale de Belgique 1850–1918*. (Official history of the Bank of Belgium, 1850–1918, issued to commemorate its centenary). Brussels.

Kaufman, G. G. (1988) 'Bank runs: causes, benefits and costs', *The Cato Journal*, 7, Winter.

Kaufman, G. G. (1990) 'Are some banks too large to fail? Myth and reality', Contemporary Policy Issues, VIII.

Kaufman, G. G. (1994) 'Bank contagion: a review of the theory and the evidence', *Journal of Financial Services Research*, forthcoming.

Kemmerer, E. W. (1932) *The ABC of the Federal Reserve System*. Princeton University Press: Princeton.

Keynes, J. M. (1936) *The General Theory of Employment, Interest and Money*. Macmillan: London.

Kindleberger, C. P. (1984; second edition 1993) *A Financial History of Western Europe*. Oxford University Press: Oxford.

King, W. T. C. (1936, reprinted 1972) *History of the London Discount Market*. Frank Cass: London.

Kisch, C. H. and W. A. Elkin (1932) *Central Banks*. Macmillan: London.

Klein, B. (1974) 'The competitive supply of money', *Journal of Money, Credit and Banking*, 6, 4.

Klopstock, F. H. (1948) 'Monetary and fiscal policy in post-liberation Austria', *Political Science Quarterly*, March.

Kneeshaw, J. T. and P. van den Bergh (1989) 'Changes in central bank money market operating procedures in the 1980's', *BIS Economic Papers*, No. 23.

Kriz, M. A. (1948) 'Central banks and the state today', *American Economic Review*, 38, June.

Kullberg, R. (1992) 'A brief history of the Bank of Finland', *Bank of Finland Working Paper*, 1/92, Research Department.

Kumcu, E. (1990) 'The regulatory power of the Central Bank of Turkey', in Korner, H. and R. Shams (eds.) *Institutional Aspects of Economic Integration of Turkey into the EC*. Verlag Weltarchiv: Hamburg.

Kuroda, A. (1992) 'Central banking in Japan: an overview', paper presented at the 19th SEANZA Central banking Course, Tokyo, November.

Laidler, D. E. (1985) *The Demand for Money: Theories and Evidence*. Dun-Donnelly: New York.

Laidler, D. E. (1991) *The Golden Age of the Quantity Theory: The Development of Neoclassical Monetary Economics*. Phillip Allan: London.

Laidler, D. E. (1992) 'Free banking: theory', in Newman, P., Milgate, M. and J. Eatwell (eds.) *The New Palgrave Dictionary of Money and Finance*. Macmillan: London.

Lampe, J. R. and M. R. Jackson (1982) *Balkan Economic History: From Imperial Borderlands to Developing Nations*. Indiana University Press: Bloomington.

Laughlin, J. L. (1933) *The Federal Reserve Act: Its Origins and Problems*. Macmillan: New York.

Lees, F. A., Botts, J. M. and R. P. Cysne (1990) *Banking and Financial Deepening in Brazil*. Macmillan: London.

Lehto-Sinisalo, P. (1992) 'The history of exchange control in Finland', *Bank of Finland Discussion Paper*, 3/92, Statistical Services Department.

Lemoine, R. L. (1929a) 'The banking system of France', in Willis, H. P. and B. H. Beckhart (eds.) *Foreign Banking Systems*. Sir Isaac Pitman and Sons: London.

Lemoine, R. J. (1929b) 'The banking system of Belgium', translated by F. Smith, in H. P. Willis and B. H. Beckhart (eds.) *Foreign Banking Systems*. Pitman and Sons: London.

Lindenlaub, D. (1993) 'The Deutsche Bundesbank', in European Association for Banking History (ed.), *Handbook on the History of European Banks*. Forthcoming.

Linklater, J. (1992) *Inside the Bank: The Role of the Reserve Bank of Australia in the Economic, Banking and Financial Systems*. Allen and Unwin: St Leonards.

Litan, R. E. (1987) *What Should Banks Do?* The Brookings Institution: Washington D.C.

Llamozas, H. E. (1990) *Complicación de Leyes del Banco Central de Venezuela*. Banco Central de Venezuela: Caracas.

Lloyd, M. (1992) 'The New Zealand approach to central bank autonomy', *Reserve Bank Bulletin*, 55, 3.

Lo Faro, F. (1929) 'The banking system of Italy', in Willis, H. P. and B. H. Beckhart (eds.) *Foreign Banking Systems*. Sir Isaac Pitman and Sons: London.

Lovell, M. (1957) 'The role of the bank of England as a lender of last resort in the crises of the eighteenth century', *Explorations in Entrepreneurial History*, 10, 1.

Lucas, R. (1976) 'Econometric policy evaluation: a critique', in Brunner, K. and A. Meltzer (eds.) 'The Phillips curve and the labour market', Carnegie-Rochester Conference Series on Public Policy, 1, North-Holland: Amsterdam.

Lutz, F. and V. Lutz (1950) 'Monetary and exchange policy in Italy', Princeton Studies in International Finance, 1.

Lutz, V. (1962) 'Italy II: The central bank and the system of credit control', in R. S. Sayers (ed.) *Banking in Western Europe*. Clarendon: Oxford.

Lyons, F. S. L. (1983) *Bicentenary Essays: Bank of Ireland 1783–1983*. Gill and Macmillan: Dublin.

Maastricht Treaty (1992) *Treaty on European Union*. Council of European Communities, Office for Official Publications of the European Communities, Luxembourg.

MacDougall, D. (1957) *The World Dollar Problem: A Study in International Economics*. Macmillan: London.

McGowan, P. (1990) 'Money and banking in Ireland – origins, development and future', Institute of Public Administration and Statistical and Social Inquiry Society of Ireland, Dublin.

McGowan, P. (1992) 'The operation of monetary policy in Ireland', Presidential Address to the Statistical and Social Inquiry Society of Ireland, Dublin, October.

McGreevey, W. P (1971) *An Economic History of Colombia, 1845–1930*. Cambridge University Press: Cambridge.

Marsh, D. (1992) *The Bundesbank: The Bank that Rules Europe*. Heinemann: London.

Martín-Aceña, P. (1987) 'Development and modernisation of the financial system, 1844–1935', in N. Sántchez Albornoz (ed.) *The Economic Modernisation of Spain*. New York University Press.

Martín-Aceña, P. (1993) 'Spain during the classical gold standard years', in Bordo, M. D. and F. Capie (eds.) *Monetary Regimes in Transition*. Cambridge University Press: Cambridge.

März, E. (1984) *Austrian Banking and Financial Policy*. Wiedenfeld and Nicolson: London.

Mastropasqua, S. (1978) *The Banking System in the Countries of the EEC: Institutional and Structural Aspects*. Sijthoff & Noordhof International: Netherlands.

Mayer, T. (ed.) (1990) *The Political Economy of American Monetary Policy*. Cambridge University Press: Cambridge.

Mazower, M. (1991) 'Banking and economic development in interwar Greece', in James, H., Hakan, L. and Teichova, A. (eds.) *The Role of Banks in the Interwar Economy*. Cambridge University Press: Cambridge.

Meek, P. (1982) *Open Market Operations*. Federal Reserve Bank of New York: New York.

Melin, H. (1929) 'The banking system of Sweden', in Willis, H. P. and B. H. Beckhart (eds.) *Foreign Banking Systems*. Sir Isaac Pitman and Sons: London.

Mengle, D. L. (1986) 'The discount window', in Cook, T. Q. and T. D. Rowe (eds.) *Instruments of the Money Market*. Federal Reserve Bank of Richmond.

Metelius, B. (1984) 'How the Riksbank became a central bank', *Sverige Riksbank Quarterly Review*, No. 1.

Meulendyke, A. (1989) *US Monetary Policy and Financial Markets*. Federal Reserve Bank of New York: New York.

Miron, J. A. (1986) 'Financial panics, the seasonality of the nominal interest rate, and the founding of the Fed', *American Economic Review*, 76, 1.

Miron, J. A. (1989) 'The founding of the Fed and the destabilisation of the post-1914 US economy', in De Cecco, M. and A. Giovannini (eds.) *A European Central Bank?* Cambridge University Press: Cambridge.

Moore, C. H. (1990) *The Federal Reserve System: Anatomy of the First 75 Years*. McFarland and Co.: London.

Moynihan, M. (1969) 'The Central Bank of Ireland', John Busteed Memorial lecture, delivered at University College, Cork, May.

Moynihan, M. (1975) *Currency and Central Banking in Ireland 1922–1960*. Central Bank of Ireland: Dublin.

Myers, M. G. (1954) 'Mexico', in Beckhart, B. H. (ed.) *Banking Systems*. New York.

Nardozzi, G. (1988) 'A central bank between the government and the credit system: the Bank of Italy after World War II', in Toniolo, G. (ed.) *Central Banks' Independence in Historical Perspective*. Walter de Gruyter: New York.

Nas, T. F. and M. Odekon (1988) *Liberalisation and the Turkish Economy*. Greenwood Press: New York.

National Bank of Greece (1928) *Annual Report*. Athens.

National Monetary Commission (1910 and 1911) Report on Banking and Central Banking. Government Printing Office: Washington D.C.

Neufeld, E. P. (1958) *Bank of Canada Operations and Policy*. University of Toronto Press: Toronto.

Newlyn, W. T. and Rown, D. C. (1954) *Money and Banking in Colonial Africa*. Oxford University Press: Oxford.

Nicholl, P. (1992) 'New Zealand's monetary policy experiment', Seminar presented at University of Western Ontario, October.

Nordhaus, W. (1975) 'The political business cycle', *Review of Economic Studies*, 42, 2.

Norges Bank (1953) 'Structural survey of Norway', Bulletin, No. 2.

Norges Bank (1985) *Act of 24 May 1985 Relating to Norges Bank and the Monetary System*. Oslo.

Norges Bank (1990) *Norges Bank*. Oslo.

Northrop, M. B. (1938) *Control Policies of the Reichsbank 1924–1933*. Columbia University Press: New York.

Norton, B. and P. Stebbingn (eds.) (1990) *Monetary Policy and Market Operations*. Papers presented at Pacific Region Central Bank Conference. Reserve Bank of Australia: Sydney.

Ogden, T. (1988) 'The Development of the Role of the Bank of England as a Lender of Last Resort.' PhD dissertation, City University.

Ogden, T. (1991) 'An analysis of the Bank of England's discount and advance behaviour 1870–1914', in J. Foreman-Peck (ed.) *New Perspectives in the Late Victorian Economy*. Cambridge University Press: Cambridge.

Olakanpo, J. O. (1965) *Central Banking in the Commonwealth*. Bookland Private: Calcutta.

Otero, M. (1948) *El Banco de la Republica 1923–1948*. Banco de la Republica: Bogota.

Palgrave, R. H. I. (1903) *Bank Rate and the Money Market in England, France, Germany, Holland and Belgium 1844–1900*. John Murray: London.

Patat, J. P. and M. Lutfalla (1989) *A Monetary History of France in the Twentieth Century*.

Patrick, H. T. (1962) 'Monetary policy and central banking in contemporary Japan', University of Bombay, Series in Monetary and International Economics, 5.

Pazos, F. (ed.) (1990) *Crecimiento Económico con Estabilidad Financiera*. Banco Central de Venezuela: Caracas.

Pellicer, M. (1993) 'Functions of the Banco de España: an historical perspective', Banco de España, Servicio de Estudios, Documento de Trabajo, No. 9330.

Peñaloza, C. L. (1984) *Nueva Historia Economica de Bolivia; Comercio, Moneda y Bancos*. Los Amigos de Libro: Bolivia.

Pereira, A. R. (1964) 'Banking in Portugal then and now', *Bankers' Magazine*, November.

Pereira, A. R. (1966) 'Banking in Portugal', in Auburn, H. W. (ed.) *Comparative Banking*. 3rd edition. Waterlow and Sons: London.

Peres, D. (1971) *Historia do Banco de Portugal 1821–1846*. (History of the Bank of Portugal). Lisbon.

Petersen, E. (1966) 'Bank of Norway 1816–1966', *Norwegian Commercial Banks Commercial Review*, No. 2.

Phelps, E. S. (1970) *Macroeconomic Foundations of Employment and Inflation Theory*. Norton: New York.

Phillips, M. J. (1992) 'Central banking – a parting view', *Reserve Bank of Australia Bulletin*, April.

Pierce, J. L. (1991) *The Future of Banking*. Yale University Press: New Haven.

Pipping, H. E. (1961) 'The origin and early development of central banking in Finland', *Bank of Finland Monthly Bulletin*, No. 12.

Plessis, A. (1982) *La Banque de France et ses deux cents actionnaires sous le Second Empire*. Droz: Geneva.

Plessis, A. (1994) 'The changing role of the Banque de France from the beginning of the twentieth century to the 1950s', in Cottrell, P. and Y. Cassis (eds.) *Financial Institutions and Financial Markets in Europe in the Twentieth Century*. Forthcoming.

Plumptre, A. F. W. (1940) *Central Banking in the British Dominions*. University of Toronto Press: Toronto.

Pollard, S. (ed.) (1970) *The Gold Standard and Employment Policies Between the Wars*. Methuen: London.

Poschinger, H. von (1878) *Bankwesen und bankpolitik in Preußen*. (3 vols.). Berlin.

Posen, A. (1993) 'Why central bank independence does not cause low inflation: There is no institutional fix for politics', in R. O'Brien (ed.) *Finance and the International Economy*. Oxford University Press: Oxford.

Prate, A. (1987) *La France et sa monnaie: essaie sur les relations entre la Banque de France et les gouvernments*. (France and its money: an essay on the relationship between the Banque de France and the governments). Juillard: Paris.

Pressnell, L. S. (1986) *External Economic Policy Since the War. Volume 1: The Post-War Settlement*. HMSO: London.

Pringle, R. and A. A. Mahate (1993) *The Central Banking Directory*. Central Banking Publications: London.

Radcliffe Report (1959) *The Committee on the Working of the Monetary System: Report. Cmnd 827*. HMSO: London.

Raman, A. (1969) *Central Banking in India: A Study of Recent Development*. Calcutta.

Ramon, G. (1929) *Histoire de la Banque de France*. (History of the Banque de France). Grasset: Paris.

Rasminsky, L. (1966) 'The role of the Central Banker today', Per Jacobsson Memorial Lecture, Rome, November.

Rasminsky, L. (1967) 'Central banking in the Canadian Financial System', Opening lecture of the 20th International Banking Summer School, Kingston, Ontario, August.

Recaman, J. (1980) *Historia Juridicia del Banco de la República. Banco de la Republica: Bogota*.

Reformas estructurales y estabilización (1991) Revista del Banco de la República. Separata Revista, No. 764 , June.

Reichsbank (1926) *Die Reichsbank 1901–1925*. Reichsbank Press.

Reichsbank (1901) *Die Reichsbank 1876–1900*. Reichsbank Press.

Report of the Royal Commission on Banking and Currency in Canada (1933).

Reserve Bank of New Zealand (1986) *Financial Policy Reform*. Hutcheson, Bowman and Stewart: Wellington.

Reserve Bank of New Zealand (1989) *Reserve Bank of New Zealand*.

Reserve Bank of New Zealand (1992) *Monetary Policy and the New Zealand Financial System*. 3rd edition. Hutcheson, Bowman and Stewart: Wellington.

Ricardo, D. (reproduced in 1993) 'Plan for the establishment of a national bank', in F. Capie (ed.) *A History of Banking*. Pickering and Chatto: London.

Rich, G. (1991) 'The orientation of monetary policy and the monetary decision making process in Switzerland', in *The Orientation of Monetary Policy and the Monetary Decision Making Process*. Bank for International Settlements, Basle.

Richards, R. D. (1929) *The Early History of Banking in England*. Frank Cass and Co.: London.

Rietti, M. (1979) *Money and Banking in Latin America*. Praeger: New York.

Rittman, H. (1986) *Deutsche Geldgeschichte Seit 1914*. (Gernam Monetary History Since 1914). Klinkhardt und Bierman: Munich.

Rockoff, H. (1975) *The Free Banking Era: A Reconsideration*. Arno Press: New York.

Rogers, J. E. T. (1887) *The First Nine Years of the Bank of England*. Clarendon: Oxford.

Roll, E. (Chairman of an Independent Panel) (1993) *Independent and Accountable: A New Mandate for the Bank of England*. CEPR: London.

Ryti, R. (1936) 'The Bank of Finland: characteristics and aims of its activities', *Bank of Finland Monthly Bulletin*, No. 12.

Sanchez, F. (1994) *Ensayos de Historia Monetaria y Bancaria de Colombia*. Terecer Mundo: Bogota.

Sannucci, V. (1989) 'The establishment of a central bank: Italy in the nineteenth century', in De Cecco, M. and A. Giovannini (eds.) *A European Central Bank?* Cambridge University Press: Cambridge.

Santoni, G. J. (1984) 'A private central bank: some olde English lessons', *Federal Reserve Bank of St Louis Review*, 66, 4.

Sarasas, P. (1940) *Money and Banking in Japan*. Heath Cranton: London.

Sayers, R. S. (1936) *Bank of England Operations, 1890–1914*. P. S. King and Son: London.

Sayers, R. S. (1957) *Central Banking After Bagehot*. Clarendon: Oxford.

Sayers, R. S. (ed.) (1962) *Banking in Western Europe*. Clarendon Press: Oxford.

Sayers, R. S. (1976) *The Bank of England 1891–1944*. (Official History of the Bank of England). Cambridge University Press: Cambridge.

Scammel, W. M. (1968) *The London Discount Market*. Elek Books: London.

Schaumayer, M. (1991) 'Central Bank independence in Austria', in Downes, P. and R. Vaez-Zadeh (eds.) *The Evolving Role of Central Banks*. IMF: Washington.

Schedvin, C. B. (1992) *In Reserve: Central Banking in Australia, 1945–75*. Allen and Unwin: St Leonards.

Schnadt, N. (1994) *The Domestic Money Markets of the UK, France, Germany and the US*. Subject Report I, City Research Project, Corporation of London.

Schwartz, A. J. (1992) 'The misuse of the Fed's discount window', *Federal Reserve Bank of St Louis Review*, 74, 5.

Schwarzenbach, E. (1929) 'The banking system of Switzerland', in Willis, H. P. and B. H. Beckhart (eds.) *Foreign Banking Systems*. Sir Isaac Pitman and Sons: London.

Schweizerische Nationalbank (1982) *75 Jahre Schweizerische Nationalbank*. (75 Years of the Swiss National Bank). Zurich.

Schweizerische Nationalbank (1992) *Functions, Instruments and Organisation*. Zurich.

Schybergson, E. (1913) *Finlands Bank: 1811–1911*. Helsingfors: Helsinki.

Seabourne, T. (1986) 'The summer of 1914', in Capie, F. H and G. E. Wood (eds.) *Financial Crises and the World Banking System*. Macmillan: London.

Sechrest, L. J. (1993) *Free Banking*. Quorum Books: Westport, CN.

Selgin, G. (1988) *The Theory of Free Banking*. Rowan and Littlefield: New Jersey.

Sen, S. N. (ed.) (1963) *The Monetary Policy of the Reserve Bank of India*. Papers read at the Indian Economic Conference, Bombay.

Shaw, W. A. (1930) *The Theory and Practice of Central Banking*. Sir Isaac Pitman and Sons: London.

Shinjo, H. (1962) *History of the Yen*. The Research Institute for Economics and Business Administration, Kobe University.

Shrivastava, N. N. (1972) *Evolution of the Techniques of Monetary Management in India*. Somaiya Publications: India.

Silva-Herzog, J. F. and R. Lecuona (eds.) (1991) *Banca Central en America Latina II: El Financiamiento Interno del Desarrollo*. Centro de Estudios Monetarios Latinoamericanos: Mexico.

Skånland, H. (1984) 'The central bank and political authorities in some industrial countries', Norges Bank Skriftserie, No. 13.

Skånland, H. (1991) 'Central bank responsibilities present and future', *Economic Bulletin*, No. 2.

Smith, V. (1936; reprinted 1990) *The Rationale of Central Banking*. Liberty Press: Indianapolis.

Sokal, M. and O. Rosenberg (1929) 'The banking system of Austria', in Willis, H. P. and B. H. Beckhart (eds.) *Foreign Banking Systems*. Sir Isaac Pitman and Sons: London.

Sommariva, A and G. Tullio (1986) *German Macroeconomic History 1880–1979*. Macmillan: London.

South African Reserve Bank (1971) *The South African Reserve Bank 1921–1951: A Short Historical Review Issued in Commemoration of the Bank's Fiftieth Anniversary*.

Sprague, O. M. W. (1910) 'History of crises under the national banking system', in *National Monetary Commission*, No. 538. Washington DC: Government Printing Office.

Steele, H. R. and F. R. Yerbury (1930) *The Old Bank of England*. Ernest Benn: London.

Stockdale, E. (1967) *The Bank of England in 1934*. Eastern Press: London.

Stokes, M. L. (1939) *The Development and Present Position of Central Banking in Canada*. Macmillan: London.

Subercaseaux, G. (1922) *Monetary and Banking Policy in Chile*. Clarendon Press: Oxford.

Sumner, S. (1990) 'The forerunners of the "new monetary economics" proposals to stabilise the unit of account', *Journal of Money, Credit and Banking*, 22, 1.

Suzuki, Y. (1987) *The Japanese Financial System*. Clarendon: Oxford.

Sylla, R. (1988) 'The autonomy of the monetary authorities: the case of the U.S. Federal Reserve System', in Toniolo, G. (ed.) *Central Banks' Independence in Historical Perspective*. Walter de Gruyter: New York.

Tagaki, R. (1960) 'Central banking in Japan', in S. G. Davies (ed.) *Central Banking in South and East Asia*. Hong Kong.

Talvio, T. (1987) *The Coins and Banknotes of Finland*. Bank of Finland: Helsinki.

Tamagna, F. (1965) *Central Banking in Latin America*. Grafica Panamericana: Mexico.

Taus, E. T. (1943) *Central Banking Functions of the United States Treasury, 1789–1941*. Columbia University Press: New York.

Teichova, A. 'Rivals and partners: reflections on banking and industry in Europe, 1880–1938', in Cottrell, P. Lindgren, H. and A. Teichova (eds.) *European Industry and Banking*. Leicester.

Thompson, J. (1979) *Inflation, Financial markets and Economic Development: The Experience of Mexico*. JAI Press: Greenwich.

Thornton, H. (1802) *An Enquiry into the Nature and Effects of the Paper Credit of Great Britain*. Hatchard: London.

Tilly, R. (1967) 'Germany 1815–1870', in R. Cameron (ed.) *Banking in the Early Stages of Industrialisation*. Oxford University Press: Oxford.

Timberlake, R. H. (1984) 'The central banking role of clearinghouse associations', *Journal of Money, Credit and Banking*, 16, 1.

Timberlake, R. H. (1993) *Monetary Policy in the United States: An Intellectual and Institutional History*. University of Chicago Press: Chicago.

Toniolo, G. (1990) *An Economic History of Liberal Italy*. Routledge: London.

Toniolo, G. (ed.) (1988) *Central Banks' Independence in Historical Perspective*. Walter de Gruyter: New York.

Treasury, Her Majesty's, and Bank of England (1980) *Monetary Control*. Cmnd 7858. HMSO: London.

Triffin, R. (1944) 'Central Banking and monetary management in Latin America', in Harris, S. E. (ed.) *Economic Problems of Latin America*. Books for Libraries Press: New York

Tudeer, A. E. (1940) *The Bank of Finland: 1912–1936*. Helsingfors: Helsinki.

Turrent Díaz, E. (1982) *Histora del Banco de México*. (Official History of the Banco de Mexico). Banco de México: Mexico.

Valerio, N. and M. E. Mata (1982) 'O Banco de Portugal: Unico Banco Emissor 1891–1931', ('Bank of Portugal: Monopoly Bank of Issue 1891–1931'), *Revista de Historia Economia e Social*, No. 10.

Van der Wee, H. and K. Tavernier (1975) *La Banque Nationale de Belgique et L'Histoire Monétaire entre les Deux Guerres Mondiales 1918–1940*. (Official history of the Bank of Belgium between the two World Wars). Brussels.

Vanthoor, W. F. V. (1992) 'The History of the Nederlandsche Bank 1814–1992', Manuscript prepared for the manual of the European Association for Banking History.

Van Wyk, H. H. (1988) 'De Nederlandsche bank, functie en werkterrein', *NIBE Bank-en Effectenbedrijf*, 25.

Vaswani, T. A. (1968) *Indian Banking System*. Lavani Publishing House: Bombay.

Vries, J de (1989) *Geschiedenis van de Nederlandsche Bank 1914–1931*. (History of the Netherlands Bank 1914–1931). Amsterdam.

Wallich, H. C. (1951) *The Financial System of Portugal*. Lisbon.

Walters, A. and S. H. Hanke (1992) 'Currency boards', in Eatwell, J., Milgate, M. and P. Newman (eds.) *The New Palgrave Dictionary of Money and Finance*. Macmillan: London.

Waris, K. (1961) 'Some features of central banking in Finland', *Bank of Finland Monthly Bulletin*, No. 12.

Watts, G. S. (1993) (Edited by T. K. Rymes) *The Bank of Canada: Origins and Early History*. Carleton University Press: Ottawa.

Werner, P. et al. (1970) *Report to the Council and the Commission on the Realisation by Stages of the Economic and Monetary Union in the Community* (The Werner Report). Supplement to Bulletin II-1970 of the European Communities, Brussels.

White, L. (1984) *Free Banking in Britain.* Cambridge University Press: Cambridge.

White, R. N. (1992) *State, Class, and the Nationalisation of the Mexican Banks.* Crane Russak: New York.

Wicksell, K. (1898; reprinted 1962) *Interest and Prices.* (Trans. by R. Kahn for the Royal Economic Society, 1936). Augustus Kelley: New York.

Wieser, F. (1893) 'Resumption of specie payments in Austria-Hungary', *Journal of Political Economy*, June.

Wikawa, T. (1929) 'The banking system of Japan', in Willis, H. P. and B. H. Beckhart (eds.) *Foreign Banking Systems.* Sir Isaac Pitman and Sons: London.

Willis, H. P. (1923) *The Federal Reserve System: Legislation, Organisation and Operation.* Ronald Press Co.: New York.

Willis, H. P. and B. H. Beckhart (eds.) (1929) *Foreign Banking Systems.* Sir Isaac Pitman and Sons: London.

Wilson, J. S. G. (1957) *French Banking Structure and Credit Policy.* London.

Wilson, J. S. G. (1962) 'The Netherlands', in R. S. Sayers (ed.) *Banking in Western Europe.* Clarendon: Oxford.

Wolf, H. (1992) 'Economic disintegration: are there cures?' in R. O'Brien (ed.) *Finance and the International Economy.* Oxford University Press: Oxford.

Wolfe, M. (1951) *The French Franc Between the Wars, 1919–1939.* Columbia University Press: New York.

Yenal, O. (1967) 'Development of the financial system', in Shorter, F. C. (ed.) *Four Studies in the Economic Development of Turkey.* Frank Cass and Co: London.

Ziegler, D. (1990) *Central Bank, Peripheral Industry: The Bank of England in the Provinces 1826–1913.* Leicester University Press: London.

Ziegler, D. (1993) 'Zentralpolitische Steinzeit? Preußische Bank und Bank of England im vergleich', *Geschichte und Gesellschaft*, 19.

Zimmerman, R. (1987) *Volksbank oder Aktienbank? Zur Gründungsgeschichte der Nationalbank.* (Public or Private Bank? The Foundation of the Swiss National Bank).

DATA REFERENCES

Brown, E. C. (1990) 'Episodes in the public debt history of the United States', in Dornbusch, R. and M. Draghi (eds.) *Public Debt Managment: Theory and History.* Cambridge University Press: Cambridge.
  US government debt to 1986

Capie, F. and A. Webber (1985) *A Monetary History of the United Kingdom.* Allen and Unwin: London.
  UK narrow and broad money to 1980.
  UK short- and long-term interest rates (monthly) to 1982

The Economist (1989) *One Hundred Years of Economic Statistics.* (Revised.). Compiled by T. Liesner. London.
  Price indices and inflation rates to 1987
  Real and current GDP (except Germany) to 1987

Exchange rates to 1987
Government deficits for France, Germany and Japan to 1987.
Federal Reserve Bulletin (various issues)
  US government deficits to 1991
  US short- and long-term interest rates (monthly) to 1991
Friedman, M. and A. J. Schwartz (1970) *Monetary Statistics of the United States.*
  Columbia University Press: New York.
  US narrow and broad money to 1969
Homer, S and R. Sylla (1991) *A History of Interest Rates.* Rutgers University Press:
  London.
  Interest rates (annual) to 1987
International Monetary Fund (1992) *International Financial Statistics Yearbook.*
  Washington.
  Residual GDP, interest rates, exchange rates, money supply, government debt and
  deficit for all five countries to 1991
Japanese Statistical Association (1987) *Historical Statistics of Japan.* Tokyo.
  Narrow and broad money (currency and bank deposits) for Japan to 1985
Mitchell, B. R. (1988) *British Historical Statistics.* Cambridge University Press:
  Cambridge.
  UK government debt and deficit to 1980
Mitchell, B. R. (1970) *European Historical Statistics.* Macmillan: London
  Narrow and broad money supply (currency and bank deposits) for France and
  Germany
  Real GDP for France 1900–1930
Sommariva, A and G. Tullio (1986) *German Macroeconomic History 1880–1979.*
  Macmillan: London.
  German government debt to 1979

Appendix A
A short history of central bank money market operations[1]

A1   Britain

Throughout the nineteenth century the Bank of England (hereafter the Bank) considered itself as primarily responsible for the protection of England's gold reserve and, in the second part of that century, the manipulation of Bank Rate (the Bank's official discount rate) had come to be seen as the channel whereby this could be achieved (Sayers 1976). As money market rates were often below Bank Rate, however, which would interfere with the ability of the Bank to raise rates in the event of a gold outflow, measures had to be developed to ensure that Bank Rate was rendered 'effective' (i.e. binding in the money market).

In other words, techniques had to be developed that would render the money market 'artificially' short of reserves, which mostly took the form of bankers' balances held at the Bank, thereby ensuring that banks had to discount paper with the Bank at the Bank's chosen rate. In more modern terms, these techniques would be referred to as open-market operations whose object was to 'force financial institutions into the discount window' of the central bank.

Of course, open-market operations might themselves be used to supply reserves to the banking system, instead of via a discount window, and this was in fact their earliest purpose in England. Since most government accounts were held at the Bank, reserves would flow into the Bank whenever taxes were paid, leading to a reduction in bankers' balances (i.e. a money market shortage), and would flow back into the banking system when the government made disbursements. This inflow to, and outflow from, the Bank was particularly marked just around the quarterly dividend payments on government stocks, and resulted in a clear pattern in market rates: acute money market shortages just before dividends were paid drove market rates

---

[1] For a recent history (i.e. over the last decade) see Kneeshaw and van den Bergh (1989), whilst detailed descriptions of current money market operations may be found in Batten et al. (1990), Kasman (1992) and Schnadt (1994).

up to Bank Rate, with rates falling below Bank Rate immediately after these payments had been made.

This seasonal fluctuation in interest rates caused considerable commercial inconvenience, leading the Bank to introduce, in 1829, a system of regular advances just prior to the four big dividend dates of the year, available to all comers with approved security wanting at least £2,000 for a minimum of ten days (see King 1936). These advances were usually made at or near the market rate, giving institutions an incentive to apply for them in anticipation of higher rates, thereby 'smoothing' the fluctuation in rates.

These quarterly advances continued for some decades, and after 1844, became available throughout the year. By this time, it had become common practice for joint stock banks to place call deposits with the discount houses (i.e. bill brokers), drawing down these call deposits whenever they needed funds. Thus discount houses in turn became the major counterparties in rediscount transactions with the Bank (Scammel 1968).

Following a speculative boom, a money market crisis occurred in 1857, during which Bank Rate was raised to 10 per cent and the Bank made enormous discounts. After the crisis had subsided, rates moved down swiftly, and the Bank became worried that this would refuel speculation. This led the Bank to announce, in March 1858, that discount houses were henceforth barred from discounting bills or receiving advances, except at the quarterly dividend periods, marking the beginning of a period during which the Bank distanced itself from the discount market. This move naturally caused discount houses to hold larger reserves, and to ration their discount activity at the first hint of trouble which, according to Bankers Magazine at the time, severely disrupted the money market:

Since the new rule came into practice, the whole machinery of the money market has been subject to a succession of jerks never before experienced; reaching such a dangerous pitch ... that men found themselves abruptly encountered by actual panic, at periods when they were congratulating themselves on the almost unparalleled soundness of trade. (Quoted in King, 1972, p. 209).

Fortunately, the 1850s ushered in a period when the money market was usually in surplus, with bankers' balances typically being above their desired levels. This meant that the market discount rate was typically below Bank Rate, which made this rate ineffective as an instrument for stemming any efflux of gold. The earliest accounts of the Bank's methods of making Bank Rate effective date back to the 1830s, when the Bank first began to withdraw cash from the money market (i.e. reduce bankers' balances) by borrowing from money market institutions (see Clapham 1944, p. 295). This borrowing typically took the form of repurchase agreements; that is, the Bank sold securities (typically Consols) spot, and repurchased them forward (Sayers 1976, p. 38). This technique was employed increasingly frequently after 1850, becoming commonplace between 1870 and 1890.

Interestingly, these borrowing operations were often insufficient to drive market rates up to Bank Rate. Thus the London joint stock banks' deposit rate, which was mechanically maintained by these banks at 1 per cent below Bank Rate, was on occasion above the market discount rate, which could fall to a rather lower level in the event of banks having excess balances. Whilst competitive pressure between the London banks prevented any co-operative agreement to lower deposit rates, it was naturally profitable (at the banks' expense) to discount bills and redeposit these funds with the banks. This led to several instances of 'fictitious' bills (i.e. written on a fictitious underlying transaction) being issued, which were of dubious credit quality, and to acute bill shortages, which drove bill rates even lower, and squeezed banking profits even further.

Thus it was not only discount houses (since 1858) but also London banks which began to distance themselves from the Bank given the absence of any clear relationship between Bank Rate and market rates, proposing at one point to move their balances to an independent clearing banker's reserve (King 1936). This put the Bank in a difficult situation between 1860 and 1890: most of the time it had to borrow reserves (via repos against consols) to support the level of market rates, whilst periodic shortages had to be met (by lending to the houses) in order to keep market rates from rising above Bank Rate and causing widespread panic.

Although the Bank did not abandon its 1858 rule limiting its lending to the discount market, this was gradually relaxed, with the market coming to rely upon the Bank to supply reserves by the early 1880s. Furthermore, when, in 1889, several increases in Bank Rate failed to be followed by a concomitant increase in market rates, the Bank began to reinforce its borrowing operations by outright sales of gilt-edged securities. One problem with this technique, however, was that the Stock Exchange market makers to whom the Bank sold these gilts were themselves insufficiently reliant upon the money market for funds, and tended to approach the Bank for advances to fund their large gilt purchases. Thus, the Bank's gilt sales did not always have the desired impact upon bankers' balances or money market rates.

In 1890, therefore, the Bank adopted another measure, namely to borrow funds (against security of government securities) directly from agents who would otherwise have lent these funds on the money market. The Council of India was an early lender to the Bank in this way and, from the mid-1890s, the Bank of Japan frequently lent directly to the Bank instead of placing funds onto the sterling money market. In the early 1900s the Bank also began to sell gilts directly to the clearing banks instead of on the Stock Exchange.

Treasury bills, whose issue had risen with the Boer War, were also used in these open-market operations. Furthermore, the issue of Treasury bills via regular weekly tenders since 1877 also aided the Bank in its objective of making Bank Rate effective, since these tenders naturally withdrew funds from the money market. Indeed, following the First World War, Treasury bills became the central medium whereby the Bank regulated the level of bankers' balances, buying or selling these as required. Although these transactions were usually conducted with the discount houses, Sayers (1957, p. 55) points out that the houses sometimes had insufficient bills (funds), in which case the Bank bought bills from (sold bills to) the clearing banks.

Bill operations with (and secured advances to) the discount houses have, since the Second World War, evolved into the primary channel whereby the Bank of England alters the reserves of the banking system. In 1981 the Bank announced that its transactions in the bill market (with the discount houses) would be the focus of its open-market operations. It is noteworthy that, since the early 1980s, the Bank predominantly acts as a lender (i.e. buys bills) rather than a borrower of reserves. At that time, large money market shortages, and a relatively small stock of Treasury bills (for the reasons behind these, consult Schnadt 1994), resulted in the Bank accumulating a large portfolio of commercial (bank) bills. When these bills mature, bankers' balances are reduced, necessitating the provision of reserves by the Bank, again through the purchase of bills. In contrast to the latter half of the previous century, therefore, it is now the case that the Bank's official discount rate (no longer known as Bank Rate) is almost always effective as the natural consequence of its commercial bill portfolio. In the unlikely event of a money market surplus, the Bank will simply purchase Treasury bills.

A2   Germany

Since the formation of the Reichsbank in 1876, and until the early 1970s, banks in Germany have relied primarily upon two channels to obtain reserves from the central bank. First, they have been able to discount short-term paper with the central bank (i.e. via a discount window) and, secondly, they have been able to borrow on a secured basis from the central bank (i.e. via a lombard facility).

From its establishment in 1876 the Reichsbank was an active participant in the bill business, and between 1876 and 1914 its average portfolio varied between 10–15 per cent of all the bills outstanding (Bopp 1953). Although the Reichsbank was authorised to sell (i.e. rediscount) bills, in fact it always held the bills it had purchased until maturity. Virtually no limits were placed upon the amount of bills the Reichsbank would purchase, as its management subscribed to the 'real-bills' doctrine. However, bills had to carry at least two signatures of known solvency, and had to have a maturity of at most three months.

Although the Reichsbank recognised that its public responsibilities might be compromised if it sought to maximise profits, its managers were not indifferent to the Bank's profitability. In particular, the President noted in 1880 that 'the Reichsbank should not look for business but neither should it decline a proper opportunity to invest its idle funds in safe, bankable paper' (quoted in Bopp, 1953, p. 38). This attitude led the Bank, between 1880 and 1896, to compete with the larger commercial banks by discounting prime bills at preferential rates that were often as much as 1.5 per cent below its official discount rate. Thus, during this period, the Reichsbank periodically lowered its preferential discount rates towards, and even below, existing market rates when its policy should have been the opposite, namely an attempt to raise market rates towards its official discount rate (see Bopp 1953).

Another notable feature of Reichsbank policy during the period before World War I was a seasonal fluctuation in its discount rate. Payment habits in Germany were such that many rents, social insurance premiums, interest and salaries were paid quarterly and in cash. These seasonal variations were particularly large in the fall and winter as cash was needed to finance the harvest – and Christmas – and due to the practice of commercial banks increasing their cash holdings in anticipation of the publication of their year-end balance sheets. Instead of treating these increased cash demands as temporary, the Reichsbank responded by first raising its discount rate and then lowering it again as soon as its reserves had been restored to a satisfactory level.[2] In addition, the Bank tried to discourage discounting by accepting only longer-dated bills. Of course, this only served to exacerbate the problem, as banks only required the extra cash for short periods, after which they would lend their excess balances on the call market, causing market rates to fall sharply. Thus, unlike the Bank of England, or the Federal Reserve, whose discount windows served to smooth seasonal fluctuations in market rates, the behaviour of the Reichsbank was such that these fluctuations persisted despite its discount window.

The Reichsbank first used open-market operations in order to make its discount rate effective in February 1901. These operations were prompted by the fact that the Treasury had begun to borrow more heavily from the Bank – by selling Treasury bills – the previous year. Armed with an increasing portfolio of government debt, the Reichsbank would, on occasion, drain reserves from the banking system by open-market sales of debt.

---

[2] See Bopp (1953, pp. 47–50) for several possible explanations for this overly cautious behaviour on the part of the Reichsbank.

These operations did not become part of a coherent open-market strategy, however, and were interrupted by the beginning of the First World War in 1914 and the subsequent hyperinflation. The new Reichsbank, which was established in 1924, was initially prohibited from purchasing government debt, and this made open market operations virtually impossible in the inter-war period. During this period, however, the Reichsbank continued its discount and lombard activities, although it occasionally imposed quantitative constraints over these in order to constrain credit growth (Northrop 1938). Indeed, these facilities became the predominant features of the central banking operations of the Reichbank's successor, in 1948, the Bank Deutscher Länder which, nine years later, became the Bundesbank.

In 1948 German banks became obliged, for the first time, to meet minimum reserve requirements. In order to meet their reserve needs, which were now well defined, they continued to discount bills with the Bank deutscher Länder and later the Bundesbank. However, each bank received a discount quota, which stipulated the maximum amount of bills which they could discount at the central bank. Additional reserve needs were then satisfied via the lombard facility, although at a rate which was above the discount rate.

In the mid-1980s, the Bundesbank began to supply reserves, on a regular basis,[3] by offering banks the opportunity to sell government (and other) securities to it on a repurchase basis (Deutsche Bundesbank 1989). Since these repurchase agreements were offered at a lower rate than the lombard rate, they became the primary source of reserves (along with the discount quotas) from the Bundesbank, with the lombard facility only being used to meet peak reserve needs. As always, therefore, the lombard rate remains a ceiling for short-term interest rates. In order to prevent money market interest rates from falling too far below the rate on repurchase argeements (which currently signifies the Bundesbank's 'official' rate), the Bundesbank offers banks the option of investing in three-day Federal Treasury bills at a rate between its repo rate and its discount rate (Deutsche Bundesbank 1989).

A3   The United States

Throughout the nineteenth century, and until 1914, the United States had no institution which resembled the central banks that had been established elsewhere. However, some central banking functions were undertaken by

---

[3] The Bundesbank first offered transactions under repurchase agreements in April 1973, at a time when lombard facilities were restricted. However, such repurchase agreements did not become a regular mechanism for providing reserves until 1984 (see Deutsche Bundesbank 1983 and 1985).

the so-called Independent Treasury (established in 1841; see Taus 1943). These included what may be seen, in the modern sense, as the first open-market operations, although they were clearly not described as such in the 1840s. The first operations, in 1847, took the form of a purchase of government securities for resale at later date (i.e. a reverse repo) by the Independent Treasury, 'with a view of relieving the pressure upon the money market of New York' (quoted in Timberlake, 1993, p. 79). This pressure arose due to cash flows into the Treasury (i.e. through tax payments or debt issues) and due to seasonal fluctuations in cash usage.

Throughout the period 1853–5, the Treasury redeemed debt for the same reasons, and these purchases eventually totalled $38 million out of a total of $63 million of debt (Timberlake 1993). In 1887 it was decided that, instead of purchasing (i.e. redeeming) securities, the Treasury would deposit fiscal balances with national banks, although banks were required to pledge government securities against these deposits. Then, in 1888, it was again decided that securities purchases would be used to offset money market pressures, and this method continued to be used throughout the 1890s and early twentienth century (Timberlake 1993).

With the formation of the Federal Reserve System in 1914 (comprising twelve regional Federal Reserve Banks and a Federal Reserve Board in Washington) banks began to obtain reserves by discounting eligible paper at the 'discount window' of their regional Reserve Bank. Initially, the system operated on a decentralised basis, with each Reserve Bank posting its own set of discount rates. In order to increase their earning assets, and to foster the secondary market in certain assets such as banker's acceptances, Reserve Banks also undertook frequent open-market asset purchases, either outright or a resale basis (Meulendyke 1989).

In the early 1920s it became apparent that these purchases affected short-term interest rates and hence Benjamin Strong, the Governor of the New York Federal Reserve Bank, argued that the operations of the Reserve Banks should not only become co-ordinated, but should be undertaken by the New York Fed (since New York was the major banking and financial centre). Strong's efforts led to the formation of the Open Market Investment Committee (OMIC) in 1923, which attempted to co-ordinate the open-market operations of the Reserve Banks (Meulendyke 1989). Only some years later, however, with the formation of the Federal Open Market Committe (FOMC) in 1935, was the power of individual Reserve Banks to buy or sell securities without the permission of the FOMC formally removed.

Discount window borrowing remained substantial during the 1920s, although it fluctuated with the Reserve Banks' open-market operations. Throughout the decade, however, the Federal Reserve had begun to implement non-price rationing of discount window funds, first by discouraging continuous borrowing from the window (1926) and then by specific statements that banks should not borrow from the window for speculative purposes (1929) (Mengle 1986). Soon afterwards, during the 1930s and 1940s, the pattern of borrowing changed due to the monetisation of gold inflows by the Treasury, which left banks with ample reserves and little need to borrow reserves from the discount window. Similarly, during this period the FOMC had little need to engage in open-market operations to offset seasonal cash demands or flows into Treasury accounts.

During World War II the Federal Reserve was forced, under an agreement with the Treasury, to peg the rate at which it would buy Treasury bills and longer-term debt, causing both the discount window and open-market operations to be largely redundant. After the war, in 1951, the Fed was permitted to resume an active monetary policy, and withdrew its support of the government bond market by adopting a so-called 'bills-only' open-market strategy: that is, only Treasury bills were to be used in its open-market operations, although these assets could be bought (or sold) either on an outright or on a resale (repurchase) basis. It was also during this period that the trading desk of the New York Fed developed the practice, which it maintains to the present day, of operating via a number of dealers, all of whom are contacted simultaneously and invited to participate in its operations (for details see Meek 1982 and Meulendyke 1989). Finally, the Fed also reinforced its non-price rationing of discount window funds.

Until 1960 the Federal funds rate had played a limited role as an indicator of reserve availability, and had typically traded below or at the Fed's discount rate. The rapid development of interbank markets during the 1960s, together with the advent of active liability management by banks, led to the Fed funds rate becoming a central indicator of 'reserve pressure' within the banking system. In 1965 the Fed funds rose above the discount rate for the first time, and has remained above it for most of the subsequent period (see Goodfriend and Whelpley 1986). This positive spread between the Fed funds rate and the discount rate reflects the non-price costs of obtaining discount window funds. By pushing banks further 'into' the window (i.e. by increasing the degree of reserve pressure, possibly via open-market operations), therefore, the Fed could engineer a higher Fed funds rate without raising the discount rate. Policy changes are thus not only signalled via changes in the discount rate, but also via a change in the perceived 'target' level of the Fed funds rate.

This arrangement for achieving a particular Fed funds rate can be summarised as the use of open-market operations to maintain a desired level of discount window borrowing, and has remained unchanged since the 1960s (see Schnadt 1994). Although the Fed announced, in 1979, that it was adopting a different operating procedure, in practice its operations remained unchanged. However, open-market operations were no longer employed to 'smooth' the level of bank reserves as much as before, which led banks to rely more heavily on the discount window. This in turn resulted in large fluctuations in the Fed funds rate, which was one of the reasons why it was discontinued in 1982.

REFERENCES

Batten, D. S., Blackwell, M. P. Kim, I., Nocera, S. E. and Y. Ozeki (1990) 'The conduct of monetary policy in the major industrial countries: instruments and operating procedures', IMF Occasional Paper, July.

Bopp, K. R. (1953) *Reichsbank Operations, 1876–1914*.

Clapham, J. (1944) *The Bank of England: A History*. Cambridge University Press: Cambridge.

Deutsche Bundesbank (1983) 'The Bundesbank's transactions in securities under repurchase agreements', *Monthly Report of the Deutsche Bundesbank*, No. 5, May.

Deutsche Bundesbank (1985) 'Recent developments with respect to the Bundesbank's securities repurchase agreements', *Monthly Report of the Deutsche Bundesbank*, No. 10, October.

Deutsche Bundesbank (1989) 'The Deutsche Bundesbank: its monetary policy instruments and functions'. 3rd edition. Deutsche Bundesbank Special Series, No. 7.

Flink, S. (1930) *The German Reichsbank and Economic Germany*. Harper and Brothers: London.

Goodfriend, M. and W. Whelpley (1986) 'Federal funds', in Cook, T. Q. and T. D. Rowe (eds.) *Instruments of the Money Market*. Federal Reserve Bank of Richmond.

Kasman, B. (1992) 'A comparison of monetary policy operating procedures in six industrial countries', *Federal Reserve Bank of New York Quarterly Review*, Summer.

King, W. T. C. (1936, reprinted 1972) *History of the London Discount Market*. Frank Cass: London.

Kneeshaw, J. T. and P. van den Bergh (1989) 'Changes in central bank money market operating procedures in the 1980's', *BIS Economic Papers*, No. 23.

Meek, P. (1982) *Open Market Operations*. Federal Reserve Bank of New York.

Mengle, D. L. (1986) 'The discount window', in Cook, T. Q. and T. D. Rowe (eds.) *Instruments of the Money Market*. Federal Reserve Bank of Richmond.

Meulendyke, A. (1989) *US Monetary Policy and Financial Markets*. Federal Reserve Bank of New York. New York.

Northrop, M. B. (1938) *Control Policies of the Reichsbank, 1924–1933*. Columbia University Press: New York.

Sayers, R. S. (1957) *Central Banking After Bagehot*. Clarendon: Oxford.

Sayers, R. S. (1976) *The Bank of England 1891–1944*. Cambridge University Press: Cambridge.

Scammel, W. M. (1968) *The London Discount Market*. Elek Books: London.

Schnadt, N. (1994) *The Domestic Money Markets of the UK, France, Germany and the US*. Subject Report I, City Research Project, Corporation of London.

Taus, E. T. (1943) *Central Banking Functions of the United States Treasury, 1789–1941*. Columbia University Press: New York.

Timberlake, R. H. (1993) *Central Banking in the United States*. University of Chicago Press: Chicago.

Appendix B
A short history of central bank objectives and functions

B1   Sveriges Riksbank

Founded in 1668

Forerunner

Stockholms Banco (The Stockholm Bank) had been privately chartered in 1657 by Johan Palmstruch, although the charter reflected considerable government influence over the bank. Although it initially only made loans against security and received deposits, the bank began to issue notes convertible into coin in 1661, thereby becoming the first bank of issue in Europe. However, over-issue led to the bank becoming unable to redeem its notes, resulting in the imprisonment of its founder and the reorganisation of the bank as a state institution under Parliament in 1668.

Motivation for founding

The over-issue of notes by Stockholms Banco precipitated its closure and replacement in 1668 by a state owned bank, the Riksens Ständers Bank (Bank of the Estates of the Realm).

Original objectives and functions

The Riksens Ständers Bank (hereafter the Bank) continued the lending and deposit business of its predecessor but, given the fate of the Stockholms Banco, was expressly forbidden from issuing notes of any kind. Although it was state owned, the administration of the Bank was under the charge of a commission chosen by the Riksdag (Parliament), and was not responsible to the government.

Evolution of objectives and functions

The ban on note issue did not prevent the Bank from issuing so-called transfer notes in 1701, which basically functioned as bank notes. Moreover, in 1789, a National Debt Office was set up by the Riksdag to issue notes for government funding purposes, and for some time the National Debt Office supplanted the Bank as the primary note issuer.

A monetary reform in 1834 culminated in the redemption, well below par, of all outstanding Bank and National Debt Office notes, and the issue of new Bank notes redeemable in silver. By this time, however, several private note issuing banks had already been chartered, and their notes now competed with those of the Bank. The establishment after 1864 of the first joint stock banks (known as enskilda banks, interesting insofar as their stock carried unlimited liability) also saw the gradual erosion of the Bank's commercial lending and deposit business.

For the greater part of the nineteenth century, therefore, the Bank basically comprised a state commercial bank, acting neither as a monopoly note issuer, nor as a lender of last resort. Indeed, a state proclamation in 1824 prohibited state participation in, or support of, private banking. The Bank did engage in foreign exchange policy, however, and was explicitly charged with maintaining the external value of the krona. This became a central function of the Bank after the formation of the Scandinavian Monetary Union in 1875 with Denmark and Norway, two years after each of these countries adopted the gold standard.

In 1867 the Bank was renamed Sveriges Riksbank. Towards the end of the nineteenth century a lengthy debate over the status and role of the Riksens Ständers Bank culminated in the Riksbank Act of 1897, which gave the Riksbank the sole right to issue notes as from 1904. The notes of private issuing banks were thus gradually withdrawn, and banks given compensation in the form of favourable discount rates by the Riksbank until 1910.

After 1897 one of the functions of the Riksbank became, though not explicitly, lender of last resort. Furthermore, in 1899 the Riksbank established a clearing institution through which banks could facilitate interbank payments, via accounts held at the Riksbank. The Riksbank did not, however, regulate and supervise banks. This task was undertaken by a government controlled Bank Inspection Board, which monitored banks' adherence to regulations specified in a Bank Act of 1911.

The Riksbank Act also limited the note issue of the Riksbank to twice its metal reserves, although this restriction was amended shortly after the outbreak of World War I, and again in 1918, giving the King and Parliament together the right to permit the issue of additional notes in the event of a national crisis (such as a war). Although convertibility was suspended at the outbreak of the war, the reserves of the Riksbank actually increased (due to large exports), leading to a resumption of convertibility two years later. The gold standard was abandoned in 1932.

The aftermath of World War II saw a break from the traditional monetary regime, as exchange and credit controls were imposed and political pressure was put on the Bank to maintain a 'low' discount rate. The Governor of the Bank objected to this policy, and eventually chose to resign in 1948 in protest. For several decades the policies of the Bank remained subservient to government policies, although it did attempt to resist these on occasion. In 1957, for example, the Board chose to raise the discount rate without prior approval by the government, which resulted in the eventual resignation of the Chairman, and his replacement with a former Finance Minister.

During the 1980s policy emphasis shifted towards liberalisation and deregulation, and a more market-oriented approach. This has led, in turn, to a lessening of political pressure on the policies of the Riksbank.

Although a new Act was adopted in 1934, the fundamentals of the 1897 Riksbank Act were in force for almost a century until a new Riksbank Act in 1988. In this latter Act it was clearly stated that the Riksbank was Sweden's central bank, and that its functions should be those of a central bank. The position of the Governor was also strengthened, and the Government no longer had the right to appoint the Chairman of the Board of Directors.

Independence

It is noteworthy that it is stated in the Swedish constitution that the Riksbank is the central bank of Sweden and an authority under the Parliament. The Riksbank is responsible for exchange rate and monetary policies. It is administered by the eight members of the Board of Directors, seven of which are elected by Parliament for a term ending at the next general election. These seven members elect an eighth member to act as Governor of the Bank.

The 1988 Riksbank Act states that the Bank shall decide the system that shall apply for establishing the external value of the krona, and that the Bank owns and manages the country's foreign exchange reserves and, further, determines its own budget. The Act does not, however, specify a clear monetary policy objective. To promote a coordinated monetary policy, the Act states that the Bank shall consult with the Cabinet Minister appointed by the government prior to making a monetary policy decision; once such consultation has been made the Bank may, however, make its own decision.

Although the Bank may not accept instructions from anyone but the Riksdag, the post-World War II period saw the Riksbank coming under political pressure to conduct monetary policy in accordance with the general policy of the government. Furthermore, foreign exchange and credit policy regulations, until they were all abolished in the 1980s, required decisions by both the Riksbank and the government.

REFERENCES

Bank for International Settlements (1963) 'Sveriges Riksbank', in *Eight European Central Banks*. BIS: Basle.

Clayton, G. (1962) 'Sweden', in R. S. Sayers (ed.) *Banking in Western Europe*. Clarendon Press: Oxford.

Hörngren, L. and A. Westman-Mårtensson (1991) 'Swedish monetary policy: institutions, targets and instruments', *Arbetsrapport*, No. 2, May. Sveriges Riksbank: Stockholm.

Jonung, L. (1993) 'The rise and fall of credit controls: the case of Sweden 1939–89', in Bordo, M. D. and F. Capie (eds.) *Monetary Regimes in Transition*. Cambridge University Press: Cambridge.

Melin, H. 'The banking system of Sweden', in Willis, H. P. and B. H. Beckhart (eds.) *Foreign Banking Systems*. Sir Isaac Pitman and Sons: London.

Metelius, B. (1984) 'How the Riksbank became a central bank', *Sveriges Riksbank Quarterly Review*, No. 1.

The Sveriges Riksbank Act (1988)

B2   Bank of England

Founded in 1694

Forerunner

None. The Bank of England was the first chartered bank in the UK.

Motivation for founding

The primary motivation was the necessity for raising government funds to finance the war against France, although the view had become current that a bank was needed to 'stabilise' financial activity in London, which saw periodic fluctuations in the availability of currency and credit. An original proposal in 1693, by William Paterson, for a government 'fund of perpetual interest', was turned down in favour of another proposal by Paterson (in 1694) to establish a company known as the Governor and Company of the Bank of England whose capital, once raised, would be lent in its entirety to the government.

Original objectives and functions

An ordinary Finance Act, now known as the Bank of England Act 1694, stipulated that the Bank was to be established via stock subscriptions which were to be lent to the government. A Governor, Deputy Governor and twenty-four Directors were to be elected by stockholders (holding £500 or more of stock).

Under its original charter the Bank was allowed to issue bank notes, redeemable in silver coin, as well as trade in bills and bullion. The notes of the Bank competed with other paper media of exchange, which comprised notes issued by the Exchequer and by private financial companies. In addition, customers could maintain deposit accounts with the Bank, which were transferable to other parties via notes drawn against deposit receipts (known as accomptable notes), thus providing an early form of cheque.

An early customer of the Bank was the Royal Bank of Scotland, which made arrangements to keep cash at the Bank from its inception. Loans were extended, predominantly in the form of discounting of bills, to individuals and companies, and the bank undertook a large amount of lending (often via overdrafts) to the Dutch East India Company and, from 1711, the South Sea Company. The Bank also acted as a mortgage lender, although this business never took off, and ceased some years later.

Finally, an important function of the Bank was the remittance of cash to Flanders and elsewhere for the wars against Louis XIV, which was facilitated through correspondent arrangements with banks in Holland.

Evolution of objectives and functions

In 1697, the renewal of the Bank's charter for another ten years saw the passing of a Second Bank Act, which increased the capital of the Bank and prohibited any other banks from being chartered. This monopoly was strengthened at the next renewal of the Bank's charter in 1708, when any association of six or more persons was forbidden to engage in banking activity, precluding the development of any other joint stock banks. The Bank's position as banker to the government was consolidated in 1715 when it was decided that subscriptions for government debts issues would be paid to the Bank, and further that the Bank was to manage the government debt (the Ways and Means Act).

The Bank also encouraged the use of its notes over other media of exchange by persuading the Treasury to increase the denomination of Exchequer bills. By 1725 the Bank's notes had become sufficiently widely used so as to be preprinted for the first time. Although a number of private banks had developed by 1750, both in and outside of London, none competed seriously with the Bank in the issue of notes. By 1770 most London bankers ceased to issue notes, using Bank of England notes (and cheques) to settle balances among themselves in what had become a well developed clearing system. Furthermore, in 1775, Parliament raised the minimum denomination for any non-Bank of England notes to £1, and two years later, to £5, effectively guaranteeing the use of Bank of England notes as the dominant money.

In Scotland, on the other hand, no note issuing monopoly existed, and banks were free to issue notes, although two banks dominated, namely the Bank of Scotland and the Royal Bank of Scotland. Furthermore, several private note-issuing banks were in business in Ireland, and the Bank of Ireland was established in 1783. These banks relied on the bank of England to obtain silver and gold, particularly during times of financial stress such as 1783 and 1793.

Following the dramatic rise in government expenditures after 1793 due to the war against France, which caused a large rise in the Bank's note issue, the Bank's gold holdings fell sharply. Thus convertibility was suspended in 1797, and resumed again only in 1821. This period thus saw a further consolidation of the Bank as a note issuer, since it began to issue small denomination notes (given the shortage of silver/gold coin), which became legal tender in 1812. Furthermore, in 1816, silver coin ceased to be legal tender for small payments. The government also moved most of its accounts to the Bank in 1805 (in 1834 all government accounts were finally moved to the Bank).

During the early part of the nineteenth century, smaller country banks had proliferated throughout England and Wales, many issuing their own notes. Given the prohibition on joint stock banking, the capital of these banks was usually small, and they regularly became insolvent, especially when the demand for cash (coin) became strong. This contrasted sharply with Scotland, where joint stock banking and branch banking were permitted, and relatively few failures occurred. Following a severe banking crisis in 1825, during which many English country banks failed, an Act renewing the Bank's charter (in 1826) abolished the restrictions on banking activity outside of London. This led to the establishment of several joint stock banks, and the Bank opened several branches throughout England.

Thus the semblance of a banking 'system' began to emerge by 1830, with the Bank of England as the 'central' bank. The practice of banks placing surplus funds with bill brokers also emerged, with the Bank beginning to extend secured loans to these brokers on a more or less regular basis. In 1833 joint stock banks were finally allowed to operate in London, although they were not permitted to issue notes and thus were essentially deposit-taking banks only. The same Act specified that Bank of England notes were legal tender, and the Bank was also given the freedom to raise its discount rate freely (until then Usury Laws had placed a ceiling on interest rates) in response to cash outflows.

The position of Bank of England notes was consolidated in an important

Act, passed in 1844, restricting all note issuers from expanding their note issue above existing levels, and prohibiting the establishment of any new note issuing banks. The 1844 Act also separated the issue and banking functions of the Bank into different departments, and required the Bank to publish a weekly summary of accounts.

Given that it did not pay interest on its deposits, the deposit activity of the Bank could never really compete with that of other banks, which expanded rapidly from 1850 onwards. In 1854, joint stock banks in London joined the London Clearing House, and it was agreed that clearing by transfer of Bank of England notes would be abandoned in favour of cheques drawn on bank accounts held at the Bank. Ten years later the Bank of England itself entered this clearing arrangement, and cheques drawn on bankers' accounts at the Bank became considered as paid (i.e. cash).

Although the Bank had, from the beginning of the nineteenth century, periodically bought or sold Exchequer bills to influence the note circulation, explicit open-market borrowing operations to support its discount rate began in 1847. From 1873 until 1890 the Bank almost always acted as a borrower rather than a lender of funds, as there were typically cash surpluses. As a result, the Bank introduced the systematic issue of Treasury bills via a regular tender offer in 1877. Treasury bills had a much shorter maturity (three to twelve months) than Exchequer bills (five or more years), and were to play an important role in raising funds at the outset of World War I.

By 1890, the Bank's role as lender of last resort became undisputed when it orchestrated the rescue of Baring Brothers and Co., a bank whose solvency had become suspect, threatening to cause systemic problems. Earlier, in 1866, the failure of a discount house, Overend, Gurney and Co., had precipitated a financial panic, during which the Bank discounted large amounts of bills and extended considerable loans.

Throughout the nineteenth century, the Bank streamlined its discount facilities. In 1851 it overhauled its discount rules, stipulating that only those parties having a discount account could present bills, and that these bills had to have a maturity of under ninety-five days and be endorsed by two creditworthy firms. In the latter part of the century, however, the Bank gradually came to favour discount houses, often by presenting them with better rates of discount, and the range of firms doing discount business with the Bank declined.

Until World War I the Bank pursued a discount policy which was aimed at maintaining its gold reserves, and which was conducted largely independently of the government. During World War I, however, a clash occurred between the Bank Governor (Cunliffe) and the Chancellor (Law), during which the government made clear that it bore the ultimate responsibility for monetary policy, and that the Bank was expected to act on its direction. This position, which was implicitly maintained during the inter-war period, was formalised in 1946, when the Bank was nationalised by the newly elected post-war Labour government.

Although the Bank Act of 1946 left the administration of the Bank largely unaltered (although the number of Directors was reduced from twenty-four to sixteen), it gave the government statutory authority over the Bank, and gave the Bank statutory authority over the banking system. The relationship between the Bank and the banking system was further defined by the Banking Act of 1987, which gave the Bank, in its role as banking supervisor, the objective of protecting the interest of depositors.

Independence

Between 1844, when the Bank first began actively to alter its discount rate in response to gold flows (for the century prior to this the discount rate was held, with few exceptions, between 4 per cent and 5 per cent), until World War I, the Bank remained relatively independent in the formulation and implementation of discount policy. No statutory provisions detailed the relationship between the Treasury and the Bank.

This state of affairs began to change during World War I when, in 1917, following a public disagreement between the Bank and the Treasury, the Bank was threatened with nationalisation. Thereafter, the position of the Bank became less independent, with the Governor in 1937 (Norman) claiming: 'I am an instrument of the Treasury'. However, only after the nationalisation of the Bank, in 1946, did the government gain statutory authority over monetary policy, which it retains to the present date. The Bank's responsibility, therefore, is to advise on monetary policy, and to carry out the policy that has been agreed with the government.

Recently, the issue of increased independence for the Bank has come under investigation and, although no official steps in this direction have been announced, the Treasury has given the Bank greater discretion over the timing of interest changes than it has had in the past.

REFERENCES

Acres, W. M. (1931) *The Bank of England from Within*. Oxford University Press: Oxford.

Andréadès, A. (1909) *A History of the Bank of England*. P. S. King and Sons: London.

Bagehot, W. (1973) *Lombard Street*. Kegan, Paul and Co.: London.

Bank for International Settlements (1963) 'Bank of England', in *Eight European Central Banks*. BIS: Basle.

Bowman, W. D. (1937) *The Story of the Bank of England: From its Foundation in 1694 until the Present Day*. Herbert Jenkins: London.

Chapham, R. A. (1968) *Decision Making: A Case Study of the Decision to Raise the Bank Rate in September 1957*. Routledge and Kegan Paul: London.

Clapham, J. H. (1944) *The Bank of England: A History*. (Official History of the Bank of England.) Cambridge University Press: Cambridge.

Clay, H. (1957) *Lord Norman*. Macmillan: London.

Feavearyear, A. E. (1963) *The Pound Sterling: A History of English Money*. 2nd edition, revised by E. V. Morgan. Clarendon: Oxford.

Fforde, J. (1992) *The Bank of England and Public Policy 1941–1958*. (Official History of the Bank of England.) Cambridge University Press: Cambridge.

Geddes, P. (1987) *Inside the Bank of England*. Boxtree: London.

Giuseppi, J. (1966) *The Bank of England: A History from its Foundation in 1694*. Evans Brothers Limited: London.

Hennessey, E. (1992) *A Domestic History of the Bank of England 1930–1960*. Cambridge University Press: Cambridge.

Richards, R. D. (1929) *The Early History of Banking in England*. Frank Cass and Co.: London.

Rogers, J. E. T. (1887) *The First Nine Years of the Bank of England*. Clarendon: Oxford.

Sayers, R. S. (1936) *Bank of England Operations, 1890–1914*. (Official History of the Bank of England). P. S. King and Son: London.

Sayers, R. S. (1957) *Central Banking After Bagehot*. Clarendon: Oxford.

Steele, H. R. and F. R. Yerbury (1930) *The Old Bank of England*. Ernest Benn: London.

Stockdale, E. (1967) *The Bank of England in 1934*. Eastern Press: London.

Smith, V. (1936) *The Rationale of Central Banking*. P. S. King and Son: London.

Ziegler, D. (1990) *Central Bank, Peripheral Industry: The Bank of England in the Provinces 1826–1913*. Leicester University Press: London.

B3   Banque de France

Founded in 1800

Forerunner

Napoleon persuaded the stockholders of the Caisse des Comptes Courants, a joint stock discount and note issuing bank, and one of the two largest such banks in Paris, to dissolve this company and form a new bank known as the Banque de France, partly financed by additional issues of stock and by government funds. The Caisse des Comptes Courants was itself modelled on, and shared personnel with, another bank, the Caisse d'Escompte.

Motivation for founding

The collapse of the assignat regime (1789–1795), during which the over-issue of fiat money drove a hyperinflation, left the French financial system in considerable disarray at a time when the government had a large and ongoing war financing requirement. To restore financial confidence, and to improve state revenue, a more efficient system of tax collection was imposed (1799) and the Banque de France established (1800), primarily to manage the public debt and ease the discounting of government paper. However, these steps were an integral part of a wider impetus to create a more centralised bureaucracy.

Original objectives and functions

The Caisse des Comptes Courantes had been one of two large note issuing discount banks in Paris, and also accepted deposits. The Banque de France (hereafter the Banque) continued the business of its predecessor, although the emphasis in discounting shifted in favour of government paper and that in deposit-taking to government deposits. Its bank notes were denominated in francs and convertible into silver.

The administration and management of the Banque was undertaken by a committee of directors, but was heavily influenced by the government (Napoleon). Soon after its foundation the government sold a large part of its shares in the Banque, although this did little to make management of the Banque more independent. The Banque was first chartered in 1803, and statutes first issued in 1808 in the form of an Imperial Decree. These governed the Banque's operations, with some modifications, until the statutes became legally ratified (Codified) in 1936.

Evolution of objectives and functions

Two years after the dissolution of the Caisse des Comptes Courants its main competitor, the Caisse d'Escompte du Commerce, was also induced (unwillingly) to merge with the Banque de France, thus substantially reducing competition in both the discounting and the note-issuing business. However, one year later, in 1803, the government granted the Banque de France the exclusive right to issue notes in Paris, ordered all existing note-issuing banks there to withdraw their notes, and forbade the formation of any new note-issuing banks in France except by the consent of government. The government also reserved the right to grant all privileges of issue, and to fix the maximum of such issue.

Permission was granted in 1817–18 for three (regional) banks of issue to be formed, although their business was severely constrained, i.e. their notes were legal tender only within a restricted area. By 1838 six more banks had been founded, prompting the Banque to open several branch offices (each of which had a monopoly in their area) and pressurising the government to refuse to grant any more bank charters. This reinforced the position of Banque de France notes and, during a banking crisis in 1848, all these banks felt forced to become branches of the Banque, securing its note monopoly.

From its inception the Banque was under continuous pressure from Napoleon to discount large amounts of government paper at favourable rates. Already in 1805 the Banque had over-issued notes relative to its specie reserves due to excessive discounting of government paper, and had to impose a partial suspension of its notes into coin. This was seen as the outcome of poor management, and consequently the stockholder – elected management was replaced by a new system of administration in 1806, led by the Governor and two deputy – Governors appointed by the head of state. Complementing these Governors, but only in an advisory capacity, were fifteen directors (Regents), nine of which were elected by the 200 biggest shareholders from among the merchant banking community (Haute Banque) and three of which were selected from civil servants at the Ministry of Finance, and three (non-voting) censors (Censeurs) chosen from the Paris business community.

The government placed a ceiling of 6 per cent on the Banque's discount rate, which was lowered to 5 per cent in 1806, then to 4 per cent in 1807, and fluctuated between 4 per cent and 5 per cent until 1852. To maintain its specie reserves, therefore, the Banque resorted to rationing of credit or the purchase of specie at a premium rather than raising its discount rate. After 1850, increased specie mobility prompted the Banque to change its discount rate more freely, and this rate began to move in harmony with Bank rate in England (although changes were usually less severe). Discount rate changes were almost always decided upon by the government, and implemented through the Governors rather than the directors of the Banque, even though there was no explicit legislation providing for such government intervention.

Excessive government financing demands on the Banque resulted in the partial suspension of convertibility in 1813, and between 1848 and 1850 to a total suspension of convertibility. During this period notes were declared legal tender, and a ceiling on the note issue announced. Although the legal tender status of notes was abolished in 1850, it was reintroduced during the Franco-Prussian War in 1870, and remained in force since then.

After 1850, several joint stock banks began to emerge, although the development of banking was much slower in France than in England. The use of cheques, for example, remained limited until the turn of the century. The Banque de France remained by far the most extensive bank until the early 1900s, having a branch network which extended to 160 sites in 1900 and 259 sites in 1928.

In 1889 the Banque de France acted as a lender of last resort to the

Comptoir d'Escompte de Paris, which was the first joint stock bank. In 1901 the Banque set up the Paris Clearing House, although this took the form of an association of which the Banque was only one of several members.

Since 1936, when convertibility of the franc was suspended, the Banque has managed an Exchange Stabilisation Fund on behalf of the Treasury for purposes of regulating the external value of the franc. After World War II, in 1945, the National Credit Council and the Commission for the Control of Banks, both of which included the Governor of the Banque either as president or vice president, were established for purposes of regulation and supervision of banks.

In 1993 the main objectives of the Banque de France were reformulated according to the Act on the Status of the Banque de France and the Activities and Supervision of Credit Institutions. The Act states that the that the Banque '... shall formulate and implement monetary policy with the aim of ensuring price stability ... shall regulate the exchange rates between the franc and other currencies on behalf of the State [and] ... shall ensure the smooth operation and the security of payment systems.'

Independence

From its establishment in 1800 until 1936 there existed no provision for direct government involvement in the administration of the Banque, although policy decisions were almost always determined by the government in collaboration with the Governors.

In 1936, an Act of Parliament codified the statutes of the Banque, and gave the government the means to intervene more directly in the activity of the Banque. The fifteen directors were replaced by twenty councillors (which together with the Governors made up the General Council), of which seventeen were nominated by the government (the number of councillors has subsequently been reduced to ten).

In 1945 the Banque was nationalised, with all shares being transferred to the State. In 1973 a reform of the Banque's statutes was undertaken, which stated that the Banque operated 'on behalf of the State and within the framework of the general instructions issued by the Minister of Economic Affairs'. Furthermore, the Banque was to 'help in the preparation and participate in the implementation of the Government's monetary policy'.

During the early 1990s the government confirmed its intention to increase the independence of the Banque in accordance with the provisions of the Maastricht Treaty and, in 1993, an autonomous, nine-member Monetary Policy Committee (headed by the Governor of the Banque) took authority over monetary policy, rendering the Banque formally independent.

REFERENCES

Bank for International Settlements (1963) 'Banque de France', in *Eight European Central Banks*. BIS: Basle.

Banque de France (1992) *The Banque de France: History, Organisation, Role*. Direction de la Communication, Paris.

Baumgartner, W. (1971) *La Banque de France*. Historia: Paris.

Bigo, R. (1927) *La Caissse d'Escompte (1776–1973) et les Origines de la Banque de France*. Presses de Universitaire de France: Paris.

Bouvier, J. (1988) 'The Banque de France and the State from 1850 until the present day', in G. Toniolo (ed.) *Central Banks' Independence in Historical Perspective*. Walter de Gruyter: Berlin.

Cameron, R. (1967) 'France 1800–1870', in R. Cameron *Banking in the Early Stages of Industrialisation*. Oxford University Press: Oxford.

Conant, C. A. (1909) *A History of Modern Banks of Issue*. G. P. Putnam's Sons: London.

Goodman, J. B. (1992) *Monetary Sovereignty: The Politics of Central Banking in Western Europe*. Cornell University Press: London.

Lemoine, R. L. (1929) 'The banking system of France', in Willis, H. P. and B. H. Beckhart (eds.) *Foreign Banking Systems*. Sir Isaac Putnam and Sons: London.

Mastropasqua, S. (1978) *The Banking System in the Countries of the EEC: Institutional and Structural Aspects*. Sijthoff & Noordhof International: Netherlands.

Palgrave, R. H. I. (1903) *Bank Rate and the Money Market in England, France, Germany, Holland and Belgium 1844–1900*. John Murray: London.

Patat, J. P. and M. Lutfalla (1989) *A Monetary History of France in the Twentieth Century*.

Plessis, A. (1985) *La Politique de la Banque de France de 1851 à 1870*. Libraire Droz: Geneva.

Prate, A. (1987) *La France et sa monnaie: essaie sur les relations entre la Banque de France et les gouverments*. (France and its money: an essay on the relationship between the Banque de France and the Governments). Juillard: Paris.

Ramon, G. (1929) *Histoire de la Banque de France*. (History of the Banque de France). Grasset: Paris.

Smith, V. C. (1936) *The Rationale of Central Banking*. P. S. King and Son: London.

Wilson, J. S. G. (1957) *French Banking Structure and Credit Policy*. London.

Wolfe, M. (1951) *The French Franc Between the Wars, 1919–1939*. Columbia University Press: New York.

B4   Suomen Pankki (Bank of Finland)

Founded in 1811

Forerunner

None. The Bank of Finland was the first bank in Finland, and remained the only one until 1861 (although several small savings institutions had been established in the 1820s).

Motivation for founding

Being part of the kingdom of Sweden until 1809, and then annexed to the Russian Empire as an autonomous Grand Duchy, Finland had several currencies which circulated alongside one another, including Russian and Swedish notes and coins. A major initial aim of the Bank of Finland was to drive Swedish money out of circulation, replacing this with its rouble notes, although this was not achieved until the early 1840s.

Original objectives and functions

The Bank of Finland was founded mainly upon the same principles on which the Bank of Sweden (see Sverige Riksbank) was based, although its activities were at first restricted to accepting deposits and issuing small denomination banknotes. Although the Bank of Finland was based upon the Bank of Sweden, which was independent of the Government and subordinate to the Diet, Finland's dependence on Russia and the uncertain position of the Diet meant that this was impossible. Consequently the Bank acted as the government's bank, and was formally subordinate to the Senate (government) of the Grand Duchy. The practical management of the Bank was in the hands of a three-member Board (elected by the Tsar), and its functions were laid out in the Bank's original charter, 'His Imperial Majesty's Gracious Regulations for an Office of Exchange, Lending and Deposits in the grand Duchy of Finland'.

Evolution of objectives and functions

Following a monetary reform in 1840 (due to decisions by Sweden and Russia to return to the silver standard), the Bank began to issue large denomination rouble notes redeemable in silver, develop its business in domestic and foreign bills and issue State loans. During the 1840s the Bank also established several branch offices. After the Crimean War (1853–1856), during which convertibility was suspended, the Bank began to use its bill discount rate as an instrument for regulating credit conditions.

In 1860 Finland obtained its own monetary unit, the markka, and the Bank was granted the right to issue markka denominated notes and coin (equal to one quarter of a rouble). The markka was linked to silver in 1865, replacing the rouble (which ceased to be legal tender) as the dominant means of payment. This paved the way for the Bank to become established as the major holder of foreign exchange reserves. In 1878 Finland adopted the gold standard, and the markka became convertible into gold. Only in 1886 was the Bank finally given the sole right to issue banknotes in Finland.

Following the establishment of the first commercial banks in the latter half of the nineteenth century, which held their cash funds at, and obtained credit from, the Bank of Finland, the Bank began to act as the banker's bank. Although it originally competed with commercial banks for private customers (by offering interest bearing deposits), the Bank increasingly began to act as leader and convenor of the negotiations engaged in by commercial banks as regards interest rates, and also began rediscounting bills and granting secured loans to provide reserves to the banks. This relationship was further strengthened in 1906, when interbank clearing was introduced at the Bank. By this time the Bank had also become established as the lender of last resort, having rescued Kansallis-Osake-Pankki (a commercial bank) in the early 1890s.

The Bank ceased to accept interest bearing deposits in 1875, thus restricting its explicit competition with other commercial banks. It did, however, maintain banking relationships with domestic non-bank firms (the oldest being Hackman and Co. from 1842) as well as with foreign commercial banks (especially in Russia and Scandinavia). These relationships, including direct lending to the business sector, were maintained until the 1980s, when all such financing arrangements and business with private customers was discontinued.

Following the reassembly of the Estates during the 1860s, the Bank became independent of the government and was made subordinate to the four Estates (1868). Decision-making was transferred to a Parliamentary Supervisory Board, elected by the Estates, consisting of one permanent member from each Estate as well as a deputy and additional members. The day-to-day management of the Bank, however, remained in the hands of the Board of Management. In 1875, administration of State finances was transferred from the bank to a newly formed Treasury. Furthermore, the Bank was given a new and explicit objective, namely to maintain a secure and stable monetary system, in addition to its existing objective of promoting and facilitating the circulation of currency. These have remained the main objectives of the Bank until the present.

With the outbreak of World War I, Finland effectively abandoned the gold standard and, by the end of the war, the value of the markka had declined to an eighth of its prewar value. Finland declared independence in 1917, although this did not lead to any significant changes in the organisation of the Bank, since this was already a fully fledged and independent (of the government) central bank. In 1925 new regulations for the Bank of Finland were imposed which, although amended several times, are still in force today. These pertained to all aspects of the Bank's activities, including the tasks of the Parliamentary Supervisory Board.

In 1926 Finland returned to the gold standard, only to abandon it again during the Great Depression five years later. During the inter-war period, the interest rate was actively used as a means of monetary control, although this began to change in the late 1930s. During and after World War II, extensive financial regulations were introduced, which remained in force until the early 1980s. These comprised an interbank agreement on deposit rates, restrictions on bank lending rates, exchange controls, regulation of bond issues and a quota system for banks' borrowing at the Bank with an associated penalty rate schedule. Furthermore, the Bank only relinquished its commercial lending activities (especially to large exporting concerns) in the 1960s.

Independence

Since 1868, fifty-seven years after its formation, the Bank of Finland has not been subordinate to the Government. Instead, it is under the 'guarantee and care' of the Diet (Parliament since 1907), although this involves no direct intervention in the Bank's activities.

Parliament appoints nine Bank Supervisors who control the administration of the Bank. They are appointed at the first ordinary parliamentary session after elections to Parliament, for a term of four years (the next election). Whilst Bank Supervisors meet monthly, they do not administer or manage the Bank. This is done on a full-time basis by the Board of Management (a chairman and at most five members), being appointed by the President on the proposal of the Supervisors.

The Bank is wholly free to decide whether or not credit should be granted to the Government, and to fix the amount, terms and maturity of this credit. Government borrowing from the bank has been the exception rather than the rule.

REFERENCES

Bank of Finland (1984) *Currency Acts and Regulations for the Bank of Finland.* Helsinki.
Bank of Finland (1991) 'Financial markets in Finland', *Bank of Finland Monthly Bulletin*, Special Bulletin.
Bank of Finland (1992) *The Bank of Finland.* Helsinki.
Kullberg, R. (1992) 'A brief history of the Bank of Finland', *Bank of Finland Working Paper*, 1/92, Research Department.
Lehto-Sinisalo, P. (1992) 'The history of exchange control in Finland', *Bank of Finland Discussion Paper*, 3/92, Statistical Services Department.
Pipping, H. E. (1961) 'The origin and early development of central banking in Finland', *Bank of Finland Monthly Bulletin*, No. 12.
Ryti, R. (1936) 'The Bank of Finland: characteristics and aims of its activities', *Bank of Finland Monthly Bulletin*, No. 12.

Schybergson, E. (1913) *Finlands Bank: 1811–1911*. Helsingfors: Helsinki.
Talvio, T. (1987) *The Coins and Banknotes of Finland*. Bank of Finland: Helsinki.
Tudeer, A. E. (1940) *The Bank of Finland: 1912–1936*. Helsingfors: Helsinki.
Waris, K. (1961) 'Some features of central Banking in Finland', *Bank of Finland Monthly Bulletin*, No. 12.

B5   De Nederlandsche Bank

Founded in 1814

Forerunner

None, although there were several previous endeavours to establish a public credit institution.

During a severe money market crisis in January 1773, the Municipality of Amsterdam established a temporary loan bank, called the Fund for Maintaining the Public Credit which advanced money against collateral of domestic securities or merchandise. After the crisis abated, however, the fund was liquidated, without loss, in September 1773.

A related institution was established following another money market crisis in 1781. Though originally intended to be operative for the period of only one year, problems arose at the time of expiration, so that the Municipality of Amsterdam took over the bank in 1783, resulting in the foundation of the Muncipal Loan Chamber. This time the institution was founded for twelve years, which term was extended for another twelve years. Nevertheless the bank was not successful because it continued making loans without collateral to private merchants and to the East-India Company. It was liquidated in 1807.

In 1795, the year that the French occupied the Netherlands, the provisional government of the province of Holland established the General Loan Bank for facilitating the collection of a capital tax. This institution was to grant secured advances which could be used to pay this tax and then be repaid over a period of three years, after which the institution was to be liquidated. In fact, repayment took much longer, and a proposal was made to transform the institution into a General National Loan, Discount and Deposit Bank, based to a large extent upon the example of the Bank of England. This was not adopted, however, and the institution was eventually liquidated in 1803.

Motivation for founding

Following the end of French occupation of the Netherlands in 1813, economic conditions were extremely depressed, with trade, traditionally a source of prosperity, having fallen to very low levels. At the initiative of King William I, and based upon the earlier proposal for the General National Loan, Discount and Deposit Bank, it was decreed that De Nederlandsche Bank (hereafter the Bank) would be established in March 1814 in order to promote economic recovery.

Original objectives and functions

The tasks undertaken by the Bank included the rediscounting of trade bills, the extension of secured advances, trading precious metals and receiving current account funds for the government. The issue of convertible bank-notes was not explicitly a function, but was implicit in the Bank's authority to make its payments in specie or bank notes, the regulation of which (i.e. cover provisions) was left to the Bank's judgement until 1847, when it was decreed that the note issue was to be a fixed absolute amount.

The Bank was established as a private company, under a charter which was originally set at twenty-five years. The Bank was governed by a Managing Board, consisting of a permanent President and Secretary, and five Directors with appointments of two and a half years. The President and Secretary were appointed by the Sovereign, whilst the Directors were proposed by the principal shareholders.

Evolution of Objectives and Functions

During the first three decades of its existence, the activities of the Bank remained limited. Public confidence in a new banknote was low following the experience with French assignats. Also, the fact that the Bank of England (in 1797) and the Banque de France (in 1805 and 1814) had suspended convertibility diminished the confidence of the Dutch people in bank notes. Another important explanation for their low acceptance was that Amsterdam bankers and cashiers feared competition from the Bank. Furthermore, the development of trade, and hence lending, was slow, and the Bank's clientele was limited to Amsterdam, since it did not have branches elsewhere.

In 1838, therefore, the Charter was renewed for another twenty-five years, at which time the Bank was granted the right to discount other paper besides bills, and extend its deposit activities to the private sector. The Bank still had no special privileges as regards note issue, besides that its notes were exempt from stamp duty (which was intended as a commercial incentive).

Following the growth of a number of new credit institutions during the 1840s, the Netherlands Bank began to rediscount their promissory notes issued to customers, thereby beginning to deal less frequently with non-financial firms and more with banks. This position of bankers' bank was consolidated with the first Bank Act of 1863 (following the expiry of the second twenty-five year Charter), which established a number of subsidiaries to the Bank in the form of a branch in Rotterdam and agencies and correspondents throughout the Netherlands.

The Act of 1863 also, for the first time, formally restricted other institutions from issuing banknotes without permission of the State, and changed the legal status of the Bank to that of a limited company. Furthermore, the Bank's note issue was no longer limited in absolute amount, but had to be a specified fraction of the Bank's bullion reserve. By 1870 the Bank dealt almost exclusively with other banks, also acting as a lender of last resort (the first instance of lender of resort operations occurred during a financial crisis in 1857). Its sole instrument consisted of the discount rate, with open market operations only being used much later (from 1937 onwards).

At about the turn of the century, the Bank informally began to supervise the banking system, monitoring those banks which regularly discounted paper with it. By 1920 banks regularly consulted the bank about their lending activities, and in 1931 began, voluntarily, to submit quarterly returns to the Bank concerning their credit positions. Only after World War II, however, following the Bank Act of 1948, was the bank formally charged with supervision of the banking system.

During the aftermath of World War II the Bank was nationalised, and the objectives and functions of the Bank redefined in the Bank Act of 1948. This stated that 'it shall be the duty of the Bank to regulate the value of the Netherlands monetary unit in such a manner as will be most conducive to the nation's prosperity and welfare, and in so doing seek to keep the value as stable as possible'. The Bank also no longer undertook any commercial banking functions, and its agencies (branches) were given the task of servicing the banknote issue.

Independence

Although the government did not hold any shares in the Bank between 1847 (when it sold all its shares) and 1948 (when the Bank was nationalised), it has always retained the right to appoint the senior management of the Bank, namely the President and Secretary of the Governing Board. Furthermore, following a Bank Act in 1903, the government has been allowed to obtain non-interest bearing credit from the Bank, initially limited to fifteen million guilders, and then to one hundred and fifty million guilders.

Government influence over the Bank was formalised after its nationalisation in 1948, when it was specified for the first time that the Minister of

Finance could give directions to the Governing Board 'as he thinks necessary for the Bank's policy to be properly coordinated with the Government's monetary and fiscal policies'. This authority has never been exercised, however, and the Bank has typically implemented monetary policy with considerable independence.

It is envisaged that the government's statutory right to Bank credit, as well as its authority to give instructions to the Bank, will soon be abolished in accordance with the requirements of the Maastricht Treaty.

REFERENCES

Bank for International Settlements (1964) 'Nederlandsche Bank', in *Eight European Central Banks*. BIS: Basle.

De Nederlandsche Bank (1964) *De Bank 1814–1964*. (Jubilee Issue on the Occasion of the 150th Anniversary of the Netherlands Bank.) Amsterdam.

De Nederlandsche Bank (1968) *De Instrumenten van de Monetaire Politiek in Nederland*. (The instruments of monetary policy in the Netherlands). Amsterdam.

De Nederlandsche Bank (1991) *Bank Act 1948 and Articles of Association*. Amsterdam.

den Dunnen, E. and S. de Wilde (1992) 'Instruments of money and foreign exchange market policy in the Netherlands', *NIBE Serie Bank-en Effectenbedrijf*, 31.

Gaarden, A. van der (1964) 'The Netherlands Bank–150 years old', *Amsterdamsche Bank Quarterly Review*, No. 144, June.

Jong, A. M. de (1929) 'The banking system of Holland', in Willis, H. P. and B. H. Beckhart (eds.) *Foreign Banking Systems*. Sir Isaac Pitman and Sons: London.

Jong, A. M. de (1934) 'The origin and foundation of the Netherlands Bank', in J. G. Van Dillen (ed.) *History of the Principal Public Banks*, Martinus Nijhoff: The Hague.

Jong, A. M. de (1967) *Geschiedenis van de Nederlandsche Bank*. (History of the Netherlands Bank, in two volumes, 1814–1864 (I) and 1865–1914.) De Nederlandsche Bank: Amsterdam.

Mastropasqua, S. (1978) *The Banking System in the Countries of the EEC: Institutional and Structural Aspects*. Sijthoff and Noordhoff International Publishers: Alphen aan den Rijn.

Vanthoor, W. F. V. (1992) 'The History of the Nederlandsche Bank 1814–1992', Manuscript prepared for the manual of the European Association for Banking History.

Van Wyk, H. H. (1988) 'De Nederlandsche bank, functie en werkterrein', *NIBE Bank-en Effectenbedrijf*, 25.

Vries, J de (1989) *Geschiedenis van de Nederlandsche Bank 1914–1931*. (History of the Netherlands Bank 1914–1931.) Amsterdam.

Wilson, J. S. G. (1962) 'The Netherlands', in R. S. Sayers (ed.) *Banking in Western Europe*. Clarendon: Oxford.

B6   Oesterreichische Nationalbank (Austrian National Bank)

Founded in 1816

Forerunner

None. Although an attempt was made in 1703 to create a national bank which would issue notes for purposes of funding the Treasury. The bank was liquidated soon after its establishment as the government was unable to meet its redemption obligations on these notes.

Motivation for founding

Throughout the end of the eighteenth century and the beginning of the nineteenth century, the Austrian government borrowed heavily by issuing paper notes, which could be used for the payment of taxes and circulated as media of exchange. Excessive issues, however, especially during the Napoleonic Wars, frequently led to large depreciations in the value of these notes, causing widespread disruption. Consequently, the need arose for an issuing bank which was seen as independent of the state.

Original objectives and functions

Two statutes, the 'Hauptpatent' and the 'Bankpatent', established the Priviligierte Oesterreichische Nationalbank (Chartered Austrian National Bank; hereafter the Bank) in 1816. The Bank was established as a joint stock company, and its administration modelled upon that of the Banque de France.

The Nationalbank was authorised to accept deposits and discount bills (commercial paper), and given the exclusive right to issue notes convertible into silver, although it was not obliged to maintain any specific ratio of specie to its note issue. An important function of the Bank was the gradual replacement of previously issued state paper notes with its own notes, although this process was to take over three decades. Initially, the National-bank did not serve as the government's bank, and the government was limited in its ability to borrow from the Bank.

Evolution of objectives and functions

The charter of the Nationalbank was renewed in 1842, along with its monopoly over the note issue, although the exclusive privilege to discount paper and the ability to make mortgage loans was withdrawn.

The uprising in Hungary, the Crimean War and the Italian struggle imposed huge financing requirements on the state, which borrowed heavily from the Nationalbank. In 1848, therefore, convertibility of Nationalbank notes was suspended. The state then resumed issuing its own unbacked, but interest bearing, notes, some of which were declared legal tender. Convertibility into silver was restored in 1858, only to be suspended again the following year.

Constitutional changes in 1867 formed the Austro-Hungarian Monarchy and led, after some time, to a renaming of the Nationalbank as the Austro-Hungarian Bank in 1878. The Governor of the new Bank was appointed by the Emperor and nominated by the Finance Ministers in each of the two parts of the empire.

By this time, several banks had been established, beginning with the Austrian Discount Company in 1853 and the Creditanstalt in 1855. A clearing-house became operational in 1864 on the initiative of the Creditanstalt, although the volume of clearing remained relatively small. A stock market crash in 1873 led to a dramatic reduction in the number of joint stock banks, and it was only after the turn of the century that a significant increase in the number of banks began to occur again.

The falling price of silver during the 1870s led, in 1877, to substantial increases in the circulation of silver coins, leading the government to restrict the private coining of silver in 1879. The silver standard (known as the 'limping silver standard', given that currency was not convertible) was finally abolished in 1891, when it was decided to adopt a gold standard and a new currency unit, the Krone (crown). As before, however, notes remained inconvertible.

At the outbreak of World War I, the Bank Act, which had (since 1892) specified the minimum specie reserve which had to be held by the Austro-Hungarian Bank, was suspended, and large loans were extended to the government. The Bank was also relieved of its obligation to publish its balance sheet, and it was only after the convening of the Bank's Board some four years later that details of the Bank's wartime activities became public.

In 1918 the Austro-Hungarian Monarchy broke down, leading to the formation of independent states of Austria, Hungary, Czechoslovakia, and Yugoslavia. All of these so-called Successor states shared the Krone as a common currency, and it was decided to partition the currency issue amongst them. The post-war peace treaty (signed at Saint-Germain) stipulated the liquidation of the Austro-Hungarian Bank, which effectively led to all Successor states issuing their own currencies.

Given its poor post-war condition, Austria was able to continue to use its 'portion' of the Austro-Hungarian Bank as a legally independent (from Hungary) bank of issue. However, large redemptions of war loans generated extremely high inflation which, in 1922, led to plans for financial reconstruction (the Geneva Recovery Programme), including the establishment of a new central bank to be known as the Austrian National Bank.

Undertaking all the conventional central banking functions, the main function of the Bank was to reintroduce convertibility of currency into gold. For this purpose it was to hold a minimum specie reserve of 20 per cent, with excess note issues being taxed. The Bank was organised as a joint stock institution, administered by a General Council comprising a President (appointed by the government) and thirteen members (appointed by shareholders).

At the outset of World War II the Bank was put into liquidation and annexed to the Reichsbank until 1945, during which time reichsmarks were put into forced circulation in Austria. After the war, the government undertook a major monetary reform, re-establishing the Bank and depriving reichsmarks of their legal tender status. The statutes of the Bank were revised in 1955 (and amended again in 1984), with the main objective of the Bank becoming the maintenance of the internal and external value of the currency.

Independence

The independence of the Bank has passed through stages, becoming particularly limited during wartime, when the Bank has been called upon to finance government expenditures. Since 1955 the bank has enjoyed considerable independence, and remains a joint stock company only partly owned (50 per cent) by the Federal government. Government borrowing from the Bank is limited to a specified maximum, and Article 41 of the National Bank Law states that 'the Federal Republic must not issue any paper currency or adopt measures which are liable to hinder the bank in the performance of the functions entrusted to it'.

REFERENCES

Austrian National Bank (1991) *Striking a Balance: 175 Years of Austrian Central Banking*. Vienna.

Bachmeyer, O. (1960) *Die Geschichte der Österreichischen Währungspolitik*. (The History of Austrian Monetary and Exchange Rate Policy). Vienna.

Kamitz, R. (1949) 'Die Österreichische Geld-und Währungspolitik von 1848 bis 1948' ('Austrian monetary and exchange rate policy from 1848 to 1948') in H. Mayer (ed.) *Hundert Jahre Österreichische Wirtschaftsentwicklung 1848–1948*. Vienna.

Klopstock, F. H. (1948) 'Monetary and fiscal policy in post-liberation Austria', *Political Science Quarterly*, March.

März, E. (1984) *Austrian Banking and Financial Policy*. Wiedenfeld and Nicolson: London.

Sokal, M. and O. Rosenberg (1929) 'The banking system of Austria', in Willis, H. P. and B. H. Beckhart (eds.) *Foreign Banking Systems*. Sir Isaac Pitman and Sons: London.

Schaumayer, M. (1991) 'Central Bank independence in Austria', in Downes, P. and R. Vaez-Zadeh (eds.) *The Evolving Role of Central Banks*. IMF: Washington.

Wieser, F. (1893) 'Resumption of specie payments in Austria-Hungary', *Journal of Political Economy*, June.

B7   Norges Bank

Founded in 1816

Forerunner

None. Norges Bank (hereafter the Bank) was the first Norwegian-owned bank in Norway.

Motivation for founding

Until 1814 Norway had been under Danish jurisdiction, being part of a union with Denmark. One year earlier, the Danish State was rendered bankrupt by its expenditures in the Napoleonic wars, and a monetary reform declared (see the entry under Danmarks Nationalbank). A constitutional assembly in Norway thus began drafting an act to establish a Norwegian bank, whose purpose was to issue notes, convertible into silver and denominated in dalers, accept deposits, lend money and undertake transfers of money.

Original objectives and functions

The Norges Bank Act of 1816 established the Bank with the main purpose of issuing currency whose value was to be maintained through convertibility into silver. To this end a minimum specie reserve equal to 50 per cent of its notes had to be held. However, the Bank's notes were originally convertible below par, with par convertibility only being gradually achieved (in 1842).

In addition to note issue, over which the Bank was granted a monopoly in 1818, the Bank undertook commercial banking functions which included the taking of deposits, the transfer of money, and lending via the rediscounting of bills and the extension of mortgages. Indeed, mortgage loans formed the bulk of the bank's assets for the first half of the nineteenth century.

Although the Bank was to be established as a joint stock company, its public flotation was unsuccessful. Thus capital was raised via a 'forced subscription' payable in silver, and shareholders' normal voting and control rights were taken over by the Storting (parliament).

The administration of the Bank was made up of two bodies: a fifteen-member Board of Representatives, and a five-member Board of Directors. The President and Vice President of the Board of Representatives was appointed by the Crown, whilst all other governing members were elected by Parliament. Ultimate authority over the discount rate rested with the Bank (until World War II).

Evolution of objectives and functions

With the emergence of savings and commercial banks during the nineteenth century, the commercial banking functions of the Norges Bank gradually decreased, and by the end of the century it began to play more of a role as a bankers bank. An interbank clearing system was established in 1898, administered by the Bank. The Bank also played the role of lender of last resort for the first time in 1899, during a severe financial crisis.

However, Norges Bank did not supervise or regulate banks. Savings banks were supervised by the Ministry of Finance from 1887, and by a separate governmental body, the Inspectorate of Saving Banks, from 1919. Five years later, following new laws for savings and commercial banks, another government supervision authority for both bank groups was established.

Norway adopted a gold standard in 1873. The new monetary unit, the krone, had the same gold content as the Danish kroner and Swedish krona, all which circulated at par throughout these countries under the Scandinavian Currency Union (formed in 1875). This prompted the Norges bank to hold foreign exchange reserves, a role which it retains today.

In 1892 the Norges Bank Act was revised, with the Bank of England as a model. Greater flexibility was introduced into the ability to issue currency, and the status of the Bank as the government's bank was formalised.

The gold standard was abandoned in 1914 (World War I), readopted in 1928 at its pre-war parity, and then abandoned again during the Great Depression in 1931. The external value of the krone dominated inter-war policy concerns, and in 1932 an advisory committee on economic policy was appointed by the government on which the Norges Bank was not represented. This implied that the Bank was no longer the sole expert on monetary policy issues, although it retained ultimate authority over the discount rate.

Between 1940 and 1945 (World War II) the Germans occupied Norway, financing much of their occupation expenses via increases in the note issue of the Bank. This resulted in a considerable post-war inflation, and led to further attrition of the Bank's policymaking authority as the government effectively took control of interest rate policy and the discount rate. At the end of 1949 the Bank was nationalised. Finally, in 1965, a new Act established that interest rates and credit volumes were to be regulated by the government.

Independence

In 1985, the relationship between the Norges bank and the Government was stated for the first time. The 1985 Act Relating to Norges Bank and the Monetary System states that Norges Bank shall conduct its operations in accordance with the political and economic guidelines drawn up by the government. Before taking decisions of special importance, the Bank shall submit the matter to the Minister of Finance. According to the Act, the Bank may be instructed by Royal Decree (e.g. by the government) to act in specific ways. In such cases the bank will be given the opportunity to state its opinion, and the Storting (parliament) shall be notified as soon as possible. However, the government has never used its right to instruct Norges Bank.

REFERENCES

Act of 24 May 1985 Relating to Norges Bank and the Monetary System, Oslo.
Bang, P. and J. P. Holter (1991) *Norges Bank 175 År*. (Norges Bank 175 Years). Norges Bank: Oslo.
Norges Bank (1953) 'Structural Survey of Norway', Bulletin, No. 2.
Norges Bank (1990) *Norges Bank*. Oslo.
Petersen, E. (1966) 'Bank of Norway 1816–1966', *Norwegian Commercial Banks Commercial Review*, No. 2.
Skänland, H. (1984) 'The central bank and political authorities in some industrial countries', *Norges Bank Skriftserie*, No. 13.
Skänland, H. (1991) 'Central bank responsibilities present and future', *Economic Bulletin*, No. 2.

B8   Danmarks Nationalbank

Founded in 1818

Forerunner

The first bank in Denmark, the Kurantbanken (Currency bank) was established in 1736, and had the sole right to issue notes, which were convertible into silver. Having over-issued notes as a result of financing government expenditures, however, convertibility could no longer be upheld, and the bank folded.

In 1791 another bank was established, known as the Specie Bank, which met the same fate, largely as the result of government expenditure during the Napoleonic wars. This led to increasing inflation, and culminated in the 'Statsbankerot' (State bankruptcy) in 1813.

In order to restore monetary stability, a provisional institution known as the Rigsbank was set up in 1813 as a forerunner to the Nationalbank. In addition to the sole right to issue notes, the Rigsbank (later the National-bank) had a 'first priority' right to all property mortgages in Denmark. In this way the Nationalbank could be funded via mortgage instalments.

Motivation for founding

The Nationalbank was founded in order to restore monetary stability after the 'state bankruptcy' and inflation which ensued from excessive govern-ment expenditure during the Napoleonic wars.

Original objectives and functions

Stabilisation of the monetary system was the main priority of the National-bank, whose task it was to bring the value of banknotes up to par so as to restore redeemability into silver. First, sufficient notes were withdrawn from circulation to make them reach parity with coin. This was achieved by 1845, when notes were declared redeemable once more.

The Nationalbank's second, and less important, task was to pay interest on the liabilities taken over from its bankrupt predecessor(s). Finally, the bank was expected to facilitate the allocation of credit by acting as a commercial bank, although this task had the lowest priority.

The rules governing the Nationalbank were embodied in a Royal Charter, which was granted for a period of ninety years. The Nationalbank was established as a private corporation in which debtors under mortgage could obtain shares, although their right as shareholders was restricted to receiv-ing dividends. The management was vested in a co-optative Board of Directors and a Board of Governors (one Governor to be appointed by the Crown and the others by the Board of Directors).

Evolution of objectives and functions

While the Nationalbank's efforts were concentrated on restoring the par value of notes, little ordinary banking activity was carried out. However, the Bank did begin to rediscount bills and grant secured loans during the 1830s.

Being the only bank, the demand for Nationalbank credit was strong, and its commercial banking activity increased.

With monetary stabilisation achieved, however, the first private bank was established in 1846, with several commercial banks and mortgage credit institutions emerging shortly thereafter. The Nationalbank thus shifted its activity towards acting as banker to these banks. The Lender of Last Resort activities of the Nationalbank only developed some time later, during a bank crisis in 1908 in which a number of banks heavily committed to builiding activities foundered. The Nationalbank did not play the role of banking supervisor and regulator, however, and this role was (is) undertaken by the Danish Financial Supervisory Authority, under the Ministry of Industry.

Like several other European countries, Denmark moved from a silver to a gold standard in 1873. This took place under the Coinage Act of 1873, which replaced the existing currency unit, the rigsdaler, with the krone. This was given the same gold content as the Norwegian krone and the Swedish krona, and in 1875 a Scandinavian Currency Union was set up under which all these currencies served equally as legal tender throughout the Union until World War I, when the gold standard was abandoned.

The Nationalbank's role as central bank was sealed in 1914 when, by agreement between the Bank and the Treasury, it became the sole banker to the Danish government. Following World War I, the exchange rate became the focus of policy, and attempts were made to restore the pre-war gold parity. In 1927 Denmark adopted a gold bullion standard, although this only lasted until 1931 when, along with Sweden, Norway and several other countries, Denmark followed Britain off the gold standard, effectively pegging its currency to the pound. Following this, responsibility for exchange rate policy was transferred to the Danish government. Exchange controls were also implemented, the administration of which was undertaken by the Nationalbank.

With the impending expiry of the Nationalbank's Royal Charter, which had been extended for another thirty years in 1908, the statutory basis of the bank was revised under the Danmarks Nationalbank Act of 1936. Existing shareholders were bought out, and the Bank reconstituted as a self-governing institution whose profits (after allocations) accrued to the government. The Board of Directors was supplemented with members of parliament, and a committee of directors established as a link between the Board of Directors and the Board of Governors, who still administered the Nationalbank and determined monetary policy. The objective of the Nationalbank, according to the 1936 Act, is to 'maintain a safe and secure currency system ... and to facilitate and regulate the traffic in money and the extension of credit'. This Act has not been modified.

As in many other countries, the pre-and post-World War II period was characterised by regulations on banking activity and foreign exchange markets, particularly the imposition of capital controls, many of which were only removed in the 1970s and 1980s. During the 1950s, the Nationalbank's remaining activities as a commercial bank, which included direct lending to business and accounts carried for private customers, were unwound. In the middle of 1970, it was agreed that the government would no longer borrow from the Nationalbank, but would instead issue debt on the open market.

Independence

The Nationalbank was originally set up as a private company under Royal Charter, although it was dissolved under the drafting of the 1936 Act, which replaced the Charter. This Act left the authority for monetary policy in the hands of the three-member Board of Governors, whilst governance was shared between the Board of Directors and the Committee of Directors. The Board of Directors, which includes members of parliament, elects two of the Governors (the Crown appoints the Chairman). The Royal Commissioner (i.e. Minister for Economic Affairs) and the Minister of Finance are entitled to take part in deliberations, but neither have voting rights as regards discount rate decisions.

REFERENCES

Clayton, G. (1962) 'Denmark', in R. S. Sayers (ed.) *Banking in Western Europe*. Clarendon: Oxford.
Danmarks Nationalbank (1983) *The New Building*. Copenhagen.
Danmarks Nationalbank (1991) *Central Bank Responsibilities and Tasks*. Copenhagen.
Glindemann, P. (1929) 'The banking system of Denmark', in Willis, H. P. and B. H. Beckhart (eds.) *Foreign Banking Systems*. Sir Isaac Pitman and Sons: London.
Handsen, S. (1954) 'The Danish banking system', *Bankers' Magazine*, December.
Hoffmeyer, E. (1960) 'Structural changes on the money and capital markets', *English Summary of a Study by the Author*. Copenhagen.
The National Bank of Denmark Act, By-Laws, etc. (1937). Copenhagen.

B9   Banco de Portugal

Founded in 1846

Forerunner

The Banco de Portugal was formed from the merger of two institutions, the Banco de Lisboa (established in 1821 as the first commercial bank in Portugal) and the Companhia Confiança Nacional (or National Surety

Company, a finance company set up in 1844 to make loans to the government).

From its inception the Banco de Lisboa, which enjoyed a note issuing monopoly, had been involved in financing the government. Increasing funding demands, especially during the 1840s, resulted in the government becoming unable to meet its obligations to the Bank, leading to a suspension of convertibility of its notes. For similar reasons the Companhia Confiança Nacional had to suspend its payments, prompting the government to merge and replace these two institutions in 1846 with the Banco de Portugal (hereafter the Bank).

Motivation for founding

The inability of the Banco de Lisboa and the Companhia Confiança Nacional to service their liabilities caused substantial monetary disruption. To restore credibility in the monetary system the government sought to withdraw these liabilities, replacing them with notes of the newly formed Banco de Portugal.

Original objectives and functions

The operations of the Banco de Portugal were subject to rules laid out in its founding charter, although its objectives and functions were vague. The Bank issued convertible bank notes (notes were convertible into gold), over which it initially held a monopoly throughout the entire country. Four years later, however, this monopoly was reduced, holding only in the district of Lisbon.

No formal reserve requirement was stipulated, but the Bank was forbidden from extending long term credit or making mortgage loans. During its first decades, therefore, the Bank operated primarily as a note-issuing commercial bank, discounting commercial paper and undertaking foreign exchange transactions.

The Bank was established as a joint stock company whose shares were publicly held. It was administered by a Board of Directors elected by the shareholders.

Evolution of objectives and functions

Following a new law on joint stock companies (including banks) in 1867, the Bank's note issuing monopoly was further eroded, and resulted in a proliferation of note issuing banks outside Lisbon. A banking crisis occurred in 1876, with many banks suspending payments on their notes. Although this prompted the Directors of the Bank to call for legislation restricting note issue, it was not until another crisis in 1891 that the Bank's monopoly over the note issue finally became statutory.

Although the Bank was not formally entrusted with acting as a lender of last resort until World War II, it did undertake this function during the banking crises in the 1870s and the 1890s. Rediscounting bills presented by banks also became common practice.

No official clearing system was operated in Portugal until 1926, and there is no evidence that the Banco de Portugal had established any informal clearing arrangements prior to this. Furthermore, the Bank only became informally involved in regulating and supervising the banking system in 1925 (formally in 1975). From the 1890s, when banking first became supervised, this task was undertaken by government departments.

When it was founded, the Banco de Portugal had no formal obligation to lend to the state, nor was it the state bank. This changed in 1887, when the Bank became the state's bank. After 1891 the Bank also became a large creditor to the state.

For most of the nineteenth century the Banco de Portugal was legally committed to a discount rate of 5 per cent, although this could be changed, by decree and by its own request, usually to deal with external drains. At least until 1888, when a government appointed governor became able to veto decisions by the Board of Directors, the Bank enjoyed substantial independence from the government in its daily operations.

Independence

Until 1931 government influence over the Bank had grown steadily, but remained informal. In 1931 a reform of the Bank's statutes occurred which, although it incorporated rules limiting the expansion of the Bank's notes and its lending to the government, at the same time increased formal government influence over the Bank. According to the reform, the government could appoint two of the three vice-Governors, and part of the Bank's decisions became vested in a Stabilisation Committee, where representation of government appointed officials equalled other officials.

Government influence over the Banco de Portugal increased in 1974 when it was nationalised, and its functions and objectives redefined in 1975 in a Decree-Law (revised in 1990). Under this law the Governor and other members of the Board of Directors were appointed by the Cabinet, on a proposal by the Finance Minister.

REFERENCES

Bank of Portugal (1990) *Organic Law.*
Bank of Portugal (1993) *Correspondence.*

Clayton, G. (1962) 'Portugal', in R. S. Sayers (ed.) *Banking in Western Europe*. Clarendon Press: Oxford.

Pereira, A. R. (1966) 'Banking in Portugal', in Auburn, H. W. (ed.) *Comparative Banking*. 3rd edition. Waterlow and Sons: London.

Pereira, A. R. (1964) 'Banking in Portugal then and now', *Bankers' Magazine*, November.

Peres, D. (1971) *Historia do Banco de Portugal 1821–1846*. (History of the Bank of Portugal). Lisbon.

Valerio, N. and M. E. Mata (1982) 'O Banco de Portugal: Unico Banco Emissor 1891–1931', ('Bank of Portugal: Monopoly Bank of Issue 1891–1931'), *Revista de Historia Economia e Social*, No. 10.

Wallich, H. C . (1951) *The Financial System of Portugal*. Lisbon.

B10   Deutsche Bundesbank

Founded in 1957 (Prussian Bank founded in 1846)

Forerunner

The Bundesbank is the last of a sequence of public note-issuing banks, beginning with the Royal Giro and Loan Bank established by Frederick the Great in 1765 for purposes of economic reconstruction following the Seven Years' War. This was reorganised as the Prussian Bank in 1846, which subsequently became the Reichsbank in 1876, issuing currency known as the Mark. Following a hyperinflation in 1923 a new public bank of issue, the Rentenbank, was established to restore monetary confidence, issuing a currency known as the Rentenmark. The next year a 'new' Reichsbank resumed operation, issuing the Reichsmark.

After World War II, and another large (but suppressed) inflation, the Reichsbank was dissolved, and its role assumed in 1948 by a two-tier system of regional central banks organised around the Bank deutscher Länder, which issued currency known as the Deutsche Mark. The following year the German Constitution scheduled for the establishment of a Federal Bank which would merge the existing two tier arrangement into a single independent central bank with a number of regional main offices. This institution, formed in 1957, was the Deutsche Bundesbank.

Given that the Reichsbank, and after it the Bank deutscher Länder were central banks before the establishment of the Bundesbank, this section differs from others in that it presents the founding and evolution of the Prussian bank, the Reichsbank, the Bank deutscher Länder and the Bundesbank in turn.

Founding, objectives and evolution

In the first decades of the nineteenth century a wide variety of coins, including foreign coins, circulated throughout Germany, contrasting with conditions in England or France, for example. Not only were the coins of different weights and denominations, but they were also from different standards, although the silver standard was dominant. Paper money was also used, although to a much lesser degree, and showed a similar variety.

Several note-issuing banks had arisen, among them the Prussian state bank (the Royal Bank), although their note issue never became substantial. In addition, most states issued paper money (which was not always convertible into specie) to cover fiscal financing needs, with a notable example being Prussian treasury notes issued to fund its war effort against Napoleon. The note-issuing privileges of banks were often withdrawn (e.g. that of the Royal Bank was withdrawn in the early 1830s) to achieve wider circulation of state issued paper money.

(i) The Prussian Bank (1846–1875)   Increasing demands for bank notes due to a growing economy led the Prussian Government to establish the Prussian Bank in 1846. Partly owned, and totally managed, by the government (the bank's head was the Prussian Minister of Trade), the Prussian bank functioned as a bank of issue and a discount bank (another institution, the Prussian Sea Trading Corporation, later known as the Prussian State Bank, served as the government's bank). The decree which established the Prussian bank also stated that its task was to prevent any great rise in the rate of interest, and the bank was forbidden to raise its lending (or lombard) rate above 6 per cent. The same decree also specified both a minimum specie reserve ratio (to notes) of one third and an absolute maximum on its note issue. This maximum was lifted in 1856, however, in order to give the Prussian bank an advantage over other note-issuing banks, particularly the small state note issuers, whose circulation had remained unrestricted. The position of the Prussian bank was further strengthened by a banking crisis the following year, during which the Prussian bank also acted as a lender of last resort.

By the 1870s the circulation of Prussian bank notes accounted for about two thirds of all bank notes, although the use of such notes remained limited next to coins, which represented about 75 per cent of circulating media at the time. Following the formation of the German Reich in 1871, increasing demands to unify the coinage system resulted in two Coinage Acts, in 1871 and 1873, which adopted a new monetary unit, the Mark, and a new monetary standard, namely gold instead of silver. The second act also required the withdrawal of all state issued paper money by 1876, and imposed a minimum denomination on bank notes (100 Marks) which greatly reduced the circulation of extant bank notes.

(ii) The Reichsbank (1876–1948) The monetary unification which followed the formation of the German Reich also resulted in the replacement of the Prussian bank with the Reichsbank, whose functions and organisation remained essentially the same as those of its predecessor. That is, the Reichsbank was the government's bank, a discount bank, and an issuer of convertible bank notes, holding one third of its note issue in the form of specie (coin). In addition, the Reichsbank was 'to regulate the monetary circulation of Germany, to facilitate clearings, and to see to it that available capital is productively employed' (Banking Act 1875). Thus the Reichsbank sometimes acted as a direct lender to business, and acted as the lender of last resort to the banking system.

The Reichsbank was privately owned, but under government management, with the Chancellor of the Reich at its head and a Directorate of civil servants headed by a President conducting day-to-day business. However, the Reichsbank remained relatively free from government interference, and was not subordinated to fiscal needs as in many other countries. For the remainder of the nineteenthth century the Reichsbank, like other central banks, pursued a policy of altering its discount rate to maintain its specie stock at the designated level. By the turn of the century the Reichsbank had begun using open-market operations to influence market interest rates (i.e. make its discount rate binding by forcing banks to borrow from it) and had also become the major custodian of foreign reserves. In 1909 Reichsbank notes became legal tender for the first time.

With the advent of World War I the Reichsbank effectively became an instrument to finance the war and its aftermath. Germany left the gold standard and the Reichsbank was no longer obliged to maintain any proportion between its note issue and its specie reserves. The fiscal burden of reparation payments following the war led to an increasing note issue and culminated in a hyperinflation in 1923. To restore monetary confidence a new currency, 'backed' by property and known as the Rentenmark, was issued by a new, independent and privately managed bank known as the Rentenbank.

In 1924 a Banking Act established a new, and independent, Reichsbank, administered by a General Council composed of domestic and foreign representatives. The Reichsbank now had to maintain a specie (and foreign exchange) reserve equal to at least 40 per cent of its note issue, and its lending to the government was restricted to small amounts. However, this independence began to be eroded in 1930, when all foreign influence in the administration of the Reichsbank ceased. By 1933 the right to appoint and dismiss members of the Reichsbank's Directorate was transferred to the

President of the Reich, and in 1937 the Reichsbank was made subject to Hitler's instructions. The note issue dramatically expanded again as a result of war financing, and another huge – but suppressed, due to price controls – inflation ensued after World War II.

(iii) The Bank deutscher Länder (1948–1957) At the end of World War II, Germany was divided into four zones, and the Reichsbank ceased to function as the German central bank. Instead, a federal or two-tier system of central banks (like the Federal Reserve System of the US) was established in 1948, with a number of regional central banks, or Landeszentralbanken, being co-ordinated by a co-ordinating central bank, known as the Bank deutscher Länder. The regional central banks did not issue notes and simply facilitated a more federal or decentralised decision making structure, as the regional central bank Presidents elected the President of the Directorate of the Bank deutscher Länder and the President of the Central Bank Council (which took policy decisions).

The capital of the Bank deutscher Länder was owned by the regional central banks, and its articles of establishment were lacking in any provision which would have subordinated the Bank to any political body. Initially, the Bank was subject to international supervision, although this was discontinued in 1951. The Bank had the exclusive right to issue notes, undertook open market operations, could dictate discount rates and minimum reserve requirements, and acted as the government's bank. Credit extension to the government could not exceed a stated maximum.

(iv) The Deutsche Bundesbank (1957–) The West German constitution of 1949 had already provided for the establishment of the Bundesbank, which would essentially centralise the existing two tier central banking system whilst retaining the independence and functions of the Bank deutscher Länder. In 1957, therefore, the Bundesbank replaced the Bank deutscher Länder with the regional central banks becoming its main offices. Although the capital of the Bundesbank was owned by the State, it has autonomy to pursue its main objective, namely to safeguard the value of the German currency, i.e. price stability. The Federal Government takes decisions concerning the exchange rate regime and capital controls. Banking regulation and supervision is undertaken by a government institution, the Federal Office for Control of the Banks (or Bundesaufsichtsampt fur Kreditwesen).

Independence

Although they have been subject to the government's instructions, German central banks have remained relatively independent until the First World

War. Independence was again severely compromised before and during the Second World War. Given the inflations which followed both of these episodes, the Bundesbank was established as an extremely independent institution, dedicated to price stability.

Monetary and credit policy is determined by the Bundesbank on its own authority, and the Bundesbank may employ and develop monetary policy instruments at its discretion. There is no binding obligation to grant credit to the government, neither is the Bundesbank obliged to report to Parliament and the Federal Government.

REFERENCES

Bopp, K. R. (1953) *Reichsbank Operations 1876–1914*. University of Pennsylvania.

Deutsche Bundesbank (ed.) (1976) Währung und Wirstschaft in Deutschland 1876–1975. (Money and the Economy in Germany 1876–1975). Fritz Knapp: Frankfurt/M.

Deutsche Bundesbank (1988) *30 Jahre Deutsche Bundesbank: Die Entstehung des Bundesbankgesetzes vom 26 Juli 1957*. (30 Years of the Deutsche Bundesbank: Origins of the Bundesbank Statute of 26 July 1957). Frankfurt/M.

Deutsche Bundesbank (1989) *The Deutsche Bundesbank: Its Monetary Policy Instruments and Functions*. 3rd edition. Deutsche Bundesbank Special Series No. 7.

Fengler, H. (1992) *Geschichte der deutschen Notenbanken vor Einführung der Mark-Währung*. Regenstauf.

Francke, H. and M. Hudson (1984) *Banking and Finance in West Germany*. Croom Helm: London.

Holtfrerich, K. L. (1988) 'Relations between monetary authorities and governmental institutions: the case of Germany from the nineteenth century to the present', in G. Toniolo (ed.) *Central Banks' Independence in Historical Perspective*. Walter de Gruyter: New York.

Hottfrerich, K. L. (1989) 'The monetary unification process in 19th century Germany: relevance and lessons for Europe today', in M. de Cecco and A. Giovannini (eds.) *A European Central bank? Perspectives on Monetary Unification after Ten Years of the EMS*. Cambridge University Press: Cambridge.

James, H. (1985) *The Reichsbank and Public Finance in Germany 1924–1933*. Fritz Knapp Verlag: Frankfurt.

Lindenlaub, D. (1993) 'The Deutsche Bundesbank', forthcoming in European Association for Banking History (ed.), *Handbook on the History of European Banks*.

Northrop, M. B. (1938) *Control Policies of the Reichsbank 1924–1933*. Columbia University Press: New York.

Poschinger, H. von (1878) *Bankwesen und bankpolitik in Preußen*. 3 vols. Berlin.

Reichsbank (1901) Die Reichsbank 1876–1900. Reichsbank Press.

Reichsbank (1926) *Die Reichsbank 1901–1925*. Reichsbank Press.

Rittman, H. (1986) *Deutsche Geldgeschichte Seit 1914*. (German Monetary History Since 1914). Klinkhardt und Bierman: Munich.

Tilly, R. (1967) 'Germany 1815–1870', in R. Cameron (ed.) *Banking in the Early Stages of Industrialisation*, Oxford University Press: Oxford.

Ziegler, D. (1993) 'Zentralpolitische Steinzeit? Preußische Bank und Bank of England im vergleich', *Geschichte und Gesellschaft*, 19.

B11   Banque Nationale de Belgique

Founded in 1850

Forerunner

None. From 1795 until 1814 the area which eventually became the kingdom of Belgium was incorporated into the French Republic-Empire, and from 1914 until the National Revolution of 1830 it formed part of the kingdom of the United Netherlands. Consequently, both Dutch florins and French francs represented the main media of exchange, with the franc being the more widely used.

Belgium did have a number of banks in 1850, including the first ever joint stock bank, Société Générale de Belgique, which was chartered by William I in 1822 to contribute towards the commercial progress of the Belgian Provinces. These banks could issue notes convertible into specie, discount bills, accept deposits and make advances. In addition to these banks, a number of investment trusts (or holding companies) had been established, which held shares in many of the industrial concerns founded by the Societe Generale.

Motivation for founding

Although banking had developed in Belgium, the use of bank notes remained comparatively limited, with metallic currency being widely used. The limited acceptability of bank notes, reinforced by a banking crisis in 1838–9, in turn constrained the extension of bank loans and the financing of enterprise throughout the 1840s. In 1848 the Paris Revolution triggered a widespread banking crisis in France and Belgium, culminating in the suspension of convertibility of bank notes in both of these countries.

This prompted a reform of the Belgian banking system, whose principal element was the establishment of a specialised bank of issue in 1850, the Banque Nationale de Belgique, which would permit the separation of note issue from ordinary banking activity. The largest note issuing banks were persuaded to abandon this business, and in return could subscribe to the entire capital of the newly formed Banque Nationale. In effect, therefore, the Banque Nationale became the sole note issuer. However, the charter of the Banque Nationale includes a clause which permits the government, by special law, to establish other note issuing banks.

Original objectives and functions

Whilst the Banque Nationale was a privately owned joint stock bank, the government appointed the Governor, who served as its chief executive officer, and a Special Commissioner, who oversaw its operations and reported to the Minister of Finance.

In addition to note issue, the Banque Nationale was permitted to discount bills, but these had to be of short maturity (120 days) and excellent credit quality (three reputable names). Industrial securities could not be held as assets, and government bonds could only be purchased up to an amount not exceeding its own capital and surplus. The Banque Nationale did, however, serve as the fiscal agent to the Treasury.

No fixed rule dictated the issue of notes, but the Banque Nationale was obliged to maintain (under normal circumstances) a metallic reserve equal to one third of its note issue. An important function was the rediscounting of paper offered by banks, so furnishing an 'elastic' supply of its notes and reducing the need for banks to hold large stocks of notes. The Banque Nationale was also intended to serve as a lender of last resort to the banking system.

Evolution of objectives and functions

Banque Nationale notes rapidly gained currency, and the use of these notes increased rapidly throughout the rest of the nineteenth century. Branches were soon established in most of the major cities, making it possible for local bankers to readily discount paper, reducing their need to hold cash deposits at the Banque Nationale. As in France, the use of deposits, and also cheques written on these deposits, remained limited until World War I, with notes (and coins) being the primary medium of exchange. Branch banking thus also remained extremely limited until World War I.

In 1865, Belgium entered what was known as the Latin Currency Union with France, Italy and Switzerland, which standardised the gold and silver coinage in these countries in terms of weight, standard and diameter for a period of fifteen years (and then continued by mutual agreement). Furthermore, silver coins were declared legal tender in each country, with governments accepting coins minted anywhere in the Union (up to a prespecified limit).

In 1871, however, Germany adopted the gold standard, causing a large inflow of demonetised German and Austrian coins into the Union for recoining. In 1873, therefore, silver coinage for individuals was effectively suspended. When the Union was renegotiated (in 1878), the members agreed to retain silver coins as legal tender, but placed limits on the quantity of coins which could be minted, and this remained the case until the eventual dissolution of the Union in 1925.

Up until World War I the Banque Nationale had held to the rule that its lending to government could not exceed its capital (plus surplus), but this was exceeded at the beginning of World War I as large advances were made by the Banque Nationale to the government. As in many other countries, gold convertibility was suspended in 1914. Thereafter, the maximum amount of Treasury notes allowed to be discounted by the Banque Nationale was periodically increased, reaching Bfr 1.5 billion by 1939. In that year another reform of the statutes of the Bank raised this limit to Bfr 5 billion.

Just after the start of World War I the right of note issue was (temporarily) withdrawn from the Banque Nationale by the German authorities, and granted instead to the Société Générale. Furthermore, in 1918 Germany engaged in forced repatriation of German marks held by the Banque Nationale by forcing it to convert these into interest yielding deposits held (by the German authorities) with Belgian banks.

After World War I, banking became considerably more concentrated, with larger banks absorbing smaller ones, effectively becoming branch banks in the process. Furthermore, banks could operate as universal banks, and owned large share portfolios. Until 1935 banks were not subject to any special legislation/regulation, apart from that prohibiting the issue of notes.

In 1935, following large losses which had been incurred by banks on their shareholdings during the Depression, banking legislation eliminated universal banking, causing banks to split into commercial banks and holding companies. Although commercial banks could underwrite share issues, these holdings had to be sold within six months. Furthermore, a Banking Commission – an independent agency, headed by a president and six members, all appointed for six years by Royal decree – was established to undertake banking regulation and supervision, and the imposition of liquid asset ratios was amongst the first regulations. In 1937 it was decreed that banks would have to submit monthly statements to the Banque Nationale.

The 1939 statute specified that the Minister of Finance 'shall have the right to control all the bank's operations' (Article 29) through the appointment of a Government Commissioner. However, a subsequent Article (30 bis) specified that the Minister of Finance and Government Commissioner could not oppose decisions of the Bank concerning the definition and implementation of monetary policy, the conduct of foreign exchange operations and the smooth operation of the payments system.

Independence

Although the Banque Nationale remains a joint stock company, 50 per cent of its shares are held by the government. A royal decree of 1939 articulated the activities, organisation and attributions of the Banque Nationale which, with some modifications, constitute its current statutes. These do not contain an explicit objective for the Banque Nationale, although its annual reports frequently assert that monetary stability is its ultimate objective.

The Banque Nationale is directed by a Governor and administered by a Board of Directors (of not less than three and not more than six members) assisted by a Council of Regency (comprising the Governor, Directors and ten regents). Although both the Governor and the Directors are appointed by the King, candidates for the Board of Directors are proposed by the Council of Regency. The government can object to any decision by the Banque Nationale (through a Government Commissioner, who supervises all its activities), but cannot compel it to take any action.

In 1993, and in accordance with the Maastricht Treaty, an Act was passed which gave the Banque Nationale greater independence. The Act now states that the government cannot oppose a decision taken by the Bank which relates to the key tasks of the central bank as contained in the Maastricht Treaty, i.e. the implementation of monetary and foreign exchange rate policy, the mangement of foreign reserves, and the promotion of the smooth operation of the payments system. Furthermore, the new Act also prohibits the extension of credit by the Banque Nationale to the government.

REFERENCES

Bank for International Settlements (1963) 'Banque Nationale de Belgique', in *Eight European Central Banks*. Allen and Unwin: London.

Cameron, R. (1963) 'Belgium 1800–1875', in R. Cameron *Banking in the Early Stages of Industrialisation*. Oxford University Press: Oxford.

Chlepner, B. S. (1943) *Belgian Banking and Banking Theory*. The Brookings Institution: Washington D.C.

Conant, C. (1909) *A History of Modern Banks of Issue*. G. P. Putnam's Sons: London.

Eizenga, W. (1994) 'The National Bank of Belgium and monetary policy', *SUERF Papers on Monetary Policy and Financial Systems*, No. 17.

Janssens, V. (1975) 'Le Franc Belge: un siècle et demi d'histoire monétaire', Manuscript, Vlaamse Economische Hogeschool.

Kauch, P. (1950) *La Banque Nationale de Belgique 1850–1918*. (Official history of the Bank of Belgium, 1850–1918, issued to commemorate its centenary). Brussels.

Lemoine, R. J. (1929) 'The banking system of Belgium', trans. F. Smith, in H. P. Willis and B. H. Beckhart (eds.) *Foreign Banking Systems*. Pitman and Sons: London.

Palgrave, R. H. I. (1903) *Bank Rate and the Money Market in England, France, Germany, Holland and Belgium 1844–1900*. John Murray: London.
Quaden, G. (1991) 'The recent reform of monetary policy in Belgium', *National Westminster Bank Quarterly Review*, February.
Van der Wee, H. and K. Tavernier (1975) *La Banque Nationale de Belgique et l'histoire monétaire entre les deux Guerres Mondiales 1918–1940*. (Official history of the Bank of Belgium between the two World Wars). Brussels.

B12   Banco de España (Bank of Spain)

Founded in 1856

Forerunner

In 1782 the Banco Nacional de San Carlos was established by the state (the bank itself was private), and extended loans, discounted bills and serviced the considerable debt issued by the state to alleviate revenue shortfalls arising from the discontinuation of metal shipments from the colonies. The bank was the only institution authorised to issue its own notes.

By 1800 the increasing indebtedness of the state resulted in an inability to redeem its debt which, comprising most of the assets of the Banco Nacional, led to its collapse. In 1829 the bank was recapitalised, becoming the Banco Español de San Fernando and taking over the note issuing privileges of its predecessor and its function as state bank.

In 1844 two other note banks were authorised but, following a crisis in 1847, one of these was merged with the Banco Español de San Fernanado, giving rise to the Nuevo Banco Español de San Fernando. When new banking legislation was introduced in 1856, this bank was renamed the Banco de España (hereafter the Bank).

Motivation for founding

A phase of economic prosperity, and a liberal government, resulted in new banking legislation being passed in 1856. This prescribed that there should not be more than one bank of issue in any county town, that new banks were to limit their issues to three times their capital and hold coin reserves of one third of their issue, and imposed a minimum denomination of 100 reales on banknotes.

These measures were clearly aimed at strengthening the position of the existing state bank, which was renamed the Banco de España. In addition, government influence over the Bank (and the banking system) increased, as the new legislation specified that the government was to appoint the Governor of the Bank (from a list of three nominees proposed by shareholders) as well the Royal Commissioners which would manage the other banks of issue.

Original objectives and functions

The Banco de España took over all the functions of its predecessor, namely to act as the government's bank, to issue bank notes, to undertake commercial lending and deposit activity, and to discount paper.

The Bank was privately capitalised, and its profits did not accrue to the state. However, note issue was subject to periodic contracts with the state, and the governor of the Bank was appointed by the state.

Evolution of objectives and functions

At the first renewal of its charter in 1874, burgeoning public deficits resulted in the Bank obtaining the exclusive right to issue bank notes, but only in exchange for a loan of 135 million pesetas to the state. All other issuing banks were given the option to continue as ordinary commercial banks or to become branches of the Banco de España (which many of them opted to do given their weak state).

At the same time the Bank's notes were declared legal tender (although these were still convertible into gold), and the maximum limit on note issue raised from three to five times the bank's capital. Gold convertibility was abandoned in 1883, and the limit on note issue raised in 1891 and 1898 (thereafter it was no longer applicable in practice). During this period a major activity of the Bank was meeting the needs of the public finances.

After a decade of fiscal stability, deficits reemerged in 1908. Difficulties with placing government debt led to the imposition of a system of automatic pledging of government debt at the Bank at 'non-penal' interest rates from 1917. This automatic pledge remained in force for the next forty years, and thus made the Bank into a passive supplier of liquidity (at favourable rates) throughout this period. It was replaced, in 1957, by a similar system of automatic rediscounting, under which specified private financial instruments were automatically rediscountable at the Bank in unlimited amounts.

Although the Bank's regulations did not specify its relationship with other banks, banking crises in 1913–14 saw the Bank acting as a lender of last resort. In 1921 a General Banking Act was passed which, for the first time, regulated the Bank's activities as a private bank (i.e. it became responsible for rediscounting bills offered to it by other banks) and as a central bank (i.e. the Bank, under the authority of the government, became responsible for managing the external value of the peseta). The state also strengthened its influence over the Bank by taking control of the note issue.

The 1921 Banking Act established a Banking Supervisory Council (i.e. a self-regulatory body) and specified that the Banco de España should supervise banks. The Bank did not perform this task initially, however, since its commercial activities still made it a competitor of other banks. Thus the banking system remained essentially self-regulated by local Banking Boards until 1938, when supervisory responsibility was transferred to the Ministry of Finance. Following the nationalisation of the Bank in 1962, supervision again became its responsibility.

Whilst private banks had accounts with the Banco de España since the turn of the century, these were used primarily for purposes of pledging public debt and/or rediscounting bills rather than for interbank clearing. Several private clearing houses were established in 1922 under the authorisation and supervision of the Banking Supervisory Council, and it is only since 1976 that banks began to utilise a wholesale payment system provided and overseen by the Bank.

In 1931 government influence over the Banco de España increased, when it was declared that rediscount rates were to be set by the Minister of Finance, and this decision was formally ratified in 1938. Dependence on the government became total in 1962 when the Bank was nationalised, and legislation was passed which stated that 'monetary authority ... shall be exercised permanently by the government through the Minister of Finance'. Nationalisation of the Bank finally saw the integration and elaboration of all the functions commonly undertaken by other central banks. The Bank's objective was stated as the pursuit of a 'monetary and credit policy ... most suited to the country's interests'.

Although the purpose and functions of the Banco de España were redefined in 1980, these remained essentially the same as before, as did the Bank's autonomy.

Independence

Although it was established as a wholly private bank, the independence of the Banco de España has never been substantial, and was steadily eroded over time until its nationalisation in 1962.

During the nineteenth century, for example, the limit on the Bank's note issue was readily increased whenever state financing demanded this, and the limit abandoned altogether in 1898. Moreover, from 1917, for the next forty years, the Bank was forced to purchase public debt at 'non-penal' interest rates. In 1931 the government explicitly took control of the Bank's discount rate, a decision which was formally ratified in 1938 and which remained in force until 1977.

In 1993 a Draft Act facilitating the autonomy of the Banco de España was drawn up, and is expected to be approved in 1994. Under this Act, the definition and implementation will become the responsibility of the Bank, and government financing by the Bank legally forbidden.

REFERENCES

Banco de España (1970) *El Banco de España: Una Historia Economica.* (The Bank of Spain: An Economic History). Madrid.

Banco de España (1982) *El Banco de España: Dos Siglos de Historia 1782–1982. (The Bank of Spain: Two Centuries of History 1782–1982). Madrid.*

Banco de España (1983) (Compiled by G. Perez de Armiñan) Legislacion Bancaria Española (Spanish Banking Legislation). Sixth edition. Madrid.

Conant, C. A. (1909) *A History of Modern Banks of Issue.* G. P. Putnam's Sons: London

Hamilton, E. J. (1945) 'The foundation of the Bank of Spain', *Journal of Political Economy*, 53.

Hamilton, E. J. (1946) 'The first twenty years of the Bank of Spain', *Journal of Political Economy*, 54.

Martín-Aceña, P. (1987) 'Development and modernisation of the financial system, 1844–1935', in N. Sántchez Albornoz (ed.) *The Economic Modernisation of Spain.* New York University Press.

Martín-Aceña, P. (1993) 'Spain during the classical gold standard years', in Bordo, M. D. and F. Capie (eds.) *Monetary Regimes in Transition.* Cambridge University Press: Cambridge.

Pellicer, M. (1993) 'Functions of the Banco de España: an historical perspective', Banco de España, Servicio de Estudios, Documento de Trabajo No. 9330.

B13   Nippon Ginko (Bank of Japan)

Founded in 1882

Forerunner

None.

Motivation for founding

Following the overthrow of the feudal system in 1867, the new Meiji government began to issue inconvertible paper money. In 1872 private banks were authorised to issue their own notes (the banking system was based upon the National Banking System of the US) which were initially convertible into silver. In 1876, however, legislation was introduced which permitted these banks to redeem their notes in government money, leading to a vast expansion in the overall note issue.

Efforts were made in 1878 to impose monetary stability by reducing the note issue and restoring the specie convertibility of all notes; these included a prohibition on the establishment of private banks, government suspension of new issues of notes and the issue of (interest bearing) government bills instead. Another element in this monetary reform included the formation of the Bank of Japan, a joint stock bank with a majority shareholding by the government, whose major initial task was to assist the government in retiring inconvertible bank notes.

Original objectives and functions

A primary initial objective of the Bank of Japan was to implement a reduction in the stock of inconvertible bank notes, and the Bank did not at first issue its own notes. Instead, it became the government's bank and the custodian of the government's specie reserves. When (in 1885) these had become sufficiently large relative to the outstanding stock of government paper money, the Bank began to issue its own notes which, along with government notes, became convertible into silver in 1886 (unlike many other countries, therefore, Japan did not adopt a gold standard during the 1880s).

Besides the retirement of inconvertible notes, the bank was also expected to serve a broader purpose, namely to consolidate the banking system and promote industrialisation (these were explicitly incorporated into the Bank of Japan Law of 1882). The Bank did not function as a commercial bank, and was prohibited from making advances against real property and owning real property or shares. The Bank was permitted to purchase and sell government bonds and specie, discount domestic and foreign bills and accept bankers' deposits. In a memorandum outlining the rationale of the Bank, the Minister of Finance noted the importance of an institution which would supply currency to the banking system, both to smooth out seasonal fluctuations in interest rates, and to avoid banking crises. Informally, therefore, the Bank served as a lender of last resort from its inception.

Ownership of the Bank was split between the government (50 per cent) and the (Japanese) public (50 per cent), but the Governor, Vice Governor and four directors which made up the Assembly of Officers (or Governing Board) were all appointed by the government (although directors were nominated by public shareholders). The charter of the Bank specified that the government 'shall control all the operations of the Bank' (Article 24), and policy was essentially dictated by the Minister of Finance.

Evolution of objectives and functions

In 1883 banking regulations were amended so that private banks would lose their right to issue notes upon expiration of their existing charters. This finally occurred in 1899, when private bank notes ceased to be issued, and coincided with the retirement of all the paper money which had previously been issued by the government.

In 1884 the Convertible Bank Note Regulation was passed, authorising the Bank to issue its own notes. Although this was based upon similar regulations elsewhere (Germany and Belgium), which usually stipulated the legal maximum note issue or minimum specie reserve, no such criteria were adopted in Japan: note issue remained at the discretion of the Minister of Finance, and was often raised substantially through government borrowing from the Bank.

A war indemnity paid to Japan by China in 1895 increased gold reserves sufficiently for the gold standard to be adopted in 1897. Unlike many other countries, who suspended the gold standard at the onset of World War I, Japanese gold reserves actually increased due to its exports. Suspension of convertibility did occur in 1917, however, following the Russian revolution, and continued until 1930. Convertibility was briefly resumed in 1930, but abandoned again in 1931 and never restored.

During World War II (1942) the Bank of Japan Act was amended (modeled on the Reichsbank Act of Germany), with the objectives of the Bank becoming 'the regulation of the currency, the facilitation of credit and finance, and the maintenance and fostering of the credit system, pursuant to the national [economic] policy'. In addition, management of the Bank became totally subordinate to the Minister of Finance (Article 43) (see below), and the government ownership share in the bank was increased to 55 per cent.

Although private clearing houses had already been established in 1879 (Osaka) and 1887 (Tokyo), these were remodelled after the UK Town Clearing system in 1896 and 1891 respectively, with banks using accounts at the Bank of Japan for settlement purposes. From its inception the Bank had been providing clearing and settlement services to the government, banks and other financial institutions. More recently, in 1988, the Bank has introduced an electronic settlement system (BOJ-NET).

The Bank also became involved, at an early stage, in prudential oversight of financial institutions, and monitored their lending activity. In 1928, following a recommendation of the Financial System research Council, the Bank started on-site examination of those banks which had an account with it. This supervisory role received statutory backing in 1942, when the Bank was formally charged with maintaining and fostering the credit system.

Independence

Originally management of the Bank was undertaken by an Assembly of Officers, comprising a Governor, Vice Governor and four directors.

However, in 1942, following the amendment of the bank of Japan Law, the Governor and Vice Governor were deprived of any voting rights, and the Governor authorised to regulate and control the affairs of the bank on his own authority.

In 1949 a seven-member Policy Board was established, and was given sole authority over interest rate policy and thenceforth took sole responsibility for changing the official discount rate. This Board was composed of a Governor, four (Cabinet-appointed) members taken from the banking, commercial or industrial sector, and two (non-voting) government representatives.

Override provisions, which give the Minister of Finance the ultimate power to make important policy decisions, have been in force since 1942, although it is widely understood that it would be extraordinary if the government resorted to these provisions, and they have never been enacted. The Bank has thus enjoyed independence in practice.

REFERENCES

Bank of Japan Law
Bank of Japan (1964) *The Bank of Japan: Its Function and Organisation*. Economic Research Department. Tokyo.
Bank of Japan (1982) *Nippon Ginko Hyakunenshi*. (Centennial History of the Bank of Japan). Tokyo.
Kuroda, A. (1992) 'Central banking in Japan: an overview', paper presented at the 19th SEANZA Central banking Course, Tokyo, November.
Patrick, H. T. (1962) 'Monetary policy and central banking in contemporary Japan', University of Bombay, Series in Monetary and International Economics, 5.
Sarasas, P. (1940) *Money and Banking in Japan*. Heath Cranton: London.
Shinjo, H. (1962) *History of the Yen*. The Research Institute for Economics and Business Administration, Kobe University.
Suzuki, Y. (1987) *The Japanese Financial System*. Clarendon: Oxford.
Tagaki, R. (1960) 'Central banking in Japan', in S. G. Davies (ed.) *Central Banking in South and East Asia*. Hong Kong.
Wikawa, T. (1929) 'The banking system of Japan', in Willis, H. P. and B. H. Beckhart (eds.) *Foreign Banking Systems*. Sir Isaac Pitman and Sons: London.

B14   Banca d'Italia

Founded in 1893

Forerunner

Italian unification in 1861 led to the formation of the National Bank in the Kingdom of Italy (previously the National Bank of Sardinia) which, together with three other banks, constituted the earliest note-issuing banks in Italy (notes were convertible into silver). Following heavy lending to the state (to finance its war with Austria) these banks were allowed to suspend the convertibility of their notes between 1866 and 1883. Two other note issuing banks were subsequently authorised (in 1863 and 1871), and their notes become legal tender along with the notes of the existing banks. At the same time the government imposed limits on the note issue of individual banks.

Although convertibility was restored in 1883, and the discount policy of banks subjected to government authority in 1885, note issues expanded dramatically throughout the 1880s, culminating in a banking crisis in 1893. This resulted in the collapse of one issuing bank and, as part of a government rescue operation, the merger of two others (from Tuscany) with the National Bank to form the Banca d'Italia.

Motivation for founding

A banking crisis in 1893 resulted in the (government co-ordinated) merger of three existing banks of issue to form the Banca d'Italia.

Original objectives and functions

The Banca d'Italia (hereafter the Bank) was organised as a joint stock bank which was privately owned. Shareholders elected the governing body of the Bank, the Bank Council, as well as the Governor of the Bank, although this appointment was subject to the sanction of the government.

The Bank continued the note issuing and the commercial banking business of its predecessors, and the latter included accepting deposits, discounting bills and making advances (including advances to the government). In this regard, therefore, the Banca d'Italia was largely indistinguishable from, and competed with, the other two note-issuing banks which had also survived the 1893 banking crisis, namely the Bank of Sicily and the Bank of Naples. The Bank was granted the privilege of issuing 80 per cent of the total note issue, whilst the other two banks were allocated 15 per cent and 5 per cent respectively.

Given their low specie reserves, the notes issued by these banks were not convertible (and did not become convertible until 1927). However, the government imposed maximum issue limits and it was decreed that issuing banks had to achieve a 30 per cent specie reserve by 1907. Notes issued in excess of these imposed limits had to be covered in full by specie, but notes advanced to the Treasury were exempted from this provision. Finally, the government precluded these banks from extending mortgage loans.

As far as note-issuing banks were concerned, therefore, the only distinguishing feature of the Banca d'Italia seems to have been its role as the official depository for state funds, especially in the provinces.

Evolution of objectives and functions

Between 1894 and 1926 the Banca d'Italia remained the largest of three large note-issuing banks, and its leading – some would say central banking – role was reinforced by its being the main advisor to the state in monetary and banking matters. Furthermore, during financial crises (1907 and 1911) the Bank extended lender of last resort loans to the wider banking system, although usually by leading consortia of commercial banks.

In 1910, however, responsibility for setting the discount rate of the Banca d'Italia (and the other note issuing banks) was transferred to the Treasury Minister. Furthermore, in 1926, in preparation for the resumption of gold payments, the Fascist government decided to increase the international standing of the Banca d'Italia by stripping other banks of their note issuing privileges. At the same time lending limits and reserve requirements were imposed upon commercial banks, and a regulatory agency was created (under the control of the Banca d'Italia) to supervise banks. Thus although the Bank continued to function as a privately owned commercial bank after 1926, it had effectively become a central bank.

During a major banking reform in 1936 the Bank ceased to be a joint stock company, becoming an institution incorporated under public law (i.e. existing shareholders were bought out and new shares issued which could only be held by other institutions incorporated under public law). At the same time the Bank could no longer conduct discount and lending business with non-bank customers, and became officially responsible for the smooth functioning of the payments system. Lastly, the Bank was obliged to extend a credit line to the Treasury equal to 15 per cent of projected government expenditures, and no formal limit was specified as to the government debt which could be held by the Bank.

From 1936 administration of the Bank was undertaken by a shareholder-elected Board of Directors (twelve), headed by the Governor of the Bank. Although the Governor had considerable discretion in formulating monetary policy, the authority for this rested ultimately with the government. In 1947 this authority was formally vested in the Interministerial Committee for Credit and Saving.

Independence

Although the Banca d'Italia remained a private institution between 1893 and 1936, government influence over its discount rate and its advances to the government was considerable.

Following its incorporation under public law in 1936, government influence of the Bank increased, with authority for monetary policy becoming formally vested in a government department in 1947. In practice, however, the Bank has enjoyed greater independence during the post-war period than its legal position suggests. Only in 1993 was the Bank legally granted the freedom to set the discount rate autonomously, and a bill drafted to abolish advances to the Treasury.

The Directorate of the Bank (consisting of the Governor, the Director General and two Deputy Director-Generals, all appointed by the Board of Directors) has the responsibility for carrying out its tasks.

REFERENCES

Bank for International Settlements (1963) 'Banca d'Italia', in *Eight European Central Banks*. Allen and Unwin: London.

Ciampi, C. A. (1987) 'The functions of the central bank in today's economy', in P. Ciocca (ed.) *Money and the Economy: Central Bankers' Views*. St Martin's Press: New York.

Lo Faro, F. (1929) 'The banking system of Italy', in Willis, H. P. and B. H. Beckhart (eds.) *Foreign Banking Systems*. Sir Isaac Pitman and Sons: London.

Lutz, F. and V. Lutz (1950) 'Monetary and exchange policy in Italy', *Princeton Studies in International Finance*, 1.

Lutz, V. (1962) 'Italy II: the central bank and the system of credit control', in R. S. Sayers (ed.) *Banking in Western Europe*. Clarendon: Oxford.

Goodman, J. B. (1992) *Monetary Sovereignty: The Politics of Central Banking in Western Europe*. Cornell University Press: London.

Nardozzi, G. (1988) 'A central bank between the government and the credit system: the Bank of Italy after World War II', in Toniolo, G. (ed.) *Central Banks' Independence in Historical Perspective*. Walter de Gruyter: New York.

Sannucci, V. (1989) 'The establishment of a central bank: Italy in the 19th century', in De Cecco, M. and A. Giovannini (eds.) *A European Central Bank?* Cambridge University Press: Cambridge.

Toniolo, G. (1990) *An Economic History of Liberal Italy*. Routledge: London.

B15   Swiss National Bank

Founded in 1907

Forerunner

None. Following the establishment of the first note-issuing bank in 1836, banking developed rapidly in Switzerland, but remained completely unregulated until 1874 when, in a revision of the Federal constitution, authority to legislate note-issuing banks was given to the Federal government. Hereafter, all note-issuing banks were required to hold a specie (gold) reserve of 40 per cent and to redeem the notes of other banks in specie.

In 1881, further legislation limited the circulation of any individual bank to twice its capital, and required weekly reports to be submitted to a Federal Council. The Federal Assembly also reserved the right to fix the aggregate issue of notes and apportion this among banks. At no time, however, were bank notes guaranteed by the government or made legal tender.

Motivation for founding

Competition between issuers implied a wide variety of notes and discount rates, often leading to sustained outflows of specie. Support for centralisation and standardisation of note issue increased towards the end of the nineteenth century, and the ability to confer a note-issuing monopoly passed to the Federal Government in 1891.

However, disagreements about the form (i.e. state vs privately owned) and location of a central bank of issue delayed its establishment until 1907, when Parliament finally voted in favour of a Swiss National Bank, organised on a joint stock basis, with ownership being spread between the cantons (63 per cent) and private shareholders (37 per cent).

Original objectives and functions

According to the Federal Constitution, the National Bank's chief function was to regulate the country's money circulation and facilitate payment transactions. To this end the Bank issued convertible notes (against which it had to hold specie reserves of 40 per cent) and discounted eligible short-term paper at a specified discount rate.

The Bank also immediately became the government bank (i.e. it accepted, and paid interest on, government deposits, administered the national debt and participated in the issue of government bonds), the bankers bank (i.e. it managed the clearing system and acted as lender of last resort, although the latter function was not formally specified), and a custodian of gold and foreign exchange. Regulation and supervision of the banking system was not a function of the Bank: this task was entrusted (in 1934) to the Federal Banking Commission, an autonomous body elected by the Federal Council.

The framework for the activity of the Bank was provided by the National Bank Law of 1905. Administration of the Bank was undertaken by a forty-member Bank Council, of which fifteen members were elected by stockholders and twenty-five by the Federal Government. In addition, a Bank Committee comprising the Chairman and Vice Chairman of the Bank Council, and eight other Bank Council members, undertook more detailed supervision and control of the Bank. Daily management of the Bank, and decisions regarding monetary policy, were (and still are) the responsibility of a Governing Board of three members, appointed by the Federal government on recommendation of the Bank Council.

Evolution of objectives and functions

Up to 1914 (and again between 1925–1936) the gold standard dictated Bank policy. With the onset of World War I, gold convertibility was suspended, and large loans made to the government. Throughout the war, government influence over the bank (and the banking system) was considerable. Convertibility was again suspended in 1936.

The National Bank Law was amended in 1921, 1953 and 1978. After 1953 the Bank abolished convertibility into gold, its notes were declared legal tender, and the overall objective of the Bank became the pursuit of a credit and monetary policy 'serving the interests of the country as a whole'. Following the abolition of fixed exchange rates in 1973, the Bank's main objective has been to stabilise the price level.

Independence

The National Bank is largely independent, as neither the Federal Council nor Parliament may issue policy Directives to the Bank's Governing Board. This Board, which is responsible for monetary policy, consists of three full time members appointed for six years by the Federal Council.

REFERENCES

Bank for International Settlements (1963) 'Schweizerische Nationalbank', in *Eight European Central Banks*. Allen and Unwin: London.

Hoffmann, M. (1987) *Die Geschichte des Schweizerfrankens*. (The History of the the Swiss Franc). Zurich.

Hoffmann, M. (1992) *Geld-, Währungs-und Bankenschichte der Schweiz*. (The History of Swiss Money, Exchange Rates and Banking). Zurich.

Rich, G. (1991) 'The orientation of monetary policy and the monetary decision making process in Switzerland', in *The Orientation of Monetary Policy and the Monetary Decision Making Process*. Bank for International Settlements, Basle.

Schwarzenbach, E. (1929) 'The banking system of Switzerland', in Willis, H. P. and B. H. Beckhart (eds.) *Foreign Banking Systems*. Sir Isaac Pitman and Sons: London

Schweizerische Nationalbank (1982) *75 Jahre Schweizerische Nationalbank*. (75 Years of the Swiss National Bank). Zurich.

Schweizerische Nationalbank. (1992) *Functions, Instruments and Organisation*. Zurich.

Zimmerman, R. (1987) *Volksbank oder Aktienbank? Zur Gründungsgeschichte der Nationalbank.* (Public or Private Bank? The Foundation of the Swiss National Bank).

B16   Federal Reserve System

Founded in 1914

Forerunner

In 1791 the First Bank of the United States was established, modelled upon the Bank of England, and acted as a collector of and depository for public funds, issued notes and made loans to the Federal government. Organised as a joint stock bank, with private shareholders constituting the majority owners, the First Bank's twenty-year charter failed to be renewed in 1911 due to political opposition.

Government support for a new national bank resurfaced some years later, and the Second Bank of the United States was established in 1817, also as a private bank under a charter lasting twenty years. Like its predecessor, the Bank initially acted as the government bank, and issued its own notes, which competed with those of the numerous state banks that had arisen. Under the management of Nicholas Biddle, the Second Bank increased its commercial activity and assumed an active role in maintaining the nation's specie reserves.

Opposition to the Second Bank from President Jackson (supported by the state banks) resulted in the Bank's federal charter failing to be renewed, although the Bank received a state charter from Pennsylvania in 1936. The Bank then began to engage in risky lending ventures, however, which culminated in its failure in 1841.

The need for a safe and reliable government depository prompted the Independent Treasury Act of 1841, under which public receipts had to be in specie (or Treasury notes) and would be held and managed by the Treasury itself. This was immediately repealed, during which time several state banks acted as official depositories, although a second Act was passed successfully in 1846. In practice, however, the arrangement imposed large and periodic reserve imbalances upon the banking system, with the result that public funds were often placed with state banks anyway.

For the remainder of the nineteenth century, and until 1914, the United States had no institution which resembled the central banks that had been established elsewhere, although central banking functions were undertaken by the Independent Treasury (i.e. offsetting money market fluctuations through open market operations) and the New York Clearinghouse Association (i.e. clearing, and the provision of liquidity, in the form of loan certificates, during crises).

Motivation for founding

Since 1863 US banking operated according to the so-called National Banking System, under which all issuing banks were compelled to cover (fully) their note issues by holdings of Treasury debt. Whilst this effectively created a uniform national currency (and provided the government with a ready source of revenue), the arrangement rendered the supply of currency (notes) 'inelastic' since it meant that banks first had to obtain government debt before they could expand their note issue. Restrictions on branch banking compounded this problem, making it even more difficult for banks to meet sudden increases in the demand for notes. Finally, banks faced strict reserve requirements, which meant that they could not even use the notes which they had.

Not surprisingly, the National Banking System was prone to frequent banking panics. A particularly severe banking crisis in 1907 prompted increasing support for banking reform and the establishment of a mechanism which would render the currency supply more 'elastic'. A National Monetary Commission was set up in order to investigate this issue, and concluded that the formation of a decentralised system of central banks, as opposed to a single central bank, was the most appropriate solution.

Original objectives and functions

Under the Federal Reserve Act of 1913, twelve Federal Reserve banks were to be established under the umbrella of the Federal Reserve Board and designated the Federal Reserve System (the Fed, or the System). The Federal Reserve Board had seven members, including the Secretary of the Treasury, the Comptroller of the Currency and five members appointed by the President with the approval of the Senate. As such, there was considerable government influence over the affairs of the Bank. Federal Reserve Bank stock was owned by the banks which became members of the System, who elected six of the nine directors of each Bank, with the remaining three directors appointed by the Board of Governors.

The functions of the Fed included currency issue (currency was redeemable in gold, and had to be 40 per cent backed by gold or gold certificates), the provision of banking services to the government, the provision of discounting and clearing facilities to member banks, and the regulation and supervision of member banks. The System also became the custodian of the nation's gold and foreign exchange reserves, was considered as the lender of last resort and was committed to maintaining 'orderly' government debt markets.

Initially, each Bank conducted its own open-market operations, although it was proposed in 1915 that this function be centralised into one organisation which would undertake transactions for the System as a whole. This lead to the establishment (in 1923) of the Open Market Investment Committee, which became responsible for the open market policy of the System, to be implemented by the Federal Reserve Bank of New York given the concentration of money market activity in the city.

Evolution of objectives and functions

Although Federal Reserve Banks were originally free to set different discount rates, authority over these rates was (implicitly) transferred to the Federal Reserve Board in 1927, after which these rates did not vary across Banks.

From its establishment (at the outset of World War I) the Federal Reserve typically accepted the discount rate which was decided by the Treasury, given its stated objective of maintaining an orderly market for government securities. In 1933 it was proposed that the two Treasury officials no longer sit on the Board of Governors, and they were finally unseated in 1935.

Following the Great Depression (1933), however, government influence over the Fed increased significantly due to the Thomas Amendment, which gave the Secretary of the Treasury power over the credit policy of the Fed, and the Emergency Banking Act 1933, which effectively forced the System to cooperate with the government, otherwise its policy would be overridden. Additional changes during the 1930s were also aimed at centralising authority within the Fed, and the Federal Reserve Board (which became the Board of Governors in 1935) was granted the power to alter reserve requirements and set deposit interest rate ceilings.

Throughout the following decades Treasury influence over the Fed remained substantial, especially due to the growing Federal debt which accompanied World War II. In 1950 disagreements between the Fed and the Treasury became public, exemplifying the continuing struggle between them over discount policy. Following an Accord in 1951, the Fed agreed to co-operate with the Treasury in future, but reduced its level of commitment to maintaining orderly markets in public securities.

Independence

The Federal Reserve was not established as an independent institution, although the nature of its dependence has not been formally specified. As in many other countries, government influence over the Fed has been at its strongest during periods of upheaval and crisis (i.e. the World Wars, the

Great Depression), which have been accompanied by substantial increases in the level of government borrowing.

The Fed has periodically had policy disagreements with Treasury (some of them public), however, and in 1979 even changed its operating procedures to implement higher interest rates when this was politically undesirable. In practice, therefore, the independence of the Fed has depended to a significant extent on the character of the Chairman of the Board of Governors.

REFERENCES

Beckhart, B. J. (1972) *Federal Reserve System*. Columbia University Press: New York.

Belongia, M. T. (1991) *Monetary Policy on the 75th Anniversary of the Federal Reserve System. Proceedings of the 14th Annual Conference of the Federal Reserve Bank of St Louis*. Kluwer: Boston.

Board of Governors of the Federal Reserve System and the United States Treasury Department (1963) *The Federal Reserve and the Treasury: Answers to Questions from the Commission on Money and Credit*. Prentice Hall: Englewood Cliffs.

Burns, A. F. (1985) *Reflections of an Economic Policymaker: Speeches and Congressional Statements 1969–1978*. American Enterprise Trust for Public Policy Research: Washington D. C.

Clark, L. E. (1935) *Central Banking under the Federal Reserve System*. Macmillan: New York.

Clifford, A. J. (1965) *The Independence of the Federal Reserve System*. University of Pennsylvania Press: Philadelphia.

Fforde, J. S. (1954) *The Federal Reserve System 1945–1949*. Clarendon: Oxford.

Friedman, M and A. J. Schwartz (1963) *A Monetary History of the United States, 1867–1960*. Princeton University Press: Princeton.

Hurst, J. W. (1983) *A Legal History of Money in the United States 1774–1970*. University of Nebraska Press: Lincoln.

Johnson, G. G. (1939) *The Treasury and Monetary Policies 1933–38*. Harvard University Press: Cambridge MA.

Kemmerer, E. W. (1932) *The ABC of the Federal Reserve System*. Princeton University Press: Princeton.

Laughlin, J. L. (1933) *The Federal Reserve Act: Its Origins and Problems*. Macmillan: New York.

Mayer, T. (ed.) (1990) *The Political Economy of American Monetary Policy*. Cambridge University Press: Cambridge.

Miron, J. A. (1989) 'The founding of the Fed and the destabilisation of the post-1914 US economy', in De Cecco, M. and A. Giovannini (eds.) *A European Central Bank?* Cambridge University Press: Cambridge.

Moore, C. H. (1990) *The Federal Reserve System: Anatomy of the First 75 Years*. McFarland and Co.: London.

Smith, V. (1936) *The Rationale of Central Banking*. P. S. King and Son: London.

Sylla, R. (1988) 'The autonomy of the monetary authorities: the case of the U. S.

Federal Reserve System', in Toniolo, G. (ed.) *Central Banks' Independence in Historical Perspective.* Walter de Gruyter: New York.

Taus, E. T. (1943) *Central Banking Functions of the United States Treasury, 1789–1941.* Columbia University Press: New York.

Timberlake, R. H. (1993) *Central Banking in the United States.* University of Chicago Press: Chicago.

Willis, H. P. (1923) *The Federal Reserve System: Legislation, Organisation and Operation.* Ronald Press Co.: New York.

B17   South African Reserve Bank

Founded in 1920

Forerunner

None, although proposals for a central bank were regularly made by the Afrikaner Bond (a political organisation) since 1879, and further proposals were prompted by the formation of the Union of South Africa in 1910.

The formation of the Union did not change the banking regulations which had hitherto applied in the respective colonies. Typically, several commercial banks issued notes payable in gold (and denominated in pound sterling), but had to observe either a maximum issue limit (e.g. equal to their capital in the Cape Province) or a minimum specie reserve (e.g. 30 per cent in the Orange Free State).

Motivation for founding

Unlike in many other countries, gold convertibility was not suspended in South Africa at the beginning of World War I, although an embargo was placed on gold exports. Following World War I, when the pound depreciated against the dollar, it became profitable to smuggle gold from South Africa and sell it abroad. This placed commercial banks in the difficult position of having to redeem their notes at par but restore their gold reserves at a premium, and they called for a suspension of convertibility.

This situation prompted a 'Gold Conference', which resolved to establish a Mint, lift the gold export embargo, and thereby 'naturalise' exchange rates between South Africa and Britain. At the same time, the Conference wanted to unify banking regulations so as to reduce the potential for inflation. This latter aim led the Government to consult overseas experts (in particular, Henry Strakosch, a London financier), who advised that the conservation of specie reserves would be best achieved via the issue of (temporarily in-convertible) gold certificates by a central 'Reserve Bank'. It was also argued that the transfer of monopoly note issue to this Reserve Bank would simplify the control of inflation.

In 1920, therefore, a Currency and Banking Act was passed, facilitating the establishment of the South African Reserve Bank (hereafter the Bank) which would begin business the following year. The provisions of the Act were based largely on the operation of the Bank of Java (and, thereby, the Nederlandsche Bank) and the Federal Reserve System.

Original objectives and functions

According to the 1920 Act the Bank was to be the sole currency issuer (this was achieved in 1924), the custodian of the country's gold and foreign exchange reserves, a bank of rediscount and lender of last resort, and the custodian of the cash reserves of the banking system. This last function meant that the Bank provided interbank clearing and settlement services. Originally, the Bank was not the government bank, although government accounts were transferred to the Bank in 1927.

Although the Bank issued inconvertible gold certificates, inconvertibility was deemed to be a temporary measure (and was only granted until 1923), and the Bank had to hold a specie reserve of 40 per cent of its note issue. Other banks in the Union had to hold reserves (at the Bank) equal to 13 per cent of their demand liabilities and 3 per cent of their time liabilities.

The Bank was founded as a private company, with 30 per cent of its capital being allotted to the commercial banks and 70 per cent to the public. Administration of the Bank was undertaken by a Board of eleven Directors. Of these, five (including the Governor and Deputy Governor) were appointed by the Governor-General (i.e. the government) and the remainder by shareholders.

Evolution of objectives and functions

Three years after it was passed, the Currency and Banking Act was amended, prompted by the near failure of a large bank in 1922 (which had necessitated substantial lending by the Bank) and by the desire to maintain the inconvertibility of Bank notes (since their parity with gold had not yet been achieved). Consequently, amendments to the Act in 1923 included extensions to the types of financial assets which the Bank could purchase (these were again extended in 1930) and to the period of inconvertibility (this was extended to 1925).

In addition, the three banking representatives on the Board of Directors were removed, being replaced by further representatives from the commercial arena, as it was felt that banking representatives compromised the Board's ability to discuss the Bank's discount policy openly and independently.

In 1925 it was decided (on the advice of the Kemmerer-Vissering Commission) that convertibility of notes into gold specie (not bullion, as in Britain) would be resumed, and this was maintained until 1931 when, along with most other countries, South Africa abandoned the gold standard. Thereafter, and until World War II, South Africa effectively remained part of the sterling 'area', since the Bank maintained a fixed parity with the pound, and kept most of its non-gold reserves in that currency.

In 1941 the Bank was, for the first time, authorised to invest in government securities in excess of its capital and reserves. The following year a major revision of banking regulation occurred (the Banking Act of 1942), which saw the imposition and supervision of liquidity requirements by the Bank for the first time.

With the renewal of the Bank's charter (due to expire in 1945) in 1944, the amended Currency and Banking Act was replaced by the Reserve Bank Act, under which the Bank's currency monopoly was extended indefinitely, and many of the existing restrictions on its ability to discount and make advances and investments were abolished. Contrary to the tendency in many other countries, the Bank remained privately owned, although the maximum individual shareholding was reduced (from £10,000 to £5,000).

The most recent revision of the Bank's statutes occurred in 1989, when the primary objectives of the Bank were stated for the first time, being the pursuit of 'monetary stability and balanced economic growth in the Republic'.

Independence

No formal division of monetary responsibilities between the Bank and the government has existed, nor has any attempt been made to lay down administrative constitutional arrangements governing coordination between these two bodies. Throughout the Bank's history there has been regular consultation and close co-operation between it and the Treasury in all matters relating to monetary policy, and the two are regarded as jointly constituting the monetary authority.

In 1956, for example, the Minister of Finance stated that 'the Reserve Bank is an autonomous statutory institution, deliberately divorced from political control, and no Minister of Finance has the right to dictate credit policy to the Reserve bank, nor has any Minister attempted to do so'. This remains the position to date, as a recent Commission of Inquiry into the monetary system (the De Kock Commission) has reiterated this joint responsibility for monetary policy.

REFERENCES

Arndt, E. H. D. (1928) *Banking and currency development in South Africa 1652–1927.*
Juta & Co.: Cape Town.
Barker, H. A. F. (1952) *The Principles and Practice of Banking in South Africa.* Juta
& Co.: Johannesburg.
De Kock, G. (1954) *A History of the South African Reserve Bank 1920–52.* J. L. Van
Schaik: Pretoria.
De Kock Commission (1985) *Final Report of the Commission of Inquiry into the
Monetary System and Monetary Policy in South Africa.*
Du Plessis, E (1980) 'Structure and operation of the Reserve Bank and its relation-
ship to the Government', *Modern Business Law*, July.
Falkena, H. B. (1989) *The Mechanics of the South African Financial System.* Mac-
millan: London.
Olakanpo, J. O. (1965) *Central Banking in the Commonwealth.* Bookland Private:
Calcutta.
Plumptre, A. F. W. (1940) *Central Banking in the British Dominions.* University of
Toronto Press: Toronto.
South African Reserve Bank (1971) *The South African Reserve Bank 1921–1951: A
Short Historical Review Issued in Commemoration of the Bank's Fiftieth Anni-
versary.*

B18   El Banco de la Republica (The Bank of Colombia)

Founded in 1923

Forerunner

None. The banking history of Colombia, prior to the establishment of the
Banco de la Republica in 1923, was a continuous struggle to adopt the gold
standard and avoid excessive paper money issues stemming from civil wars
and fiscal requirements.

In 1886, notes issued by the Banco Nacional (a state bank established in
1881) became recognised by the government as legal tender, and all other
banks were banned from issuing notes. These notes, however, soon became
inconvertibile due to a fiscal crisis. Despite obtaining special privileges and
being the government's bank, the Banco Nacional did not develop into a
proper central bank. An overissue of notes led to the Banco Nacional's
liquidation in 1896, although the notes that had been issued by the Banco
continued to be the legal tender until 1905, when the law which had
established the monetary system expired.

When political stability returned, the introduction of monetary stability
became a priority. So, in 1903 the Government started considering projects
and, by the end of the year, the Junta Nacional de Amortización (an
independent body) was created. Although it was granted reserves in order to

replace the paper peso with a gold peso, and a law was passed to prohibit the issue of paper money for fiscal reasons, convertibility was not restored.

A second attempt to introduce gold convertibility and to stabilise the currency was made in 1905, with the creation of a private bank, the Banco Central, which was to have the sole right of issuing banknotes. However, its existence was short-lived, and it was liquidated in 1909, without having fulfilled its main purpose.

Then, in 1909, the Junta de Conversión was created to assume central banking responsibilities and to introduce the gold standard. Although the Junta ultimately failed to achieve this – like its predecessors – it would intervene in the foreign exchange market using gold to maintain the external value of the peso. Indeed, between 1910 and the establishment of a central bank in Colombia in 1923, exchange rate fluctuations of the peso were minimal.

Motivation for founding

During the early twentieth century, constant attempts were made to establish a centralised banking system and to move away from inconvertible paper money. Most experts were in favour of a central bank primarily to promote the gold standard, which they believed would curb exchange and price instability. Hence, after 1917 different projects which supported a central bank were presented in the Congress.

In 1922 a law providing for the establishment of a central bank was passed and a charter approved. Furthermore, Edwin Kemmerer (an economics professor at Princeton) was invited by the government to modernise the country's banking system in accordance with the expanding needs of the economy. At the time of his appointment, banks remained few in number, credit was scarce, and capital mobility was restricted.

The influence exerted by the Kemmerer mission on the establishment of the Banco de la República is debatable, as the foundations for a central bank were already in place when Kemmerer reached Colombia. Many of the elements of the 1922 central banking law also appeared in the 1923 law. However, the mission undoubtedly reinforced the changes which were taking place by influencing public opinion in favour of the reorganisation of the financial system and by increasing foreign confidence to invest in Colombia.

Original objectives and functions

The Bank was granted a monopoly of issue for twenty years, with its notes being convertible into gold. Its notes became legal tender, and the government began undertaking the task of withdrawing from circulation all the heterogeneous inconvertible notes which had served as currency. The Bank also became the fiscal agent, but was subject to a legal limit (equal to 30 per cent of its capital) on the amount it could lend to the government.

The 1923 law stated explicitly that the Bank should be at the centre of the banking system in Colombia, and that all the important banks of the country should hold accounts with the Bank. This is one of the fundamental differences between the Bank's final charter and the original 1922 central banking law, which contained no such provision. The Bank could receive deposits from commercial banks, as well as buying and selling securities from them, and also became responsible for the liquidity of the banking system.

According to the founding law of the Banco de la República (hereafter the Bank), it had a mixed ownership as the State, banks and the public all held parts of the equity capital. The Bank was administered by a Board of Directors (the Junta Directiva) which consisted of nine members, three of which were government officials while the remainder came from the banking sector.

Evolution of objectives and functions

The first amendment to the charter of the Bank occurred in 1925, when the participation of representatives of the productive sectors in the Junta Derictiva was introduced, despite strong opposition from the commercial banks. Four further amendments to the initial law of 1923 are also important, occurring in 1951, 1963, 1973 and most recently in 1991.

The years 1946–1954 were a turbulent period in the social and political history of Colombia. The Bank extended significant credits to the commercial banks and government, either directly or through debt purchases. A revision of Bank's charter in 1951 changed the objectives of the Bank, with the aim of monetary policy becoming aimed at accelerating economic development. For this purpose the Bank was granted new powers over monetary policy.

Further changes to the objectives and functions of the Bank occurred in 1963, aimed this time at coordinating monetary and other economic policies, and tightening the government's direction over the Bank. A monetary body known as the Junta Monetaria was established, which diminshed the status of the Bank. The Junta became the supreme monetary authority, and its objectives were to determine monetary policy and the external value of the currency. The Junta consisted of four members, including the Director of the Bank and was presided over by the Minister of Finance.

In 1973 the Bank was nationalised, although the Junta Monetaria continued to be the supreme monetary authority. The powers of the Junta

Monetaria were strengthened, and now included the determination of banks' reserve requirements. Finally, the Fondo de Estabilización was created to undertake open market operations.

The current law, dating from 1991, re-assigns the responsibility for monetary policy, and for credit and exchange rate policy, to the Bank, and is aimed at maintaining the autonomy of the Bank. The objectives and functions determined by the charter of 1991 relate to its roles as issuing bank, fiscal agent and bankers' bank.

Independence

The founding charter of the Banco de la República granted it a degree of independence, as it stressed the private rather than the public character of the Bank. Only three out of nine (later ten) members of the Junta Directiva, the Board of Directors of the Bank, were appointed by the government. However, during the 1940s and 1950s, commercial banks and powerful interest groups (such as the National Coffee Growers Federation) exerted pressures on the Bank, which weakened its resolve to constrain monetary growth and diminished its independence.

It is noteworthy that, in 1963, the Bank was the only central bank in Latin America which had not been nationalised. However, the revision of its charter in that year significantly increased the influence of the government on the Bank. Furthermore, the Bank lost the authority to determine monetary policy, which shifted to the Junta Monetaria, leaving the Bank to implement policy as determined by the Junta.

The key personalities on the Junta Monetaria were the Minister of Finance and the Governor (or, General Manager, as this title is known) of the Banco de la República (who was elected by the Junta Directiva). The Minister of Finance was thus able to influence and dominate the activities of the Bank and the course of monetary policy. This dominance increased in 1973, when the Bank was nationalised.

The 1991 charter of the Bank, however, aimed to restore the autonomy of the Bank. Although the Junta Directiva (the Board of Directors) was still chaired by the Minister of Finance, he had the same voting power as other members of the Junta. This Junta now consisted of seven members, of which the President of the Republic was not allowed to nominate more than two during a term of office. Finally, any credits or advances to the government require the unanimous approval of the Junta.

REFERENCES

Aguirre Carrillo, E. (1991) *La Genesis de la Banca Central*. Banco de la República: Bogotá.

Banco de la República (1990) *El Banco de la República: Antecedentes, Evolución y Estructura*. Bogotá.

Banco de la República (1991) *LXVIII Informe anual del Gerente a la Junta Directiva*.

Banco de la República (1994) *Kemmerer y el Banco de la República: Diarios y Documentos*. Bogotá

Díaz-Alejandro, C. F. (1976) *Foreign Trade Regimes and Economic Development: Colombia*. National Bureau of Economic Research: New York.

Drake, P. W. (1989) *The Money Doctor in the Andes, The Kemmerer Missions 1923–1933*. Duke University Press: London.

Joslin, D. (1963) *A Century of Banking in Latin America*. Oxford University Press: Oxford.

La Banca Central en la Reforma Constitucional: explicación de la propuesta del Gobierno, 759 (January 1991).

McGreevey, W. P. (1971) *An Economic History of Colombia, 1845–1930*. Cambridge University Press: Cambridge.

Otero, M. (1948) *El Banco de la Republica 1923–1948*. Banco de la Republica: Bogota.

Recaman, J. (1980) *Historia Juridicia del Banco de la República*. Banco de la Republica: Bogota.

Reformas estructurales y estabilización (1991) *Revista del Banco de la República*. Separata Revista, No. 764 , June.

Sanchez, F. (1994) *Ensayos de Historia Monetaria y Bancaria de Colombia*. Terecer Mundo: Bogota.

Tamagna, F. (1965) *Central Banking in Latin America*. Centro de Estúdios Monetarios Latinoamericanos: México.

B19   Banco Central de Chile

Founded in 1925

Forerunner

None. However, proposals for a central bank had been made prior to 1925. As early as 1845, for example, the government established a committee to study the possibility of creating a state bank. Its proposals were rejected, although a state bank to foster agricultural activity (Caja de Crèdito Hipotecario) was created some years later.

Between 1918 and 1924 several concrete proposals for a central bank were put before the government but, as before, these were always rejected due to disagreements over its functions and objectives.

Motivation for founding

In 1925 the services of a Princeton professor, Edwin Kemmerer, were contracted by the President to evaluate and restructure the country's banking system, which at that time consisted of a number of banks, and the state, issuing inconvertible paper notes. The primary objective was to bring about monetary stabilisation by moving from a paper to a gold standard. This had been attempted several times previously, but had never been successfully maintained for any significant period of time. The legislation proposed by Kemmerer included the creation of a central bank.

Original objectives and functions

Based to some extent upon the Federal Reserve (particularly in that part of its capital was owned by commercial banks) the Banco Central de Chile (hereafter the Bank) acquired the monopoly to issue currency, which was convertible into gold. Against its note issue the Bank had to hold a minimum specie reserve of 50 per cent, and was taxed whenever this was not met. Interestingly, the Bank's statute (known as the First Organic Law) included an article (72) under which suspension of convertibility would lead to the Bank being declared bankrupt and liquidated. Not surprisingly, this clause was suspended in 1932, and the bank not liquidated, when convertibility was abandoned.

The Bank immediately became the government depository and fiscal agent. In addition the Bank was authorised to accept (non-interest bearing) deposits, as well as discount bills and make advances to financial and non-financial entities, although differential discount rates were applied to these two groups (banks faced lower rates than non-banks). The Bank also acted as the clearing agent for the banking system, and was expected to play the role of lender of last resort in the event of a crisis.

Ownership of the Bank was divided into four classes of shares, state (10 per cent), domestic commercial banks, foreign banks and the general public. Administration was undertaken by a ten member Board of Directors, of which three members were appointed by the government, three by banks, one by general shareholders, with the remaining three being representatives of agricultural, labour and commercial associations. The President of the Bank was elected by the Board of Directors.

Evolution of objectives and functions

Although the Bank was initially restricted from purchasing government securities in excess of 30 per cent of its paid up capital and reserves, legislation in 1932 gave the government authority to override this. In that year the Bank was also ordered to grant substantial credits, at preferential rates, to the government and to agricultural, mining, and industrial concerns.

Such preferential discount rates became a distinct feature of Bank practice throughout the interwar and post-World War II period, reflecting the desire to develop and sustain these sectors of the economy. At times this led to an extremely complicated rate structure, with over thirty different rates applicable at any one time.

Another role adopted by the Bank was the support of commodity markets, in particular copper. The Bank acted as a purchaser and exporter of copper, in turn utilising the foreign exchange for its exchange rate policy and for the allocation of foreign currency for government expenditures and 'essential' imports.

The Bank's Organic Law was revised in 1953, establishing the Bank as an autonomous entity of indefinite duration, and described its primary objective as 'striving towards the orderly and progressive development of the country's economy, through a monetary and loan policy that would, while trying to avoid inflationary or depressive trends, allow for better use of the country's productive resources'. In addition, the Bank was authorised to vary banks' reserve requirements and gained the ability to impose quantitative and qualitative controls over credit institutions. The Bank did not, however, supervise credit institutions, which had been entrusted to a government Superintendent of the Banks since 1926.

Another revision of the Bank's Organic Law occurred in 1960, which included the withdrawal of shares owned by the general public, a change in the composition and election of the Board of Directors and the creation of an Executive Committee to administer and manage the Bank. Although this Committee retains the management function, administrative authority, and the formulation of monetary and exchange rate policy, it was transferred to a five-member Monetary Council in 1975. This Council is chaired by the President of the Bank who, along with the other members (all from the government), are all appointed by the Minister of Finance.

In the latest revision of the Bank's Organic Law, in 1990, the objectives of the Bank became 'the stability of the currency system' and 'the due payment of internal and foreign debts'.

Independence

Frequent, and often substantial, inflations have occurred subsequent to the establishment of the Banco Central de Chile, usually generated by excessive government expenditures financed by the Bank. In addition, the Bank has almost always conducted a discount policy aimed at facilitating development through the provision of subsidised credit. Clearly, therefore, the Bank has not been independent.

Between 1940 and 1960, for example, parliamentary advisors were appointed who obstructed and delayed decisions by the Bank regarding its monetary or exchange rate policies. During this period the Bank often made public its disagreement with the government over policies which it saw as a source of inflation and disinvestment.

Since 1975 a Monetary Council has formulated monetary and exchange rate policy. Its five members are all appointed by the Minister of Finance and, apart from the President of the Bank, are all either government ministers or government representatives.

REFERENCES

Banco Central de Chile (1988) 'Banco Central de Chile'. Official publication.

Banco Central de Chile (1990) *Constitutional Organic Act of the Central Bank of Chile*.

Hirschmann, A. O. (1963) *Journeys Toward Progress: Studies of Policymaking in Latin America*. The Twentieth Century Fund: New York.

Kisch, C. H. and W. A. Elkin (1932) *Central Banks*. Macmillan: London.

Subercaseaux, G. (1922) *Monetary and Banking Policy in Chile*. Clarendon Press: Oxford.

Tamagna, F. (1965) *Central Banking in Latin America*. Grafica Panamericana: Mexico.

Triffin, R. (1944) 'Central Banking and monetary management in Latin America', in Harris, S. E. (ed.) *Economic Problems of Latin America*. Books for Libraries Press: New York.

B20   Banco de México

Founded in 1925

Forerunner

None. The first note issuing bank was established in Mexico in 1864. By 1882 four such banks had arisen, as no laws existed which forbade this activity. One of these banks, the Banco Nacional Mexicano, served as the state bank, and received various concessions, in return for which it granted credit to the government.

After a financial crisis in 1884, which left the Treasury bankrupt, the government turned to the Banco Nacional for assistance, which resulted in the bank's notes becoming the only notes acceptable for payments to the government (the bank was also permitted to merge with a mortgage bank, and was renamed the Banco Nacional de Mexico).

The crisis of 1884 prompted a review of the regulations governing bank note issue, and new regulations were formalised in the Banking Law of 1897. These included restrictions on banks' total note issue (to three times their paid up capital) and a minimum specie reserve requirement (equal to 50 per cent of their note issue).

A revolution occurred in 1910, and the ensuing political turbulence had dramatic consequences for the banking system. The government secured large loans from the banks, which led to inflation and a decline in the acceptability of notes. In 1913 bank notes became 'forced currency'.

One year after the Constitutionalist government came to power in 1815, banks were given a deadline to raise their note cover to 100 per cent, otherwise they were to be liquidated. Naturally none of the banks could meet this condition, with the result that they were all placed under government control. Given that most of their assets comprised loans to the government, however, the banks could not be liquidated, and so their liabilities were simply 'frozen'.

From 1816 onwards, therefore, bank notes became practically worthless, and the supply of circulating media was substantially reduced. Indeed, until the formation of the Banco de Mexico in 1925, the primary circulating media in Mexico consisted of silver and gold coin.

Motivation for founding

Since the coming to power of the Constitutionalist government in 1915, a central bank of issue under government control had been proposed as a measure for stabilising the prevailing monetary disarray. A detailed proposal was submitted in 1917 but, given the depleted specie reserves of the government, could not be implemented without domestic and foreign credit. Considering the disorganised condition of the government's finances, such credit was not forthcoming, and the proposal was shelved.

This scenario was repeated a number of times until, in 1925, the government achieved a budget surplus, and was finally able to finance the establishment of a central bank.

Original objectives and functions

According to the Organic Law of the Banco de México (hereafter the Bank), the Bank was authorised to issue notes, convertible into gold, 50 per cent of which would be covered by specie reserves. Furthermore, the Bank was to function as the government's bank and as banker to the commercial banks. The latter activities were essentially commercial in nature, however, and included accepting deposits of commercial banks, discounting paper and extending loans. Indeed, during its early years the bank acted as a commerical bank, and was perceived as a competitor by the other trading banks.

The Bank was established as a joint stock corporation, although most of its shares (over 90 per cent) were purchased by the government. Management was undertaken by an Administrative Council, made up of nine government nominated councillors. The Council was responsible for all decisions regarding note issue, rediscount operations and lending.

Evolution of objectives and functions

For the first several years the Bank was unsuccessful in its central banking functions: its note issue actually declined between 1925–31, mainly due to low public confidence in the Bank, whilst commercial banks were hostile to the Bank. On the other hand, according to Bett (1951) the Bank 'developed a considerable commercial business' although 'it is an unfortunate blight upon the Bank that much of this business was conducted with favourites of the government' (Bett 1951, p. 51).

A new monetary law became effective in 1931, which repealed the convertibility of bank notes into gold. At the same time the Adminstrative Council of the Bank was replaced by a Junta Central Bancaria (Board of Directors), whose decisons were subject to a veto by the minister of finance. Further, gold was demonetised and a monetary role for silver, of which Mexico was a major producer, was reinstated. An increase in the world price of silver in 1934 threatened to provoke a massive currency drain leading to a temporary demonetisation of silver between 1935 and 1936, leaving only Bank of Mexico notes as legal tender.

With the onset of World War II the Bank gained wide powers to use selective reserve requirements and interest rate ceilings and floors to channel credit to selected sectors. These marked the beginning of a long phase of direct intervention in the financial sector, which culminated in the nationalisation of the banking system in 1982. This move was prompted by economic crises which had resulted in a loss of confidence in the peso, accompanied by enormous speculation against the currency and capital flight. In 1990, however, the banks were privatised again, marking the retreat of State from the banking system.

Independence

The independence of the Bank of Mexico was, until 1993, never substantial. Legislation passed in 1993, however, has given the Bank substantial independence, in addition to giving the Bank a constitutional mandate to pursue price stability. The Bank is free to determine interest rate policy, and this is not subject to any override provision (see the remarks by the Governor of the Bank of Mexico included elsewhere in this volume).

REFERENCES

Banco de Mexico (1993) *Iniciativa de Reforma Constitucional Para Dotar de Autonomia al Banco de Mexico.*
Banco de Mexico (1993) *Ley Del Banco de Mexico.*
Bett, V. M. (1957) *Central Banking in Mexico.* University of Michigan: Ann Arbor.

Goldsmith, R. (1966) *The Financial Development of Mexico*. Development Centre of the OECD: Paris.

Mancera, M. (1994) 'Politica economica de mexico para 1994', En Occasion del Seminaro, Organizado por la Asociacion Nacional de Ex-Alumnos del Itam, A.C., March.

Mancera, M (1994) 'Remarks on "Modern Central Banking"'. This volume.

Myers, M. G. (1954) 'Mexico', in Beckhart, B.H . (ed.) *Banking Systems*. New York.

Thompson, J. (1979) *Inflation, Financial Markets and Economic Development: The Experience of Mexico*. JAI Press: Greenwich.

Turrent Díaz, E. (1982) *Historía del Banco de México* (Official History of the Banco de Mexico). Banco de México: Mexico.

White, R. N. (1992) *State, Class, and the Nationalisation of the Mexican Banks*. Crane Russak: New York.

B21   Bank of Greece

Founded in 1928

Forerunner

None. However, the National Bank of Greece, which was founded in 1842, undertook a quasi-central banking role. The National Bank was one of the first note-issuing banks in Greece, and was by far the largest commercial bank, discounting bills, accepting deposits and making agricultural and mortgage loans.

Although the National Bank was organised as a joint stock company, with the state holding only a 20 per cent share, it was often coerced into lending heavily to the government. This resulted in its notes becoming 'forced currency' (i.e. inconvertible into specie) from 1877 onwards.

The Bank obtained a note-issuing monopoly over most of Greece in 1892 (the only exception being the Ionian islands and Crete until 1920), but its statute required it to hold a minimum specie reserve equal to 33 per cent of its note issue (even though these notes were inconvertible).

The large deficits run by the Greek and other Balkan governments led them to raise a substantial amount of funds externally. When, towards the end of the nineteenth century, these countries' ability to repay their European creditors became doubtful, a European Financial Commission was given control over budgetary affairs so as to guarantee repayment. This included the imposition of a total ban on the issue of any new notes by the National Bank between 1898 and 1910, and the placing of absolute limits on its note issue thereafter.

Motivation for founding

Following World War I, the ability of the Greek government to repay its European creditors again became suspect, and had resulted in a forced loan being made by the National Bank in 1922 which violated the international control agreement negotiated previously. Following an international dispute, the League of Nations agreed to support Greece's external borrowings, but under the condition that an independent note-issuing bank was established.

This led to some debate over whether the National Bank should be altered to play this role (the League of Nations position), or an entirely new institution set up (the Greek position). The latter view prevailed, and the Bank of Greece was established in 1928 by a Charter which was contained within the Geneva Protocol (of 1927).

Original objectives and functions

The Bank of Greece (hereafter the Bank) was given a monopoly over the issue of bank notes, which had to be convertible into gold. A minimum specie reserve ratio of 40 per cent of its note issue had to be observed, and the Bank's statutes stated that 'the first duty of the bank shall be to ensure that the gold value of its notes remains stable'.

The Bank was also given the task of being the government's bank, although lending to the government was limited to the purchase of government bonds (up to a stated maximum) and short-term advances (also up to a specified maximum). In addition the Bank discounted bills, accepted deposits, and made secured advances to banks and non-financial firms.

The Bank's role as a banker to the other commercial banks, and as a custodian of foreign exchange, was limited, since commercial banks were not compelled to hold either domestic or foreign reserves with the Bank. This put the Bank into a weak position as regards the implementation of discount and exchange rate policy, which was practically non-existent before 1931.

Although the Bank was organised as a joint stock company, the National Bank of Greece initially purchased the entire share capital of the Bank. The state (and its affiliations) was restricted to holding a maximum of 10 per cent (in total) of the Bank's capital. Administration was undertaken by a Governing Board comprised of a Governor, two Deputy Governors, and nine Directors (at least five to come from the industrial, commercial or agricultural sector). Whilst the first Board was appointed by the government for a period of three years, its successors were to be entirely elected by the shareholders.

Evolution of objectives and functions

The Bank initially played a limited role as a central bank, given its lack of control over the reserves of commercial banks and the dominant position of the National Bank. The government viewed the Bank as a price which had to be paid for foreign financial assistance, and often threatened to merge it with the National Bank.

This position changed considerably during 1931, when many countries left the gold standard. The Greek government decided to maintain convertibility, but this proved to be unsustainable given large outflows of specie as well as an increasingly fragile banking system. Before the drachma was eventually devalued in 1932, the Bank had been given increased powers to supervise all foreign exchange transactions and to impose minimum reserve requirements upon banks (although these did not have to be held at the Bank). During 1931 the Bank also undertook lender of last resort operations, and its advances to the banking system rose dramatically.

World War II ushered in dramatic increases in the note issue, and inflation, resulting from the German occupation which began in 1941. Following World War II, a Civil War broke out which continued until 1950, during which time inflation reached high levels. In 1946 a Central Loans Committee was established, which had authority as to the pricing and allocation of credit by the banking system, effectively usurping the policy role of the Bank. Further, a General Inspectorate of Banks was set up to monitor banks' advances. Selective credit controls, administered by the Central Loans Committee, remained a dominant feature of the financial system throughout the sixties and seventies.

Independence

Although its founders intended the Bank to be independent from the government, exemplified by the statutory restriction over state ownership of the Bank's share capital to at most 10 per cent, in practice the Bank has not been independent. Restrictions over Bank advances to the government have constantly been raised, for example, and the ability of the Bank to alter its discount rate has been constrained by the fact that the interest rate on government paper is administratively set by the government. Furthermore, exchange rate policy is formulated by the government, with the Bank acting as a consultant.

The Bank has forwarded proposals to the government which will increase its independence and render its Statute compatible with the Maastricht Treaty. Since January 1994, for example, the Bank has been prohibited from extending credit to the government.

REFERENCES

Bank of Greece (1928) *Annual Report*. Athens.
Bank of Greece (1975) *Statutes*. Sixth edition. Athens.
Delivanis, D. and W. C. Cleveland (1950) *Greek Monetary Developments 1939–1948*. Indiana University Publications, Social Science Series No. 6.
Eulambio, M. S. (1924) *The National Bank of Greece: A History of the Financial and Economic Evolution of Greece*. S.C. Vlastos: Athens.
Halikias, D. J. (1978) *Money and Credit in a Developing Economy: The Greek case*. New York University Press.
Lampe, J. R. and M. R. Jackson (1982) *Balkan Economic History: From Imperial Borderlands to Developing Nations*. Indiana University Press: Bloomington
Mazower, M. (1991) 'Banking and economic development in interwar Greece', in James, H., Hakan, L. and Teichova, A. (eds.) *The Role of Banks in the Interwar Economy*. Cambridge University Press: Cambridge.
National Bank of Greece (1928) *Annual Report*. Athens.

B22   Banco Central de Bolivia (Central Bank of Bolivia)

Founded in 1929

Forerunner

A multiple note-issuing system existed in Bolivia at the turn of the twentieth century, with all banks being able to issue their own notes, convertible into gold since 1907 (the gold standard was subsequently suspended, in 1914). A desire to increase the efficiency of the monetary and banking system, however, led to the creation of the Banco de la Nación Boliviana in 1911 which, three years later, was reorganised and granted the sole right to issue banknotes. Although the Banco de la Nación Boliviana was the only legal bank of issue, the notes of other banks remained in circulation until 1928.

When the Banco de la Nación Boliviana was reorganised in 1914, its board consisted of seven members, three of whom were chosen by the Government and four by the stockholders. Later, in order to increase its influence on the board, the government reduced the number of members to five, thereby procuring a majority, as it continued to appoint three out of the five members.

Although the charter of the Banco de la Nación Boliviana determined that the bank should limit its loans to the government to 20 per cent of its capital, this limit was repeatedly and significantly exceeded in practice.

Motivation for founding

In the 1920s Bolivia was a growing export economy in which commercial exports far exceeded imports. Nevertheless, the government typically ran large budget deficits, which were met by debt issues and loans from the Banco de la Nacion. In addition, the underdeveloped banking system meant there was often a lack of credit for the productive sectors of the economy.

Although the official exchange value of the boliviano was relatively stable during the early 1920s, attempts to return to the gold standard were unsuccessful, and the currency remained inconvertible. A growing fiscal crisis in the 1920s (remarkable since it occurred during a period of unusual political stability under civilian rule) prompted the government to invite Edwin Kemmerer (a monetary expert from Princeton) to rationalise and modernise the monetary, banking and fiscal systems. Kemmerer's mission was also intended to restore foreign investors' confidence in Bolivia.

Instead of the establishment of an entirely new central bank, Kemmerer suggested the reorganisation of the Banco de la Nación Boliviana, which was transformed into the Banco Central de Bolivia. The banking arrangements which existed prior to Kemmerer's appointment thus continued, although with two (supposed) changes. First, the Government's monetary demands upon the new central bank were subject to new limits. Secondly, commercial banks had been facing strong competition from the Banco de la Nación Boliviana, which the new central bank was intended to cease. However, the new central bank continued to have a dual character, undertaking both central banking and commercial banking functions.

The central bank law was promulgated in July 1928, but preparations for the opening of the Banco Central de Bolivia took a whole year, with the result that it started operations in July 1929.

Original objectives and functions

The Banco Central de Bolivia (hereafter the Bank) was granted the monopoly of issue, and became the Government's bank. Its charter stated that loans to the Government could not exceed 25 per cent of its paid-up capital (35 per cent in an emergency). Furthermore, the Bank could purchase, sell and hold government bonds and the debt of official agencies. Although the Bank's loans to the Government had to be reduced to this newly imposed quota during the first year of operation of the Bank, a decree in October 1930 allowed additional credits to the Government. The Bank also continued to operate partly as a commercial bank.

The Bank's ownership was mixed, as the state, banks and the public held parts of equity capital. The first law created a Board of nine Directors, of which two were appointed by the Government, two were chosen by the subscribing commercial banks and two by the public stockholders. Of the remaining three Directors, one was from the Association of Mining Industries, one represented the national chamber of commerce, and one represented agricultural associations.

Evolution of objectives and functions

The Banco Central de Bolivia was nationalised in 1939, but continued to operate under the 1928 charter.

In 1945 the Bank was reorganised, and the monetary and banking departments were separated. It undertook central banking functions through its monetary department and it engaged in general operations with the public in competition with commercial banks through the banking department (which was further subdivided into an Industrial Section and a Commerce Section).

Each department now had its own Board of Directors. Additionally, there was a General Board of Directors to which was entrusted the general policies of the Bank. Six members of this General Board were appointed by the government, and the remaining five by the banks, commerce and industry.

A National Monetary Stabilisation Council was created in 1956, under the immediate direction of the President of the Republic. Its members included ministers of the National Economy, Finance, Mines, Petroleum, Labour and Social Security, the Vice-President of the Planning Board and the Director of the Bank. The main objective of this Council was to coordinate the activities of its various members so as to achieve and maintain monetary stability in the country. The National Monetary Stabilisation Council in effect exercised control over all major decisions of the Bank.

In 1970 the organisation of the Bank was modified, with the banking department being separated from the Bank to serve as the foundation for the creation of the Banco del Estado, a state-owned development bank. Furthermore, the task of banking supervision, which had until this time been undertaken by an independent government agency, was transferred to the Bank. In 1987, however, a Superintendency of Banks and Financial Institutions was established to carry out the task of supervision.

Independence

Reflecting the tenets of central banking of the 1920s, there was some measure of independence in the founding law of the Bank. Following the nationalisation of the Bank in 1939, and the increased representation of the Government on its Board in the 1945 revision of its charter, this autonomy was considerably limited.

With the establishment of the National Monetary Stabilisation Council the independence of the Banco Central de Bolivia was further reduced, and the President of the Republic had discretionary powers in appointing the Directors of the central bank.

In 1990, the Bolivian Congress passed an Act which clearly defined the nature of the Bank as the country's sole monetary authority, and as the regulatory and governing body of banks and other financial institutions (supervision remained with the Superintendency). Further, the composition and terms of the Bank's Board of Directors were modified in 1993. According to the new legislation, the President of the Republic would appoint the President of the Bank and its five Directors from a list of candidates approved by a two-thirds majority of the Chamber of Deputies.

Finally, a new Law is presently before Congress which aims to make the Bank independent, granting it full powers over the formulation and execution of monetary policy, with the explicit objective of price stability. This Law also places overt restrictions on the granting of credit to the government.

REFERENCES

Drake, P. W. (1989) *The Money Doctor in the Andes: The Kemmerer Missions 1923–1933*. Duke University Press: London.
Joslin, D. (1963) *A Century of Banking in Latin America*. Oxford University Press: Oxford.
Peñaloza Cordero, L. (1984) *Nueva Historia Economica de Bolivia; Comercio, Moneda y Bancos*. Los Amigos de Libro: Bolivia.
Tamagna, F. (1965) *Central Banking in Latin America*. Centro de Estúdios Monetarios Latinoamericanos: Mexico.

B23   Türk Ye Cumhur Yet Merkez Bankasi (Central Bank of the Republic of Turkey)

Founded in 1930

Forerunner

None. The monetary experience of the Ottoman Empire during the nineteenth century was rather turbulent. Originally on a silver standard, the government began to issue interest-bearing Treasury notes for the first time in 1839. Over-issues led to a heavy discount on these notes, and in 1844 a bimetallic standard was adopted as part of a monetary reform. Government spending remained high, however, due to the Crimean and other wars, resulting in a declaration of bankruptcy by the state in 1875.

During this time, the first commercial bank had been established in Constantinople (in 1856), known as the Ottoman Bank. In 1863 the government turned to the bank to manage its increasingly disorganised finances, and to obtain funds, and in return the bank obtained a charter for note issue. An infusion of capital from France (led by the Credit Mobilier) led to the bank being renamed the Banque Imperiale Ottomane. Hereafter the bank was both a commercial, investment bank and a state bank, collecting and transmitting taxes via a branch network and servicing the public debt.

The Banque Imperiale Ottomane remained the only note-issuing bank before and after the dissolution of the Ottoman Empire following World War I (currency in circulation mainly consisted of coins until the war). During the war, the Banque Imperiale Ottomane did not increase its note issue substantially, causing the government to increase the issue of its own notes. Upon dissolution, the Empire lost virtually all its territory, part of which became the Turkish Republic in 1923. Although the legal position of the Banque Imperiale became uncertain, and it was prohibited from issuing new notes, its existing note issue was retained as legal tender.

Motivation for founding

Following World War I, and the League of Nations conference in Brussels, the idea that each country should have a central bank became widely held, and Turkey was no exception. Throughout the 1920s the Turkish lira depreciated steadily, accelerating during 1929 as a result of a build-up in Turkey's foreign debt. This led the government to impose exchange controls in 1929, and to establish a consortium of banks in 1930 for the purposes of stabilising the currency. The establishment of a central bank was seen as a more permanent means of stabilising the internal and external value of the Turkish lira, and motivated the formation of the Central Bank of the Republic of Turkey (hereafter the Bank) in 1930.

Original objectives and functions

According to the Central Bank Law of 1930, the Bank was given the right to issue notes, and was to serve as the government's bank and as a banker to the commercial banks (this included management of the clearing system and supervision of banks). The Bank was precluded from operating as a commercial bank.

The statutory objectives of the Bank included the regulation of the volume and circulation of currency, and taking the necessary measures (i.e. exchange controls, foreign exchange intervention) to protect the internal and external value of the currency. The latter responsibility, however, was shared with the government.

The Bank was organised as a joint stock company, with shares being issued to the government (restricted to 25 per cent), special law banks (which were owned by the government), commercial banks and the public.

Administration of the Bank was undertaken by a Board, comprising a Governor and six Directors.

Evolution of objectives and functions

The Central Bank Law of 1930 was supposed to be followed by a Stabilisation Act, which would determine the powers of the Bank to increase the note issue as well as the gold cover of its notes. This was never enacted, however, given the worldwide failure to return to gold convertibility, with the result that the government's ability to obtain credits from the Bank was never severely constrained. Indeed, subsequent amendments to the Act, in 1934, 1940 and 1955, enabled the Treasury and many state economic enterprises to obtain credit from the Bank more easily.

In 1933 the Bank was charged with forming and managing a Bank Liquidation Fund, which was financed by banks and would be used to repay bank depositors (in full) in the event of a bank failure. Although the Bank was authorised to rediscount securities and undertake open-market operations these did not occur very often due to the lack of development of a money market, which remained the case until the 1980s.

In 1968 the government embarked on the (second) Five Year Development Plan, centred upon an import substitution strategy with heavy subsidies to industrial and mining activity. These subsidies included cheap Bank credit, with the result that the statutory objectives of the Bank were explicitly amended, in 1970, to include the 'conduct of monetary and credit policy in conformity with the Development Plans and the Annual Programmes ...'. Furthermore, government ownership in the Bank was increased to a minimum of 51 per cent.

Up until the mid-1980s, therefore, the Turkish banking system remained heavily regulated and financial markets underdeveloped. Consequently, a series of IMF and World Bank supported initiatives aimed at liberalising the financial system were implemented in 1984–5.

Independence

Although the original laws of the Bank stated that it was to be independent of the government, and restricted government ownership of the Bank to 25 per cent, the Bank was not in fact independent. Through its ownership of the special law banks, the government held a majority of shares in the Bank. Furthermore, until 1970 monetary policy was not formulated by the Bank's Board, but by a Committee for the Regulation of Bank Credit, which comprised government ministers, commercial bank representatives, and the Governor of the Bank.

Under the revision of its laws in 1970, the Bank became obliged to support the selective credit subsidies of the government. Although these have reduced during the 1980s, the first objective of the Bank remains 'to conduct monetary and credit policies in conformity with the Development Plans and Annual Programs . . .'.

REFERENCES

Akyüz, Y. (1989) 'Financial system and policies in Turkey in the 1980's', Discussion Paper No. 25, United Nations Conference on Trade and Development.

Fry, M. J. and M. R. Farhi (1979) *Money and Banking in Turkey*. Bo aziçi University Publications: Istanbul.

Issawi, C. (1980) *The Economic History of Turkey 1800–1914*. University of Chicago Press: Chicago.

Kumcu, E. (1990) 'The regulatory power of the Central Bank of Turkey', in Korner, H and R. Shams (eds.) *Institutional Aspects of Economic Integration of Turkey into the EC*. Verlag Weltarchiv: Hamburg.

Nas, T. F. and M. Odekon (1988) *Liberalisation and the Turkish Economy*. Greenwood Press: New York.

The Law on Türkiye Cumhuriyet Merkez Bankasi (1970) and (1985).

Yenal, O. (1967) 'Development of the financial system', in Shorter, F. C. (ed.) *Four Studies in the Economic Development of Turkey*. Frank Cass and Co.: London.

B24   Reserve Bank of New Zealand

Founded in 1933

Forerunner

None. A state bank, the Colonial Bank of Issue, was established in 1850 in response to the perceived lack of circulating media and banking facilities in the new colony. The Colonial Bank was given a monopoly over the note issue (at that time only one commercial bank, the Union Bank of Australia, issued notes), which in turn discouraged the development of other banks as note issue usually promised the highest profits. As the Colonial Bank did not extend loans or mortgages, the availability of credit actually remained just as restricted as it had ever been. The Colonial Bank was thus closed in 1856.

In the 1860s, five commercial banks were chartered in New Zealand, three of which were Australian, and issued notes convertible into gold. These banks were required to hold gold reserves equal to at least 30 per cent of their note issue, although they typically held more. As most trade in New Zealand and Australia took place with Britain, these banks also held substantial sterling reserves in London, which could be exchanged for gold if necessary.

Although the government adopted one of these banks, the Bank of New Zealand, as its fiscal agent in 1862, and acquired a substantial shareholding in the Bank during a financial crisis in 1893 which had threatened the solvency of the Bank, it did not interfere in the credit policies of the Bank and did not seek to make it into a central bank.

Until 1914, therefore, the monetary system of New Zealand was essentially one of free banking, linked to the international gold standard. With the suspension of gold convertibility at the onset of World War I, however, the New Zealand pound was effectively free to fluctuate against sterling, although banks attempted to maintain parity between the two currencies. When sterling convertibility was restored in 1925, New Zealand did not follow, implying that it was again up to banks to maintain parity between the New Zealand pound (NZ£) and sterling. This situation, which persisted until 1931, put New Zealand on a sterling exchange standard, again under free banking.

Motivation for founding

With four of the six banks in New Zealand being Australian, trade conditions in Australia tended to have a considerable influence over monetary conditions in New Zealand. A trade deficit between Australia and Britain, for example, caused these banks to lose sterling reserves, and consequently led to a depreciation of the NZ£ against sterling (as banks sought to stem their loss of reserves).

Such a situation arose in the late 1920s, and led to a sustained divergence between the NZ£ and sterling. At the same time the banks were becoming increasingly unpopular, due to the impression that they were contributing to the Great Depression.

In response to this situation the government, in 1931, imposed exchange controls, and sought the advice of Sir Otto Niemeyer (formerly of the British Treasury), who had also been consulted by the Australian government on their monetary situation. In his report, Niemeyer proposed the establishment of a central bank. Owing to the Depression, however, the central bank proposal was pushed into the background, but resurfaced again in 1933, when it culminated in the Reserve Bank of New Zealand Act.

Original objectives and functions

Based to a large extent on the Bank of England, the Reserve Bank of New Zealand (hereafter the Reserve Bank) was given a monopoly over the note issue, against which it had to hold reserves of 25 per cent (this requirement could be suspended by the Minister of Finance). The Bank also became the fiscal agent of the government, and could extend advances to the government up to a specified maximum (equivalent to four months revenue). In addition the Bank was authorised to accept deposits, discount securities, make secured advances and buy and sell gold and securities.

The Reserve Bank Act stipulated the transfer of commercial banks' gold reserves to the Bank, which met with strong opposition from the banks. Although reserve requirements were not imposed upon banks, it was envisaged that the Bank would organise a clearing system based upon banks' deposits with the Reserve Bank.

Although the political opposition (the Labour Party) argued strongly for the Bank to be state-owned, the government chose to organise it on a joint stock basis, with share ownership being widely dispersed.

Management was undertaken by a Board comprising a Governor, Deputy Governor and seven directors, three of which were appointed by the government and four by shareholders. The Secretary of the Treasury was made a non-voting member of the Board. The political ambivalence towards the independence of the Bank was reflected in the fact that no statutory definition of the relationship between the Bank and the Treasury was formulated.

Although the Niemeyer report had emphasised price stability as the Bank's primary objective, the Bank's statute stated that its objective was 'to exercise control . . . over monetary circulation and credit in New Zealand, to the end that the economic welfare of the Dominion may be promoted and maintained.' It was also decided that the Bank would act to maintain a fixed exchange rate to sterling, which had been the government's policy since 1931.

Evolution of objectives and functions

Following the election of the Labour government, the Bank was duly nationalised in 1936, and its primary objective replaced by the duty of '[giving] effect . . . to the monetary policy of the Government as communicated to it from time to time by the Minister of Finance'. Furthermore, the restrictions on government borrowing from the Bank were eased. Finally, the Bank's influence over the commercial banks was increased, as it was given the power to impose and vary banks' reserve requirements.

Given the absence of a domestic money market, the Bank's initial operations consisted of acting as the government's banker, and of purchasing and selling foreign exchange. Partly as a result of interest rate ceilings, which had been introduced during the Depression, sustained outflows of foreign exchange occurred during the mid-1930s. Consequently, exchange controls were imposed in 1938, and strengthened in 1940. Outflows of reserves became a recurring problem, and exchange controls remained in place until the 1980s.

During World War II, the sectoral composition of banks' loan portfolios began to be regulated by Selected Advance Controls imposed by the Bank, and these were retained, even broadened, after the War, remaining effective until the 1960s.

For much of the post-war period, therefore, monetary policy remained the responsibility of the government, and was implemented through direct controls over bank lending, interest rates and foreign exchange transactions. These were typically accompanied by relatively high rates of inflation and low rates of growth. This led the newly elected government in 1984 to implement financial reforms, which included abolishing most direct controls, freeing the exchange rate and reducing inflation in the medium term.

This reform process culminated in a revision of the Reserve Bank Act in 1989, which now states that 'the primary function of the bank is to formulate and implement monetary policy directed to the economic objectives of achieving and maintaining stability in the general price level'. At the same time, the Bank became independent in the sense that it could decide on how to operate policy to achieve this objective.

Independence

Since its establishment in 1935, and until 1989, the independence of the Reserve Bank has been severely limited, with authority for monetary policy typically resting with the government. Following the revision of the Reserve Bank Act in 1989, however, the Bank has become one of the most independent central banks.

The Bank now has a clear statutory objective, price stability, and it is obliged to set out specific targets (jointly determined by the Minister of Finance and the Bank) whereby its policy performance may be assessed. Whilst the Bank has the sole authority to formulate and implement monetary policy, a formal 'override' provision exists whereby the government may change this policy. However, such changes must be made public, are strictly temporary, and exist to facilitate the political accountability of the Bank's policies.

REFERENCES

Brash, D. T. (1993) 'Reconciling central bank independence with political account-
    ability – the New Zealand experience', Address to the European Policy Forum,
    June.
Dawe, S. (1993) 'Reserve Bank of New Zealand Act 1989', unpublished manuscript.

Hawke, G. R. (1973) *Between Governments and Banks: A History of the Reserve bank of New Zealand*. A. R. Shearer: Wellington.

Lloyd, M. (1992) 'The New Zealand approach to central bank autonomy', *Reserve Bank Bulletin*, 55, 3.

Nicholl, P. (1992) 'New Zealand's monetary policy experiment', Seminar presented at University of Western Ontario, October.

Olakanpo, J. O. (1965) *Central Banking in the Commonwealth*. Bookland Private: Calcutta.

Plumptre, A. F. W. (1940) *Central Banking in the British Dominions*. University of Toronto Press: Toronto.

Reserve Bank of New Zealand (1986) *Financial Policy Reform*. Hutcheson, Bowman and Stewart: Wellington.

Reserve Bank of New Zealand (1989) *Reserve Bank of New Zealand*.

Reserve Bank of New Zealand (1992) *Monetary Policy and the New Zealand Financial System*. 3rd edition. Hutcheson, Bowman and Stewart: Wellington.

B25   Bank of Canada

Founded in 1934

Forerunner

None. The gold standard was adopted by the united provinces of Canada (now Ontario and Quebec) in 1853. Following confederation in 1867, the federal government issued convertible Dominion notes, which served as legal tender and were partly covered (25 per cent) by a gold reserve (issues beyond a specified level were, however, 100 per cent backed by gold).

Although the government had a monopoly on small denomination (i.e. below $5) notes, which were *de facto* inconvertible, banks issued convertible notes subject to limits based upon their paid-up capital. No specie reserve requirements were imposed upon banks.

Banks typically had many branches, which accepted one another's notes at par, returning them via a well developed system of clearinghouses (formalised under the Canadian Bankers Association in 1901). One of the largest banks, the Bank of Montreal (founded in 1817), served as the government's bank.

Prior to 1914, banks would manage their liquidity by holding reserves and via call loans held in New York (and, to some extent, liquid securities drawn on London) given the absence of a domestic money market. During banking crises in 1907, and again in 1914, when such call loans proved insufficient to meet reserve needs, the government acted as a lender of last resort, making advances to banks against collateral.

This lending arrangement was formalised under the Finance Act, which was introduced as an emergency measure in 1914, but was subsequently amended (1923) and maintained for some twenty years. Thus a discount window of sorts was in operation in Canada after 1914, administered by the Treasury, although the discount rate was not actively used as a policy instrument to regulate credit conditions.

Canada returned briefly to the gold standard between 1926 and 1928, but thereafter the gold standard was suspended and, in 1931, abandoned.

Motivation for founding

Although proposals for a central bank were regularly made from about 1913 onwards, especially after the International Financial Conference in Brussels in 1920 which had called for central banks to be established in every country, none was seriously (or popularly) received until 1933. In that year, Prime Minister Bennett expressed concern about the absence of any mechanism for settling international balances directly with Canada (this was done indirectly, via New York), which a central bank would remedy.

At the same time the idea of establishing a central bank served two other political ends, namely the need for an active government response to the Great Depression and the need to regulate what was perceived as an unduly concentrated and powerful banking system. There is little evidence that a central bank was seen as a necessary institution for purposes of regulating the currency issue following the suspension of the gold standard in 1931.

Thus, in 1933, the Prime Minister asked Lord MacMillan, a known supporter of the idea of a central bank, to conduct a Commission of Inquiry into banking in Canada, and there was little doubt as to the outcome of the Commission. The Commission duly recommended the formation of a central bank, to be called the Bank of Canada, modelled to a large extent upon the Bank of England.

Original objectives and functions

The Bank of Canada (hereafter the Bank) Act of 1934 gave the Bank a monopoly over the note issue, and provided for the gradual withdrawal of Dominion bank notes over a number of years. Although the gold standard was no longer in operation, the Bank was required to hold gold reserves equalling 25 per cent of its note issue.

The Bank was directed to act as the fiscal agent of the government (federal and provincial, although the latter was never used), authorised to discount specified tradable securities and make advances against tradable securities, and permitted to deal in securities, foreign currencies and bullion. Commercial banks were required to hold 5 per cent of their deposit liabilities in the form of a deposit at the Bank and, in addition, had to transfer their entire holdings of gold coin and bullion to the Bank.

The Bank did not, however, manage the clearing system, but became an active participant in clearing arrangements. Similarly, the Bank did not regulate or supervise commercial banks, but played an advisory role in this capacity. Regulation and supervision was undertaken by a government body, the Inspector General of Banks from about 1925, which subsequnetly (during the 1980s) became the Office of the Superintendent of Financial Institutions.

The Bank was organised as a privately owned institution, with shares being offered for public subscription. Management was vested in a Board of Directors, comprising a Governor, Deputy Governor and seven Directors, elected by shareholders. An Executive Committee, comprising the Governor, Deputy Governor, one Director (selected by the Board) and the Deputy Minister of Finance (who had no vote), was given the power to decide the Bank's discount rate.

The only reference to the objectives of the Bank occur in the preamble to the Bank Act: 'to regulate currency and credit ... to control and protect the external value of the national monetary unit ... and generally to promote the economic and financial welfare of the Dominion ...'

Evolution of objectives and functions

Soon after its establishment, government control over the Bank increased. In 1936 further shares were issued which were purchased by the government, giving it ownership of 51 per cent of the Banks' shares. Additional Directors were appointed to give the government a majority on the Board, and while the existing Directors were permitted to conclude their terms of office, the election of Directors by private shareholders was discontinued. Two years later the Bank was nationalised completely, with all shares owned by the public being redeemed, and the number of Directors was increased to eleven.

With the advent of World War II in 1939, exchange controls were introduced, administered by the Foreign Exchange Control Board. This Board was directly responsible to the government, and effectively usurped the Bank's policymaking position. The gold reserve provisions in the bank were suspended in 1940, and the Bank was instructed to sell its entire bullion stock to the Foreign Exchange Control Board. This Board was eventually dissolved in 1951.

The absence of a domestic money market meant that open market operations were scarcely used during the 1930s and 1940s, and the discount rate did thus not constitute a very effective policy instrument. This changed in the early 1950s, however, when initiatives to develop a domestic money market finally succeeded, and monetary restriction was deliberately employed to counter the perceived threat of inflation arising from the Korean War.

Independence

During the late 1950s the governor of the Bank, James Coyne, sought to follow a low inflation policy, which conflicted with the overall economic policy of the government. This conflict culminated in a public clash between Coyne and the government which eventually led to his resignation in 1961, leaving little doubt as to the government's ultimate authority regarding monetary policy.

Following this dispute, the Bank Act was amended in 1967 to reflect the ultimate responsibility of the government in formulating monetary policy. In the event of a disagreement between the Bank and the government, the Minister of Finance may issue a directive to the Bank as to the policy it must follow. This directive must be in writing, in specific terms, and applicable for a specified period. In practice, however, it is not anticipated that such directives would need to be issued, and this has not occurred to date.

REFERENCES

Bank of Canada (1990) *Bank of Canada Act*. February.
Bordo, M. D. and Redish, A. (1987) 'Why did the Bank of Canada emerge in 1935?' *Journal of Economic History*, June.
Dick, T. J. O. and J. E. Floyd (1993) 'Canada and the gold standard 1871–1914: a durable monetary regime', in Capie, F. and M. D. Bordo (eds.) *Monetary Regimes in Transition*. Cambridge University Press: Cambridge.
Howitt, P. (1993) 'Canada', in Fratianni, M. U. and D. Salvatore (eds.) *Monetary Policy in Developed Economies*. Greenwood Press: London.
Jamieson, A. B. (1957) *Chartered Banking in Canada*. Ryerson Press: Toronto.
Neufeld, E. P. (1958) *Bank of Canada Operations and Policy*. University of Toronto Press: Toronto.
Olakanpo, J. O. (1965) *Central Banking in the Commonwealth*. Bookland Private: Calcutta.
Plumptre, A. F. W. (1940) *Central Banking in the British Dominions*. University of Toronto Press: Toronto.
Rasminsky, L. (1966) 'The role of the central banker today', Per Jacobsson Memorial Lecture, Rome, November.
Rasminsky, L. (1967) 'Central banking in the Canadian Financial System', Opening lecture of the 20th International Banking Summer School, Kingston, Ontario, August.
Report of the Royal Commission on Banking and Currency in Canada (1933).

Stokes, M. L. (1939) *The Development and Present Position of Central Banking in Canada*. Macmillan: London.

Watts, G. S. (1993) (Edited by T. K. Rymes) *The Bank of Canada: Origins and Early History*. Carleton University Press: Ottawa.

B26   El Banco Central de La República Argentina (Central Bank of the Argentine Republic)

Founded in 1935

Forerunner

None. Throughout the nineteenth century the lack of control and coordination of money and banking in Argentina led to frequent abuses and periods of instability. In 1877, a law was passed which authorised all commercial banks to issue bank notes on the condition that they bought government bonds, and an Oficina de Inspección was created to control the system. However, excessive note issues led, in 1890, to a financial crisis which culminated in the liquidation of virtually all commercial banks (including the Banco Nacional in 1891).

As a result of the crisis, which also affected the economic and political state of the country, two institutions were created in an attempt to centralise currency issue. These were the Caja de Conversión (1890) and the Banco de la Nación Argentina (1891), which played an important role in the development of the financial and monetary system in Argentina prior to the establishment of a central bank.

The Caja was a public organisation, and was granted a note issuing monopoly. It was administered by a five member board, and aimed at providing a uniform monetary system and, eventually, establishing the convertibility of the currency. This was achieved in 1902, and was sustained without interruption until the outbreak of the First World War. During this time the Banco de la Nación Argentina, whilst acting as a commercial bank, undertook central banking functions in that it was the government bank and could act as the bankers bank. In 1912 a Clearing House ('Cámara Compensadora') was created as an autonomous office for which the Banco de la Nación Argentina was responsible.

Motivation for founding

The first attempt at establishing a central bank was made in 1917 when the so called Proyecto Piñero was prepared. A second and more serious attempt was made in 1931 when a commission suggested a scheme for a central bank, although this never became law.

With the Great Depression, and the combination of reduced exports and the impossibility of borrowing, Argentina suffered heavy reserve losses and exchange rate depreciation. Consequently, it was one of the first countries to abandon the Gold Exchange Standard in 1929, which severed the close dependence of the money supply on the balance of payments. None the less, in 1931, foreign exchange controls had to be introduced, and it became obvious that the country lacked the necessary tools to control monetary developments in the economy. Central banking reform was required.

In 1933 a scheme was prepared by a Commission under the direction of Otto Niemeyer, a Director of the Bank of England, and was presented to the National Government. It became law in 1935. That same year the Banco Central de la República Argentina started operations.

Original objectives and functions

The primary aim of El Banco Central de la República Argentina (hereafter the Bank) was to adapt the circulating currency to the needs of business and to maintain stable monetary and credit conditions. The Bank took over the note issuing function of the Caja de Conversión. The Banco de la Nación Argentina was transformed into a purely commercial bank, with the Bank taking over as the financial agent and banker for the government. A provision of the charter gave authority to the Bank to buy and sell government securities, and also to create and issue its own obligations. However, it was prohibited from guaranteeing or endorsing government obligations, although it was authorised to grant credit to the government for limited periods, in order to cover temporary budget needs.

The Bank was required to keep at least 25 per cent of its reserves in the form of gold and foreign exchange with a view to securing the internal and external value of the peso, and was allowed to intervene in the exchange market as agent for the government.

Furthermore, it was given powers to regulate credit and to maintain the liquidity of the banking system. The original charter also introduced a commercial banking inspection system, which was entrusted to the Bank.

The capital of the new Bank was distributed between the government and the commercial banks. A Board of Directors, on which the government, the banking institutions and the principal sectors of the economy were represented, was responsible for the administration of the Bank and the policy it followed.

Evolution of objectives and functions

In 1946 the Argentinian regime changed from a parliamentary to an authoritarian system. The Bank was immediately nationalised and, in 1949, substantial amendments to its charter were introduced. The major change was that all banks were required to maintain deposits with the central bank, and various financial institutions were combined to form a more centralised system.

Changes in the charter of the Bank again coincided with the restoration of a parliamentary regime in 1957. The underlying aim in the new charter was to transform the Bank into an institution which would be responsible for economic and monetary stability in the country. For this reason there was an attempt to grant the bank a degree of autonomy within the confines of government policy and changes in the Board were introduced. The part that the Bank played as monetary authority with regard to commercial banks and other financial institutions was strengthened. Furthermore, there was a shift from the use of direct controls to instruments related to general market direction.

In 1964, amendments were made to the charter to expand the limits up to which the Bank could make temporary advances to the Government or could hold Government securities in its portfolio. These limits were related to the level of reserves received from commercial banks.

Independence

The first charter of the Bank was intended to limit the influence of the government on the Bank, although the government determined the election of the Governor and Deputy Governor. Nevertheless, the country's other banks could exert a great influence on the central bank as they held the majority of the stocks of the Bank and determined the election of eleven out of twelve directors.

With the nationalisation of the Bank in 1946, and its charter amendment in 1949, the Minister of Finance assumed the Presidency of the Bank, and the composition of the Board was altered, with all its members being appointed directly or indirectly by the Executive. Whilst the 1957 changes in the Bank's charter were intended to grant greater autonomy to the Bank, the government continued to be the sole owner of the Bank and its directors were still appointed by the Executive.

It is difficult to argue, therefore, that the Bank has ever been independent, and the government has frequently shaped the policy of the Bank to support its own economic objectives. Recently, however, discretion over monetary policy, either by the government or the Bank, has been abrogated by a Currency Board mechanism linking the peso to the US dollar.

REFERENCES

Arnaudo, A. (1987) *Cincuenta Anos de Politica Financiera Argentina, 1934–1983*. El Ateneo: Buenos Aires.

Diaz-Alejandro, C. F. (1970) *Essays on the Economic History of the Argentine Republic*.

Difrieri, J. (1967) *Moneda y Bancos en la República Argentina*. Abeledo-Perrot: Buenos Aires.

Ford, A. G. (1962) *The Gold Standard 1880–1914: Britain and Argentina*. Clarendon: Oxford.

Hueyo, A. (1958) *El Banco Central: Aspectos Fundamentales y Antecedentes de su Implantación en la República Argentina*. Francisco A. Colombo: Buenos Aires.

Joslin, D. (1963) *A Century of Banking in Latin America*. Oxford University Press: Oxford.

Tamagna, F. (1965) *Central Banking in Latin America*. Centro de Estudios Monetarios Latinoamericanos: Mexico.

B27   Reserve Bank of India

Founded in 1935

Forerunner

None. There had been numerous proposals before 1935 for a state bank, however, dating back to as early as 1773 when the General Bank of Bengal and Bahar was established and performed, albeit only very briefly (nine months), some of the functions typically attributed to central banks. Proposals for a central bank became especially frequent after the early 1920s, when the League of Nations conferences in Brussels and Genoa advocated that all countries should have a central bank.

By that time, the Imperial Bank of India had been established (in 1920) and, although a purely commercial bank, it in fact undertook several central banking functions. The Imperial bank served as the government's bank and the bankers' bank, setting up a number of branches (including one in London), and offering cash transfer, clearing and correspondent banking services.

Currency was issued by the government, however, and consisted of two tokens, paper notes and silver rupees. Although India had been on a gold standard since 1898 (the free coinage of silver had been prohibited since 1893) very little gold was coined and used as currency.

Motivation for founding

The idea that each country should have a central bank became widely held during the 1920s, and India was no exception. Already in 1913 a commission of inquiry (The Chamberlain Commission, of which Keynes was participant) into Indian currency had advocated the formation of an Indian central bank. The need for a central bank also arose due to the existing separation between the reserves of the banking system (held by the Imperial Bank) and the country's specie and foreign exchange reserves (held by the government).

The recommendation for a central bank was repeated by another commission (the Hilton-Young Commission) in 1926, which finally led to the drafting of the gold standard and Reserve Bank of India bill in 1927. This bill foundered over the question of the ownership of the Bank, however, and it was only after the Great Depression that another bill (the Reserve Bank of India bill) was eventually passed (in 1934).

Instead of transforming the Imperial Bank of India into the central bank, it was decided to establish a new institution, to be known as the Reserve Bank of India, which would take over the central banking functions undertaken by the Imperial Bank. This was in order to preserve the successful commercial relationships that had been formed between the Imperial Bank and other banks which, it was believed, would be compromised if the status of the Imperial Bank changed to that of a central bank.

Original objectives and functions

The Reserve Bank of India (hereafter the Bank) Act states that the objective of the Bank was to 'regulate the issue of bank notes and [keep] reserves with a view to securing monetary stability ... and generally to operate the currency and credit system of the country to its advantage' and to this end defined several 'central banking' functions for the Bank.

These included the monopoly over the issue of currency, acting as the government's bank, the bankers' bank (including the imposition of reserve requirements and the management of the clearing system), open market operations (including lender of last resort), the management of specie and foreign exchange reserves, and the regulation and supervision of (some) financial and non-financial institutions.

In compensation for the removal of a core part of the business of the Imperial Bank, the Reserve Bank Act stipulated the payment of commission to, and the maintenance of interest-free balances with, the Imperial Bank by the Reserve bank for a number of years.

The Bank was established as a private company, with shares sold to the public, companies and banks. Administration of the Bank was vested in a Central Board of Directors comprising a Governor and (not more than four) Deputy Governors appointed by the government, fourteen directors nominated by the central government, and one government official.

Evolution of objectives and functions

During the pre-World War II period Bank Rate was never altered (it remained at 3 per cent between 1935–51), and in fact had little influence over commercial rates generally, mainly because banks continued to apply for (cheaper) advances from the Imperial bank, with which they had a close relationship, and which continued to discount traditional commercial bills (known as hundis). The Reserve Bank, on the other hand, only stood ready to discount bills created under the Indian Negotiable Instruments Act, which most commercial banks did not hold in any great quantity.

The early relationship between the Bank and other commercial banks was often difficult, and is well illustrated by the refusal (in 1938) of an ailing bank to provide the Reserve Bank with information regarding its financial position. Consequently, the Bank refused to lend, threatening a larger crisis, although this did not materialise.

The only regular customers of the Bank before and during the war, therefore, were the central and state governments, who borrowed increasingly heavily to finance wartime expenditures. As in other countries, this resulted in many of the regulations concerning the minimum reserve asset backing for the note issue to be suspended.

The Bank was nationalised in 1949, which increased the influence of the government over the Bank: the Central Board was reduced to eleven members (including the Governor plus two Deputies), all appointed by the government. In the same year the Bank's influence over the banking system was also extended, via the Banking Companies Act, which brought a much larger number of hitherto unregulated financial institutions under the regulatory and supervisory reach of the Bank.

In 1955 the Imperial Bank, until then the largest commercial bank, was nationalised and, together with ten other state banks, converted into the State Bank of India. The stated aim of this move was to apply financial resources more intensively to (state) selected sectors of the economy for the purpose of fostering economic growth and development. This aim led, in 1967, to the announcement of a policy of 'social control' over the financial system.

Amongst other things, this policy included the establishment of a National Credit Council to determine the sectoral allocation of credit, the appointment of a minimum number of directors representing these sectors in the Boards of banks, the imposition of restrictions over the lending policies of banks, and the extension of the powers of the Reserve Bank over the banking system. In 1969, the policy of social control culminated in the nationalisation of the fourteen largest registered banks. Six more banks were nationalised in 1980.

The Reserve Bank has played a unique role in establishing a number of specialised institutions such as agricultural banks, mortgage banks, mutual funds and insurance companies, and many of these were subsequently hived off from the Reserve Bank when they became independently viable. Since the mid-1980s the Reserve Bank has also initiated steps to shift monetary management from 'direct' controls to more indirect methods. Furthermore, in 1991 major financial reforms were undertaken: reserve requirements were lowered, money markets were encouraged, and a market in government securities was developed.

Independence

Contrary to the spirit of the League of Nations conferences in the early 1920s (which had provided the impetus for the Reserve Bank), the Bank has not been independent from the government, which has typically determined its policies. According to a Minister of Finance in 1957: 'we can, in matters where Government's policies are to be carried out, issue directives ... the Reserve bank can hold a different opinion though they have to act according to the directives ...'

The Bank's independence was compromised soon after its establishment, as state governments from time to time indulged in unauthorised overdrafts which, for political reasons, the Bank could not prevent. Furthermore, from about 1955, and certainly after 1967, the Bank was expected to exercise detailed control over the allocation of credit by banks to different sectors of the economy under the government's policy of 'social control'.

In recent years, however, a scheme for the regulation of overdrafts to State governments has been put into place, which has led to a significant improvement in the fiscal discipline of the States. Furthermore, a major reform is currently underway aimed at phasing out – over a period of three years – the automatic monetisation of the government via the sale of *ad hoc* Treasury bills to the Bank. For 1994–95 a ceiling on such monetisation has been fixed which, if it is exceeded, will result in the Reserve Bank selling government paper into the market to reduce the level of its government securities. This step is expected to contribute to fiscal discipline and improve the Reserve bank's scope for effective monetary management.

REFERENCES

Almaula, N. I. (1960) *Operations of the Reserve Bank of India 1935–54*. Asia Publishing House: London.

Bagchi, A. M. (1987) *The Evolution of the State Bank of India 1806–1876*. Oxford University Press: Bombay.

Gupta. O. P. (1934) *Central Banking in India*. Hindustan Times Press: Delhi

Hasan, K. S. and L. N. Blythe (1973) *Banking in India*. Macdonald and Evans: Plymouth.

Iengar, H. V. R. (1962) 'Central banks and governments', speech delivered under the joint auspices of the Democratic Group of Indian Merchants' Chamber, the

Commerce Graduates Association and the Progressive Group, Bombay, January.

Jha, L. K. (1985) 'Redefining the role of RBI and the government', Commerce, September 7.

Olakanpo, J. O. (1965) *Central banking in the Commonwealth*. Bookland Private: Calcutta.

Raman, A. (1969) *Central Banking in India: A Study of Recent Development*. Calcutta.

Rangarajan C. (1988) 'Issues in Monetary Management'. Presidential Address at the 71st Annual Conference of the Indian Economic Association held under the auspices of Jadavpur University at Calcutta.

Rangarajan, C. (1993) 'Autonomy of Central Banks'. Tenth M. G. Kutty Memorial Lecture, Calcutta.

Reserve Bank of India (1970) *History of the Reserve Bank of India 1935–51*.

Reserve Bank of India (1983) *Functions and Working*. 4th edition.

Reserve Bank of India (1985) *Report of the Committee to Review the Working of the Monetary System in India*.

Sen, S. N. (ed.) (1963) *The Monetary Policy of the Reserve Bank of India*. Papers read at the Indian Economic Conference, Bombay.

Srivastava, N. N. (1972) *Evolution of the Techniques of Monetary Management in India*. Somaiya Publications: India.

Vaswani, T. A. (1968) *Indian Banking System*. Lavani Publishing House: Bombay.

B28   El Banco Central de Venezuela (The Central Bank of Venezuela)

Founded in 1940

Forerunner

None. Until the 1920s, the Venezuelan economy was predominantly agricultural, and its monetisation was far from complete. Six of the country's eleven commercial banks issued their own currency, with the Banco de Venezuela being the largest in terms of note issue, capital and turnover (by 1939 it had 67 per cent of the total issue). The Banco de Venezuela also performed limited central banking functions, as it was the government's bank and held a contract (with the government) which made it responsible for the circulation of currency in accordance with the rules of the gold standard.

The character of the economy began to change in the late 1920s, however, owing to the growth of the oil industry. Exports of oil grew rapidly, and led to a tremendous increase in foreign currency revenues, necessitating the creation of a structured foreign exchange market. In 1937, a separate institution, the Officina National de Centralición de Cambio, was created by the National Government to control the foreign exchange market, a respon-sibility which since 1934 had been the province of the Banco de Venezuela (in accordance with government policy).

Motivation for founding

The growth of the oil industry increased the number, the size and the complexity of commercial transactions. At the same time, profound poli-tical, economic, and social changes were taking place. The establishment of a central bank and the modernisation of the financial system of the country began to be discussed in a serious way, following the Latin American trend for creating central banks which had flourished in the early 1920s (and again after the beginning of the Great Depression).

Unlike many other Latin American countries, however, there was little foreign intervention in the establishment of a central bank in Venezuela, nor was it prompted by heavy external or public debt. Instead, the initiative for a central bank seemed to stem from the political and economic changes taking place in the country, and the belief that a central bank could facilitate economic development. Following a Mission to the United States and other Latin American countries, therefore, the Banco Central de Venezuela was established in 1940.

Original objectives and functions

The main objectives of the Banco Central de Venezuela (hereafter the Bank) according to its first charter were, firstly, to centralise the issue of bank notes and to establish a uniform currency and, secondly, to regulate monetary circulation according to the needs of the economy. The Bank obtained the exclusive right to issue bank notes and became the only financial agent of the National Government, the states, municipalities, autonomous institutions and State companies. In addition, the Bank was required to maintain both the internal and external value of the bolivar, to centralise national reserves and to regulate and to oversee trade in gold and foreign exchange.

The Bank was established as a private institution, but the government owned 51 per cent of the shares while the remainder was in private hands. The Board of the Bank consisted of one President (who was elected by the Shareholders' Assembly) and eight Directors (four of which were appointed by the government, and the others being elected). It is noteworthy that the Bank's first charter explicitly prohibited the extension of credit to the government, the states and the municipalities.

Evolution of objectives and functions

Three amendments to the initial Law of 1939 have occurred, the first in 1960, the second in 1974, a year after the general increase in oil prices, and the most recent in 1992.

In 1960, it was explicitly stated that the Bank should create and maintain monetary, credit and exchange conditions that encouraged the stability of the currency, fostered economic equilibrium and promoted the economic development of the country. Additionally, the Bank was authorised to exercise the rights and assume the obligations of Venezuela at IMF.

In 1974, the objectives and the functions of the Bank remained virtually as before, with the most notable addition to the statute being that the Bank 'should assure the continuity of the country's international payments'. The Bank also obtained the right to mint coins, an authority that was previously held by the National Government.

The current Law (1992) states explicitly that one of the major objectives of the Bank is monetary stability. To this end the Law grants extensive powers to the Bank to regulate interest rates and bank reserves.

Independence

Although its founders intended to establish an independent central bank, it is difficult to argue that the Bank has been independent in practice. In 1974 the Bank was nationalised and the government became the sole owner of its shares. The juridical structure of a limited liability company remained but, under the new charter, the government obtained the right to appoint the majority of Directors (i.e. the number of Directors was reduced to seven, with four being chosen from high ranking officials of the government).

In 1992 the Central Bank Law was again revised, with one aim being to increase the autonomy of the Bank. The number of directors was again reduced, of which only three were designated by the President of the Republic. The 1992 Law also prohibits the Banco Central de Venezuela from granting direct credits to the National Government, and from guaranteeing the obligations of the Republic or of any other public entity. The crisis of 1994, however, revealed the fragility of the Bank's autonomy from the government, the final outcome of which has yet to become clear.

REFERENCES

Banco Central de Venezuela (1992) *The Law of the Central Bank of Venezuela.* Caracas.

Crazut, R. J. (1990) *El Banco Central de Venezuela: Notas sobre su Historia y Evolución, 1940–1990.* 4th edition. Banco Central de Venezuela: Caracas.

Escobar, J. B. (1992) *Jurisprudencia del Máximo Tribunal de la República Relacionada con el Banco Central de Venezuela, 1940–1990*. Volumes I and II. Banco Central de Venezuela: Caracas.

Llamozas, H. E. (1990) *Complicación de Leyes del Banco Central de Venezuela*. Banco Central de Venezuela: Caracas.

Pazos, F. (ed.) (1990) *Crecimiento Económico con Estabilidad Financiera*. Banco Central de Venezuela: Caracas.

B29   Reserve Bank of Ireland

Founded in 1942

Forerunner

The Bank of Ireland was established in 1783 as the government's bank (the entire capital of the Bank was lent to the government), in return for which it received a partial monopoly over the issue of notes (no other body exceeding six partners could establish an issuing bank). Notes were convertible into gold, and the Bank maintained an exchange rate that put the currency on a par with sterling. After a period during which convertibility was suspended (1797–1821) in both Ireland and England, the prior relationship with sterling was restored.

The Bank of Ireland's position as a nascent central bank suffered a setback when, in 1817, the Irish and British exchequers were merged, robbing the bank of its intimate relationship with government. Furthermore, in 1821, the Bank of Ireland's monopoly note issue was restricted to a fifty-mile radius around Dublin, and in 1824 joint-stock banks were permitted to issue notes (outside of this fifty mile radius), thus competing with the Bank in this regard. Finally, in 1826, the Irish pound was effectively amalgamated with sterling, and ceased to have a separate identity.

Unlike the Bank of England, therefore, the Bank of Ireland did not attain a dominant position within the Irish financial system during the nineteenth century. Instead, the Bank coexisted with several other note-issuing banks, most of whom also developed a reasonable branch network. Most financial dealings with the continent were cleared through London, whilst the Bank of Ireland itself had a last resort relationship with the Bank of England, from which it was able to draw gold or notes in times of crisis. This situation persisted until the Irish Banking Act of 1845, which prevented any further note-issuing banks from being established. Furthermore, the Act placed limits on the circulation of the existing issuers, with the result that Bank of England notes gradually became the dominant media of exchange.

With the formation of the Irish Free State in 1922 the Bank of Ireland was asked to act as the financial agent of the new government. Its role as commercial bank, however, made it unwelcome as a candidate for a central bank with regulatory powers over other commercial banks, and it consequently did not become a central bank. Instead, in 1926 a Coinage Act was passed which authorised the Minister of Finance to issue token currency of limited legal tender (sterling also retained limited legal tender). In order to control the issue of this currency, a Commission of Inquiry (headed by Professor Parker-Willis, a former Director of Research of the Federal Reserve Board) proposed the establishment of a Currency Commission, which was to maintain parity between this new Irish currency and sterling. The Currency Act of 1927 gave legislative form to these proposals, and a Currency Commission was duly set up, issuing and regulating currency until the establishment of a new central bank in 1942.

Motivation for founding

In 1934 a Second Commission of Inquiry was set up to examine the Irish banking and credit system, and recommended (some years later, in 1938) that the Currency Commission be replaced by another monetary authority with expanded powers, namely a central bank. The Act encompassing these recommendations, the Central Bank Act, was eventually passed in 1942.

Original objectives and functions

The primary objective of the Central Bank of Ireland (hereafter the Bank) was to '[safeguard] the integrity of the currency and ... [ensure] that, in what pertains to the control of credit, the constant and predominant aim shall be the welfare of the people as a whole'. To this end the Bank was authorised to issue currency, accept deposits, rediscount bills, purchase government bonds and make advances. Initially, however, the Bank did not have the statutory right to restrict credit by direct quantitative limit, nor could it influence credit conditions via open-market operations. No bills were discounted until 1955.

Furthermore, the Bank did not immediately obtain duties undertaken by many other central banks. For example, the Bank did not become the government's bank (this function was performed by the National Bank of Ireland), nor did it become the custodian of the reserves of the commercial banks or of the external assets of these banks.

The Bank was owned by the government, and administered by Governor and a Board of (at most) eight Directors who were appointed by the President on the advice of the Government.

Evolution of objectives and functions

The operations of the Bank expanded only gradually over the next two decades. In 1958 banks were required to settle all clearances via accounts held at the Bank. Then, in 1965, the administration of exchange control was delegated to the Bank, and in the same year the Bank obtained the power to advise banks to restrict credit growth.

Under the Central Bank Act of 1971 the bank acquired the exchequer accounts, and thus became the government's bank. Furthermore, the Bank also gained the responsibility for licensing and supervising banks. These powers were extended under another Central Bank Act, in 1989, at which time the Bank's Board was also extended from eight to nine members.

Independence

The Bank is owned by the government, and its Governor and Board selected by the government. Furthermore, under the Bank's original Act, the Minister of Finance had the power to request the Bank's Governor 'to consult and advise him in regard to the execution and performance of the Bank'. Whilst this made the Bank formally dependent upon the government, this clause has never been invoked, and independence has been recognised as important. In 1942 the Minister of Finance noted that the Bank 'will be independent in the carrying out of its functions. This independence is possessed by almost every central bank throughout the world and is a very desirable provision.'

In practice, therefore, the Bank has had a degree of independence; there has been cooperation between the Bank and the Treasury; and the Bank has been a limited funder of government.

REFERENCES

Barrow, G. L. (1975) *The Emergence of the Irish Banking System, 1820–1845*. Gill and Macmillan: Dublin.
Bodenhorn, H. (1992) 'Free banking in Ireland', in K. Dowd (ed.) *The Experience of Free Banking*. Routledge London.
Central Bank Act (1942) (1971) (1989).
Central Bank of Ireland (1992) 'Summary material relating to the role, functions, structure and independence of the Central Bank of Ireland', Manuscript, Monetary Policy Division, March.
Central Bank of Ireland (1992) *Annual Report*. Dublin.
Doherty, J. (1993) 'The evolution of central banking in Ireland', in Central Bank of Ireland, *Annual Report 1992*, Summer.
Hall, F. G. (1949) *The Bank of Ireland 1783–1946*. Hodges, Figgis and Co.: Dublin.

Lyons, F. S. L. (1983) *Bicentenary Essays: Bank of Ireland 1783–1983*. Gill and Macmillan: Dublin.

McGowan, P. (1990) 'Money and banking in Ireland – origins, development and future', Institute of Public Administration and Statistical and Social Inquiry Society of Ireland, Dublin.

McGowan, P. (1992) 'The operation of monetary policy in Ireland', Presidential Address to the Statistical and Social Inquiry Society of Ireland, Dublin, October.

Moynihan, M. (1969) 'The Central Bank of Ireland', John Busteed Memorial lecture, delivered at University College, Cork, May.

Moynihan, M. (1975) *Currency and Central Banking in Ireland 1922–1960*. Central Bank of Ireland: Dublin.

B30   Reserve Bank of Australia

Founded in 1959 (formerly the Commonwealth Bank, founded in 1911)

Forerunner

The Commonwealth Bank had been established in 1911 and, by most accounts, had come to resemble a central bank before World War II. Thus this summary begins with the founding of the Commonwealth Bank, and traces its evolution into the Reserve Bank.

For much of the nineteenth century, media of exchange in Australia comprised gold and silver coin and, from the 1820s, bank notes convertible into coin. With the formation of the Commonwealth of Australia (i.e. Federation) in 1901, authority was given to the Federal government to regulate banks and the issue of notes. Under this authority, the government permitted the Treasury to issue convertible notes (backed by a gold reserve of 25 per cent) in 1910, whilst at the same time taxing (at 10 per cent) the note issue of all issuing banks, thus effectively creating a monopoly note issue for the Commonwealth Treasury.

Motivation for founding

Proposals for a state bank had been heard since the 1840s, usually for an institution resembling the Bank of England. A host of reasons were forwarded, over the years, to motivate such a bank, ranging from the regulation of 'excessively profitable' banks and the provision of cheap credit (both private and public), to the creation of a national note issue and support for the banking system. In addition, a severe banking crisis in the early 1890s, together with Federation in 1901 are usually cited as important events which motivated discussion of a state bank.

In 1910 the Minister for Home Affairs of the newly elected Labour Government, King O'Malley, put forward a substantial proposal for a national bank which would issue notes, act as the government's bank, hold the reserves of other banks, and control the currency. This proposal was supported by the Prime Minister (Andrew Fisher), culminating in the Commonwealth Bank Bill of 1911, which established the Commonwealth Bank.

Original objectives and functions

Contrary to the intention of O'Mally, the Commonwealth Bank did not issue notes since legislation from 1910 had created a de facto note issuing monopoly for the Treasury. The Commonwealth Bank, therefore, was predominatly a commercial bank, acting also as the government's bank, whose objective was to compete with the established commercial banks and make a profit. In practice, however, the early relationship between the Commonwealth Bank and other commercial banks tended to be more cooperative than competitive, as the first Governor of the Bank did not embark on an aggressive campaign to compete with commercial banks in their traditional business.

Unlike most other banks, no capital was raised for the establishment of the Commonwealth Bank, as it was started with a (temporary) government loan, to be repaid from the profits of the Bank. All the business of the Commonwealth Bank was managed by a single Governor who, without shareholders or a Board of Directors to restrict him, consequently assumed wide powers.

Evolution of objectives and functions

Throughout the First World War, the activity of the Commonwealth Bank was centred around its function as the government's bank. This changed in 1920, however, when the Treasury handed over the note issue to a separate issue department of the Commonwealth Bank, modelled upon that of the Bank of England. Authority over this department was not given to the Governor, however, but to a Notes Board (of which the Governor was a member).

A highly restrictive – and unpopular – note issue policy between 1920–23 led to a reorganistion of the management of the Commonwealth Bank in 1924. A Board of Directors, appointed by government and made up of a Governor, the Secretary of the Treasury and six Directors, was charged with the management of the Bank. Although the Bank was given the power to fix and publish a discount rate, this had little impact given the absence of a money market and the extremely limited use of trade bills. Finally, during the reorganisation of 1924 other banks were required to settle their inter-bank obligations via accounts held at the Commonwealth Bank.

The Commonwealth Bank emerged from the Depression with responsi-bility over the exchange rate and foreign exchange reserves, although interest rate changes were usually initiated by another trading bank, the Bank of New South Wales. It was not until the Second World War that interest rates finally came under the control of the Commonwealth Bank (1941), essentially to guarantee the cheap money policy of war finance. Other war-time regulations included the imposition of Special Accounts, into which trading banks were to place funds in proportion to their asset growth (i.e. these were essentially reserve requirements).

Following the war, the Commonwealth Bank Bill (1945) was passed, which replaced all existing banking legislation and, for the first time, clearly defined the role of the Commonwealth Bank as a central bank. The Bank was to 'pursue a monetary and banking policy directed to the greatest advantage of the people of Australia', and would contribute to 'the stability of the currency' and to the 'maintenance of full employment'. The existing Board of Directors was abolished, and sole managerial authority vested in the Governor, who was to be aided by an Advisory Council comprised of Treasury officials. However, this Advisory Council was in turn replaced by a Board of Directors (which had the same structure as the original Board) in 1951 The ultimate authority over the policy of the Bank continued to rest with the government.

In 1959, under the Reserve Bank Act, the central banking functions of the Commonwealth Bank were separated from its commercial, functions, and marked the point at which the Commonwealth Bank, now renamed as the Reserve Bank, was formally defined as 'the central bank of Australia'. The trading and savings activities of the Commonwealth Bank were continued as part of a separate entity, the Commonwealth Banking Corporation. Few changes of substance were incorporated into the Act, however, and the emphasis was on continuity. The system of Special Accounts introduced in 1941 was phased out, and replaced by a formal system of reserve require-ments. In the same year, a short-term money market was finally established, and the Reserve Bank offered a secured lending faciltiy to authorised dealers within this market to deal with seasonal cash shortages.

Independence

Until the early 1980s the Reserve Bank (and previously the Commonwealth bank) did not have a high degree of independence from government. For example, government security yields were, for many years, set by the

Treasury; changes in bank interest rates and reserve requirments (both of which the Bank was empowered to regulate) had to have the prior approval of the Treasury; monetary targets were decided upon by the Treasury and announced in the budget speech. Deregulation during the early 1980s, however, has scrapped many regulations and controls, essentially leaving the short-term interest rate as the only policy instrument. Since then, therefore, the independence of the Bank has increased in practice. The ultimate authority for policy remains with the government: in the event of policy disagreement, for example, the views of both parties are tabled in Parliament, with the elected government having the final say. Such a dispute has never occurred.

REFERENCES

Butlin, S. J. (1983) 'Australian Central Banking, 1945–59', *Australian Economic History Review*, 23, 2.

Butlin, S. J. (1986) *The Australian Monetary System 1851–1914*. Ambassador Press: Sydney.

Campbell Committee of Inquiry into the Australian Monetary System (1981) *Final Report*. Australian Government Publishing Service: Canberra.

Copland, D. B. (1929) 'The banking system of Australia', in Willis, H. P. and B. H. Beckhart (eds.) *Foreign Banking Systems*. Sir Isaac Pitman and Sons: London.

Fraser, B. (1991) 'Some observations on the role of the Reserve Bank', Speech at Annual General Meeting of CEDA, Sydney, November.

Fraser, B. (1993) 'Reserve Bank independence and all that', *Reserve Bank of Australia Bulletin*, December.

Giblin, L. F. (1951) *The Growth of a Central Bank: The Development of the Commonwealth Bank of Australia 1924–1945*. Melbourne University Press: Melbourne.

Gollan, R. (1968) *The Commonwealth Bank of Australia: Origins and Early History*. Australian National University Press: Canberra.

Johnston, R. A. (1989) 'The Reserve Bank's role in economic management', *Reserve Bank of Australia Economic Bulletin*, May.

Linklater, J. (1992) *Inside the Bank: The Role of the Reserve Bank of Australia in the Economic, Banking and Financial Systems*. Allen and Unwin: St Leonards.

Norton, B. and P. Stebbingn (eds.) (1990) *Monetary Policy and Market Operations*. Papers presented at Pacific Region Central Bank Conference. Reserve Bank of Australia: Sydney.

Olakanpo, J. O. (1965) *Central Banking in the Commonwealth*. Bookland Private: Calcutta.

Phillips, M. J. (1992) 'Central banking – a parting view', Reserve Bank of Australia Bulletin, April.

Plumptre, A. F. W. (1940) *Central Banking in the British Dominions*. University of Toronto Press: Toronto.

Schedvin, C. B. (1992) *In Reserve: Central Banking in Australia, 1945–75*. Allen and Unwin: St Leonards.

B31   Banco Central do Brazil (Central Bank of Brazil)

Founded in 1965

Forerunner

The Superintendencia da Moeda e do Crédito (hereafter the Sumoc) – which formulated economic policy, supervised banks and conducted monetary research – may be considered to be the forerunner of the Central Bank of Brazil (hereafter the Bank). The Sumoc was formed in 1945 to unify and carry out banking regulation after the Second World War. The banking structure at this time was relatively complex, with central banking functions being divided between the Banco do Brazil, a commercial bank, and various agencies of the Treasury.

The Banco do Brazil was a private bank established under Brazilian commercial law, although the majority of its stock was owned by the Treasury. It consisted of two commercial banking departments and, additionally, several departments with full central banking functions, the most important of which were the Rediscount Department (Cared), the Agency for Banking Supervision and Operations (Camob) and the Foreign Exchange Department.

Before the creation of the Sumoc in 1945, the function of note issue was discharged by two institutions. Currency could be issued directly by the Treasury (for its own use or when asked by the Agency for Banking Supervision and Operations (Camob) for loans to banks), or by the Banco do Brazil when this was requested by the Rediscount Department (Cared).

Between 1945 and 1965 central banking functions in Brazil were thus undertaken both by the Sumoc and by the Banco do Brazil. Monetary regulation was the responsibility of the Sumoc, while currency was issued by the Treasury at the request of the Banco do Brazil. During this period the Banco do Brazil also acted as a commercial bank, representing a competitive threat to the expansion of the other commercial banks.

Motivation for Founding

After the end of the Second World War, Brazil experienced unprecedented rates of growth, but inflation also began to increase.

In 1964 an attempt was made to centralise central banking functions. Furthermore, the power of the privileged Banco do Brazil constituted a continuous threat to other commercial banks, who found it difficult to compete with a bank that could issue notes and whose deposits were virtually guaranteed by the government. There were doubts on both sides, therefore, whether the Banco do Brazil was the appropriate institution to assume the responsibility of being banker to the commercial banks.

In 1965, therefore, a new central bank, the Banco Central do Brazil was established. The Banco do Brazil, although it retained the right to request the Treasury to issue currency, became a purely commercial bank. It has remained the largest and most important commercial bank, and is still controlled by the government. Whilst conducting the complete range of commercial banking functions it also executes government policy in critical areas, such as rural credit.

The establishment of the Bank did little to reduce the complex manner in which central banking functions were organised in Brazil. The same law that provided for the creation of the Bank also created a National Monetary Council (Conselho Monetário Nacional, CMN). This Council became responsible for determining monetary and exchange rate policy, and also assumed the role of banking regulator and supervisor.

The CMN consisted of nine members, three of which became members because they held public offices (the Minister of Finance, the President of the Banco do Brazil, and the President of the National Economic Development Bank). The remaining six members were appointed by the President of the Republic with the consent of the Senate. The Council chose four out of the six fixed-term appointees to become the directors of the Board of the Bank for six years, one of whom would be president of the Central Bank. As a result, the members of the Board of the Central Bank were all members of the CMN.

Original objectives and functions

The usual central bank objectives and functions were assumed by the Bank, although they were not explicitly stated in its charter. For example, the Bank became responsible for providing currency, acting as a banker to the banks and as a fiscal agent of the Treasury, and became the custodian of foreign exchange reserves. According to the 1964 charter the Bank also had to implement the policy decisions of the CMN regarding interest rates, and undertake the function of banking supervision.

Despite the Bank having all the appearances of a central bank, some functions continued to be exercised by other institutions. The Executive branch of the Government retained most of its former authority in matters relating to money and credit creation, and currency issue remained under the control, though now indirectly, of the Minister of Finance. The Banco do Brazil, through the 'movement account', also retained the privilege of issuing money.

Evolution of objectives and functions

The Cental Bank Board increased its limited power to determine monetary policy in 1967, when the membership of the National Monetary Council was increased to ten and the Board of the Central Bank gained a fifth member. The requirement that the Board of the Central Bank consist only of members of the National Monetary Council was maintained. Nevertheless, majority voting power in the National Monetary Council was now in the hands of the Board of the Bank. In addition, the term of office of the members of the Board was increased from six to seven years.

Reforms in 1986 were a landmark in the history of the Bank. Many measures were introduced to simplify the complicated relations between the Federal Treasury, the Central Bank and the Banco do Brazil. The Banco do Brazil was classified as a commercial bank rather than a monetary authority. Another group of resolutions sought to include in the fiscal budget all current expenditures of the government that were carried out by the Bank.

Central bank credit control was complicated by the so-called 'movement account' which permitted the Banco do Brazil to continue to issue money in spite of the fact that there was a central bank in the country. In 1986 this practice was abolished, depriving the Banco of what was a significant contribution to its profits. It was subsequently compensated by being permitted to engage in new types of activities, such as accepting rural savings deposits.

Independence

The period 1965–67 probably represents the only time during which the Bank experienced a limited degree of independence. The first real test of the stability and independence of the Central Bank Board occurred in 1967, when a new President of the Republic was chosen, and a constitutional amendment passed which granted him unprecedented powers. This made it clear that the appointment of the members of the Board of the Central Bank was entirely at the discretion of the President.

The existence of the National Monetary Council (CMN) as the superior decision-making body has further restricted the powers, functions and independence of the Central Bank. Most members of the Council can be replaced at the discretion of the President, and the terms of their office are not predetermined, which makes them vulnerable to political pressure. Since 1974 the entire Bank Board can be dismissed at the discretion of the President.

A proposed reform in 1994 aims to reduce the number of members of the

CMN, thereby increasing the relative importance of the Bank's Governor, who also serves as the deputy chairman of the CMN.

REFERENCES

Almeida, J. R. N. (1992) 'Essays on Brazilian monetary polices and history, 1945–1988'. Unpublished MPhil thesis, the George Washington University.

Lees, F. A., Botts, J. M. and R. P. Cysne (1990) *Banking and Financial Deepening in Brazil*. Macmillan: London.

Rietti, M. (1979) *Money and Banking in Latin America*. Praeger: New York.

Silva-Herzog, J. F. and R. Lecuona (eds.) (1991) *Banca Central en America Latina II: El Financiamiento Interno del Desarrollo*. Centro de Estudios Monetarios Latinoamericanos: Mexico.

Tamanga, F. (1965) *Central Banking in Latin America*. Centro de Estudios Monetarios Latinoamericanos: Mexico.

B32   El Banco Central de Uruguay (The Central Bank of Uruguay)

Founded in 1967

Forerunner

The Banco de la República Oriental de Uruguay (hereafter the Banco de la República) created in 1896, is considered to have been the first central bank to be established in Latin America.

Prior to the establishment of the Banco de la República, a multiple note-issuing system had prevailed, with foreign banks also able to issue notes. The country had been on the gold standard, with short interruptions since 1865. The first attempt to centralise note issue was made in 1890, when the Banco Nacional, a private bank established in 1887, was granted a monopoly over the note issue. However, this institution very quickly went bankrupt, due to its attempt at reconciling two (conflicting) interest groups within Uruguayan society. One group, known as the 'oristas', made payments abroad in gold, and could benefit from high interest rates. They thus required monetary stability for the successful conduct of their business, and supported convertibility to gold. The other group, the 'papelistas', which included small farmers, manufacturers and members of the government in their ranks, found the shortage of credit and high interest rates an obstacle to economic prosperity. They favoured an inconvertible paper currency and expanded credit facilities. Needless to say, the liberal extension of credit by the Banco Nacional, together with the attempted maintenance of convertibility, soon led to its bankruptcy.

The foundation of the Banco de la República in 1896 followed the crisis of 1890 and the failure of the Banco Nacional. The Banco de la República was founded as a state bank and undertook commercial as well as central banking functions. It consisted of three departments, the Currency Department, the Banking Department and the National Savings and Discount Fund. Each department was under separate administration while the general policy of the Banco de la República was determined by a Board of Directors.

The Banco de la República retained its original form (apart from being nationalised in 1911) for seventy years after its creation in 1896. Constitutional reform in 1966 led to it being replaced by the Banco Central de Uruguay.

Motivation for founding

Uruguay experienced double digit inflation for the first time in the late 1950s, generated by increases in the money supply due to increased fiscal and private borrowing. In 1959 a programme to establish internal and external equilibrium was introduced which, in addition to fiscal and exchange measures, included restrictions on central bank credit to the private sector and to banks. Whilst these measures were effective in curbing credit from the Currency Department of the Banco de la República to other banks, the Banking Department of the central bank increased credit to the government and to the public, thereby failing to constrain money supply growth.

A plebiscite was organised in 1966 to approve constitutional reforms. The new constitution provided for the establishment of a central bank which would be established as an autonomous entity. Thus the Banco Central de Uruguay was founded, beginning operations the following year. As a result, the Banco de la República became a purely commercial bank and took on the more specialised role of development bank.

Original objectives and functions

The original objectives and functions of the Banco Central de Uruguay (hereafter the Bank) were much the same as those of the Banco de la República (see below). The Banco de la República was granted the right to issue notes, became the government's bank and managed the foreign reserves of the country.

The establishment of the Bank, like its predecessor, was aimed at promoting credit and at channelling the resources of the country to the productive sectors of the economy for the benefit of the nation. It is noteworthy that the Bank could not rediscount bills for other commercial banks, as it was considered that this function had previously fostered inflation.

Evolution of objectives and functions

Changes to the objectives and functions of the Banco de la República while it operated as a central bank were aimed at strengthening its central banking character. Amendments to its charter, from the beginning, specifically promoted the centralisation of the issuing of bank notes. The Banco de la República shared the responsibility with the Investment and Economic Development Commission for the preparation of national plans and projects and the coordination of financial activities aimed at increasing national production and productivity.

A notable amendment to the charter of the Banco de la República occurred in 1964, when it was stated that the Currency Department was to maintain a quantity of money in circulation such as was required for balanced economic growth. As mentioned above, this provision did not inhibit inflation as had been hoped.

Independence

Whilst the statute of the Banco de la República, and of the Banco Central del Uruguay in its turn, have provided for some degree of independence, the history of both Banks confirms that they have never been fully independent. The central government, with the consent of the senate, appoints the majority of the members of the Board of the Banco de la República, and the term of office of the Directors of the Bank coincides with that of the President of the country. There are currently plans to grant a greater degree of autonomy to the Bank.

REFERENCES

Banco de la República Oriental del Uruguay (1964) *Carta Organica.* Montevideo.
Finch, M. H. J. (1981) *A Political Economy of Uruguay since 1870.* Macmillan: London.
Tamagna, F. (1965) *Central Banking in Latin America.* Centro de Estudios Monetarios Latinoamericanos: Mexico.

Conference proceedings

Presentation: Professor Charles Goodhart

The purpose of our paper has been to review the question of how, and why, central banks developed over the course of their history into their present state. Although this is a celebration of the tercentenary of the Bank of England, our paper has tried to cover a much wider canvas, concentrating on those functions and features common to virtually all central banks. In any case the Bank has been extremely well served by its historians, most notably Clapham, Sayers and more recently John Fforde.

Indeed, the second appendix of our long paper was taken up with potted histories, constructed in a systematic manner within a standardised framework, of some thirty-two major and long-lived central banks around the world, with in each case a bibliography of major reference works.

In the longer run it will probably be this part of our work, primarily written and organised by my co-author, Norbert Schnadt, that will prove of most use to future students of central banking. We are most grateful for the extensive assistance in preparing these summary histories that we have had from the central banks concerned, but the editorial responsibility, final decision and stated authorship remains with us, Forrest Capie, Norbert and myself, since these potted histories are not to be treated as an authorised version, even if they have frequently been much assisted, for which we thank you.

Within the relatively short time available this morning, I can do little more than summarise the contents of the first, and more general, part of our paper before picking up a selection of the more important themes. We have tried to emphasize the development of the main functions of a central bank; in its role as the guarantor of the value of the currency, whether via the gold standard, an intermediate target, or by the direct pursuit of price stability; its role as banker to the government, and as banker to the other commercial banks, rather than restricting ourselves to a purely chronological ordering. It is, moreover, always difficult to distil order and logic from the often disjointed sequence and happenstance of historical data. This can result in creative tensions between the personas of the historian in the economic historian and his economist *döppelganger*. The historian in the economic historian is perhaps more comfortable with the uniqueness of events and happy to explain each change as the product of a number of factors specific to that change. The economist in the economic historian is always tempted to look for generalisations, and we succumb to that temptation in spite of the difficulties. But both have an essential role to play. At this juncture I want to emphasise the full extent to which this paper is joint work with my co-author Forrest Capie. He shares the responsibility for all this work, especially the errors. For those wanting a clue about who wrote what, all I will say is that Forrest is happy to end a sentence with a preposition, whereas that is something which I will not put up with. At least not in print.

It is, perhaps, the tensions and stresses within the lives of both individuals and institutions, and how they have attempted to deal with these, that are most interesting and illuminating. Let me now focus my comments around three such areas of tension. The first concerns an issue, the relationship between central and commercial banks, where there was once serious rivalry, but which has now been largely resolved. In their earlier years, prior to the latter part of the nineteenth century, central banks were generally expected to carry out a commercial banking function; in some cases, in the European countries when they were first established, they offered the only sources of commercial banking services in that country, and for a longer period they were often the most important and largest commercial bank in their country. Consequently, the early relationships between central banks and commercial banks were often ones of business rivalry and competition. This adversarial relationship was resolved around the early twentieth century in most cases, with a few exceptions, by a largely uncodified concordat, whereby, in return for the central bank's withdrawal from commercial banking, the commercial banks voluntarily accepted the central bank's leadership – even by such informal mechanisms as the Governor's eyebrows.

Indeed, the relationships between central bank and commercial banks have passed through three main phases during our historical period. The first thus involved a shift from a competitive, and even adversarial, relationship, towards the acceptance by the central bank of its (lender of last resort) responsibility for the health of the banking system as a whole. In the second period, which ran from some time around the beginning of this century to about the early 1970s, most central banks were able to maintain this role with, at the same time, a very limited hands-on direct regulatory or supervisory function, because of the cartelised, protected, club-type structure of the banking, and indeed of the wider financial system, which fostered self-regulation.

However, competition, enhanced by information technology, and driven on by inflation, financial instability and de-regulation, has since undermined that cartelised system, but has also resulted in a marked worsening in the risk-return profile of banks in many countries in the last two decades.

The response has been, of course, to require higher capital ratios from banks in relation to their assessed risks. But competition, at least in wholesale financial markets, is now international, and the imposition of tougher capital requirements by one country's authorities in isolation would involve a comparative competitive disadvantage on the banks over whom that regulatory authority had jurisdiction. This was the incentive for central banks, and other bank regulators, to attempt to translate such regulation, and the adoption of common, international (capital adequacy) requirements onto an international, multilateral plane via, in particular, the BIS.

This has not been an easy exercise. Differences between the major countries involved in commercial laws, in accounting practices, in the customary practices and activities of banks, have meant that the achievement of a level playing field cannot be exact or complete. This will continue to generate some friction. It is probably even harder to measure risk, particularly on an *ex ante* basis, in a manner that is generally accepted as both reasonably simple and accurate. There are, for example, so many forms of risk, credit risk, interest rate risk, liquidity risk, foreign exchange risk, etc, etc. In a world where covariances are not unity, and hedging practices are not only possible but practicable, risks should clearly not be calculated just on an additive basis, but more sophisticated measures will often be controversial, complex and sometimes beyond the capacity of smaller banks to operate.

Moreover, there are dangers that this exercise will distort banking business into areas where the risk/return trade-off has been, somewhat artificially, influenced by the regulatory authorities. Meanwhile, the general increase in the need for bank capital is perceived as burdensome, and there is a perception that the traditional business of banking, at least in those countries with advanced, efficient, and competitive capital markets, is under threat and in potential decline. Another aspect of this same syndrome is that non-bank institutions may be moving into core banking business, while banks are trying to diversify into other areas. The dividing lines between the functional roles of financial institutions are becoming fuzzier.

Under these circumstances Central Bank regulators are under increasing pressure to reassess which institutions and functions they should regulate and supervise; and what exactly are the principles involved. As we note, bank regulation largely evolved thus far as an accretion of *ad hoc* responses to particular crises. In the growing flux of structural change, such an approach becomes increasingly unsatisfactory.

The second area of tension, that I want to highlight, relates to the great debates about how monetary policy should be conducted, whether by rules or discretion. For us economists, the Bank of England is special in having been the main subject of the first of the two great sustained monetary debates in history. It was also intimately involved in the recent second debate, of Monetarists versus Keynesians, amidst such landmarks as the Radcliffe Report, the Green Paper on Monetary Control and the Medium Term Financial Strategy. Although the first debate was concentrated in this country, whereas the second has been more worldwide, with its epicentre perhaps in the USA, the circumstances, conduct and outcome of these two debates are nevertheless uncannily similar. Both debates arose out of the perceived failings of the system to achieve the desired objective, currency stability. The currency debates in the 1800s initially grew out of discussions and analysis of the causes and effects of the suspension of convertibility in the UK (1797–1821) and its association with contemporary inflation, though this was further spiced by analysis of the determinants of monetary disturbances in the 1820s and 30s. Similarly the monetarist/Keynesian debate arose out of increasing concern with the endemic, and steadily worsening, medium-term inflationary experience in most developed countries in the 1960s and 1970s.

In both cases the Currency/Monetarist School advocates emphasised the essentially monetary causes of the prior inflation, whereas the Banking/Keynesian School pointed to non-monetary supply-side shocks, such as harvest failures, oil shocks, labour wage-push. In both cases, that argument has mostly been settled in favour of the Currency/Monetarist position.

Since the cause of the failure was assessed in both cases, by the Currency/Monetarist School, as arising from a failure of monetary management, an excessive rate of growth of the relevant aggregates (bank notes in the nineteenth century, some preferred monetary aggregate in the twentieth century), the obvious answer for them was to introduce appropriate controls (rules) on such monetary growth.

The Currency/Monetarist School in both instances won the intellectual battle about how to reform the monetary system, somewhat aided in the UK by the fact that the Prime Minister, in the 1840s, and then in the 1980s, was in each case of their persuasion. Peel's Bank of England Act, 1844, for example, faithfully reproduced the main proposals of the Currency School; and central banks in all major industrialised countries adopted some form of intermediate monetary target during the 1970s, and these were reinforced in several major countries by the end of the decade.

Yet in both cases the Currency/Monetarist School lost the war. The rules, which had been so carefully worked out, depended for their efficacy on an underlying, implicit assumption that the structure of the monetary system would remain unchanged. But the very introduction of these new rules helped to change that structure. This is particularly clear in the nineteenth century. The restriction on note issue led the commercial banks to place more emphasis on marketing their chequable deposit accounts, as the Banking School had warned.

In the 1980s the new set of policies, bringing with them high and variable nominal interest rates in a context of deregulation and enhanced competition, led to the introduction of financial innovations, for example new interest-bearing forms of chequable deposits, that helped to undermine the prior predictability of velocity and of the demand-for-money functions. The break-down of these prior regularities was, perhaps, even quicker and more complete in the 1980s than in the mid-1800s, but had been less well foreshadowed in the debate. This was partly because such prior regularities had appeared to be 'robustly' and 'significantly' established by the novel and arcane science of econometrics, an exercise to which I also plead guilty. Mere practitioners could hardly be expected to challenge Chow tests and the like!

In practice the new monetary rules did not work as had been intended. Financial disturbances were not averted by the 1844 Bank Act, which had to be temporarily rescinded three times shortly thereafter. This experience led to the publication of *Lombard Street*, wherein Bagehot argued that the centralisation of banking reserves with the Bank of England, which had in effect been taken further by the 1844 Bank Act, made it more rather than less essential for the Bank of England to act as a central bank for the public good to preserve systemic stability. The proposed separation of function, which lay behind the division of the Bank into Issue and Banking Departments, soon ceased to hold.

Again, in the more recent episode, experience of achieving monetary targets was mixed at best, and monetarists claimed that their policies had not been properly or seriously attempted. These operational debates became quite inflamed in the early 1980s. They were not resolved, and there was little meeting of minds. What happened, instead, in most but not all of the relevant countries, was the breakdown in the predictability of velocity. That meant that it became difficult or impossible in those countries to select a generally acceptable intermediate monetary target. But without that, there was no point left in monetary base control, though the movements in high-powered money could remain a useful information variable.

What more general lesson, if any, can we infer from observing the similarities of these two episodes? One possible lesson is that economists are good at explaining to central bankers the causes, and consequences, of the latter's past failures, but much less good at designing ways of improving the system. Their proposed 'rules' tend to be conditioned – to a far greater extent than often realised – on implicit assumptions about market structures and infrastructures. Given the continuing rapid pace of the evolution of such structures, central banks will surely aim to retain their discretionary flexibility.

The third area of tension, and perhaps the one of most immediate policy relevance, concerns the question of the appropriate relationship between the central bank and government. Indeed, this provides the main focus of Stanley Fischer's companion paper. But this is not just a present issue. Throughout the history of central banks there has been an inherent tension between their aim to maintain the value of their currency and their function as banker to the (central) government. Central banks have almost invariably been established by an Act of government, for example through a government charter, and have been designated as banker to the government. Governments have a natural preference for cheap finance from their own bank, and, particularly when the existence of the state is threatened, notably by war, they have both the power and the incentive to force the central bank to give priority to their immediate needs.

One of the incentives for governments to found the earlier-established central banks was, indeed, that these could provide an additional source of funds, particularly in times of war or other crises. But another incentive, particularly among those central banks founded around the time of the end of the Napoleonic Wars, and for the Second Bank of the United States, was that the state had generated very high inflation through the 'excessive' issue of government paper currency, to meet its wartime expenditures, described in Denmark by the splendid term 'Statsbankerot' (State bankruptcy). The establishment of a, somewhat independent, commercial banking institution, whose note issue was to be convertible into specie, either through legal restrictions on issue, or through the exercise of discretion by the Bank's directors, was perceived as a means of restoring monetary stability.

It is, perhaps, worth noting at this juncture that, while the maintenance of the value of the currency has, historically, almost always been achieved via the same instrument, varying the central bank's discount rate, this objective has not always meant the same thing. Under the classical gold standard the objective was cast in terms of metal convertibility: that is, the value of central bank notes was expressed in terms of their metal (gold) 'content'. The purchasing power of currency relative to goods in general (ie to a price index) was thus only indirectly an objective of central banks, with gold acting as the true nominal anchor. In the absence of fluctuations in the value of gold relative to goods, however, the maintenance of a fixed parity between currency and gold amounted to the same thing. But economists then, and subsequently, have argued that any such assumption was unwarranted, and many alternative intriguing suggestions, for example for a compensated dollar or indirect convertibility, have been proposed by academics. Be that as it may, with the gradual erosion of the gold standard throughout the first half of the twentieth century, and its replacement everywhere by a pure fiat standard, the objective of central bank policy has now been recast in terms of price stability. The value of central bank notes has come to be understood as the inverse of the price level, the price of a particular bundle of goods, and monetary authorities try to achieve (often implicit) price level or inflation targets.

Historically the principal factors influencing government/central bank relations over almost two centuries have been the prevailing political conditions (essentially peace/war), the dominant political/economic philosophy of the time, and the exchange-rate regimes. As in much of economic life, there has been an alternating pattern, in this case of relative dependence and independence. Such a pattern of alternating regimes is not uncommon in economic history. It has, for example, appeared in the case of switches between periods of fixed and floating exchange rates.

When we turn to changing fashions in relation to monetary policy, there are perhaps three important elements to the explanation. First, are the underlying political conditions. Secondly, within that we can try to identify some short-term factors that trigger change. And thirdly, there is a difference according to the simplicity or complexity of the task confronting the Central Bank.

In very broad terms, the period from the origins of central banking at the beginning of the nineteenth century through to the First World War is the period when *laissez-faire* emerged, dominated, and then faded. That was a period when the state tended to keep its distance, particularly in trade and monetary matters. The belief that the gold standard, the prevailing international monetary system, provided a largely automatic means of adjustment, was important to this philosophy. A considerable degree of independence therefore obtained, particularly in so far as it related to the central bank assisting in the smooth working of the gold standard. The period from the First World War to the 1970s has in contrast been the age of the state, of economic management, of socialism. It was in this period that there was a move to greater government control, and of more dependent central banks. This era is probably over now and we may be entering another of relative economic freedom.

The second area of explanation lies in the immediate proximate cause or trigger for change. Within the very broad underlying political conditions that I have just set out there have been some factors, not always exogenous, which have provoked a change. War, or a similar type of crisis, is the most obvious. The state has always been tempted to gain control over resources; that is, the revenue motive has never been far away. In times of crisis such as war there is an obvious incentive to ensure greater control over resources, and independence is likely to suffer and even disappear. Other triggers have been: the acquisition of sovereignty by former colonial countries; rapid inflation leading in due course to greater independence, because of the perceived responsibility of the monetary financing of governments for such inflation, and deflation leading to less independence, as greater government intervention becomes desired.

The third element in the story concerns the simplicity or complexity of the central bank's operations. When the role of the central bank is relatively clear-cut, when there is for example a single objective, especially if that is a technical one, as in the maintenance of convertibility under the gold standard, there is more likelihood of independence. At the other extreme, with the advent of Keynesian economics a range of possible objectives was opened up. What weakens, or perhaps destroys, the independence of an agent of government with delegated powers is the complexity in the range of choices.

Currently, with the recent break-down in the stability of demand-for-money functions, which I have already mentioned, central bankers have been left, largely unchallenged now by monetarist critics, to use their single main instrument, i.e. the control over short-term interest rates, in the light of their own discretion for the, generally agreed, objective of achieving medium-term price stability. The main operational problem is that interest rate changes affect the economy (and also monetary expansion) with a considerable, and varying lag. Consequently, central bankers need to vary interest rates in response to deviations of the uncertain *future* rate of inflation (from the desired, say, 0 to 2 per cent rate), rather than react to current data. This means that the forecasts of future price inflation, say 1 to 2 years hence, now play a central role in the conduct of monetary policy (as in the Bank of England quarterly forecast).

Especially, however, given the uncertainty of such forecasts, there remains considerable room for political, and other interest group, pressures to be applied to central banks, usually to defer interest rate increases at (politically) inconvenient moments. The 'time inconsistency' literature suggests that it has been the incentive structure (both for politicians and for central banks) rather than technical/operational limitations that has hindered the attainment of price stability.

It is in this context that the campaign for central bank independence has developed. In this approach the central bank is to be statutorily mandated to give primacy to the achievement of price stability, and provided with freedom from any government constraint, and autonomy to vary short-term interest rates to that end.

Besides the theoretical arguments for central bank independence, the case for it has been strengthened by the empirical evidence that, in recent decades, the more independent central banks have presided over lower inflation but had largely similar growth/employment outcomes compared with their more dependent colleagues.

The counter-claim has been made that there is little evidence that more independent central banks can directly lower the unemployment cost of lowering inflation (the loss function). Rather, it is suggested that more independent central banks are established where there is, in any case, a dominating political constituency for low inflation. While this may well be so, an independent central bank by its own actions, words and reputation can help to extend and to sustain that constituency.

This latter view, that the establishment of an independent central bank will largely succeed, or fail, depending on its 'political' skills in holding together a low inflation constituency, implies that the passage of Acts to grant such independence will not of themselves be a panacea. A danger in this context is that 'independence' may get oversold as the solution to all the ills of the monetary system, just as monetary targeting, exchange rate floating, and so many prior economic nostrums were often given exaggerated credence in some quarters, to their own subsequent detriment.

It is, perhaps, inevitable that there will be some degree of hype in the promotion of new ideas, in order for them to overcome the barrier of inertia. Fortunately, it is hardly necessary to remind central bankers of the merits of a cautious scepticism. This will stand them in good stead during the next 300 years.

Let me turn finally to our conclusions.

First, if the fundamental, evolutionary criterion of success is that an organisation should reproduce and multiply over the world, and successfully mutate to meet the emerging challenges of time, then central banks have been conspicuously successful. As can be seen from table 1.2 of our paper, their numbers have multiplied, and continue to grow alongside the growth in the number of separate nation states. Their existence is treated as a crucial aspect of political sovereignty. When a new nation state seeks to establish itself, the foundation of an independent central bank will be an early item on the agenda, slightly below the design of the flag, but above the establishment of a national airline. But the latter comparison should carry a health warning, in that appurtenances of national sovereignty are not, by that same token, necessarily economically essential or even efficient.

Indeed, if we should judge an institution by the effect of its actions, the recent record has been mixed. Price stability has not been achieved, as the article in the *Bank of England Quarterly Bulletin* on 'Inflation over 300 years' in the May 1994 issue showed. From the 1960s onwards, but particularly in the 1970s, there was the worst episode of endemic inflation that has occurred during periods of peace and political stability – without much excuse in the form of exogenous events such as gold discoveries. While current opinion attributes more of the blame to politicians than to central banks for that, the trend to central bank independence will put the latter on their mettle. Should central banks fail to achieve price stability in the next decade, or so, despite being given both a mandate and operational autonomy for that end, then alternative, more exotic proposals, some of which, such as Free Banking, envisage the removal of central banking altogether, may come onto the agenda. Moreover, in so far as there has been success in reining back inflation in recent years, this has gone hand in hand, in Europe at least, with rising average unemployment levels that have mirrored the 1930s in proportionate extent, if not in equivalent distress or potential political unrest. This is hardly an indication of the 'credibility' of monetary policy, which was supposed to act in the opposite direction, to lower the loss ratio.

Besides their macro objective of price stability, central banks have a micro objective of maintaining financial stability, especially in the core areas of the payment system and the commercial banks who operate that. In the last few years, the number and size of banking institutions who have failed, and have had to be bailed out by the authorities, have risen to levels last seen in the 1930s. While there have been recent episodes in which the authorities have been conspicuously successful in averting systemic financial failure, e.g. the LDC debt problem in 1982 and the 1987 stock market collapse, their handling of the property bubble and bust, 1988–93, has not been so sure. Recent developments have thrown up difficult micro-level problems, such as the universalisation and globalisation of financial institutions, the danger of moral hazard, the 'too big to fail' syndrome, the growth of over-the-counter derivatives, with which central banks have been struggling, not always successfully, to find answers.

That same globalisation has led to a massive expansion of international capital flows and foreign exchange dealing. In the face of this, the authorities in general, and central banks in particular, have seemed increasingly incapable of maintaining a stable international exchange rate regime. Floating exchange rates have behaved poorly, and pegged exchange rates have been blown asunder. Where do we go now from this?

So, looking at the record of domestic price stability, financial market stability, or international monetary order, the recent record is at best spotty. Despite their institutional success, central banks cannot afford to be complacent. There is much to learn, and much room for improvement.

Discussion

Alan Greenspan

Over the years, the Bank of England has served to a considerable extent as an example and inspiration for all of the central banks represented here today. It is natural, therefore, at an event marking the tercentenary of the

Bank to reflect on the public policy role of a central bank in general. I would like to thank Governor George for this opportunity to do so.

Charles Goodhart's paper, written with Forrest Capie and Norbert Schnadt, 'The development of central banking', is an extremely useful, thorough, and wide-ranging overview of the history of both the art of central banking and of the core policy issues that have both tested and formed that art.

I would like to take advantage of the fact that Goodhart and his colleagues have covered the ground so well and have provided a comprehensive and well-documented account of the development of central banking. Accordingly, in my remarks today, I plan to elaborate on what I see as some of the guiding principles of a central bank's public policy role. The guiding principle that runs throughout the history of central banking is that the fundamental strategic policy goal of a monetary authority should be macroeconomic price stability.

Goodhart makes the point right at the start of his paper that, historically, central banks have had as their main objective maintenance of the value of the currency, primarily in terms of gold in the early days of central banking and in terms of goods in general in modern times. The importance of price stability as an ongoing policy regime rarely surfaced when money was tied to gold. Inflation could not prevail in such a system excepting the rare episodes of substantial new gold discoveries. The consequences of chronic inflation, as distinct from specific, usually war related episodes, were rarely a subject for analyses.

In recent decades, however, it has become increasingly clear that inflation even at moderate levels is destructive of economic vitality. Evidence is beginning to mount to indicate a strong negative relationship between the degree of inflation on the one hand and the rate of growth of productivity on the other, and the direction of causation appears to run from lower inflation to productivity growth, rather than the other way around.

Moreover, while evidence of a short-run trade-off between inflation and employment seems to hold in periods of low inflation expectations, the trade-off rapidly deteriorates as inflation expectations rise. In the end, as actual inflation mounts, jobs are lost, not gained. Hence, a longer-term strategy of price stability is also a strategy to foster maximum gains in standards of living and employment.

Regrettably, maintaining such a long-term strategy too often confronts the problem of what I would label 'political time preference'.

In this regard, Professor Goodhart raises some interesting questions with respect to the currently debated degrees of central bank independence. His working definition, 'the right to change the key operational instrument without consultation or challenge from government', is as a first step appropriate. It is also important to define how the individuals who exercise that right are appointed. A central bank, which wields significant power within a democratic society through its monopoly on the issuance of the currency, must be appropriately accountable to the electorate.

If the central bank is given the cardinal obligation to preserve the value of the currency, which, as Professor Goodhart points out, is explicit or implicit pretty much throughout the current world of central banking, then the question is what is the appropriate time preference with which such an institution makes its key operational decisions? Who is to determine whether a trade-off of longer-term stability is of value relative to short-term costs, other than the electorate? One may appropriately argue that ill-advised short-run perspectives on the part of a central bank lead to inflationary instabilities in the longer run. But if the desired time frame in which the electorate chooses the central bank to function is short, it may well be argued that it is up to the electorate to realise what those consequences are and to adjust accordingly. That, of course, is the nature of a democratic society.

But is the electorate's time preference as short-sighted as many, especially political commentators, allege? Here it is important to distinguish between opinions and actions. The former do not have to adhere to reality, the latter must operate in an environment with consequences. It is quite possible, indeed too often disturbing, to find that society holds diametrically contradictory positions. The electorate, for example, may desire a lower budget deficit but simultaneously eschew increases in revenues or reduction in outlays. While contradictions can be held in political value preferences and reflected in elections, they generally cannot be maintained in the real world. Consumers cannot both spend and save the same income, nor can one indefinitely deplete one's capital. Political choices may be fudged, but the arithmetic of the real world more often than not forces real choices.

What does one then infer as to the will of the electorate as reflected through its choices in the market place? There is, clearly, quite a different time preference structure in the market place than that which is inferred in the political context. In modern societies, investment time frames can run twenty, thirty, perhaps even fifty years or longer. Indeed, the infrastructure of a modern industrial society could not function in a decision time frame of significantly shorter dimension. There is, thus, an implied time preference or, as some economists maintain, a revealed time preference of the society based on its economic choices in the market place on a day-by-day basis. That value system, of course, creates the level of interest rates, the rates of return on investments, the distribution between consumption and savings, indeed, the whole structure of any functioning competitive capitalist society.

To be sure, preferences in the market place are weighted by purchasing power rather than by the one-person-one-vote principle. Weighting by purchasing power is inappropriate for fundamental political decisions, but, for economic decisions it has distinct advantages: it provides a strong incentive for participants to consider carefully the alternatives, and it allows intensity of preferences to play a role. The net result is a more efficient and prosperous growing economy, from which all citizens gain.

For central bank policy, the revealed time preference emerging out of the market place is clearly the appropriate standard. Inconsistent choices or unachievable political wishes cannot be the base guiding central bank policy for very long.

In the United States considerable attention was paid in the original Federal Reserve Act (1913) to insulate the board members from short-term political pressures. Fourteen-year terms were established to enable longer-term time preferences to govern the institution. Once in office, members of the board cannot be removed by the President of the United States over a policy dispute. In addition, regional Reserve Bank presidents – who are selected at some remove from political channels – were also included in the monetary policy-making Federal Open Market Committee when it was formed by statute in 1935. Finally, to prevent political pressure from being applied on monetary policy makers, via the power of the purse, the Federal Reserve is not required to depend upon appropriated funds to meet its expenses.

The issue of rules versus discretion addressed by Professor Goodhart also raises critical questions for the implementation of monetary policy. Implicit in any monetary policy action or inaction, is an expectation of how the future will unfold, that is, a forecast.

The belief that some formal set of rules for policy implementation can effectively eliminate that problem is, in my judgement, an illusion. There is no way to avoid making a forecast, explicitly or implicitly. For example, a rule might stipulate that a particular monetary aggregate should increase at some fixed percentage change quarter-over-quarter. If so, past relationships would imply that the economy would follow a preordained path. The forecast implicit in the procedure is that the relationship between the particular monetary aggregate and an economic process would remain unchanged. Or, as Professor Goodhart put it, the relationship rests 'on implicit assumptions about market structures and infrastructures'.

I am not saying that monetary aggregates are without value, or that intermediate targets should not be sought. I am saying, however, that their use requires just as much of a forecast as the broader, so-called discretionary policy procedures.

Regrettably, there are no simple models that can be inferred out of some complex set of econometric techniques that can provide a definitive guide for monetary policy, or for that matter economic policy in general. The relevant conceptual model, which drives the economy, is clearly changing too rapidly for the standard econometric techniques to derive a useful structure. None the less, there is no alternative to some conceptual framework, irrespective of whether it is a subset of perceived, though temporary, dominating forces, or an elaborate model.

Of course, any particular rule or set of rules guiding central bank policy is often, as econometricians say, a reduced form of a broader model. There is clearly no rigid distinction between model-based 'discretionary policy' and those policies that are on automatic pilot with a specific target in mind. The latter is a version of the former. There is a continuum that exists between evermore complex models and some modular rule.

I wish there were a simple way to remove fallible human judgement from central bank policy making, as policy by 'rule' would endeavour to do. It would make it a lot easier, especially for central bankers. Regrettably, there is no available option of that nature in the world that confronts us on a day-by-day basis.

Finally, whether a central bank's goals are determined outside the institution or decided internally, central banks need freedom from short-run political pressures to meet these goals, given political propensities to sacrifice long-run objectives for short-run gains. Central bankers themselves need to keep their long-run objectives clearly in mind as they consider short-run tactics. Professor Goodhart's paper has discussed how these trade-offs have influenced the development of central banking and the course of economic history, recognising the intellectual and political forces that necessarily have played, and will continue to play, important roles.

The paper that we are discussing today concludes with the following: 'Despite their institutional success, central banks cannot afford to be complacent. There is much to learn, and much room for improvement.' In light of the circumstances under which central banks must operate, as we know from our own personal experience and from the historical evidence so well exposited by Goodhart and his colleagues, those closing sentences can serve as a fitting benediction for my remarks as well.

Discussion

Jean-Claude Trichet

It is quite a challenge to engage in a brief discussion of the wealth of subjects dealt with in this study. It is a brilliant assessment of three centuries of central banking and it is bound to become an authoritative work on the matter. All too often the day-to-day demands for immediate action push consideration of the long term into the background, and yet the lessons of the past shed light on the present and can show the way to the future. I should like to share with you some of the thoughts that came to me as I read the text. These thoughts express the point of view of a gentleman, or an 'honnête homme', as the term was understood in France at the time the Bank of England was founded, but a gentleman who is also an economic policy maker. It seems to me that this symposium is fully in line with this outlook.

I should like to start by expressing my conviction, and I believe that I share this conviction with Professor Goodhart and the other authors of the study, Forrest Capie and Norbert Schnadt, that the central bank is a key to the smooth operation of the economy. Of the three functions mentioned – macroeconomic stabilisation, banker for the government and banker for the banks – I think the first is certainly now the most important. The function of banker for the government was the first central bank task to emerge, but it has come to be carried out in a very indirect way. The credibility of monetary policy aimed at a macroeconomic objective of price stability helps provide the governments that are sound managers of public finances with financing on the best terms. The third function, that of banker for the banks, is part of the more general task of ensuring the stability of the financial system. Yet, this stability is more the consequence than the cause of a stable macroeconomic environment. All in all, the passage of time has brought an astonishing reversal in central banks' priorities.

Let me review the three central bank functions in succession and look at how they have evolved. Ensuring macroeconomic stability has become the most important, in my view at least, and this is because stability can no longer be achieved through automatic mechanisms, as it was in the past. In the days of the gold standard, when the notes issued by the Banque de France could be exchanged for gold or silver, there was no need to use the interest rates as much as today to stabilise the exchange rate of the national currency.

But these automatic mechanisms have disappeared and active policy must now be used to ensure the stability of the currency. Policy based on quantitative targets is one of the solutions that have been found to make up for the disappearance of the automatic mechanisms. France started implementing this type of policy in 1977. On this point, the study speaks of the relative ineffectiveness of monetary targeting in the fight against inflation in the late 1970s and suggests that most countries dropped such policies in the mid-1980s. There is no denying that there were some problems, but my own assessment of policies for controlling monetary aggregates would be less pessimistic.

First of all, monetary targeting was the first step towards dropping wholly discretionary monetary policies. On this point, I should like to express a reservation about the conclusion of the study that the leading countries' monetary policies are now mainly discretionary, with the regulation of demand as their short-term goal and price stability as only a medium-term goal. While I agree that price stability is also a medium-term goal, I do not think that we can attribute a different short-term goal to monetary policy. Indeed, the new statutes governing the Banque de France make no mention of the goal of regulating activity. I think that laying down rules in monetary matters is both possible and worthwhile, and that setting intermediate targets could be more necessary than before for the adequate use of monetary policy instruments. But I accept the need for cautious scepticism – to use the words of the study – in reading their conclusion.

This brings us to a second argument, namely that prices, interest rates and exchange rates cannot take the place of a money supply growth target. It is a tricky business to interpret changes in the slope of the yield curve because they reflect both expectations about the outcome of monetary policy and the public's spontaneous expectations as to economic activity and inflation. These interpretation problems are compounded at the long end of the yield curve by the growing integration of financial markets. The exclusive use of an exchange rate target is not an overall monetary policy solution either, because it is only valid for small countries with open economies dealing with dominant partners that in turn have a good grip on inflation. in other cases, it seems to me that the announcement of a target for a money aggregate could provide a very useful 'anchor' for the formation of nominal expectations.

I do not believe that the short-term problems encountered along the way in controlling what can be large deviations of the aggregates from their medium-term trends are significant enough to call the usefulness of intermediate objectives into question. There are difficulties here, but I continue to think these targets are essential because they give the authorities enough advance warning of inflation dangers for timely action to be taken. Tracking the ultimate goal of price stability alone raises the danger that the central bank will not be able to anticipate trouble. Of course, the erratic swings seen in the aggregates, mainly as the result of greater volatility on open and deregulated markets, require some adaptation. First of all, we must take a medium-term view. This is what we did explicitly in France with the announcement of our monetary objective for 1994. The intermediate objectives and the indicators should also be diversified. That is why, in France, we now target a financing aggregate, Total Domestic Debt, in addition to the M8 aggregate, and we look at both of them simultaneously. The comprehensive coverage of this financing aggregate means it is less affected by substitutions. Nowadays, it is essential to have a wider view on monetary and financial phenomena to be able to interpret the overall situation that financial innovation has made so much more changeable. But I agree with Charles Goodhart that this is more of an art than a science.

The second central bank function mentioned in the study is that of banker for the government. The change in this role has been the opposite of that in the previous function. In many cases, this role was the original task of central banks, along with the issue of bank notes, but it then became secondary to the role of banker for the banks. The pace of change was stepped up recently, and for several central banks, independence from the government has become the priority. This independence is a factor in the credibility and effectiveness of monetary policy, but it is obviously incompatible with the role of banker for the government as it was perceived in the last century.

The study shows how central bank independence has become a key means of enhancing the effectiveness of monetary policy. However, it is no miracle cure. We are warned, for example, that central bank independence is not sufficient, if it is not backed up by relative stability in public finances. Today, the Banque de France can unhesitatingly be classified as one of the independent central banks. Since the first of January, a collegial body called the Monetary Policy Council, which does not include any government representatives, has full powers to frame and implement monetary policy. And the Banque de France is accountable to Parliament. The independence of the Banque de France was granted as part of the process towards monetary integration in Europe and I wish to convince the authors of this study that this integration will occur. The current situation in Europe is unique in that Monetary Union is taking place after a long period of peace. It is the result of an intellectual consensus and a political conviction that the people of Europe have ratified. Monetary Union is the prolongation of the Single Market and of long-standing coordination in which the efforts of each have helped build up an outstanding potential for the future.

Finally, I should like to speak about the central banks' role as banker for the banks. In the nineteenth century, this came to be their main task, in France and elsewhere, as the growth of credit and the banking system made a lender of last resort an absolute necessity.

On this point, I should like to give you a few details about how the Banque de France played this role at different times in its history.

First, a few words on the Bank's support for institutions in difficulty. The criteria governing this support were less vague than the authors seem to think. The Bank could not have prevented the fall of the Crédit Mobilier because the institution founded by the Péreire brothers called into question the status of the Banque de France as the central bank. The Union Générale bankruptcy in 1882 was dealt with according to the precepts of Bagehot and the discounting facilities for other banks were increased to prevent a chain reaction. In 1889, the Banque de France bailed out the Comptoir d'Escompte because it was solvent. The list of rescue operations could be rounded out by the episode in 1931, when the Treasury, rather than the Banque de France, acted as the lender of last resort to prevent the Banque Nationale de Crédit from going under.

The second detail that I should like to deal with relates to the competition that the Banque de France had from the big deposit-taking banks, particularly after 1880. The study mentions that the Banque de France countered competition from commercial banks by attempting to increase its direct discounting of bills, thus acting more like a commercial bank than a central bank. This brings us to the matter of the Banque de France branches. I should point out that the branches were set up at the request of the government, when the right to issue notes was renewed.

In the same vein, the study presents the competition between the Banque de France and the commercial banks as a factor that blunted the effectiveness of the central bank's discount policy, as the rates on the money market were supposedly too loosely linked to the official discount rate. Even though the large banks did not rediscount their bills with the Banque de France, monetary policy was not hindered, because at the time, it was based on virtually automatic adjustments aimed mainly at keeping interest rates low and stable.

Let me stress once again that the central banks' role as banker for the banks is to my mind inextricably linked to central bank supervision and regulation of the financial system as a whole. Many central banks, including the Banque de France and the Bank of England, take part in the regulation of the banking and financial system, and I think it is perfectly logical for them to do so. Equally, I recognise and respect the different views taken by others.

I should like to conclude by expressing my conviction that the role of central banks is being re-evaluated. At one point, Milton Friedman said that money is too important to be left in hands of central banks. We have come a long way since he made that judgement. The public realises that monetary stability is a precious and fragile asset and that an independent institution must be given the task of preserving it. A shift in mentalities on this point has been particularly noticeable in France in the last few years. Our central banks have an long and rich history. The issues that they are now confronting show how essential their future role is and underline the scope and the importance of their tasks.

Discussion

Yasushi Mieno

First of all, I would like to offer my sincere congratulations on the Bank of England's tercentennial anniversary. I would also like to express my gratitude to Governor George, whom I deeply respect for his integrity, for giving me the opportunity to join this symposium today. It is impressive to see the 'Old Lady' of 300 years old defying Keynes' famous words: 'In the long run, we are all dead.' The Lady appears to be very much alive and is, as she has always been, a distinctive leader in the club of central bankers.

The paper submitted by Professor Goodhart and his colleagues on the development of central banking is a timely and valuable contribution to our profession, given the recent wide interest in central bank independence. It skillfully combines historical perspective, economic analysis, and the practical viewpoint of a former central banker.

Since the paper covers a broad range of issues, let me concentrate on only a few and express my views referring to the experience of the Bank of Japan since its foundation in 1882.

To us central bankers, it is self-evident that the primary macro-policy objective of a central bank is 'price stability'. Even if the central bank law of a country does not explicitly state this, our belief in price stability is unshakable.

Frankly speaking, however, in spite of our firm belief, it is sad to admit that price stability has not been achieved for any lengthy period in modern history. It is thus worth asking ourselves what is responsible for this gap between belief and reality.

In the course of our Bank's 110-year history, we encountered hyper-inflation several times as a result of civil disturbance and war. On such occasions, inflation became uncontrollable because central bank objectives were overruled by the pursuit of national objectives. A stable international political framework, therefore, is vitally important for us to carry out our mission.

However, hyper-inflation caused by war is an extraordinary phenomenon, and its duration is usually not very long, either. Hence, as a second historical experience which is much more relevant for us today, I need to touch upon economic policy in the 1960s and 1970s. While we objected to the growth-oriented attitude prevalent at that time, we accommodated price pressures in the end. In this sense, I must admit that the Bank of Japan was also influenced by the idea of attaining growth at the expense of price stability which, in effect, condoned mild inflation. When shocks such as oil crises hit the economy operating with rapid monetary growth in the early 1970s, we had to pay a high economic cost in the form of annual inflation above 20 per cent and a subsequent deep recession.

This experience can be regarded as a case in which the principle of central banking was pushed aside to accommodate people's desires in modern democracy. One lesson I learnt from this is that there is no such thing as 'an appropriate rate of inflation'. Or if there is, it is unsustainable.

In the late 1980s we encountered a third new challenge, the birth and expansion of asset price bubbles along with general price stability. In hindsight, asset price bubbles accelerated economic growth and eventually increased inflationary pressures. But with actual price developments remaining subdued, at least initially, monetary policy action was taken a bit too late. Of course, monetary policy should not be aimed at asset price stability. Yet, we cannot ignore asset prices, given that any large fluctuation can have a serious adverse impact on financial systems. I think the question still remains as to how we should treat asset prices in formulating monetary policy.

Japanese historical experience, as I have discussed, leads me to two general propositions. First, democratic society has an inflationary bias. Second, the threat of inflation takes on a different shape every time.

Nobel laureate James Buchanan once argued in his book *Limits to Liberty* that while people tend to doze off, they are at the same time conscious of their weakness and set an alarm clock, thereby managing to control themselves. If you replace the doze with inflation and the alarm clock with central bank independence, you will see the role of the central bank in maintaining price stability. In this sense, a framework which entrusts monetary policy management to an independent central bank could be evaluated as a product of human wisdom acquired through historical experience.

Then, how can one fulfill the role of a good central banker who 'takes away the punch bowl just when the party is getting going?' What is more, this party is held for different reasons each time, and the time lag it takes for the guests to get drunk differs each time!

While the determination to achieve price stability is most necessary, it is not sufficient. Also, there is no convenient rule that can replace discretionary, often lonely, judgements.

I do not have a panacea for price stability. However, there are two suggestions I can make from my own experiences, limited as they are *vis-à-vis* the 300 years' rich history here. First, a deep understanding of history helps us obtain a good insight into future problems, no matter in what guise they may emerge. Second, what is absolutely necessary is the general public's understanding of price stability and their quiet but firm support of the central bank's objectives. Such public support, in turn, could only be gained through consistent policy efforts and results over decades.

After all, a keen sense of fiduciary responsibility, systematic efforts to enforce the most appropriate policies, modest confidence in such policies to improve daily life, not necessarily in the short-run, but in the medium to long term, and ceaseless efforts to communicate with the general public – these, I believe, are the very foundations of 'constructive accountability'.

The paper submitted by Professor Goodhart and others discusses the relationship of the central bank with the macroeconomy, the government, and private banks, and provides interesting insights into each aspect. If I may, I would like to add another item to this list, and that is the central bank's relationship with other central banks, or cooperation among central banks.

The banking relationship between the Bank of Japan and the Bank of England dates back to 1896 when we opened a demand deposit account at the Bank of England. Ever since then, the cooperative relationship between the two banks has gradually strengthened. It was none other than former Bank of England Governor Norman who most strongly advocated central bank co-operation, and his view eventually led to the foundation of the BIS. The progress of financial globalisation and liberalisation make central bank co-operation and the exchange of views all the more necessary in such areas as macroeconomic conditions, settlement systems, and prudential oversight and supervision, all of which are preconditions for sound monetary policy management today. By emphasising the importance of this point, I would like to conclude my comments.

Open Session

Alexandre Lamfalussy

My question is basically about disclosure – disclosure of the decision-making process in monetary policy: why a decision is taken and on what basis? I think that this is particularly important in a world where discretion must and is bound to play a relatively important role. I think there are two angles to this – disclosure is essential for the process of democratic accountability; but it can also shorten the timespan between the decision and its impact on the economy and price formation. Now could I ask the Panel how they look at the present state of disclosure and in what direction they think we should go?

Alan Greenspan

I think, as Alexandre correctly points out, that if we are going to have independent central banks then implicit in that independence is accountability. You cannot in a democratic society have an institution which is either fully or partly dissociated from the electoral process and which has powers that central banks inherently have. So the question really amounts to how does one position the central bank with respect to the issue of disclosure and accountability – which are related questions.

The position that we take is that the burden of proof is against the central bank: that is, we have to demonstrate that either delayed disclosure or non-disclosure is a policy which is required for us to implement our statutory goals. We have struggled with this, and have concluded that we should make available to the electorate what it is we think, why we are doing what we are doing and in a very general way under what conditions we would behave differently.

Where the central bank has a single governor with discretion, he or she has the capability of contemplating with oneself in a closet, and the issue of disclosure does not arise; but when you are dealing, as a number of our central banks are, with a committee form of decision-making, we then get to the issue of to what extent disclosure inhibits the deliberative process.

Now when it is argued that, in a public forum and amongst public people, individuals should not have a level of discussion and a level of insight different from what they have in private, then I must say I know very few human beings to which that would apply. It may be regrettable, but it is a fact – and it is clear that if you are deliberating in public, which is another way of saying that you make your minutes immediately available, then there is an inhibition which I think undercuts the quality of the discussion. In that regard I think the argument is very strongly for the deliberative process to be either secret for a while or secret for a long while, and the question is only the timeframe in which one makes that particular judgement. And this gets to the question as to whether one has minutes and to what extent one publishes those minutes and when.

As far as the Fed is concerned, by the nature of our deliberations in the Federal Open Market Committee, we have a considerable amount of contingency planning in the sense that if x occurs it is the consensus of the group that policy would shift to y. It's a debatable question as to whether if these contingencies are immediately made public that induces increased stablility or increased instability in the markets in which we function; and it is the conclusion of our group that it is the latter, that it's instability which is engendered and indeed makes the process of implementation of policy more difficult.

There are a number of other questions which are related to this issue: namely, does one immediately disclose all actions when they are taken? When one changes Discount Rate one obviously has to; but when one changes the degree of calibration in open market policy does one disclose it at that point or not? These are technical questions which I think are very legitimately open. In general, I think that it is very important for us central bankers to recognise that, implicit in the trend towards independence which has been discussed here at great length and will continue to be discussed, is the cost – and that cost is accountability and disclosure, and if we endeavour to restrict the latter we will surely undermine the former.

Yasushi Mieno

As I mentioned earlier, there is first of all a need for public support if we are to maintain independence of the central bank. However, the yardstick for us central bankers often happens to be different from the yardstick that the general public has, as other governors have already pointed out, and therefore I believe there is all the more need to gain the understanding of the public with regard to the measures that we employ. More specifically, when we shift our official discount rate, and the decision to do that is made by the Bank of Japan Policy Board, then immediately following that decision a statement explaining the purport of that decision will be issued and I myself will meet the press and explain in detail the intent of that decision. And apart from that, I also give regular press conferences which take place every other week, which is a practice I suppose, rather uncommon amongst central banks around the world. Last year alone I met the press in that form twenty-one times. Apart from that I think we do what my colleagues do in their countries, responding to queries in Parliament, giving lectures and also publishing regular publications and research materials of the central bank.

Jean-Claude Trichet

I would say that this question of accountability is absolutely key and particularly in a new-born central bank. I share the view expressed by Alan Greenspan on the fact that to disclose the minutes of a 'meditation' might induce more instability than stability, and that is the reason why we have decided that our own 'meditations' will not be disclosed. All members of course of the Council of Monetary Policy are sticking to the decision that has been made and support the decision that has been made, but we consider that the accountability and the disclosure must be totally open on the decision itself – why it has been taken, the inspiration of monetary policy, the relationship with the other elements of economic policy and so forth. It takes place, as Governor Mieno has said, in an encounter with the press, or through a communique; and I consider personally that the meetings with our parliament are absolutely key in this respect. I also have the experience that informal communication, informal explanation with the unions, with the political parties, with the various political circles, with entrepreneurs, and with all responsible people in our democratically open societies is absolutely key.

Charles Goodhart

The only point I would make is that the nature and form of disclosure depends on the governance structure. I think there is a difference between a central bank where the sole responsibility for the actions and success, or otherwise, of those actions rests with the central bank governor who can always be personally and individually approached with the question 'why did you do that?', and the central bank where the decisions rest more formally with a board. As has been said, if there is a failure you can always fire the central bank governor, but it is less easy to fire a board and therefore there is greater need for disclosure, in my view, if there is a board rather than if the responsibility lies with the governor individually.

Eddie George

I think the question is very relevant to our situation in the UK and I would pick up what Charles Goodhart and Alan Greenspan said about the governance question, and of course it becomes all the more important where the advice and the decision are separated, as they are constitutionally in our case – at least for the time being. It is very difficult in that situation to have real accountability unless you actually do disclose the discussion that takes place between the adviser and the decision-maker, and I think it has been a great weakness in our arrangements that we didn't have proper disclosure, proper accountability in that sense.

I do think that there are the questions that Alan touched upon on, whether disclosing the process, the discussion, the contingencies, adds to or takes away from stability in the financial markets. The view that we've taken, and obviously we'll see, is that in fact the disclosure of that process will enhance the understanding in financial markets of the nature of the process. What we had, before we went to publishing the minutes of my monthly meetings with the Chancellor, was a great deal of speculation about the nature of the discussion process which greatly exaggerated the extent of the differences. From that point of view we would hope that disclosure will actually enhance market understanding, but clearly it is something that we expect to learn more about.

Dr Courtney Blackman
(former Governor, Central Bank of Barbados)

I enjoyed Professor Goodhart's presentation very much indeed, but it still leaves me with the problem I had almost thirty years ago when I first grappled with central banking in developing countries. The theory which is implicit in Professor Goodhart's presentation does not really give us adequate insights into central banking in a developing country, and I want to suggest a slightly different over-arching concept, and that is to go back to the concept of seignorage. The reason why the independence of central banks has become so important today is because the commodity element of money has been removed. So we have in developed countries purely symbolic money, so in fact the potential seignorage is infinite and not limited as it was in the past. The basic conflict is because the governments want to get the seignorage and the central bankers want to restrict that potential. Now in the case of the developed countries, developed markets do impose a discipline on governments on the extent to which they can obtain that seignorage. Whereas in developing countries, without these developed markets, there is no discipline, and we do have cases in developing countries where in fact the governments do assume that the seignorage is infinite and behave that way. Therefore central banks in developing countries have become sources of great disfunction – I'm not naming any names but we know who they are!

So I want to suggest to Professor Goodhart, and we are interested in his response, to say that in a case where you have first of all poorly developed markets and very open economies, that developing countries have no choice but to retain a commodity element in their money supply. In other words, they have to have foreign exchange reserve holdings and they have to have specific constraints on the extent to which their central banks can expand money supply out of proportion to their foreign exchange reserves.

Charles Goodhart

All countries have to try to deal with potential fiscal irresponsibility from their governments and it is possible that it may be more difficult to do in some cases when the need for infrastructure expenditures are seen as so immediately pressing. But even so, whatever mechanisms can be obtained to try to maintain underlying price stability and help to develop financial markets and maintain freedom in those financial markets will act to encourage growth rather than vice versa. There has been in too many developing countries a tendency to try to use the monetary system at large as a milch-cow for providing cheap funds to government, not only through the direct inflation tax but possibly just as much through requiring banks to hold very large proportions of government debt, high required reserve ratios, limitations on the interest rates that financial institutions can offer or charge and all such measures which tend to go under the general heading of repressed financial systems, and have been adverse rather than beneficial to development. The more you can avoid those, and the more you can help to encourage fiscal responsibility and limitation on governments' attempts to what is feasible within the fiscal system, the better off you will be.

Richard D. Erb   (Deputy Managing Director, IMF)

I have a question that brings in the issue of exchange rate policy. There has been a trend toward greater central bank independence, and yet most governments retain control over exchange rate policy. Now this can lead to tensions at times between the government and the central bank if the exchange rate target, whether it is a fixed target or a range, is inconsistent with the underlying policy of the central bank. I wonder if one or more might comment on how this tension is to be resolved?

Jean-Claude Trichet

First of all, of course as you have mentioned, to my knowledge in all countries the ultimate decision as regards exchange rate arrangements, exchange rate devaluation and revaluation, are made by the government. It is true everywhere to my knowledge. Second, one cannot in advance foresee a situation where you would never have a conflict between the government and the central bank, and it seems to me that we all have experience of varying views. I'm not speaking for my country where, on the contrary, all the experience I have before independence as well as after independence is full agreement between the government and the central bank on what has to be done. But we have observed and we could observe here and there various views, and I would say that the ultimate decision as regards interest rate policy is taken by the independent central bank, sticking to its own responsibility. On the other hand you have a government which is obviously entitled to negotiate with others a new arrangement – or, if there is any kind of system or mechanism a new position in the system or mechanism. But your question might also be whether or not, when you have two intermediate goals simultaneously, one external goal and one domestic, as is the case in my country, you might be put in some contradiction from time to time. I will say that in our own vision, to mention my particular case, where I have this domestic economic goal I have mentioned and an external intermediate goal which is the functioning of the mechanism in which we participate, I would say that my own understanding is that they are mutually reinforcing. We don't see the contradiction that has been mentioned from time to time.

Gordon Thiessen   (Governor, Bank of Canada)

I'd like to go back to the issue of accountability because I suspect we all agree that it is so very important when you have central banks gaining increased autonomy (I like the word autonomy better than independence) in taking responsibility, having responsibility for carrying out monetary policy. But I find myself wondering if this swing of the pendulum to more autonomy can really be sustained. No matter how hard we work at disclosure, no matter how often we all appear before Parliament, as long as there are perceptions that the central bank is making judgements about some important policy trade-off. I wonder whether we all won't get pushed to far more narrowly defined objectives. I wonder if even price stability is sufficiently narrowly defined to be satisfactory, and whether we won't all end up being pushed much closer, for example, to the New Zealand example where you spell out in really some detail what the precise objective would be.

Charles Goodhart

Well, my answer to that is very simple. That's where I want to push you, and I think that it is important that price stability be quantified; otherwise I think that accountability is much harder to sustain. The quantification of price stability gives a reasonable basis for actually seeing whether you have succeeded or not. There must be a bottom line, and if there is to be a bottom line it needs to be quantified, and I have never really fully understood why so many of you talk about price stability, but when it comes to the point you're not prepared to state explicitly what it is that you mean by that.

Alan Greenspan

I don't want this to come as a shock but I happen to agree with you!

Monetary policy basically is a single tool and you can only implement one goal consistently. It's a very interesting game for central bankers to play trade-offs and try to keep several balls in the air concurrently but at the end of the day that is not really a credible outcome.

At root here is not so much central bank philosophy – it's really economic policy philosophy and it gets to the question as to whether or not monetary policy has a significant role in short-term economic stabilisation. If the Phillips curve is alive and vibrant then it's very difficult to get round that, but I suspect the evidence is increasingly for a gradual diminishment – not only of the now obviously defunct long-term Phillips curve, but I seriously question whether or not the short-term Phillips curve is going to reign indefinitely in its current role in economic policy. And if it turns out that the evidence suggests that low inflation is a necessary condition for economic growth, I think the pressure towards reserving or rather focusing central bank activity to the equivalent of the gold standard will become increasingly evident.

Whether or not that role of price stability, and what that implies, will be accepted in the political environment is really the crucial question. It is very difficult, as I think we are all aware, to communicate the issue that there is no free lunch, that seignorage in the long run is ultimately an illusion and that you cannot manipulate an economy and get effective long-term maximum sustainable growth. If that view becomes politically acceptable, then I think central banks inevitably will be moved statutorily towards price stability as the goal – and essentially the only goal – of monetary policy. I must say however that while the trend that we are all observing is in that direction, I am not at all confident that the trend is irreversible.

Yasushi Mieno

This is not a direct response to the question but let me share with you my views on price stability.

I believe that price stability is not equivalent with price indicators stability. I believe only when the economy which lies behind those price indices attain stable and sustained growth – only then can we say there is true price stability. The current consensus of G7 is to achieve in each of our countries, under their respective circumstances, non-inflationary and sustainable economic growth in the medium-term. And we are fully aware that this consensus is fraught with contradictions and is very difficult to achieve. But as a central banker I believe that we have no choice but to adhere to that very honestly.

Jean-Claude Trichet

I will tell Charles Goodhart that we are in the camp of those who are bold enough to say what we mean by price stability – I hope we are not too naive. We have said that we consider that 2 per cent or less than 2 per cent is what we would call price stability not only for this year but in the medium run. We said that at end of January as part of the overall monetary policy. So we have been much bolder on the price stability objective than we were as you might have seen on the intermediate target. I think that that is the appropriate way and I think that therefore, Charles, I would say that I totally agree with you in that respect.

Alan Greenspan

There is an interesting question which I think is going to confront us on this notion, which I would like to just put on the table.

With the increase in globalisation of the financial system, which is becoming extremely complex, increasingly powerful and increasingly swamping domestic activities in goods and services, I wonder whether we're not going to find – as Governor Mieno was implying – that the whole structure of asset prices and financial stability is going to become a necessary condition for price stability in product and service markets. It is difficult to judge how one would approach this because it presupposes that markets are not functioning wholly efficiently and that bubbles do emerge from time to time and I think there is at least some evidence, contrary to what I would like to believe is in the real world, that in fact those bubbles do exist. If that is the case, then a collateral part of the endeavour to achieve product and service price stability may also be a focus on maintaining a degree of stability in the financial system which is not indifferent to the question of asset prices and bubbles; and that raises a far more complex question than I think just a simple statutory notion that a central bank is required to maintain price stability – and I would much prefer to be in an area where I could ask that question rather than answer it.

Dr Chakravarty Rangarajan   (Governor, Reserve Bank of India)

Perhaps this is a narrow technical question that doesn't touch upon the broader issues. I address this particularly to Professor Goodhart. Starting with the instability of the demand function for money – and I think he said somewhere in the course of the discussion that what is to be manipulated is the short-term rate of interest – my question really is whether the rate of interest is in some way coordinated with the level of money supply. After all in a simplified economic system both the interest rate and the quantity of money are the equilibrium quantities that finally emerge. Therefore can we really argue that interest rate manipulation takes us away from the need to look at the quantity of money?

Charles Goodhart

No. It certainly doesn't take us away from the need to look at the quantity of money and I hope that I didn't mislead. Although the objective is price stability the question facing central bankers always is how should we adjust interest rates to achieve price stability over the horizon in which interest rates work. And in reaching that judgement they will have to assess whatever key bits of information come their way and that includes exchange rates, asset prices and very much the monetary aggregates. The fact that the monetary aggregates may not have, and have not had, a relationship with nominal incomes and prices that has been robust through financial innovations and other structural changes does not mean that they do not contain information. It is just that the information needs winnowing and certainly the central banker who did not look at what was happening to the monetary aggregates, and indeed to credit as well, would not I think be performing as I would have thought any of those on this panel here would want.

2   Modern central banking

Stanley Fischer[1]

2.1   Introduction

The practice and theory of modern central banking revolve around the inflationary tendencies inherent in the conflict between the short- and long-run effects of monetary expansion and in the temptations of monetary financing of government spending. They should also revolve around the conflict between the benefits of shielding the central bank from political pressures and the principle of accountability to the public of those who make critically important policy decisions.

The earliest central banks were set up to provide financing for governments, and to help develop the financial system, often by bringing order to the note issue.[2] As the practice of central banking developed during the nineteenth century, the central bank took on the primary responsibility for protecting the stability of the financial system and the external value of the currency. The mandate given to the central bank in legislation passed during the 1930s and 1940s – in the Great Depression and the heyday of the Keynesian revolution – typically included both monetary stability and the promotion of full employment and maximum levels of production. Then, as the inflationary forces that destroyed the Bretton Woods system gathered strength in the 1960s and 1970s, the focus of monetary policy shifted to the maintenance of the domestic value of the currency.

The trend is summarised by the contrast between the absence of a specific mandate for the Bank of England in the Bank Act of 1946[3] and the very

---

[1] International Monetary Fund, on leave from MIT I am grateful to my discussants at the conference, Don Brash, Miguel Mancera, and Josef Tosovsky for useful comments, to Guy Debelle for research assistance, and to Michael Bruno, John Crow, Charles Freedman and Mervyn King for discussions and the provision of literature.
[2] See de Kock (1974) for the historical development of central banking, as well as the interesting companion paper for this conference by Capie, Goodhart and Schnadt (1994).
[3] The Bank of England's 1694 Charter starts 'Now know ye, That we being desirous to promote the publick Good and Benefit of our People'; this section was embodied in the 1946 Bank of England Act.

262

specific goals set out for the Reserve Bank of New Zealand in the Act of 1989, 'The primary function of the Bank is to formulate and implement monetary policy directed to the economic objective of achieving and maintaining stability in the general level of prices'.

I shall start this paper by briefly reviewing the functions and goals of central banks – the mandates set out for them in legislation, and in some cases the mandates they have chosen in interpreting conflicting legislative goals. In recent years, central banks have increasingly come to emphasise the fight against inflation and to deemphasise the possibility that monetary policy can affect the level of output; I therefore turn next to the changing views of the Phillips curve trade-off, and economic analysis of the costs of inflation.

The rational expectations revolution in macroeconomics and the growing sophistication of game-theoretic models have radically changed the academic analysis of policy-making. For the first time, economists can talk analytically about such key issues as credibility, rules versus discretion, and central bank independence. I will briefly describe some of the relevant analysis of credibility and of rules versus discretion, and draw practical lessons for policy.

In the remainder of the paper I concentrate on the key issue of central bank independence, its analytics, and the empirical evidence. I conclude by describing the charter of a modern central bank.

2.2 Central bank functions and mandates

Central banks around the world perform a variety of functions. Through their control over the monetary base – their role as 'bank of issue' in an earlier terminology – all have the responsibility for managing the supply of credit and money and correspondingly determining market interest rates. Sometimes, as in Britain, the Treasury or the finance ministry makes the decisions on interest rates, and leaves only their implementation to the central bank. The central bank may be fully or jointly responsible for determining the exchange rate and managing the foreign exchange reserves. Central banks hold the reserves of the commercial banks and play a role in managing the payments system. Most are given responsibility for promoting the stability of the financial system, by supervising the banks and other financial institutions, by serving as lender of last resort, and in some countries by administering deposit insurance. The central bank is usually the government's banker; central banks often administer foreign exchange controls; in some countries they manage all or part of the national debt; the research department of the central bank may often be the best and sometimes the only policy research group in the country; the central bank may have a development banking function.

A country, particularly a developing country, derives many benefits from having a highly professional, highly respected central bank. The capacity and the reputations of, for examples, the central banks of Israel, Italy, and Mexico have all played a key role in helping bring about stabilisation and stability in their countries. But I will take a narrow perspective on central banking in this paper, by concentrating on the essential central bank function, monetary policy – management of the supply of credit and money, and thus of money market interest rates. The lender of last resort function typically accompanies this responsibility. Exchange rate and foreign reserve management can hardly be divorced from interest rate determination, though the treasury frequently shares or is responsible for these tasks.[4] Commercial bank supervision is generally the responsibility of the central bank, but in some countries is carried out in a separate agency.[5] To avoid creating a conflict between the government's desire to keep debt service low and the goals of monetary policy, management of the national debt is best left to the treasury or another agency. Whether or not the central bank is the government's banker, there is a need for coordination between the fiscal authority's management of government cash flow, and the central bank.

Control over the supply of money and credit gives the central bank potentially enormous power. In countries where the central bank has sufficient independence to determine interest rates, the goals towards which that power should be deployed are often specified in legislation. The Bundesbank is directed to conduct monetary policy 'with the aim of safeguarding the currency'; it is also required to support the general economic policy of the Federal Government, but only to the extent that this is consistent with its primary goal of safeguarding the currency.[6] The Act of August 4 1993, amended 31 December 1993, gives the Banque de France the aim of ensuring price stability, within the framework of the Government's overall economic policy. This is similar to the Bundesbank mandate, but without the provision that the price stability mandate overrides the obligation to support government economic policy. Like the Bundesbank, the Reserve

---

[4] The choice of the exchange rate system, as opposed to the management of the chosen system, is normally a central government rather than a central bank decision.

[5] The question of whether the central bank or another agency should supervise the commercial banks has been extensively discussed (see for example paragraphs 83–103 of Volume I of the Treasury and Civil Service Committee report *The Role of the Bank of England*, London: HMSO, 1993; this report is referred to henceforth as *The Role of the Bank of England*). The weight of the evidence supports the view that the supervisory function should remain with the central bank, but the issue is not crucial.

[6] I shall focus most directly on four central banks: the Bundesbank, the Reserve Bank of New Zealand, the Federal Reserve System, and the Bank of England.

Bank of New Zealand is charged with producing price stability. The Federal Reserve is given a more general charge,[7] to 'maintain long-run growth of the monetary and credit aggregates commensurate with the economy's long run potential to increase production, so as to promote effectively the goals of maximum employment, stable prices, and moderate long-term interest rates'. There are no clearly set out goals for the Bank of England; indeed there is a logical difficulty in specifying independent policy goals for a non-independent agency.

Where goals are either unclear or multiple, central banks may succeed in setting their own priorities. For instance the Swiss National Bank is required 'to regulate the country's money circulation, to facilitate payment transactions, and to pursue a credit and monetary policy serving the interests of the country as a whole'. As the SNB explained to the House of Commons Treasury and Civil Service Committee last year,[8] 'The SNB understands this ... primarily as a mandate for ensuring price stability with the instruments at its disposal'. Similarly, the Bank of Japan, whose 1942 legislation requires it to enhance the nation's general economic activities, states that 'its objectives are commonly described as "to maintain price stability" and "to foster the soundness and stability of the financial system"'.[9]

Table 2.1 presents a tabulation of the legally-specified objectives of seventy-two central banks, whose charters have been studied by Cukierman, Webb and Neyapti (1992). The objectives are scaled by the degree to which they emphasise price stability relative to other goals. These are the goals that existed in legislation as of the 1980s.[10] Two-thirds of the countries in both the overall sample and the industrialised country group include price stability among the goals of the central bank; it is also true that two-thirds of the central banks are either not given an explicit price stability mandate or are given one that is mentioned together with a conflicting goal, for example the maintenance of full employment.

In the period since the data were tabulated, several central banks have moved up in the table, among them the central banks of France and others that plan to join the European System of Central Banks, New Zealand, and Mexico. And, as we have seen, several of the central banks which do not have explicit or sole price stability targets, interpret their mandates as emphasising price stability. Increasingly, the debate over the role and mandate of central banks focuses on the question of whether the central

---

[7] This the goal of monetary policy set out in the Humphrey-Hawkins Act of 1978.

[8] *The Role of the Bank of England*, Volume II, p. 175.

[9] *The Role of the Bank of England*, Volume II, p. 165.

[10] In the overall sample, the second country whose central bank has an overriding price stability goal is that of the Philippines.

Table 2.1. *Central bank objectives*

Description	Value of objective	Number of countries	Percent of total	Industrial countries
		Full sample		
Only price stability (can override government)	1	2	3	Germany
Only price stability	0.8	6	8	Finland, Greece Ireland, Netherlands
Price stability and compatible objective	0.6	17	24	Austria, Denmark, Luxembourg, Spain.
Price stability and incompatible objectives	0.4	22	31	Australia, Iceland, New Zealand, U.S.
No objectives	0.2	10	14	Canada, Italy, Sweden, U.K.
Objectives but not price stability.	0.0	15	21	Belgium, France, Japan, Norway
Total		72		21

Source: Cukierman et al., 1992, table A.1. Data are for the 1980s.

bank should be given the sole or primary task of assuring price stability or low inflation.

Why should this be, when monetary policy affects both output and prices in the short run? The answer starts from the well-known history of the Phillips curve.

2.3   The Phillips curve

The original 1958 Phillips curve showed a century-long relationship between wage inflation and unemployment in the United Kingdom. A century surely qualifies as a long run, and so it should not be surprising that some economists of the time concluded that the curve represented a trade-off menu of choices facing the government, in which the benefits of lower inflation have to be balanced against their costs in terms of higher unemployment. The Phillips curve was brought to the United States by Paul Samuelson and Robert Solow (1960), who after presenting the menu view of the curve, warned that their discussion dealt only with the short run, and that it would be wrong to think that the same trade-off would be maintained in the longer run.[11]

---

[11] Samuelson and Solow gave two examples of how the curve would shift: first, that low inflation might shift the curve down because of its impact on expectations; second, that

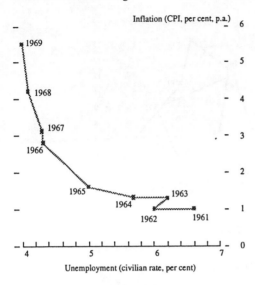

Figure 2.1 Inflation and unemployment, US 1961–1969

None the less, United States experience through the 1960s presented the appearance of a simple Phillips curve trade-off, as unemployment steadily declined and inflation gradually increased (figure 2.1). But that of course was only the beginning of the story. As the textbooks tell us,[12] even before the end of the 1960s Edmund Phelps (1967) and Milton Friedman (1968) predicted that the Phillips curve would shift as expectations of inflation adjusted to actual inflationary experience. Unemployment could not be kept permanently below its natural rate, and attempts to do so would lead only to accelerating inflation. The experience of the next two decades, shown in figure 2.2, certainly supported their prediction that the curve would shift.

The Phillips curve had been presented as an empirical phenomenon, and rationalised as an example of the law of supply and demand which asserts that excess demand causes the price of a good to rise. Friedman and Phelps pointed out that wage negotiators bargain about the real wage, and that nominal wage increases would therefore be adjusted to reflect expectations of inflation. This destroyed the theoretical basis for assuming a long-run trade-off between inflation and unemployment; the facts seen in figure 2.2

structural unemployment might rise as a result of higher unemployment, so that the curve would shift up. Both these possibilities have been central to subsequent discussions, the first as the expectations-augmented Phillips curve, the second as the phenomenon of hysteresis (Blanchard and Summers, 1986).

12 See for example, Dornbusch and Fischer (1994), chapter 16.

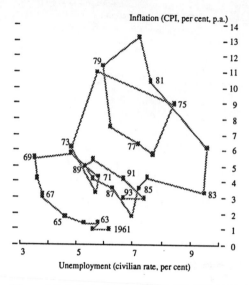

Figure 2.2 Inflation and employment, US 1961–1993

destroyed the empirical basis for assuming that there is any simple form of long-run trade-off. We shall return to the question of the long-run trade-off below.

In the Friedman-Phelps Phillips curve, it is only errors in expectations that permit unemployment to differ from the natural rate. Friedman and Phelps assumed that expectations were formed adaptively,[13] so that the monetary authority could for a time keep unemployment low by accelerating the inflation rate. As inflation accelerated, workers – forming their expectations with a lag – would continually underpredict inflation, the real wage would remain below its equilibrium level, and employment would exceed its equilibrium level. With the addition of the assumption of rational expectations, Lucas (1973) destroyed even the short-run Phillips curve trade-off. In his model, no predictable monetary policy has any effects on output, because the private sector takes the monetary policy into account, adjusts its expectations accordingly, and there is no possibility of a systematic gap between expected and actual inflation.

The Lucas no short-run trade-off view would, if correct, imply that systematic monetary policy can only affect the inflation rate, and should therefore be deployed to that end. But while the view that there is no long-run trade-off between inflation and unemployment is widely accepted,

---

[13] That is, expectations of inflation are assumed to adjust on the basis of the gap between actual and expected inflation.

the no short-run trade-off view is not. The most obvious reason not to accept the no short-run trade-off proposition is that central banks have demonstrated repeatedly that they can create recessions by tightening monetary policy. It does not take sophisticated econometric analysis to recognize that the Fed produced a recession in 1981–82 as it successfully reduced inflation. Romer and Romer (1989) have more systematically shown that Fed policy decisions to tighten monetary policy have been followed by recessions. A second reason not to accept the no short-run trade-off view is the econometric evidence that predictable monetary policy affects output and not only prices.[14]

The question remains of why there is a short-run Phillips curve trade-off. The short-run trade-off in the Lucas (1973) model is the result of confusion by buyers and sellers about the meaning of changes in nominal prices; in that model, even unpredictable monetary policy would have no real effect of any kind if there were perfect information about the current money stock or aggregate price level. A more plausible explanation is that monetary policy gets its short-run leverage from the existence of sticky wages and prices, resulting for instance from long-term and perhaps overlapping wage contracts.[15] The stickiness may result more fundamentally from costs of changing individual prices[16] or renegotiating wages.

The terms of the short-run trade-off between output and inflation may depend on the average rate of inflation. Because prices in a high inflation economy have to be changed frequently, any excess monetary expansion is likely to be taken into account in a price change within a short time. In a low inflation economy, by contrast, prices need not be changed very often, and so prices are likely to respond less rapidly to a monetary expansion. This would mean that the short-run Phillips curve is flatter in a low inflation economy than in a high inflation economy.[17]

The existence of a short-run trade-off between output and inflation is central to the day-to-day decisions confronting monetary policy-makers. There is no escaping the fact that it is almost always possible to increase

[14] See for example Mishkin (1983).
[15] See for instance, Fischer (1977); Blanchard (1986) shows how even quite short-term overlapping contracts may generate lengthy adjustment processes to nominal shocks.
[16] However, Caplin and Spulber (1987) show that in some conditions, stickiness of prices at the level of the individual firm does not translate into stickiness at the aggregate level; Caplin and Leahy (1991) examine conditions in which the Caplin-Spulber neutrality result does not hold.
[17] This theory is developed by Ball, Mankiw and Romer (1988), who present supporting evidence. The short-run Phillips curve derived by Lucas (1973) is flatter the lower the variance of the aggregate inflation rate; and since the level of the inflation rate and its variance are in practice positively correlated, the Lucas model can also be seen as predicting that the short-run Phillips curve is flatter at lower inflation rates.

output by accelerating money growth,[18] or to cause a recession by tightening credit sufficiently. Even if there is no long-run trade-off between inflation and real output, there is a short-run trade-off.

The social benefits of one part of that trade-off, the increase in output and decline in unemployment brought about by expansionary policy, appear to be obvious.[19] We need to consider the other part of the trade-off, the social costs of higher inflation, in more detail.

2.4   The costs of inflation

Reporting to the House of Commons in 1810, the Select Committee on the High Price of Gold Bullion dealt summarily with the costs of inflation (in this case high prices): 'Your committee conceive that it would be superfluous to point out, in detail, the disadvantages which must result to the country from any such general excess of currency as lowers its value.'[20] Almost two centuries later, it is still often said we lack an account of the costs of inflation that matches the intensity with which inflation is denounced by policymakers and disliked by the general public. It is more accurate to say that while there are convincing accounts of the many costs of inflation, especially in a society that has not adapted to its existence, the costs have been difficult to quantify.[21]

Table 2.2 presents a reasonably complete listing of the costs of inflation, which depend on the institutional structure of the economy and on the extent to which the inflation has been anticipated. Rather than work through the table in detail, I will summarise the major categories of costs, and then go on to discuss recent work relating the growth of output and productivity to inflation.

The most analysed cost of inflation is the money triangle or shoe-leather costs,[22] the social cost of economising on the use of non-interest bearing money. The area of the triangle depends on the magnitude of the relevant money stock and on the elasticity of money demand with respect to the nominal interest rate. For simplicity, we take currency to be the relevant

[18] The qualifier takes care of the possibility that extra monetary expansions have no effect in extreme hyperinflations.

[19] However the issue is not as analytically straightforward as it seems. If the economy is at an undistorted equilibrium, with the marginal value of leisure equal to the real wage, an expansion in output brought about by fooling workers as in the Friedman-Lucas model, does not increase their welfare. In the presence of distortions that make the natural rate of unemployment exceed the socially optimal level, or at a monopolistic competition equilibrium, an increase in output beyond the equilibrium level will be socially beneficial.

[20] Pp. cclviii–cclvix, reprinted by Arno Press, New York, 1978.

[21] Keynes (1924) provides one of the earliest analyses. I draw here on Fischer and Modigliani (1978), and Fischer (1981). See also Driffill et al. (1990).

[22] The classic reference is Bailey (1956).

concept of money. The average ratio of currency to GNP in the G-7 in 1992 was 5.2 per cent. The average inflation rate (CPI) for these seven countries for the period 1989–92 was 4.5 per cent.[23] Assuming an interest elasticity of 0.25, and that the nominal interest rate is 2 per cent when the inflation rate is zero, a reduction in the inflation rate to zero would increase the stock of currency to 7 per cent of GNP. The welfare gained as a result of that decline in inflation would amount only to 0.03 per cent of GDP.

Of course, these small welfare costs apply only at low inflation rates.[24] When inflation reaches the triple digit range, the social costs of attempting to economise on currency become high. Financial departments of firms expand at the expense of production, consumers spend time and resources delaying payments, and this social cost of inflation rises – approximately with the square of the inflation rate.

The money triangle calculation implicitly assumes the existence of non-distorting taxes to compensate for revenues lost by reducing inflation. If lump-sum taxes are available, then Friedman (1969) showed that the optimal inflation rate is not zero but rather that inflation rate which satiates the economy with real balances by driving the nominal interest rate to zero. Absent lump-sum taxes, the inflation tax may form part of an optimal tax package, so that the optimal inflation rate could be positive. However, the fiscal approach to inflation provides no clear theoretical presumption as to whether the optimal inflation tax is positive.[25]

There are two other potential effects of even a fully anticipated inflation. First, savers may substitute capital for real balances in their portfolio as inflation increases.[26] This would offset the steady state costs of the inflation. The portfolio substitution effect is bound to be small at low inflation rates, because the money displacement effect is itself small. In addition, inflation would generate menu costs – the costs of more frequent changes of prices.

---

[23] These are unweighted averages, based on data in the International Financial Statistics. The relevant base for the inflation tax includes non-interest bearing bank reserves, but since interest is paid on some bank reserves in the G-7, for instance in Italy, I work with the currency stock. The average ratio of high-powered money to GNP in the G-7 in 1992 was 7.8 per cent, and the social costs would rise proportionately if this were the relevant money stock.

[24] Lucas (1994) shows that the welfare loss depends significantly on the functional form of the demand for money.

[25] Phelps (1973) initiated the optimal tax analysis of inflation. For more recent general equilibrium analyses, see Cooley and Hansen (1991), and Chari et al. (1991). The optimal inflation tax is zero in the latter model. Faig (1988) also establishes conditions under which it is optimal not to tax money holdings.

[26] Theory makes no unambiguous predictions in this case either: in infinite horizon maximising models, such as that of Sidrauski (1967), inflation would not affect the steady state capital stock; in an overlapping generations model, or a model with a cash-in-advance constraint, it can.

Table 2.2. *The real effects of inflation*

Source of effect	Direct effect	Indirect (general equilibrium) effects
Fully indexed economy No interest paid on currency, a government (outside) liability	1. Increase in government revenue (inflation tax) 2. Economising on currency 3. Reduction in private net wealth 4. Resource costs of price change ('menu costs')	G1 Reduction in other taxes or increases in government spending. G2 Diversion of resources to transaction (shoe-leather costs) G3 Offsetting increase in capital stock, lowering real interest rate
Real effects of nominal government institutions Progressive taxation of nominal income	5. Increased real income tax bill	G5 See G1
Nominal tax base 1. Taxation of nominal interest income received by persons	6. Reduction of net of tax return on lending relative to pretax real rate	G6–10 Potential effects on cost of capital to corporations and in-individuals, with resultant effects on capital accumulation; changes in patterns of financing G9 See also G1
2. Deductibility of nominal interest paid by persons 3. Deductibility of nominal interest paid by corporations	7. Reduction of net real cost of borrowing relative to pretax real rate 8. Return to equity holders in levered corporations rises given constant debt-equity ratios, constant real pretax interest rate on bonds, and constant marginal product of capital 9. Changes in government tax receipts; net effect depends on induced changes in pretax real interest rate on bonds, differences in tax rates between debtors (including corporations) and creditors	
4. Depreciation at original cost Costs of goods sold measured at original costs	10. Return to equity holders declines 11. Tax revenue increases	G10–11 See also G1 Combined effects vary among firms, depending on nature of assets; likely shift away from use of long-lived assets; shift in inventory accounting methods from FIFO to LIFO

Table 2.2 (*continued*)

5. Taxation of nominal capital gains	12. Post-tax return to equity owners on realized gains declines if pre-tax return remains constant	
	13. Lock in effects	
Nominal accounting methods used by government	14. Distortions in interpretations of economic situation, e.g., nominal interest share in GNP rises, savings rate misinterpreted since both income and savings measured incorrectly; overstatement of government deficit	

Real effects of nominal private institutions and habits

Continued reliance on nominal annuity contracts, mortgages	15. Declining real repayment streams relative to nominal streams	G15 Possible effects on real interest rates, and therefore investment
Nominal accounting methods	16. Distortion of reports of profits; other money illusions based on confusion between real and nominal interest rates possible	G16 Effects on stock market valuation of firms; investment decisions

Real effects of unanticipated inflation through existing nominal contracts

Existing contracts for goods or services fixed in money terms or otherwise sticky	17. Redistribution between buyer and seller if quantity of services fixed by contract	G17–19 Effects on level of economic activity (Phillips curve); short-run functional income redistribution by income size
	18. Effects on quantity of services provided	
	19. Distortions of relative prices fixed at different times	
Existing debt contracts fixed in nominal terms	20. Redistribution from private to public sector	G19 Misallocations of resources arising particularly from need to search for relative price information
	21. Redistribution between private debtors and creditors	G20 Ultimately intergenerational transfers

Real effects of uncertainty of future inflation

Need to make decisions without knowledge of future prices	22. Reluctance to make future commitments without knowledge of prices; absence of safe asset	G22 Changes in patterns of asset accumulation
	23. Shortening of nominal contracts	G23 Increased transactions costs of making frequent contracts, and loss of planning ability

Table 2.2 *(continued)*

Real effects of government endeavors to suppress symptoms of inflation		
Public dissatisfaction over inflation, and governmental reactions	24. Wage and price controls	G24 Shortages, possibly pervasive; misallocations of resources
Government concern over potential bankruptcies and other financial losses resulting from a rise in interest rates	25. Control of interest rates, intervention in bond markets	G25 Instability of financial flows, with possible effects on direction and level of investment activity

Menu costs have not been measured, but it is hard to believe they would amount to much in a low inflation economy.

The familiar conclusion so far is that the costs of any fully anticipated inflation rate below say 5 per cent, in an economy whose institutions have adapted to inflation, must be moderate indeed. If inflation has significant costs, they must arise from the non-adaptation of institutions to inflation, and because inflation is often not anticipated.

The most important source of institutional non-neutrality to inflation is the tax system; within the tax system it is the taxation of capital that is most distorted by inflation. The deductibility of nominal interest and the taxation of nominal capital gains are the two main distortions. Assuming that the effective tax rate on saving rises with inflation, and making a host of subsidiary assumptions, it is possible to calculate the costs of lower rates of capital accumulation implied by higher inflation.[27] In addition, rising rates of taxation associated with inflation cause misallocations of capital among sectors, and affect corporate financing decisions. In the presence of bracket creep, rising inflation would also affect labour supply.

Taken together, such inflation-caused distortions could easily have a social cost amounting to 2–3 per cent of GNP at an inflation rate of 10 per cent.[28] However, there is a very real question of whether these costs should be attributed to inflation, for most of them could be removed by indexing the tax system. Income tax brackets have been indexed in the United States but indexation of capital taxation is generally more cumbersome and rare.

The assumption of a constant value of money is also built into private sector institutions, including the typical level-payment nominal mortgage in the United States, and accounting practices. There has been an increasing recognition of inflation in both areas in the last two decades, with a corres-

---

[27] Fischer (1981) contains one such calculation, in which an increase in the inflation rate from zero to 10 per cent has a social cost of 0.7 per cent of GNP as a result of its impact on saving.
[28] See Fischer (1981).

ponding reduction in the costs of inflation. It has also become more common to recognise the effects of inflation-caused increases in interest rates on government fiscal data, with the notion of the operational deficit gaining increasing usage in moderate-to-high inflation countries.[29]

Unanticipated inflations are associated with redistributions of income and wealth, the latter of which may be massive. Keynes (1924) argued that entrepreneurs gain from inflation, and it is often believed that labor loses. However, the direction of any redistribution of income must depend on the source of the inflationary shock and, at least in the moderate inflations in the United States, the estimated redistributions are small.

Inflation-induced wealth redistributions are larger, both between the private and public sectors, and within the private sector between debtors and creditors. Taking the Maastricht norm, at a debt to GDP ratio of 60 per cent an increase in the price level by 1 per cent reduces the value of government debt by 0.6 per cent of GDP. Unanticipated changes in the price level thus have potentially large impacts on private sector wealth. However because a reduction in the value of government debt reduces future taxes, these redistributions should be viewed as intergenerational within the private sector rather than between public and private sectors, with unanticipated inflation reducing the wealth of the old and increasing that of the young. This is certainly one source of the political unpopularity of inflation. Within the private sector, unanticipated inflation benefits the debtors. Corporations appear to gain at the expense of their lenders, though equities do not generally benefit from inflation – so that unanticipated inflation benefits neither bondholders nor equityholders. Mortgage borrowers gain at the expense of depositors and other lenders.

The wealth redistributions associated with even moderate rates of unanticipated inflation are likely to be economically and politically significant. That is all the more so when unanticipated changes in the price level are large, as they have been in the aftermath of wars. It is however difficult to estimate the social costs of such redistributions, for one group gains what another loses.

A considerable body of evidence establishes that the variability of relative prices rises with the inflation rate, for both anticipated and unanticipated inflation. In both cases, it is likely that the increased variability of relative

---

[29] The operational or inflation-adjusted deficit deducts the decline in the real value of government debt caused by inflation from the nominal deficit. In analysing inflation stabilisations, there is also a case for calculating a 'zero-inflation deficit', an estimate of what the deficit would be if inflation were reduced to zero. This would differ from the operational deficit because inflation affects other components of the budget, for example through the Tanzi effect, and because the real interest rate might change if inflation were stabilised. The zero-inflation deficit provides information about the extra fiscal effort that would be needed for a stabilisation programme to succeed.

prices distorts the allocation of resources.[30] These inflation-related distortions must be part of the explanation for the negative association between growth and inflation to be documented below.

Finally, high inflation is also more uncertain inflation.[31] There are several possible reasons for this relationship: inflation is often associated with real shocks; the higher the inflation rate, the more likely it is that the government will want to reduce the inflation rate at some point; higher inflation is a signal of a government that is losing control over the economy. Whatever the cause, the higher uncertainty is costly, potentially reducing investment,[32] and also reducing the welfare of savers forced to contend with it. The welfare costs for savers of greater uncertainty are related to the potential benefits of the introduction of indexed bonds. Sample calculations in Fischer (1981) suggest that an increase in the uncertainty of inflation typically associated with a rise in inflation within the range of recent United States experience would create no more than a modest social cost.

This long list establishes the many ramifications of inflation, anticipated and unanticipated, in a modern economy even at moderate rates of inflation. Adding together those elements in the list that can be quantified would provide an estimate of the costs of a 10 per cent inflation at 2–5 per cent of GNP. That is a sizable social cost, albeit one that could be significantly reduced by indexation.

But it remains true that such an enumeration does not capture the very strong feelings about inflation that are evident even in the less inflation-averse industrialised economies. Some of the popular attitude must derive from the belief that inflation unfairly takes away the fruits of inflation-caused nominal income increases that people incorrectly attribute to their own merit and hard work.[33] Another factor must be the disorientation of having to deal with price increases in the face of the surprisingly deeply inbuilt belief that money values are stable, a form of money illusion.[34] A further cause of the popular view must be the fear that the disorders of hyperinflation lie just over the horizon of any inflation, a fear that is more vivid in countries that have suffered hyperinflations.

Most important, the experience of inflation is rarely that of a simple

[30] For recent theoretical treatments, see Reagan and Stulz (1993) and Tommasi (1994).

[31] See Fischer (1981) and Taylor (1981).

[32] Huizinga (1991) presents a model in which uncertainty reduces investment as entrepreneurs wait for its resolution before committing themselves. It should be noted though that the general equilibrium effects of greater uncertainty on investment may differ from the partial equilibrium effects, since asset prices and interest rates can adjust in general equilibrium.

[33] Fischer and Huizinga (1982) examine public opinion polls on attitudes to inflation, but are unable to substantiate this inflation illusion hypothesis.

[34] Such money illusion appears to remain in economies that experience single digit inflation, but does not survive in prolonged moderate (15–30 per cent) inflations, where a foreign currency is often used as a unit of account and store of value.

steady rate of growth of prices at sustained full employment. Rather, inflation is usually associated with other problems, supply shocks or a lack of fiscal control. Yet another cause of the popular attitude must be the generally negative association between output growth and inflation.

2.4.1   Indexation

Many of the costs of inflation would be reduced by the introduction of indexation. This applies to the tax system, to inflation-caused wealth redistributions on debt, and to the losses to savers from the greater uncertainty associated with higher inflation. Here lies the essential case for government introduction of indexed bonds, to reduce the uncertainties confronting those saving for retirement.[35] Indexation of wages would reduce the redistribution of income associated with demand-caused inflation in the presence of long-term labour contracts, and would also make the Phillips curve steeper.

Many governments, and particularly central bankers, have long opposed indexation, on the grounds that its introduction would be a confession of failure in the battle against inflation, and would weaken the will to continue the fight.[36] In the words of Arthur Burns (1978, p. 148):

> This [indexation] is a counsel of despair ... I doubt if there is any practical way of redesigning economic contracts to deal with this problem satisfactorily. In any event, if a nation with our traditions attempted to make it easy to live with inflation, rather than resist its corrosive influence, we would slowly but steadily lose the sense of discipline needed to pursue governmental policies with an eye to the permanent welfare of our people.

Game theoretic models provide some support for this view (Fischer and Summers 1989). In models in which monetary policy has an inflationary bias because of dynamic inconsistency,[37] any change that reduces the social costs of inflation increases the equilibrium inflation rate, *and tends to worsen social welfare*,[38] essentially for the reasons given by the Radcliffe Committee and by Arthur Burns. However, it is necessary to distinguish different types of indexation. Indexing that increases the costs of unanticipated inflation to the government tends to reduce the inflation rate. Thus, indexation of taxes and of bonds that reduces the government's gains from unanticipated

---

[35] For discussion of the welfare economics of the introduction of indexed bonds, see Fischer (1983).

[36] Report of the Committee on the Working of the Monetary System (the Radcliffe Committee), 1959, para 573.

[37] The concept of dynamic inconsistency is discussed in more detail below.

[38] This result holds for the usual quadratic loss function, but may be reversed for other loss functions.

inflation would not necessarily cause higher inflation: the net effect depends on the relative extents to which such indexation reduces the social costs of inflation compared with the extent to which it reduces the government's gains from unanticipated inflation. Not all central bankers have opposed bond indexation;[39] nor has the introduction of index bonds in Britain had any obviously adverse effects on the government's will to fight inflation.

The extent of indexation in an economy is a measure of how much inflation that economy has experienced. It would thus be difficult to establish empirically whether indexation generally weakens the will to fight inflation. However, it is certainly clear from the cases of Israel and Brazil in the early 1980s that the view that the country had learned to live with inflation was instrumental in both the increases in inflation in each and the deterioration of their economic situations.

Widespread indexation that reduces the social costs of inflation for society is likely to increase inflation and quite possibly make the society worse off. Indexation that reduces the government's incentives to inflate by reducing its gains from inflation can make society better off.

2.4.2   Inflation, growth, and productivity

At least since the time of David Hume ([1752] 1955), it has been argued that a little inflation is good for growth:

The good policy of the magistrate consists only in keeping it [the money stock], if possible, still increasing; because by that means he keeps alive a spirit of industry in the nation, and increases the stock of labour in which consists all real power and riches.

Early models of money and growth likewise suggested that an increase in inflation would temporarily increase growth, and increase the steady state capital stock as investors substitute capital for real balances in their portfolio. More recent models allow for a negative association between inflation and growth, for example because inflation is associated with greater price variability and greater uncertainty, thereby reducing both the effectiveness of the price mechanism, and investment.

The context here is not the short-run Phillips curve trade-off, but rather the longer-term relationship between inflation and growth. The evidence points strongly to a predominantly *negative* longer-term relationship between growth and inflation.[40] Cross-country regressions reported in

---

[39] In his 22 February 1994 Humphrey-Hawkins testimony, Fed Chairman Greenspan indicated support for the introduction of index bonds, mainly on informational grounds.

[40] Neoclassical growth models imply that inflation would affect the level of output, but not the steady state growth rate. The new growth theory could generate a growth rate effect of inflation.

Fischer (1993) show a consistently negative association between inflation and growth. Based on a panel regression for eighty countries over the period 1961–1988, it is estimated that an increase in the inflation rate by 10 percentage points (e.g. from 5 to 15 per cent per annum) is associated with a decline in output growth of 0.4 per cent per annum. Estimation of a spline regression shows that these inflation effects are non-linear, the marginal effect on growth associated with an increase in inflation declining as inflation rises. The spline regression shows a larger though barely statistically significant effect of higher inflation on growth for inflation in the range of 0–15 per cent per annum: in this range, a 10 percentage point increase in the inflation rate is associated with a reduction in the growth rate of output by 1.25 per cent per annum.

Decomposing growth into its components due to capital accumulation, productivity growth, and an increase in the growth rate of the labour force, the negative association between inflation and growth can be traced to strong negative relationships between inflation and capital accumulation, and inflation and productivity growth, respectively. A 10 percentage point increase in the inflation rate is associated with a decline in productivity growth of 0.18 per cent per annum.

These negative associations do not, of course, establish that increases in inflation cause lower growth. If higher inflation is caused by adverse supply shocks, then the negative correlation between inflation and growth merely reflects the common impact of supply shocks. Fischer (1993) attempts to deal with this possibility by breaking the period into two at 1973, the date after which supply shocks became prominent. It turns out that the negative association between growth and inflation exists for both sub-periods. While this result is suggestive, it does not entirely dispose of the causation issue; indeed, given that policymakers do not create inflation out of a clear blue sky, it is almost certain that countries with high inflation rates are countries that are already in trouble for fiscal or other reasons, and thus that it will be either impossible or extremely difficult to deal definitively with the issue of causation.

The association between growth and inflation has also been examined for individual countries. In the Canadian case, Jarrett and Selody (1982) found that a one percentage point reduction in inflation was associated with a 0.3 per cent increase in the growth rate. The effect is too large to be causal: if it were, a decline in the inflation rate from 5 per cent to zero would increase the growth rate by 1.5 per cent, surely a trade-off anyone would be happy to make.

Rudebusch and Wilcox (1994) examine the closely related issue of the relationship between the rate of productivity growth and inflation. Using United States data, they find that an increase in inflation of 1 per-cent is

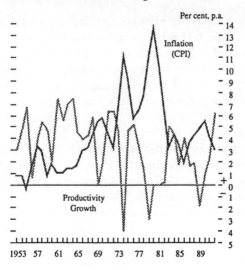

Figure 2.3 Inflation and productivity, US 1953–1992

associated with a 0.35 per-cent decline in productivity growth, an even bigger coefficient than in the Canadian case. Figure 2.3 shows United States data. The estimated coefficient for Canada and the UK is almost the same as that for the United States; it is significantly smaller and sometimes insignificant for other members of the G-7.

Rudebusch and Wilcox attempt to pin down whether the relationship is causal. One possibility is that the relationship reflects cyclical timing patterns: productivity growth is low near the peak of the cycle, when inflation is high, and high during the early part of the recovery, when inflation is typically still low. Figure 2.3 certainly suggests a strong cyclical element in the relationship. Making an adjustment for the cycle reduces the regression coefficient. Attempting to deal with the simultaneity issue econometrically, by the use of instrumental variables, Rudebusch and Wilcox find that the coefficient on inflation typically becomes insignificant. While these two approaches suggest the relationship is not causal, Granger causality tests point in the opposite direction, implying that inflation Granger-causes productivity growth rather than vice versa.

In summary, while there is a strong and suggestive negative relation between longer-term growth and inflation, and productivity growth and inflation, the statistical evidence has not yet established that the relationship is causal. One reason to suspect that the relationship is not causal is that the coefficient on inflation in the productivity growth equation is too large. Another is that the relationship does not appear particularly robust.[41]

However weak the evidence, one strong conclusion can be drawn: inflation is not good for longer-term growth.

2.5 The optimal inflation rate: zero inflation versus price level stability

The fiscal view of inflation presents one approach to determining the optimal rate of inflation. However, it is hard to believe that seigniorage can be a significant determinant of the optimal inflation rate in an industrialised economy with a sophisticated tax system. Rather the optimal inflation rate should be determined on the basis of all the costs of inflation, and of any benefits it might have.

The many costs of inflation are manifest. If there is no long-run trade-off between inflation and unemployment, or inflation and growth, at any positive inflation rate, and absent a fiscal motive for inflation, it is hard to see any benefits.[42] This would suggest a target inflation rate of zero.

Reinforcing this view is the argument that zero is the only credible target, that once the monetary authority agrees to allow some inflation, it cannot plausibly commit to fighting higher inflation. Phelps (1972, p. xvi) characterises this view[43] as

Compare 'Price Stability, Right or Wrong', which has a nice ring to it, with 'If I have but one job to give to my economy, let me give it for 5.5 per cent inflation, as against higher numbers', which is absurd.

Let me for the moment accept that the target inflation rate should be zero. The important distinction then has to be drawn between a zero inflation target and the target of price level stability.[44] With a target inflation rate of zero, the central bank aims to achieve zero inflation each period, that is, to keep the price level at its current level. A central bank committed to price level stability would aim to undo the consequences of past failures to achieve the target price level. With a zero inflation target each period, there is considerable uncertainty about price levels in the distant future. With a

---

[41] It is also puzzling that the coefficient is large and significant only for the English-speaking countries among the G-7.

[42] I do not want to rule out the possibility that the revenue motive may justify positive inflation in countries that have difficulty raising revenues in other ways.

[43] Despite the persuasiveness of the quote, Phelps does not share the view.

[44] This issue has been discussed intensively in the Bank of Canada, which will produce a conference volume on the topic shortly.

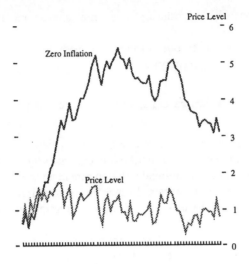

Figure 2.4 Price level, zero inflation vs price-level targeting

price level stability target, there should be much less uncertainty about price levels in the distant future.

Figure 2.4, one realisation of a stochastic simulation, illustrates the difference.[45] Each period the monetary authority achieves its target price level for that period, up to a random error. With a zero inflation target, the price level is a random walk. This means that the variance of future price levels increases linearly with their distance from the current period. With a price level target, the monetary authority is assumed each period to aim to close half the gap between the current price level and the target price level. This ensures that the actual price level stays close to the target level, and that uncertainty about future price levels is small.

The chief benefit of a price level target is that it keeps uncertainty about price levels in the distant future much smaller than it would be with a zero inflation target. The chief disadvantage is that the monetary authority with a price level target is attempting to deflate the economy half the time: the short-run target inflation rate will be negative half the time. For reasons to be discussed shortly, there are good reasons not to target negative inflation. Price level targeting is thus a bad idea, one that would add unnecessary short-term fluctuations to the economy. It is also true, as can be seen in

[45] With a zero inflation target, the price level is given by
$$p_t = p_{t-1} + \hat{\imath}_t,$$
where $\hat{\imath}_t$ is a serially uncorrelated disturbance term.
With a price level target, the price level is given by
$$p_t = p_{t-1} - 0.5(p_{t-1} - p^\star) + \hat{\imath}_t.$$

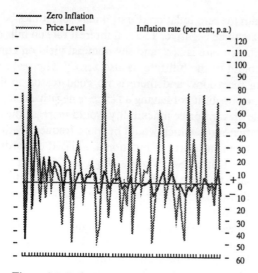

Figure 2.5 Inflation rates, zero inflation vs price-level targeting

figure 2.5, that there is more variability and uncertainty about short-term inflation rates with a price level target than with a target inflation rate.

It is sometimes said that price level stability is desirable because it would once again make long-term nominal contracting more attractive. Reference is made in this context to 99-year nominal leases, or the 100-year railroad bonds issued during the nineteenth century, a period in which a substantial measure of price level stability was achieved: in Britain, the same level of prices prevailed in 1914 as in 1881 as in 1844; setting that level at 100, prices ranged only between 70 and 130 in the period 1826 to 1914.[46] It is difficult to see much benefit from 99–year nominal leases or to make the case that 100-year bonds are an economically significant improvement over 50-year bonds, or 30-year bonds. And besides, some 100-year bonds have recently been sold in the United States.

Price level predictability is desirable for those saving for retirement. But it is far easier to provide for a stable real income stream in retirement by issuing index bonds than by trying to maintain a constant value of money.

Uncertainty about future price levels is unlikely to be much greater if the monetary authority targets a small positive inflation rate rather than a zero inflation rate. Thus there is no significant benefit from the viewpoint of the predictability of future price levels between choosing a zero inflation target and a 2–3 per cent inflation target.

So far I have accepted the zero inflation target. There are however three

[46] Data are from Keynes (1924).

good reasons not to aim for zero inflation. First, it may sometimes be useful for the real interest rate to be negative. The real interest rate on bills cannot be negative if the inflation rate is zero and the nominal yield on currency, which sets a lower bound to the bill rate, is also zero.[47] The real rate has been negative during recessions, and there is no good reason to deprive monetary policy of the possibility of having an *ex ante* negative real yield at times. Second, any downward price inflexibility would increase the output costs of negative inflation rates, which would be more frequent with a zero inflation goal.[48] Third, our measures of inflation are biased upwards. Estimates of the bias in the United States are as high as 1.5–2 per cent per annum.[49] It is very hard to see why the central bank should struggle to achieve a measured inflation rate of zero when true inflation would at that point be significantly negative.[50]

These arguments suggest that a positive though low target rate of inflation, around 1–3 per cent, would be optimal. This is in practice the range that the Bundesbank has set for itself over the years, and it is similar to the ranges specified by both the Reserve Bank of New Zealand and the Bank of Canada in recent years.[51]

The issue of a target price level versus target inflation rate none the less remains. Compare the goal of being close to a target price level that is growing at 2 per cent per annum from a given date, say January 1995, with the goal of achieving a 2 per cent inflation rate each year from 1995 on. The argument about price level versus zero inflation targeting is easily reformulated to apply to this case. With a target price path, the monetary authority attempts to offset past errors, thus creating more uncertainty about short-term inflation rates than with an inflation target. The gain is more certainty

---

[47] This argument is due to Summers (1991). There may be a small convenience yield that would allow slightly negative nominal interest rates on large denomination bills; it is also well known that nominal rates were negative at some points during the great depression, but that was a result of special tax features of bills.

[48] This argument implies money illusion.

[49] The three sources of bias are the failure to correct systematically for quality change (estimated to yield a bias of about 1 per cent per annum), 'outlet substitution bias' (the bias resulting from the inappropriate treatment of a gradual shift to lower price stores), and most remarkably the 'logarithm bias'. The last bias is caused by the practice of recording a decline in price from, say $2 to $1 as a 50 per cent decline, and a subsequent increase to $2 as a 100 per cent rise. The price of the good would be shown as having risen 50 per cent, even though it has not changed. Each of the last two sources are estimated to account for a bias of 0.3–0.4 per cent per annum. (I am indebted to Robert J. Gordon for discussion of this point.)

[50] Duguay (1993) states that the measurement bias in Canada is only 0.5 per cent per annum.

[51] In arguing for a 1–3 per cent inflation target, I am implicitly rejecting the view that a reduction in the inflation rate from 3 to 1 per cent would increase the growth rate of output by any significant amount. The regression results above do not address the relationship between inflation and growth at very low inflation rates. And in the presence of downward price inflexibility, there is reason to believe that growth would be lower at very low inflation rates.

about the long-term price level. My present view is that the inflation target with its greater short-term inflation rate certainty is preferable, despite its greater long-term price level uncertainty.

2.6   Dynamic inconsistency and inflationary bias

Inflation in most of the G-7 countries ratcheted up in the 1960s and 1970s. In the four business cycles completed in the United States between 1960 and 1981, the average inflation rate rose from 2.8 per cent to 9.9 per cent. By the end of the 1970s, the inflation rate in the United States, like that in France, the United Kingdom, Italy and Canada was higher than any conceivable account of the costs and benefits of inflation could justify. No wonder that economists felt called upon to explain the apparent inflationary bias of economic policy.

Before we proceed, it is worth asking for a moment whether there is indeed an inflationary bias to economic policy. The simple answer is yes: inflation in most countries has exceeded the optimal rate of 1–3 per cent. It was not always thus: at the ends of the Napoleonic and Civil Wars, and after World War I, Britain and the United States disinflated to get back to fixed gold parities. Certainly after World War I, this was not a wise policy and the disinflationary bias of monetary policy would have had to be explained. The price level was stable for nearly a century until 1914, and it is only in the era of fiduciary money that the inflationary bias has emerged in most countries.

The most obvious explanation for an inflationary bias in economic policy is seigniorage. As already discussed, inflation is a tax, and under certain conditions, should be used in an optimal fiscal program. But because the tax is not an explicit one, it tends to be used to excess: in Keynes's (1924, p. 46) much quoted words,

A Government can live for a long time, even the German Government or the Russian Government, by printing paper money ... The method is condemned, but its efficacy, up to a point, must be admitted. A Government can live by this means when it can live by no other. It is the form of taxation which the public finds hardest to evade and even the weakest Government can enforce, when it can enforce nothing else.

Seigniorage helps explain why inflation is on average higher in countries with less developed tax systems than in those that succeed in collecting taxes. The inflation tax is also central to the analysis of hyperinflations. But because seigniorage revenues in the major industrialised countries are relatively small as a share of GNP,[52] and perhaps because of the institutional

---

[52] For most industrialised countries, seigniorage revenue, defined as the real value of the increase in the stock of high-powered money, is less than 1 per cent of GNP. For a few

separation between the Treasury and the central bank (the inflation tax rate is not set in the budget), seigniorage appears not to receive explicit weight in the policy calculus that produces the inflation rate.[53]

The fiscal aspects of inflation should nonetheless be taken more seriously as a source of inflationary bias. Inflation tax revenues of course constitute a larger share of tax revenues than of GNP; in the 1960s and 1970s, seigniorage accounted for more than six per cent of tax (including seigniorage) revenues for several of the industrialised countries. Seigniorage considerations could help account for the increase in inflation during the 1960s and 1970s as government spending and taxes in general increased during that period. Further, a broader concept of the inflation tax, one that includes the gains that governments receive from unindexed tax brackets, and – if the inflation was unanticipated – from the devaluation of nominal government debt, renders the inflation tax explanation for an inflationary bias more plausible, especially if the inflation is unanticipated.

Nominal interest rate targeting provides a related explanation for the inflationary trends of the 1960s and 1970s. If monetary policy targets the nominal interest rate, and has no nominal anchor – that is, no monetary or price level target to tie down the price *level* – then the price level becomes indeterminate, and may move in any direction, including upwards at an increasing rate. The explanation appears straightforward: the central bank automatically accommodates any shock to money demand, including for instance one arising from an increase in output that tends to raise inflation through the Phillips curve, or an increase in the expected inflation rate. In so doing it may validate the original shock. However, this argument encounters difficulties on closer examination. Formally, it can be shown that nominal interest rate targeting may produce an indeterminate inflation rate if inflation expectations are adaptive, but will not do so if expectations are rational. More important, combining any nominal anchor with a nominal interest rate target keeps the price level determinate.[54] To put the same point less formally, a central bank that keeps its nominal interest rate constant no matter what, may produce an accelerating inflation; a central bank that raises the target nominal rate when inflation increases, need not suffer the same fate.

It is a third explanation of inflationary bias that forms the basis of most recent models of central bank independence. That is the notion of *dynamic*

countries, including Italy in the 1970s, it sometimes amounts to more than 3 per cent of GNP.

[53] Nor, as argued above, should it receive much weight in a country with a sophisticated tax system.

[54] See Blanchard and Fischer (1989, pp. 577–580) on nominal interest rate targeting; the argument traces back to Wicksell ([1898] 1965) and was developed by Friedman (1968).

inconsistency. Dynamic inconsistency is the inconsistency between the optimal policies that a policy authority would announce if its announcements were believed by the public, and the policies the authority would carry out once the public had acted on the basis of those expectations. The simplest example of dynamic inconsistency arises in the case of capital taxation. In order to encourage growth, the government should promise to tax capital at a low rate. But once the capital is in place, the government is tempted to tax it, promising all the while that this will not happen again. In the case of inflation, the government will announce that it is committed to fighting inflation. If the private sector responds by signing contracts that embody a low expected rate of inflation, the central bank is tempted to produce higher output through surprise inflation. But in a rational world, the private sector will understand the temptations that face the monetary authority, and discount its pronouncements accordingly.

Equilibrium in this game theoretic model, due to Kydland and Prescott (1977) and Barro and Gordon (1983), occurs at that point where the inflation rate is sufficiently high that the marginal cost of higher (surprise) inflation is just equal to the marginal benefit of the lower unemployment it will produce. But this equilibrium inflation rate is higher than it needs to be. It is too high because output is at the same level (the natural rate) as it would be at a lower inflation rate. All that keeps inflation from being lower is the central bank's inability credibly to promise not to create surprise inflation at lower inflation rates – to precommit, in the language of game theory. Any device or institutional change that persuades the private sector that the government will not create surprise inflation at lower inflation rates will reduce the equilibrium inflation rate.[55]

The tension between the direct benefits of lower inflation and the benefits of surprise inflation[56] that lies at the heart of these models is fundamental to modern analyses of monetary policy in general and central banking in particular. The model provides not only the basis for a theory of the role of monetary policy, but also a clear definition of credibility: a policy is credible when the private sector believes it will be carried out, and when it is correspondingly in the interest of the public sector to carry out the policy once the private sector has acted on its beliefs. Equivalently, a policy is credible if it is not dynamically inconsistent. The term credibility is of

---

[55] In his important work on the modern theory of central banking, Cukierman (1992), chapter 2) offers four reasons for an inflationary bias: the employment or short-run Phillips curve motive, a fiscal revenue motive, interest rate smoothing, and a balance of payments motive (under fixed exchange rates). Cukierman emphasises those motives that lead to dynamic inconsistency, whereas the argument here treats the revenue motive as a potentially separate cause of inflationary bias.

[56] These benefits include both the higher output available through the Phillips curve and the fiscal gains discussed above.

course used less precisely in other contexts: for instance, a central bank is said to be credible if its announcements are believed.[57]

In practice, societies find ways of dealing with dynamic inconsistency. Despite the temptations of taxing capital in place heavily, just once, capital levies are rare. Some countries had low inflation rates well before the notion of dynamic inconsistency was formalised. The patent system deals with a similar problem in the creation of knowledge.[58]

An independent central bank is one of the mechanisms that can deal with the inflationary bias of monetary policy.

2.7   Rules, discretion and central bank independence

Kydland and Prescott (1977) and Barro and Gordon (1983) saw their demonstration of the inflationary bias of discretionary monetary policy as making the case for a monetary rule, along Friedman lines. With a monetary rule firmly in place, the central bank would not be able to create surprise inflation, and the problem of dynamic inconsistency would disappear. However a monetary rule is a far cry from an independent central bank.

Friedman's (1959) argument for a constant growth rate of money rule, based on the potentially destabilising effects of active monetary policy when its effects have long and variable lags, may have led to the view that a money rule must be a constant growth rate rule. But activist feedback monetary rules are possible. The Barro-Gordon argument for a money rule would carry over to a model in which there is a potential role for an active monetary policy in offsetting shocks, thereby helping to stabilize at least inflation and perhaps also output. Given the structure of the economy, the optimal monetary feedback rule could be legislated into place and dynamic inconsistency and its inflationary bias would be prevented.[59]

More sophisticated monetary feedback rules that take account of changes in the velocity of circulation have been proposed. For instance, McCallum (1994) proposes a rule that sets the growth rate of the money base at 3 per cent per annum, with adjustments for the change in base velocity over the

---

[57] This is close to the formal definition, since announcements will not continue to be believed if they are inconsistent with reality. The more general informal definition goes beyond that emerging from the formal analysis, because it allows for credibility about policy announcements and decisions that were not anticipated at the time the private sector was making its decisions.

[58] In this case, incentives have to be provided for the creation of new knowledge, but it is in society's interests to allow the general use of the knowledge once it has been created.

[59] Friedman's (1959) argument for a constant growth rate rule is formally independent of the problem of dynamic inconsistency or the inflationary bias of monetary policy; rather, the argument is that there is no feedback in the optimal feedback rule.

past four years[60] and also for the deviation of nominal GNP from a target path. This rule is shown to produce good inflation and output performance in several small econometric models.

Note that there are two different arguments for a monetary rule in preference to discretionary monetary policy. Friedman's view is that policy-makers not bound by a constant growth rate rule would be tempted into excess activism, destabilising rather than stabilising the economy. Barro and Gordon argue that discretionary policy has an inflationary bias, but do not dispute the possibility of a stabilising activist feedback policy. Once the latter possibility is admitted, the case for a monetary rule – a rule that rigidly prescribes the behavior of a monetary aggregate – must rest on dynamic inconsistency. But there is then a trade-off between the benefits of avoiding the inflationary bias of discretionary policy and the potential cost of being bound to follow a monetary rule that is no longer appropriate.

Goodhart's law and much recent experience suggest that any monetary rule will eventually break down; in the words of Richard Sayers (1958, p. 7), 'we are doomed to disappointment if we look for rules applicable to all times and all places'. The money demand instability manifested in many countries in the 1970s and 1980s, and in Germany in the last year, has put paid to the notion of relying on any simple monetary feedback rule, much less to legislating such a rule into existence. There cannot be a case now for dealing with the problem of dynamic inconsistency by putting in place any rule that prescribes by a fixed formula the growth rate of any monetary aggregate or the behaviour of interest rates. Rather, the monetary authorities need to be given some flexibility to decide on day to day monetary policy. In this context, rules of the McCallum type can provide a useful benchmark against which to judge policy.

A fixed exchange rate peg is a form of monetary rule, one that leaves very little room for discretionary policy if the peg is taken seriously. A country that pegs to a reasonably stable currency can solve its inflationary problem. But exchange rate pegging is not danger-free: because non-traded goods prices can increase relative to traded goods prices, countries that peg frequently find themselves with overvalued currencies. In any fixed exchange rate system, the key countries need to find a way of solving their own inflationary bias problem. And as the experience of the Bretton Woods system and the European Monetary System shows, sometimes the key country acts in a way that makes it impossible to maintain the peg.[61]

---

[60] McCallum states that a four-year period is used to avoid adjusting for cyclical changes in velocity.

[61] Fixed exchange rates within a monetary union are potentially different from fixed exchange rates among countries whose central banks can make independent monetary policy decisions.

Because the fixed versus flexible exchange rate issue has been extensively investigated, and because the need remains to set overall monetary policy within a fixed exchange rate system, I shall not continue the discussion of the fixed exchange rate regime.

To retain flexibility in monetary policy while dealing with the inflationary bias of discretionary policy, Rogoff (1985) proposed the appointment of a conservative central banker, who is more averse to inflation than is society as a whole.[62] The central banker's aversion to inflation reduces the average inflation rate, but he still has the discretion to conduct stabilising counter-cylical policy.

There are two important points about the solution in the Rogoff model. First, it represents a trade-off between the reduction in the average inflation rate and the increase in the variability of output (relative to that attainable under a socially optimal policy) that is implied by the conservatism of the central banker. Second, there is an optimal degree of inflation aversion on the part of the central banker, which means that the central banker can be excessively inflation averse.

Rogoff's model provides one rationalisation for an independent central bank. The bank is given the independence to pursue activist policy, but it is expected to be more inflation averse than is society. Central banks that are given strong powers and a mandate to secure price stability, perhaps 'within the framework of the Government's overall economic policy',[63] seem to fit the Rogoff model. Based on this model, the convention has developed in empirical work of calibrating the independence of the central bank by the weight it places on inflation relative to output in its objective function.[64] By this measure of independence, a central bank can be too independent by being too monomaniacal about inflation.

Lohmann (1992) extends the Rogoff rule to allow the conservative central banker to be overruled by the government, at a cost. This produces a non-linear rule in which the central bank responds proportionately more strongly to large than to small disturbances, in such a way such that the government never actually overrules the bank.[65] The outcome under this rule is better than that under the simple Rogoff rule.

One of the reasons for central bank independence is to remove the inflation tax from the control of the fiscal authority. Debelle (1994a) extends

---

[62] Formally, both the central banker and society are assumed to prefer inflation and output levels that are close to (the same) target levels, but the central banker weights deviations of inflation from target relative to output deviations more heavily than society does.

[63] The quote is from a translation of the 1993 Act on the Status of the Banque de France.

[64] This convention is followed, for instance, in table 2.1.

[65] This result fits with experience in countries such as Canada and the Netherlands where the government has the right to overrule the central bank but has to publish its reasons for doing so – and has not so far exercised its option.

the Rogoff model to add a fiscal authority, which puts more weight on government spending than does the central bank or society. The central bank is responsible for setting the inflation rate, but the government receives the seigniorage revenue. Debelle shows that the inflation rate will be higher the greater the weight the government puts on its spending. Extending these results, Debelle and Fischer (1994) show that the inflation rate tends to be higher when the fiscal authority makes its decisions before the central bank.[66] Inflation is also likely to be higher in a situation of fiscal dominance, when the fiscal authority chooses the deficit and forces the central bank to finance it. This is a situation in which the central bank has no effective independence.

Models that include the possibility of developing a reputation present an alternative way out of the dynamic inconsistency problem. With a sufficiently long horizon, and a sufficiently low discount rate, the monetary policymaker may find it optimal to develop a reputation for anti-inflationary zeal by pursuing the dynamically consistent low inflation policy.[67]

The most important recent development in the game theory approach to monetary policy has come from applications of the principal-agent model. In this model, a principal (society) with well-defined goals has to design a contract that will motivate an agent (the central bank) to act in the principal's interests. In general the agent has access to some information that the principal does not.

Walsh (1993) and Persson and Tabellini (1993) have shown that a contract between the government and the central banker in which the central banker's remuneration declines in proportion to inflation can attain the first best equilibrium.[68] Not only does this contract remove the inflationary bias of monetary policy, but the central bank's countercyclical policy is optimally active. Accordingly, appointing a central banker who has the same loss function as society, and penalising him or her by an amount proportional to the inflation rate, enables society to obtain the first best solution.[69] This result is based on the assumption that the central bank has the same loss function as society, and that the only problem that the contract has to deal with is the inflationary bias resulting from dynamic inconsistency.

The target inflation rate in this contracting approach should be made to

---

[66] Technically, the assumption is that the fiscal authority acts as a Stackelberg leader, moving first, but taking into account the central bank's response to its choice of policy variables.

[67] Several reputational models are discussed in Fischer (1990).

[68] One example of such a contract occurs when the salary of the governor is fixed in nominal terms during his or her term of office, as for the Bank of England and the Reserve Bank of New Zealand.

[69] This result is obtained by Walsh (1993) and also by Persson and Tabellini (1993). Walsh shows that the first best can also be obtained by penalising the central bank by an amount proportional to the money stock – which is stochastically related to the inflation rate.

depend on any shocks that affect the optimal dynamically consistent inflation rate. This is done in both Canada and New Zealand, where a formula is provided to adjust the inflation target if there are supply shocks, and if indirect taxes are imposed.

Walsh and Persson-Tabellini assume that the contract will be carried out. Of course, the principal faces the temptation to behave in a dynamically inconsistent way by changing the contract *ex post*. The model therefore carries an implicit assumption that it is costly to change the contract.

The targeting approach to monetary policy that emerges from the contracting model has been implemented in New Zealand and Canada. It contrasts with the approach taken in Germany and in the new statutes of the Banque de France, where the central bank is given a more general mandate for price stability. Both the Reserve Bank of New Zealand and the Bundesbank are described as independent, but they differ in the degree of independence they have to specify short-run policy goals. The Bundesbank decides on its own on the inflation path it seeks to attain, while the Reserve Bank of New Zealand has to negotiate a target path with the government. Each central bank has full independence or discretion about the monetary policy tactics it follows to achieve these goals.

Because the term independence is not precise, some prefer to describe a central bank as autonomous,[70] or 'somewhat apart from government'.[71] Rather than fight the inevitable, I shall continue to use the term independence, but draw a distinction between *goal independence* and *instrument independence*. A central bank whose goals are imprecisely defined has goal independence: at an extreme, one could imagine endowing a central bank with the power to conduct monetary policy and giving it the goal of doing good. At the other extreme, the goal may be as precisely specified as those in New Zealand, where there is no goal independence. A central bank with a mandate for price stability but no numerical targets has more goal independence. A central bank has instrument independence when it has full discretion and power to deploy monetary policy to attain its goals. A central bank bound by a monetary rule would not have instrument independence, nor would a central bank which was required to finance the budget deficit.

The concept of *accountability* can be addressed within the contracting approach. The general notion of accountability is that there be adverse consequences for the central bank or the central banker of not meeting targets. In the optimal contract, the central banker is responsible for achieving the target inflation rate, and is penalised for failing to do so. While the penalty in the formal models appears to be monetary, public obliquy

---

[70] See for instance the evidence by Charles Goodhart in *The Role of the Bank of England*, Volume II, paragraph 3.
[71] Freedman 1993, p. 91.

would serve as well.[72] Thus even a central bank with a more general mandate could be held accountable, for instance by being required to publish a monetary policy report, or through public hearings on its performance such as the Humphrey-Hawkins hearings at which the Chairman of the Fed testifies twice a year. A central bank that is not held accountable is more likely to behave in a dynamically inconsistent way than an accountable bank – indeed any organisation that is not accountable is likely to perform worse than one that is accountable.

A subsidiary question is to whom the central bank is accountable: who is to judge whether targets were met, and to take the specified actions if they were not met. The answer implicit in the contracting approach is whoever makes the contract with the central bank. The more general answer is that the central bank should be accountable in some public forum, preferably to well-informed elected officials. An important reason to expose central bankers to elected officials is that, just as the latter may have an inflationary bias, the former may easily develop a deflationary bias. Shielded as they are from public opinion, cocooned within an anti-inflationary temple, central bankers can all too easily deny – and perhaps even convince themselves – that there is a short-run trade-off between inflation and unemployment, and that cyclical unemployment can be reduced by easing monetary policy.

Another subsidiary question is who in the central bank should be accountable. The answer must be primarily the Governor. It would also be possible to penalise the entire board for failing to meet targets, by reducing their pay. There is no reason that should not be done, for instance by fixing their salaries in nominal terms for the length of their tenure.[73]

There is an interesting contrast between the accountability of the Bundesbank and the planned European Central Bank and that of the Fed or the Reserve Bank of New Zealand. The Bundesbank is not formally accountable to any other body, whereas the Fed is. The Bundesbank arrangement, where the policy goal is not precise, and there is no formal accountability, poses a potential danger: there is very little to prevent it from pursuing a socially excessive anti-inflationary policy. While the Bundesbank holds regular press conferences, these events are not the right forum to probe the basis of monetary policy. In practice, the Bundesbank has been very careful to take public opinion with it, and to publish a serious *Monthly Report*, but the danger remains.

Before turning to the empirical evidence on central bank independence, I

---

[72] As Persson and Tabellini (1993) point out, the announcement of targets, for money or inflation, makes sense as a device to help ensure accountability.

[73] As was pointed out in New Zealand, this contract would not survive a protracted deflation, since the central bankers would then be seen as benefitting from the misery that was being inflicted on the rest of the country.

want to re-emphasise the fact that every central bank continually faces the short-run trade-off between inflation and output. To illustrate, by 1991 the Bundesbank knew that it faced rising inflation. It could at that point have tightened money and raised short term interest rates to, say, 15 per cent. Such a decision would have prevented some of the subsequent inflation, at a cost in terms of forgone output. Instead it chose to fight the inflation more gradually. In the fall of 1993, it faced another decision, of whether to cut interest rates more rapidly, tending to increase output but at the cost of a slower decline in the inflation rate. It chose not to cut interest rates rapidly, thereby disinflating more rapidly at the expense of slowing the recovery.

The Bundesbank's policy mandate to maintain the value of the currency is a far from complete guide to the crucial policy choices it has to make. Nor is a price stability mandate a sufficient guide for any central bank. That is why central banks cannot merely be given the task of keeping inflation low: they have also to be made accountable for their performance, especially their counter-cyclical performance, to be asked whether they are making the right judgement about the speed at which to reduce inflation, or to return to full employment. They cannot take refuge in the claim that there is no long-run trade-off. Again quoting Keynes (1924, p. 88). 'Economists set themselves too easy, too useless a task if in tempestuous seasons they can only tell us that when the storm is long past the ocean is flat again.'

2.8   Empirical evidence on Central Bank Independence (CBI)

There are several empirical measures of legal central bank independence (CBI).[74] I use the Grilli, Masciandaro and Tabellini (1991) or GMT index, calculated for eighteen industrialised countries as a simple sum of fifteen different legal provisions, grouped under five headings: appointments; relationship with government; constitution; monetary financing of the budget deficit; and monetary instruments. Under appointments, the central bank is more independent if the government does not appoint the governor, the longer the term of the governor, and so forth. Two provisions appear under the constitution heading: whether there is a statutory requirement that the central bank pursue monetary stability among its goals; and whether there is any legal provision that strengthens the hand of the central bank in disputes with the government. There are also two criteria under the monetary instruments head: whether the central bank sets the discount rate; and whether the central bank supervises commercial banks.

Figure 2.6 shows the key empirical result in this literature. For the period

---

[74] See Cukierman (1992), chapter 19.

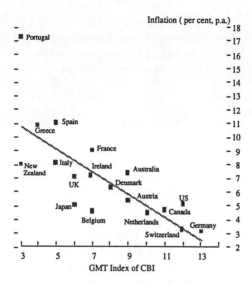

Figure 2.6 Inflation and CBI, GMT Index

1960–1992, there is a significant negative relationship between the average rate of inflation and central bank independence.[75]

This relationship is very robust for the industrialised countries. But it does not extend to a larger sample of seventy-two countries examined in Cukierman et al. (1992). For these countries, those included in table 2.1, there is a slightly positive relationship between inflation and legal CBI. For this group, Cukierman et al. find that inflation is positively and significantly correlated with the rate of turnover of central bank governors. The contrast between the results for the industrialised countries and the larger group must be due to the difference between actual and legal independence.[76]

The preceding analysis pointed most strongly to the central bank's mandate (lack of goal independence) and instrument independence as key factors in determining the inflationary bias of policy. To try to isolate these effects, I break down the GMT index of CBI into three components.[77] The first is the presence of a statutory requirement that the central bank pursue monetary stability among its goals; this is called INFOBJ. The second, EC6, consists of those measures relating to the central bank's right not to

[75] The t-statistic on CBI in the regression line shown in figure 2.6 is −4.6; R2 is 0.54.
[76] Cukierman et al. (1992) also create a questionnaire-based index of CBI for twenty-six countries. The questionnaires were answered by central bank officials. The rank correlation between the legally and questionnaire based indexes was very low for the entire group, and a bit higher (0.33) for the industrialised countries.
[77] I draw here on Debelle and Fischer (1994).

Table 2.3. *Inflation and the components of central bank independence*

Variable	(1)	(2)	(3)	(4)	(5)
INFOBJ	− 1.76	− 2.28	− 4.27		
	(1.72)	(1.61)	(1.30)		
EC6	− 1.02	− 1.02		− 1.53	
	(0.55)	(0.55)		(0.42)	
POL7-	0.41				− 0.94
	(0.45)				(0.51)
R̄2 0.44	0.44	0.44	0.37	0.42	0.12

Notes: Dependent variable is mean inflation rate, 1960–1992. Data definitions in text. Standard errors in parentheses.

finance the government, and to set the discount rate.[78] The third is a combination of legal provisions relating to appointments and the central bank's relationship with the government; this is called POL7.

Table 2.3 shows that the two variables most closely tied to inflation performance are INFOBJ and EC6. EC6, a measure of the central bank's ability to use its instruments freely, is the single variable most highly correlated with inflation. The variables grouped into POL7, which relate to appointment procedures, are not significantly related to inflation.

The most striking result of the empirical work is that CBI seems to have *no* adverse consequences. GMT (1991) and Alesina and Summers (1993) show that the improved inflation performance associated with increased CBI for industrialised countries does not come at a cost in terms of foregone growth. Similarly, for a cross-section of countries including LDCs, Cukierman et al. (1993) find that while legal independence is negatively related to growth, the coefficient is not significant; an alternative (inverse) measure of central bank independence, the frequency of turnover of the central bank governor, is negatively related to growth (and positively related to inflation). Thus improved inflation performance does not seem to come at a cost in terms of lower growth.

Figure 2.7 shows the relationship between the variability of inflation and the variability of GDP growth over the period 1960–92, for the countries for which GMT have constructed measures of CBI.[79] The association between

[78] GMT break their overall index down into a measure of political independence, which is (POL7 + INFOBJ), and one of economic independence, which is EC6 + the dummy variable that indicates whether the central bank supervises the commercial banks.

[79] Eijffinger and Schaling (1993) examine the relationship between alternative measures of CBI (Bade-Parkin (1988), Alesina (1988), GMT, and their own index) and inflation and output growth variability. They find that inflation variability is significantly negatively related only to the GMT index (in two out of three decades), and that output growth variability is not significantly related to any of the measures of CBI.

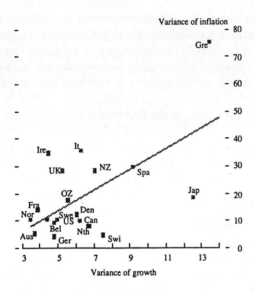

Figure 2.7 Inflation and output variability, 1960–1992

these measures of variability is positive and significant, though the statistical significance disappears if Greece is excluded from the sample.[80]

These results could reflect either reverse causation from inflation aversion to CBI, or, closely related, the presence of a third factor that produces both economic stability and CBI. Cukierman et al. (1992) have investigated the reverse causation issue econometrically and still find a negative correlation between inflation and CBI. Havrilesky and Granato (1993) include both measures of the extent of corporatism[81] and the CBI index in a regression for the rate of inflation, and find that none of the measures of corporatism separately, nor all of them together, enter significantly. By contrast, Hall (1994) argues that centralised collective bargaining at the industry level (with IG Metall setting the pattern) is at least as much responsible for low inflation in Germany as is the independence of the Bunsdesbank.

The possibility of reverse causation is sometimes used to argue that the legal position of the central bank is hardly relevant to inflation performance: if a country is inflation averse, then it will have low inflation whatever

---

[80] The standard loss function in this literature penalises deviations of the level of output from its target level, rather than the variability of output growth. Using measures of output deviations from linear and quadratic trends (of log output), we still find a positive but insignificant correlation between output and inflation variability.

[81] They include three measures of the power of organised labour, two measures of the leftward leaning of the government, and two measures of the size of the public sector.

the legal status of the central bank; if the country is not inflation averse, then the political system will always be able to get around the legal status of the central bank – as the results for the seventy-two-country Cukierman et al. (1992) sample establish. The implicit recommendation is that educating people about the costs of inflation is the best way of reducing inflation.

This is too extreme a position. In the first instance, the evidence on the costs of inflation and the relationship between inflation and growth suggests that countries benefit from being inflation averse. Even if reverse causation exists, it is probably optimal for those who want to reduce inflation to propose legislation setting up an independent central bank. There can be no better way of forcing public opinion to think about the inflation issue. And, if the country is one in which the laws are obeyed, successful legislation will lead to a different monetary policy.

While the empirical results show the gains from central bank independence, there remains an important anomaly. The Rogoff model implies that we should find a negative relationship in figure 2.7 if countries were being hit by the same shocks, and if the central banks were efficient but differed in their relative tastes for inflation and output variability. At least three factors could account for the positive relationship. If the variance of shocks differs systematically by country, then we would expect to find a positive relationship, with countries that are hit by bigger shocks[82] having greater variability of both inflation and GDP growth. Or, if some central banks are more efficient than others, they would do better at stabilising on both dimensions. Or, if more independent central banks are also more credible on inflation, they may obtain a 'credibility bonus' which makes the economy respond more rapidly to monetary policy changes.[83]

Most likely, the positive relationship between output and inflation variability in figure 2.7 reflects both differences in the magnitude of shocks affecting different economies, and differences in the efficiency with which policymakers respond to those shocks. Countries with independent central banks are likely to be countries with more disciplined governments, and thus to suffer smaller self-imposed shocks. It is also likely that more independent central banks are more efficient: they are likely to have better research staffs, and more able and experienced decision makers. I suspect that the credibility bonus explanation would also receive strong support, but return to the issue below.

---

[82] These shocks could be self-imposed, for instance greater variability of government spending.

[83] Kenneth Rogoff has pointed out that the relationship would also be positive if countries differ only in the wedge between the natural rate of unemployment and the socially optimal rate.

Table 2.4. *Inflation and output, United States and Germany*

Quarterly data	United States	Germany
Mean inflation	1.19	0.83
Variance of inflation	0.69	0.43
Mean growth rate	0.73	0.73
Variance of growth rate	0.88	1.42

Sum of squared residuals of log output against:

		Annual data
Linear trend	0.0487	0.08
Quadratic trend	0.023	0.0292

		Quarterly data
Linear trend	0.208	0.347
Quadratic trend	0.101	0.128

Note: data are for 1960–1992/3.

Despite figure 2.7, I want to argue that, for the most sophisticated central banks, there remains a trade-off between price level and output stability. Consider for instance Germany and the United States. Table 2.4 presents the mean inflation rates and growth rates, as well as the variability of inflation and growth[84] for the United States and Germany for the period 1960–92. German inflation was lower than that of the United States over the period, and growth rates were the same. The United States has more stable output and less stable inflation. No doubt the United States could have had more stable inflation, if its central bank had been more devoted to fighting inflation. Should it have had such a central bank? While the empirical results on CBI seem to say yes, since greater CBI comes with lower inflation and no evident costs, the comparison with German performance suggests there is a trade-off, and that countries have to decide how inflation averse they want their central bank to be.

We return now to the credibility bonus. In figure 2.8, we show the sacrifice ratio in recessions since 1962 against the GMT measure of central bank independence.[85] The overall relationship is positive; it is also statistically significant. This implies that more independent central banks on average pay a *higher* output price per percentage point of inflation to reduce

---

[84] Similar results hold for the variability of output around linear or quadratic trends.
[85] This relationship was discovered independently by Adam Posen (1993). The output loss and inflation measures that underlie the sacrifice ratios are from Ball (1993).

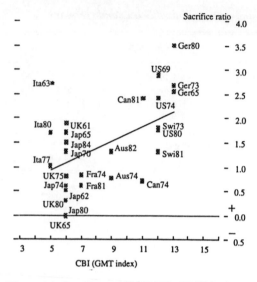

Figure 2.8 Sacrifice ratio and CBI, GMT Index

the inflation rate. A similar though weaker positive relationship holds between the output loss in recessions and central bank independence.[86]

This result is consistent with the Phillips curve being flatter in low inflation than in high inflation economies.[87] But it is none the less puzzling, because a more independent central bank should be more credible, and the public should more readily believe its anti-inflationary pronouncements. Figure 2.8 suggests that there is no credibility bonus in the labor markets for more independent central banks: they have to prove their toughness repeatedly, by being tough.

The evidence leaves little doubt that, on average, economic performance is better in countries with more independent central banks. The relationship between inflation and the elements of CBI is attributable mainly to the central bank's ability to use its policy instruments freely (instrument independence) and to the presence of a price stability goal (lack of goal independence). We further tentatively conclude that the causation in industrialised countries, where legal provisions are likely to have more force, runs at least in part from legal independence to lower inflation. As an analytic matter, we expect less price variability and greater output variability in countries with more independent central banks. Such a relationship is not

[86] The t-statistic on the CBI measure is 3.8 in figure 2.8, and 1.96 when the output loss is regressed on CBI.
[87] See footnote 17 and the paragraph to which it is attached.

visible in the aggregate data. The elements of a trade-off are present in comparing United States and German data, and there must be such a trade-off for an efficient central bank. Finally, central bank independence does not appear to bring a credibility bonus in the labour markets: even independent central banks have to fight hard and long to bring inflation down after an inflationary shock has struck.

2.9   The charter of a modern central bank

The case we have set out for an independent central bank is becoming increasingly accepted. Within the last decade, the central banks of Chile, France, Mexico, New Zealand, and Venezuela have all had their legal independence enhanced, and the Maastricht treaty requires national central banks participating in the European System of Central Banks to meet a prescribed standard of independence. And of course, there is a lively debate in Britain over the desirability of making the Bank of England, now explicitly subservient to the Treasury, independent.[88]

The argument for greater independence for the Bank of England is based on three foundations. The first is the theoretical literature on the inflationary bias of discretionary policy-making. The second is the empirical literature on central bank independence. Closely related is the third argument for greater independence, the success of the Bundesbank and the German economy over the past forty years. The Reserve Bank of New Zealand's success in reducing inflation provides further support for independence. However, the New Zealand experience has come at a time of general disinflation, and it remains to be seen how well the Bank operates as worldwide inflationary pressures build.[89]

The lessons that should be drawn from the theoretical and empirical evidence presented here are:[90]

- The central bank should have a clearly defined mandate, which includes price stability;
- The central bank should publicly announce its intermediate-term policy goals;
- The central bank should be accountable, in two senses: it should be held responsible for meeting its announced goals; and it should be required to explain and justify its policies to the legislature and the public;

---

[88] See for instance Roll et al. (1993), Vibert (1993), and House of Commons (1993).

[89] Australia, whose central bank is much less independent than that of New Zealand, was almost as successful in disinflating as New Zealand; however inflationary expectations in New Zealand at the end of 1993 were more favorable than those in Australia. See Debelle 1994b.

[90] The recommendations here are essentially the same as those in Roll et al. 1993.

- The government should have the authority to override the Bank's decisions, but the override decision should carry a cost for the government;
- The central bank should be given the authority to set interest rates and other monetary policy variables in order to achieve its policy goals;
- The central bank should not be required to finance the government deficit, and should not manage the public debt;
- There cannot be a separate responsibility for setting interest rates and the exchange rate so long as the exchange rate floats.

Let me expand briefly on each point.[91] The Bank's primary mandate should be to establish price stability, by which is meant a low (1–3 per cent) average rate of inflation. The legislation should not deny the short-run Phillips curve trade-off: hence the need for a qualifier such as 'primary', which leaves the short-run trade-off implicit; alternatively, the legislation can follow the Netherlands route and state that the mandate is for price stability 'with a view to promoting the nation's prosperity and welfare'.[92]

The Bank's inflation goals for the next three years should be announced, after consultation with the Treasury, and relative to a long-term target of, say, 2 per cent. The announcement should describe the allowances that will be made for changes in the terms of trade, interest rates, and indirect taxes in judging whether the target has been met.[93]

The Governor of the Bank should be held responsible for meeting the targets. He should be required to testify on the performance of monetary policy in meeting its preannounced goals, in public, before a House of Commons Committee, twice a year.[94] The testimony should be accompanied by the publication of a report, along the lines of the *Inflation Report*. The most difficult issue is the sanctions that should be imposed on the Bank for failing to meet its targets. Sharp public questioning is the only sanction that is now applied in the United States, and there is no explicit sanction in most countries. Public reprimand and loss of reputation is probably a sufficient sanction.

---

[91] I am not taking into account here the need to conform with the Maastricht Treaty if Britain is to become a member of the EMU.

[92] The fact that monetary policy can affect output in the short-run should not be ignored. Thus I disagree with the otherwise excellent report by Roll et al. (1993) when it states (p. 9) 'Because monetary policy eventually affects only inflation, it should be the prime instrument to deal with inflation; and this long-run effort must be sustained. [Correct, so far]. Fiscal policy therefore seems the natural countercyclical tool to mitigate short-run fluctuations in demand.' The last sentence is a *non sequitur*. Creating arrangements that prevent the use of countercyclical monetary policy will worsen economic performance.

[93] The adjustments may take the form of using a special price index for measuring inflation, such as RPIX. See for example the Bank of England's *Inflation Report*, February 1994, p. 5.

[94] It is sometimes claimed that the British system does not give House of Commons Committees the standing that Congressional committees have in the United States. That can surely change if the legislature decides it wants the change – and it should want the authority to question the Bank if it gains independence.

Although the point has not been discussed so far, it is clear that monetary policy should be the responsibility of a Monetary Policy Board or Council. Some British observers claim that a Board has worked best in federal countries such as Germany, Switzerland, and the United States, where the geographic basis for Board representation gives its members independent standing. That result is more likely to be coincidental than causal; the performance of the Monetary Policy Council of the Banque de France will shed light on this issue. This is not the place to describe detailed procedures for choosing the Board, but the French requirement that the Board be drawn from 'persons of recognised standing and professional experience in monetay, financial and economic matters' commends itself. Board members should be appointed for a lengthy term, more than five years, but well short of fourteen.

The undemocratic nature of independent central banking requires a procedure for overriding the Bank's decisions. In New Zealand, the government has the right to override the Bank's policy targets, by means of an Order in Council that lasts no more than a year. The more general Canadian provision whereby 'the Minister of Finance, with the approval of . . . the Cabinet . . . may issue a directive to the Governor as to the monetary policy the Bank is to follow'[95] is a good precedent for Britain. The directive has to be made public. This procedure has never been used in Canada, and it is clear that if it were, the Governor would have to resign. While the procedure seems to give the government an easy means of controlling the Bank, any Chancellor contemplating firing the Governor would realise that most of the Board would remain in place, and that monetary policy could not therefore be easily manipulated by the government. At the same time, the threat of the use of the directive would give the Bank pause before it set out on a policy at odds with that of the government. This gives the right balance of power.

There is one important difference between the procedures recommended here and those in New Zealand. In New Zealand the Bank has to agree on inflation targets with the government. The recommendation here is that the Bank only consult with the government in setting the inflation targets. That gives the Bank a slightly greater measure of independence, but one which is contrained by the override procedures.[96]

It goes almost without saying that the central bank needs the monetary policy tools that will enable it to meet its responsibilities. The Bank of

[95] *The Role of the Bank of England*, Volume II, p. 161.
[96] It is sometimes claimed that the British parliamentary tradition make it impossible to set up arrangements of the type discussed here. Countries with similar traditions, such as Canada and New Zealand, have done so successfully, and there is no reason Britain could not follow suit.

England has them at present, but management of government financing presents a conflict of interest of which the Bank would best be rid.

The final point concerns the interactions of exchange and interest rates. Monetary and exchange rate policies cannot be independent. Under floating rates, monetary policy affects the exchange rate. There is no other short-run policy that can affect the exchange rate. Thus the government cannot have control over exchange rate policy while the central bank has control over monetary policy. The government should have the authority to choose the exchange rate regime. If it chooses a fixed exchange rate regime, it has then essentially – though not completely – determined monetary policy. While a central bank can be more or less independent of the government in a fixed exchange rate system, its independent ability to determine the rate of inflation and interest rates is sharply curtailed.

On her 300th birthday, it is time to allow the Old Lady to take on the responsibilities of independence.

REFERENCES

Alesina, Alberto (1988) 'Macroeconomics and politics', *NBER Macroeconomics Annual*, 13–51.

Alesina, Alberto and Guido Tabellini (1987). 'Rules and discretion with non-coordinated monetary and fiscal policies', *Economic Inquiry*, 25, 619–30.

Alesina, Alberto, and Lawrence H. Summers (1988) 'Central bank independence and macroeconomic performances; some comparative evidence', *Journal of Money, Credit and Banking*, 25, 2 (May), 151–62.

Bade, Robin and Michael Parkin (1988) 'Central bank laws and monetary policy', Department of Economics, University of Western Ontario (October).

Bailey, Martin J. (1956) 'The welfare cost of inflationary finance', *Journal of Political Economy*, 64, 2 (April), 93–110.

Ball, Larry (1993) 'What determines the sacrifice ratio?', NBER Working Paper, number 4306.

Ball, Larry N. Gregory Mankiw and David Romer (1988) 'The new Keynesian economics and the output-inflation trade-off', *Brookings Papers on Economic Activity*, 1, 1–65.

Barro, Robert J. and David Gordon (1983) 'A positive theory of monetary policy in a natural rate model', *Journal of Political Economy*, 91, 4 (Aug), 589–610.

Blanchard, Olivier (1986) 'The wage-price spiral', *Quarterly Journal of Economics*, 101, 3 (Aug), 543–65.

Blanchard, Olivier and Stanley Fischer (1989) *Lectures on Macroeconomics*. MIT Press: Cambridge MA.

Blanchard, Olivier and Lawrence H. Summers (1986) 'Hysteresis and the European unemployment problem', *NBER Macroeconomics Annual*, 15–78.

Burns, Arthur F. (1978) *Reflections of an Economic Policy Maker*. Washington, D.C.: American Enterprise Institute.

Capie, Forrest, Charles Goodhart and Norbert Schnadt (1994) 'The development of central banking', Cambridge University Press, 1994.

Caplin, Andrew and John Leahy (1991) 'State-dependent pricing and the dynamics of money and output', *Quarterly Journal of Economics*, 106, 3 (Aug), 683–708.

Caplin, Andrew and Daniel Spulber (1987) 'Menu costs and the neutrality of money', *Quarterly Journal of Economics*, 102, 4 (Nov), 703–26.

Chari, V. V., Lawrence J. Christiano, and Patrick J. Kehoe (1991) 'Optimal fiscal and monetary policy: some recent results', *Journal of Money, Credit and Banking*, 23, 3 (Aug, Part 2), 519–39.

Cooley, Thomas F. and Gary D. Hansen (1991) 'The welfare costs of moderate inflation', *Journal of Money, Credit and Banking*, 23, 3 (Aug, Part 2), 483–503.

Cukierman, Alex (1992) *Central Bank Strategy, Credibility, and Independence: Theory and Evidence*. MIT Press: Cambridge MA.

Cukierman, Alex, Steven B. Webb and Bilin Neyapti (1992) 'Measuring the independence of central banks and its effect on policy outcomes', *World Bank Economic Review*, 6, 3 (Sept), 353–98.

Cukierman, Alex, Pantelis Kalaitzidakis, Lawrence Summers and Steven Webb (1993) 'Central bank independence, growth, investment, and real rates', *Carnegie-Rochester Conference Series on Public Policy*, 39 (December), 95–140.

Dawe, S. (1990) 'Reserve Bank of New Zealand Act 1989', *Reserve Bank Bulletin*, 53, 1, 21–7.

Debelle, Guy (1994a) 'Central bank independence: a free lunch?', mimeo, MIT, February.

Debelle, Guy (1994b) 'The ends of three small inflations: Australia, New Zealand and Canada', mimeo, MIT, February.

Debelle, Guy and Stanley Fischer (1994) 'How independent should a central bank be?', mimeo, MIT, April.

de Kock, M. H. (1974) *Central Banking*, 4th edition. St Martin's Press: New York.

Dornbusch, Rudiger and Stanley Fischer (1994) *Macroeconomics*, 6th edition. McGraw Hill: New York.

Driffill, John, Grayham E. Mizon and Alistair Ulph (1990) 'Costs of inflation', in B. M. Friedman and F. H. Hahn (eds.), *Handbook of Monetary Economics*, Volume 2. North-Holland: Amsterdam.

Duguay, Pierre (1993) 'Some thoughts on price stability versus zero inflation', mimeo, Bank of Canada.

Eijffinger, Sylvester and Eric Schaling (1993) 'Central bank independence: theory and evidence', Tilburg University, The Netherlands, February.

Faig, Miguel (1988) 'Characterisation of the optimal tax on money when it functions as a medium of exchange', *Journal of Monetary Economics*, 22, 1 (July), 137–48.

Fischer, Stanley (1977) 'Long term contracts, rational expectations, and the optimal money supply rule', *Journal of Political Economy*, 85, 1 (Feb), 163–90.

Fischer, Stanley (1981) 'Towards an understanding of the costs of inflation: II,' in Karl Brunner and Allan H. Meltzer (eds.) *The Costs and Consequences of Inflation*, Carnegie-Rochester Conference Series on Public Policy, Vol. 15, North-Holland, 5–42. (Reprinted in Fischer (1986).)

Fischer, Stanley (1983) 'Welfare aspects of government issue of indexed bonds', in R. Dornbusch and M. H. Simonsen (eds.) *Inflation, Debt, and Indexation*. MIT Press: Cambridge MA. (Reprinted in Fischer (1986).)

Fischer, Stanley (1986) *Indexing, Inflation, and Economic Policy*. MIT Press: Cambridge MA.

Fischer, Stanley (1990) 'Rules versus discretion in monetary policy', in B. M. Friedman and F. H. Hahn (eds.) *Handbook of Monetary Economics*, Volume 2. North-Holland: Amsterdam.

Fischer, Stanley (1993) 'The role of macroeconomic factors in growth', *Journal of Monetary Economics*, 32, 3 (Dec), 485–512.

Fischer, Stanley and John Huizinga (1982) 'Inflation, unemployment, and public opinion polls', *Journal of Money, Credit and Banking*, 14, 1 (Feb), 1–19. (Reprinted in Fischer (1986).)

Fischer, Stanley and Franco Modigliani (1978) 'Towards an understanding of the real effects and costs of inflation', *Weltwirtschaftliches Archiv*, 114, 810–32. (Reprinted in Fischer (1986).)

Fischer, Stanley and Lawrence Summers (1989) 'Should governments learn to live with inflation?' *American Economic Review, Papers and Proceedings*, 79 (May), 382–7.

Friedman, Charles (1993) 'Designing institutions for monetary stability: a comment', *Carnegie-Rochester Conference Series on Public Policy*, 39 (December), 85–94.

Friedman, Milton (1959) *A Program for Monetary Stability*. Fordham University Press: New York.

Friedman, Milton (1968) 'The role of monetary policy', *American Economic Review*, 58, 1 (March), 1–17.

Freedman, Milton (1969) 'The optimum quantity of money', in M. Friedman, *The Optimum Quantity of Money and Other Essays*. Aldine Publishing Company: Chicago.

Grilli, Vittorio, Donato Masciandaro and Guido Tabellini (1991) 'Political and monetary institutions and public financial policies in the industrial countries', *Economic Policy*, 13 (October), 341–92.

Hall, Peter A. (1994) 'Central bank independence and coordinated wage bargaining: their interaction in Germany and Europe', forthcoming, *German Politics and Society*.

Havrilesky, Thomas and James Granato (1993) 'Determinants of inflationary performance: corporatist structures vs. central bank autonomy', *Public Choice*, 76, 249–61.

Huizinga, John (1993) 'Inflation uncertainty, relative price uncertainty, and investment in U.S. manufacturing', *Journal of Money, Credit and Banking*, 25, 3 (Aug, Part 2), 521–49.

Hume, David (1955) 'Of Money', in D. Hume, *Writings on Economics*, E. Rotwein (ed.). University of Wisconsin Press: Madison.

Jarrett, J. Peter and Jack G. Selody (1982) 'The productitivity-inflation nexus in Canada, 1963–1979', *Review of Economics and Statistics*, 64 (Aug.), 361–7.

Keynes, John Maynard (1924) *Monetary Reform*. Harcourt, Brace and Company: New York.

Kydland, Finn and Edward S. Prescott (1977) 'Rules rather than discretion: the inconsistency of optimal plans', *Journal of Political Economy*, 85, 3 (June), 473–92.

Lohmann, Susanne (1992) 'Optimal commitment in monetary policy: credibility versus flexibility', *American Economic Review*, 82, 1 (March), 273–86.

Lucas, Robert E. (1973) 'Some international evidence on output-inflation tradeoffs', *American Economic Review*, 63, 3 (June), 326–34.

Lucas, Robert E. (1994) 'On the welfare cost of inflation', mimeo, University of Chicago.

McCallum, Bennett T. (1994) 'Monetary policy rules and financial stability', National Bureau of Economic Research Working Paper No. 4692, April.

Mishkin, Frederic S. (1983) *A Rational Expectations Approach to Macroeconomics*. University of Chicago Press: Chicago.

Persson, Torsten and Guido Tabellini (1993) 'Designing institutions for monetary stability', *Carnegie-Rochester Conference Series on Public Policy*, 39 (December), 53–84.

Phelps, Edmund S. (1967) 'Phillips curves, expectations of inflation, and optimal unemployment over time', *Economica*, 34, 3 (August), 254–81.

Phelps, Edmund S. (1972) *Inflation Policy and Unemployment Theory*. Norton: New York.

Phelps, Edmund S. (1973) 'Inflation in the theory of public finance', *Swedish Journal of Economics*, 75, 1, 67–82.

Phillips, A. W. (1958). 'The relation between unemployment and the rate of change of money wages in the United Kingdom, 1861–1957', *Economica*, 25, 4 (Nov), 283–99.

Posen, Adam (1993) 'Central bank independence does not cause low inflation: the politics behind the institutional fix', mimeo, Harvard University, December.

Reagan, Patricia and Rene M. Stulz (1993) 'Contracting costs, inflation, and relative price variability', *Journal of Money, Credit and Banking*, 25, 3 (Aug, Part 2), 585–601.

Rogoff, Kenneth (1985) 'The optimal degree of commitment to an intermediate monetary target', *Quarterly Journal of Economics*, 100, 4 (November), 1169–90.

Roll, Eric et al. (1993) 'Independent and accountable: a new mandate for the Bank of England'. London: Centre for Economic Policy Research, October.

Romer, Christina and David Romer (1989) 'Does monetary policy matter? A new test in the spirit of Friedman and Schwartz', *NBER Macroeconomics Annual*, 121–70.

Rudebusch, Glenn D. and David W. Wilcox (1994) 'Productivity and inflation: evidence and interpretations', mimeo, Federal Reserve Board, Washington, DC, April.

Samuelson, Paul A. amd Robert M. Solow (1960) 'Analytical aspects of anti-inflation policy', *American Economic Review*, 50, 2 (May), 177–94.

Sayers, Richard S. (1958) *Central Banking After Bagehot*. Reprinted. Oxford: Clarendon Press.

Summers, Laurence H. (1991) 'How should long-term monetary policy be determined?', *Journal of Money, Credit and Banking*, 23, 3 (Aug., Part 2), 625–31.

Sidrauski, Miguel (1967) 'Rational choice and patterns of growth in a monetary economy', *American Economic Review, Papers and Proceedings*, 71 (May), 534–44.

Taylor, John B. (1981) 'On the relation between the variability of inflation and the average inflation rate', in Karl Brunner and Allan H. Meltzer (eds.), *The Costs and Consequences of Inflation*, Carnegie-Rochester Conference Series on Public Policy, Vol. 15, North-Holland, 57–85.

Tommasi, Mariano (1994) 'The consequences of price instability in search markets: towards understanding the effects of inflation', forthcoming, *American Economic Review*.

Vibert, Frank (1993) 'The independence of the Bank of England and the Maastricht Treaty'. London: European Policy Forum, May.

Walsh, Carl (1993) 'Optimal contracts for independent central bankers: private information, performance measures and reappointment', Working Paper 93–02, Federal Reserve Bank of San Francisco, May.

Wicksell, Knut (1965) *Interest and Prices*. Augustus M. Kelley: New York. Reprints of Economic Classics.

Conference proceedings

Discussion

Dr Don Brash

Three hundred years is a long time in anyone's book. The idea of central banking only became a substantive issue in New Zealand sixty-four years ago, and a reality only sixty years ago. And for the idea itself, we stand indebted to the Bank of England, whose evangelist of the time, Sir Otto Niemeyer, advised the New Zealand Treasury that 'a full central bank of the recognised type' should be preferred to the note issue board then under consideration.

It is, therefore, somewhat ironic that the adolescent child of the mother of so many central banks around the world should be asked to respond to Professor Stanley Fischer's paper; a paper that addresses the question of the appropriate charter for the Old Lady herself. I trust that she feels a mother's sense of pride in the achievements of her offspring, and will forgive any inadvertent transgressions made in commenting on this paper!

I must say that reading Professor Fischer's paper was a humbling experience. Most of us who work in the area of monetary policy carry in our heads bits and pieces of the full picture to be drawn from theory and experience, but find it very difficult to articulate that picture with completeness and clarity. Professor Fischer's paper cuts a wide swathe through an enormous range of material – and remains lucid throughout! – something the rest of us wish we were capable of doing.

As a summary of the arguments and evidence relevant to the question of how best to structure the institutional environment to produce the monetary policy most beneficial to society's welfare, Professor Fischer's paper is a model.

There are very few areas where I have difficulties with the analysis or conclusions reached in the paper.

The paper argues that monetary policy almost always impacts on the real

309

economy in the short run, but, on the evidence, one cannot expect that output and employment effect to last. I agree.

The paper argues that the income and welfare costs of inflation are not trivial, even for that rare beast – anticipated inflation. They become even less trivial once one takes account of the impact of inflation on growth (about which there is growing understanding and evidence). I agree.

The paper avers that a strong conclusion – that inflation is not good for growth – can be drawn. I agree.

The paper argues that, notwithstanding the benefits of a constant price level target in terms of long-run price certainty, a target in terms of inflation is better. I agree.

The paper argues that with inflation as a choice variable of governments that face a range of incentives, the perception of an inflation bias can arise – a perception that itself can create an inflation bias. Mechanisms, such as the right institutional structure for monetary policy decision-making, can help deal with the inflationary bias. I agree.

The paper argues that allowing the central bank the freedom to choose the monetary policy technique – be it intermediate targetry, final targetry or whatever – within a framework that places a high but not complete weight on maintaining price stability, is preferable both to setting rules that dictate the choice of technique, and to making the central bank blind to the output consequences of decisions. I agree.

And there is much more in the paper that I agree with, including the view that the central bank should be independent within a clearly defined mandate of price stability, with announced goals that can, with cost, be overridden; that accountability should be the siamese twin of independence; that accountability ought not be diffused through unclear targets or multiple decision-makers; that even very credible central banks cannot get rid of the output costs of returning to price stability after a shock, and so on.

Where then, might I have reason to differ with Professor Fischer?

There are three areas in which Professor Fischer reaches conclusions that are not fully aligned with my views and the way the monetary policy arrangements are structured in New Zealand. Let me discuss these, starting with the easiest.

First, Professor Fischer indicates that the Reserve Bank of New Zealand framework ought to feature greater goal independence. That is, the Bank should have more of a say in the setting of the specific target of policy.

I think, in fact, that the Bank's legislation is closer to Professor Fischer's optimal prescription than he suggests. The Policy Targets Agreement (in which the policy target of 0–2 per cent CPI inflation is set) is an agreement between myself and the Minister of Finance that is required by the Act in order to provide a clear and monitorable target for policy. But in negotiating the agreement, the Minister does not have a totally free choice.

Before I sign the Policy Targets Agreement, I must be satisfied that the specific policy target is consistent with the statutory objective of monetary policy – price stability. If the Minister presses on me a target that is, in my judgement, inconsistent with price stability, I am obliged to refuse to sign. In that case, the government must use the provision in the legislation to override the price stability objective of the Act. As you are probably aware, the override provision involves an Order in Council that is very public, lasts only a year before formal renewal is required, and is therefore by no means an easy option for the government.

Thus the negotiation over the PTA is one in which I can force the hand of the Minister if and only if the Minister is seeking to fudge on the price stability objective, while the Minister can force my hand (by sacking me) if and only if I am seeking to fudge on the self-same objective.

Second, Professor Fischer suggests that the New Zealand framework is yet to show its worth, citing the similar decline of inflation in Australia over recent years. I readily acknowledge the fact that we have not yet been tested on the upside, but I would make a bit more of the gains already seen than did Professor Fischer.

Comparing Australian and New Zealand ten-year bond rates, there is a differential of around 1.5 percentage points in favour of New Zealand, notwithstanding New Zealand's worse inflation history, substantially higher government debt, and the similar positions in terms of current inflation and the economic cycle. Though the Australian fiscal position is not as sound as that in New Zealand, empirically the connection between deficits and real interest rates is not large.

It would appear, therefore, that either inflation expectations in Australia are significantly higher than in New Zealand, or that real interest rates are significantly higher in Australia. Either way, it seems eminently plausible that the monetary policy framework in New Zealand is already showing benefits beyond that shown by the record on price stability, which is now moving into its fourth year.

Thirdly, and most contentiously, Professor Fischer concludes that the right target for inflation is somewhere in the range of 1–3 per cent (he mentions 1–3, 2–3, 1–2 at different places in the text, while in his presentation to the conference on 'A Framework for Monetary Stability' in Amsterdam in October last year, he argued that there is no case for targeting an inflation rate above 4 per cent, or below 1 per cent). Of course, in New Zealand our target is 0–2 per cent.

I don't want to debate the very slim difference in its own right, especially given that Professor Fischer suggests that the bias in measuring the price index is such that 1½–2 per cent measured inflation each year represents actual price stability. We have allowed for a bias nearer ½–1 per cent. However, if the bias is indeed around 1½ to 2 percentage points, then I would have no objections to raising the midpoint of our target range from 1 per cent to 2 per cent.

I am much more interested in the question of why genuine price stability – genuine in the sense of allowing for index number distortions – might be too low a target. Professor Fischer cites two arguments:

Real interest rates might face a floor around zero because negative nominal interest rates are unlikely. This might hamper recovery from cyclical dips.

And second, in general, downward price stickiness worsens the inflation-output trade-off in the short run.

Professor Fischer is also dismissive of some of the arguments in the literature that imply optimal rates of inflation that are negative (the Friedman argument) on the grounds that they effectively assume an absence of output effects of inflation, and he is also dismissive of the argument that a zero inflation rate is the only credible inflation target. The latter argument is the monetary policy equivalent of the idea that you can't be half pregnant – either you have inflation or you don't.

Let me say that I agree with Professor Fischer that many of these arguments in favour of zero or negative inflation rates are over-drawn.

However, turning to the arguments cited for small positive inflation rates – genuinely measured – I have some difficulties. In relation to the cyclical role of real interest rates, I venture to suggest that the issue appears more important to the North American economist than to economists in other parts of the world. Lawrence Summers, who ran the argument at the Jackson Hole conference in 1992, pointed to the fact that a significant proportion of business cycle troughs in post-war US history were accompanied by negative real interest rates. New Zealand's record of negative real interest rates is not predominantly cyclical in character. Negative real interest rates in New Zealand were predominantly a feature of inflation surprises, combined with interest rate regulation.

More generally, though, is it true that nominal interest rates cannot go negative for a period, by at least one or two percentage points? While the interest rate on cash is zero – which in principle might set the floor for other rates – the linkage between cash and other assets is by no means perfect. I find it hard to imagine that significant proportions of million-dollar financial portfolios would shift into currency, given the transactions costs associated, and given the storage and risk considerations.

It is worth noting that Lawrence Summers also makes the same argument in relation to real wage behaviour during the cycle. The argument is that you need a little inflation and nominal wage growth so that real wages can fall when that is desirable. Downward nominal wage rigidity limits downward real wage flexibility when inflation is zero, it is argued.

This argument, it seems to me, is also somewhat overdone. With no inflation, on average over the business cycle there is likely to be nominal wage growth at the rate of trend labour productivity growth. Foregoing those nominal wage rises means that wages do not have to be cut in nominal terms in order to have real wages fall below trend.

Further, and this is coming on to the second point made by Professor Fischer, I usually argue that reductions in aggregate real wages can be consistent with downward nominal wage stickiness. Nominal wage stickiness, to the extent that it exists, is surely a feature of individual employment contracts. Who wants to take a pay cut? But normal staff turnover and the life-cycle features of labour markets mean that individuals' wages typically rise more rapidly than the aggregate wage bill. So, for instance, in some recent years the Reserve Bank of New Zealand has been able to hold the aggregate wage bill constant, with stable staff numbers, and with modest wage rises for most staff, by replacing highly paid retirees and resignees with lower paid recruits, and by reducing the step increase in remuneration that comes with promotion and the acquisition of greater skill and experience.

The subject of downward price inflexibility has got to be treated carefully, and not be bound by the experience of different times and different situations. The experience that I have just outlined involved no reductions in individual nominal wages. Over the last few years, as major changes have taken place in labour market arrangements in New Zealand, downward movements in individual nominal wages have in fact been reasonably commonplace. Structural change, featuring greatly intensified competition and a sharp rise in unemployment, called for substantial adjustments in prices, wages and profits. Permissive labour market legislation, in this context, allowed cuts in take home pay in some instances as high as 20 or 30 per cent – and rises just as large in other instances.

Once one moves beyond the labour market, downward price rigidities are even harder to find. Our producers and distributors who had previously been sheltered by all sorts of protective and distortionary devices suddenly found that they were competing with international suppliers whose prices were a fraction of those prevailing in New Zealand. An ability to drop prices was quickly discovered, and the same behaviour was demanded of those producers and distributors normally thought of as being in the non-traded sector.

To sum up on this point, I don't think that there is a strong analytical case for the proposition that the short-run inflation-output relationship worsens markedly at very low rates of inflation. To be sure, some worsening appears in the data. However, that is more likely to be a result of the relative absence in the data set of examples of sustained low inflation, combined with comparatively little governmental interference in pricing, than it is to be a product of something deeply inherent in pricing mechanisms.

Let me now turn to some wider-ranging points that may be of more direct relevance for the choices that face the Bank of England at this stage in her illustrious life.

We are increasingly aware that to understand what causes inflation, we have to put the spotlight on the people who determine monetary policy, and the political and institutional environment in which they are placed. Secular inflation became a matter of choice in the early part of this century, as the anchor provided by metallic standards was abandoned. But it has taken some time, and a lot of bad experience, before monetary economics really started getting to grips with the need to understand why particular monetary policy choices are made.

It is not sufficient, in my view, to know a lot about the links between monetary policy actions and their ultimate impact on the economy. Nor is it sufficient to dream up clever rules for the conduct of monetary policy that rely on the longevity of those identified linkages. One really has to get to grips with the political and institutional economics associated with the decision-making process itself. I am proud to be connected with innovations in the structure of the governance of monetary policy in New Zealand – innovations that are properly rooted in this level of economic analysis.

Having said that, I would like to make it clear that I do not pretend that we have found the holy grail. That does not yet exist. The state of knowledge in economics is such that we cannot simultaneously achieve the desired long-term results and do all that we would want to – given the capability – in the short term.

We do not have a reliable understanding of what is pushing the economy around at any given moment. We have blunt policy instruments that are not highly predictable and rapid in their short-term consequences. And the people affected by our actions are naturally and properly sceptical of our motivations and abilities. Together, these realities mean that there will be many times where we have to ride through storms that have very uncomfortable short term effects. Standing with arms folded – when a well-judged departure from the longer-term focus of policy would seem, at first sight, to be sensible – will, for the foreseeable future, be the uncomfortable but proper lot of the monetary policy maker.

Last, but not least, I would like to venture some comments on the transferability of lessons learned in New Zealand to other situations.

Professor Fischer's ideal central bank mandate is very close to the New

Zealand structure; closer still when my comments on the nature of nego-tiations on the target of policy are taken into account. That he sees such a structure as generally applicable suggests that there is a considerable degree of transferability. From my perspective, that is encouraging. We have had considerable success with the framework – it places and keeps our attention where it should be, in a manner that is obvious to all – and would like to see this success shared.

Some of the specifics might, of course, need adaptation for a different environment.

For instance, it may be more appropriate to aim at genuine price stability in a country like ours, with its particularly clean approach to government intervention in markets, than in other countries with less market flexibility.

Other features would not, however, sensibly be altered. Amongst these one should mention the linkage between monetary policy directed at price stability and exchange rate policy. The two are not independent of each other, as Professor Fischer clearly states. In structuring the decision-making process for monetary policy, one has to recognise that linkage explicitly. In our case, the government retains the ability to direct the Bank on exchange rate policy, but if (as will usually be the case) such a directive contradicts the price stability objective, the government is forced to recog-nise that, by use of the override procedure. This is something that will surely need to be addressed in the context of the arrangements for the European central bank. In the process of moving to Economic and Mone-tary Union, the different weights to be put on exchange rate and price stability by the constituent central banks could well create special diffi-culties.

In your deliberations on the future charter for central banking in Europe, I commend to you the example of New Zealand – though in so doing, I am conscious that my remarks may sound somewhat arrogant in view of the shortness of our history of central banking, and the recent nature of our adoption of the framework.

Discussion

Miguel Mancera

I am delighted to be here on the occasion of the 300th Anniversary of the Bank of England. Governor George, please accept my warmest congratula-tions. This Institution has justified cause for celebration.

Our hosts have selected a splendid theme for this session: central bank autonomy. It is indeed a topic which lends itself to serious analysis and lively debate. Stanley Fischer's paper brilliantly sums up not only the conventional wisdom but also the latest research on our subject-matter.

Reading his paper turned out to be a rewarding and, dare I say, fascinating journey. It evoked memories of the many aspects of the issue of central bank autonomy which we, in Mexico, considered and discussed – at times in a relaxed mood at others not quite so – in the process of drafting the charter of the now autonomous Bank of Mexico.

In order to describe how these issues were dealt with in my country, I would like to base my comments on Stanley Fischer's lessons to construct the charter of a modern central bank, as such lessons provide good standards to measure the quality of a particular legislation.

Lesson 1 'The central bank should have clearly defined mandate which includes price stability'

The Bank of Mexico has an unambiguous mandate – at the constitutional level – to ensure the stability of the purchasing power of the national currency. This endeavour is its priority. Not merely a primary goal which would tacitly acknowledge the validity of the short-run Phillips curve and, therefore, the merit of the trade-off it implies.

In President Salinas' proposal to amend the Constitution of the Republic in order to confer autonomy to the Bank of Mexico, it is clearly stated that price stability is not an end in itself. Rather, price stability is viewed as a necessary, albeit not sufficient, condition, to attain social equity and economic development.

Mexico suffered acute and prolonged inflation, which was closely linked to large public deficits partially financed with central bank credit. Not surprisingly, during the discussions leading to the legislation upon which the Bank of Mexico's autonomy is founded, the inflationary bias of governments issue was naturally and continuously present. It was concluded that, if the effort to control inflation is to be permanent, it is clearly fitting to keep the function of creating money separate from other functions of the State. That separation is of the utmost importance, since the public sector is permanently subject to political pressures which tend to materialise in calls for more spending and for reduced taxation.

Mexicans have paid dearly for the inflationary policies of the past. We have incurred every one of the costs of inflation listed by Stanley Fischer. We also have acquired first-hand knowledge of the sacrifices that must be made to root out this evil.

We do not dismiss the possibility, recalled by Fischer, of a Phillips curve trade-off in the short-run. Yet, in some countries, like Mexico, even that short-run relationship may not exist, except, unfortunately, when travelling on the curve's path in a south-east direction.

In such countries, the Phillips curve can hardly be used as an argument in favour of inflating. Higher inflation might not be accompanied by more growth, since such policy immediately exerts a negative effect on the expectations of economic agents. Nominal wages are promptly adjusted in response to higher expected inflation, and therefore real wages do not change and increased employment is not forthcoming. The trade-off in fact worsens and attempts to contain the deterioration usually lead to a host of interventionist policies which create distortions in addition to those brought about by inflation.

In a relatively small open economy with a recent memory of short-run exploitation of the Phillips curve and of dynamic inconsistencies, further attempts in this direction are indeed dangerous. The likely outcome of monetary expansion in the short-run will not be economic growth but capital flight and depreciation of the nominal exchange rate.

Higher inflation is always costly. Stanley Fischer points out that many of the negative effects of inflation can be avoided by means of indexation, although he also warns that widespread indexation is likely to increase inflation and possibly make society worse off. He also suggests that some types of partial indexation, which remove the incentives for the government to inflate, deserve consideration.

Notwithstanding the fact that non-comprehensive indexation can be useful, it may also be very dangerous, as it can develop into a contagious disease. Pressures are liable to build-up to make indexation extensive to various types of contracts. Once it encompasses wage contracts, a highly damaging situation ensues. This is so because indexed wage contracts, unlike other indexed contracts, never come to an end, barring the collapse of the employer. Indexation of wages is a dreadful cause of unemployment and/or perpetual inflation.

When in this context the decision to inflate is reversed, the effort may indeed cause output loss and unemployment as aggregate demand contracts, whereas prices and wages keep their momentum. This is true even in the absence of indexation.

Expectations of permanently lower inflation come about neither painlessly nor with sufficient speed. Nominal wages remain high or continue to increase. The very success in reducing inflation translates into real wages in excess of those consistent with an expansion of employment. One of the many insights in Stanley Fischer's paper points in this direction. In his own words: 'There is no credibility bonus in labour markets for more independent central banks: they have to prove their toughness repeatedly by being tough.'

Lesson 2 'The central bank should publicly announce its intermediate term goals'

Mexican law does not establish that the central bank has an obligation to publicly announce its numerical inflation targets. Still, to have and disclose them is sound policy. Uncertainty about the future price level is reduced when economic agents have information on the central bank's targets and the institution has a good track record.

It should also be pointed out that the announcement of such targets forces the central bank to work hard on attaining them. Although this may be stressing for governors, it is useful for society.

Lesson 3 'The central bank should be accountable in two senses: it should be held responsible for meeting its announced goals; and it should be required to explain and justify its policies to the legislature and to the public'

The mandate to ensure price stability over and above any other objectives offers a clear advantage in terms of evaluating the performance of the central bank. The measuring rod would be the discrepancy between targeted and observed inflation.

Certain provisions to conciliate central bank autonomy with its accountability are at the very least advisable, perhaps indispensable, in most countries. In Mexico, the central bank must submit to Congress and to the President of the Republic, three difference documents: one, in January, explaining the monetary policy it intends to follow in the current year. Then, two reports – the first one in April and the second in September – on the execution of monetary policy during the preceding semester. In addition, the Governor may be called to testify before either chamber of Congress. For 1994, the law prescribes a single document to be presented in May – instead of the three mentioned above – since the new statute became effective only last April.

In this first presentation of monetary policy, the Board of the Bank of Mexico decided to set inflation targets for the short, medium and long terms, giving economic agents the possibility of using such goals as forecasts of future price level increases. The declared intent being to facilitate the complex process of making decisions whose consequences extend over a number of years.

The Board stated that, given the current level of inflation, further reductions should not be too pronounced within rather short periods. More ambitious objectives would be ill-advised and would entail the risk of imposing severe adjustment strains on the real sector of the economy. The costs of much lower inflation in the near future were deemed too high when compared to its benefits. In other words, the Board implicitly acknowledged the short-term validity of the Phillips curve when travelling on its southeast direction.

The Board expressed that the Bank of Mexico must contribute to obtaining the inflation reduction envisaged in the government's programme for 1994, from an annual rate of 8 per cent in 1993 to 5 per cent in the current year.

As for the not precisely defined medium-term, the Board expressed agreement with the government's reiterated intention to bring Mexico's inflation rates to levels similar to those prevailing in the economies of its main trading partners.

However, once the medium-term goals are attained, the constitutional mandate to the Bank of Mexico to ensure price stability may still not be fully satisfied. It would be required that price stability also be the norm in the economies of our main trading partners. Consequently to properly serve the constitutional mandate, the Board set an explicit long-term goal of an inflation rate between zero and 3 per cent. There is international consensus that inflation within this range – or perhaps zero to 2 per cent – can be deemed representative of price stability.

Lesson 4 'The government should have the authority to override the Bank's decisions, but the over-ride decision should carry a lot of costs to the government'

The over-ride provision probably works well for those countries where the government and the central bank already agree on the desirability of keeping inflation under tight reign and also subscribe to mutually agreed inflation targets. Such a consensus facilitates the attainment of price goals. Without it, things are more difficult. Needless to say, if this accord does not exist, the override power is undesirable.

In either case, the decision to override may be taken by someone seeking to serve a short-term agenda. The end result would undermine the very principle of democratic checks and balances, which the override provision is intended to preserve. The true check on an autonomous central bank is the possibility that in the extreme the government could withdraw the Bank's autonomy. It follows that, in order to safeguard the autonomy, the central banker must be a prudent man.

No direct override provision is found in the Mexican legislation. Moreover, the indirect override, namely the removal of the members of the Board, can hardly be used unless such persons commit a crime or become physically or mentally disabled.

Lesson 5 'The central bank should be given authority to set interest rates and other monetary policy variables in order to achieve monetary policy goals'

The Bank of Mexico, in Fischer's terminology, has instrument independence. On this matter, the Mexican Constitution clearly prescribes that no authority shall order the central bank to grant credit. The exclusive power vested on the central bank to decide on the amount of its credit is indeed an essential feature of central bank autonomy. Furthermore, in order to shield the Bank of Mexico from pressures that commercial banks might exert, it may provide credit to those institutions only for monetary regulation or when acting as a 'lender of last resort'.

Lesson 6 'The central bank should not be required to finance the government deficit and should not manage the public debt'

This lesson derives from instrument independence which, as Fischer points out, is essential for the successful pursuit of monetary stability.

The Bank of Mexico may extend credit – but is under no obligation to do so – to the Federal Government, but only up to certain amount, equivalent to 1.5 per cent of total public expenditures approved in the Federal Budget, net of amortisation payments. This is a small amount, roughly equal to one third of one per cent of GDP. Should the limit be eventually exceeded, through drawings on the current account that the Bank keeps for the government, the law directs the institution to sell treasury bills in the open market. Moreover, should the need arise, the Bank is empowered to issue public debt on the Federal Government's behalf and use the proceeds to liquidate the overdraft.

Lesson 7 'There cannot be a separate responsibility for setting interest rates and the exchange rate so long as the exchange rate floats'

The Mexican government adopted, in November 1991, an exchange rate regime based on a band which gradually widens. This measure seeks a balance between two distinct objectives: the stabilisation of economic agents' inflationary expectations and the requirement for a progressively increased flexibility to face fluctuations in the balance of payments. Both objectives can be achieved since the band provides certitude as to the maximum and minimum levels the exchange rate may reach on a certain date. A band which continuously widens allows the exchange rate to increasingly accommodate variations in the demand for and supply of foreign exchange, without frequent interventions in the market by the central bank, thereby reducing the extent to which interest rate adjustments may be needed. In turn, this flexibility provides for a more stable monetary base.

When a fixed exchange rate regime or a band is selected, effective constraints are placed on monetary policy. The higher the mobility of capital and/or the narrower the band, the more binding these constraints become.

If exchange rate policy leads to an accumulation of international reserves, the resulting monetary expansion may be undesirable and cause higher inflation. In these circumstances, the central bank may choose to sterilise. Yet, its ability to do so is limited since sterilisation is not usually without cost. Once the practical limit is reached, the amount of the monetary base becomes endogenous.

In this regard, our law provides the Bank of Mexico with the power and instruments to sterilise – at government's expense – an undesired monetary expansion derived from central bank purchases of foreign currency effected to comply with the exchange regime. To this end, the Bank may issue public debt on the Federal Government's behalf, thus regaining a degree of monetary control. This provision is intended to make independent monetary policy consistent with an exchange rate regime ultimately determined by the government, as is the case in Mexico.

On a final note, let us reflect on the responsibility all central bankers share in relation to educating public opinion. Unlike economists, the public commonly adheres to the notion that the Phillips curve does hold not only in the short tern but in the long term as well. This notion can be very detrimental to the execution of monetary policy, since it nourishes pressures on the cental bank to grant excessive amounts of credit, thus promoting inflation rather than economic growth.

People often believe that the central bank can determine the level of interest rates on its own, even in the long term. To dispel myths of this sort, central bankers must work to nurture the widespread understanding of the kind of results a central bank can deliver and those which it cannot. Furthermore, the public is seldom abreast of the direct relationship between the uncertainty that inflation causes about the speed of future price increases and the risk premium thereby required to attract investment in debt instruments. Price stability is the best contribution a central bank can make towards economic development, as it removes both the distortions of inflation and the above mentioned risk premium.

A credible commitment to price stability by the central bank contributes to economic efficiency, growth and social equity. I firmly believe that the priority of monetary policy-makers must be price stability. As you might have already suspected, I am one of those inflation-averse central bankers to whom Stanley Fischer refers.

May these remarks be my small way of honouring the Bank of England, the revered Old Lady to whom I am personally grateful in the extreme for the teachings she affectionately dispensed upon me as a young man.

Discussion

Josef Tosovsky

Mr Chairman, ladies and gentlemen, let me start by wishing the Old Lady many happy returns. I must say that the Old Lady behaves often as the true mother and takes care of the young children (I am talking about the young central banks), sharing experiences and sometimes even costs. So thank you very much, Mr Governor, for all this.

Professor Fischer's paper is a brilliant summary of views on modern central banking. Of course, the paper is based on an economy with well-established market infrastructure, and I do not want to pretend that I can in any way improve it in this respect. All I can do here is to review the paper from the perspective of a transitional economy, such as our economy, but I think something from what I am going to say could be generalised for some other countries in Central and Eastern Europe.

My first batch of comments concerns the issue of inflation. First of all I would like to make a clear distinction between once-for-all price jumps and a genuine tendency to inflate. Of course, standard measures do not make any distinction between these two elements, but for central bankers there is always a problem and dilemma – what to do with these price jumps and whether to accommodate them, or to fight them by squeezing monetary policy and credits. This distinction is also very important for another issue – the cost of inflation and the cost of disinflation – because these two concepts may involve completely different policy actions as well.

There is no doubt that it is very difficult to recognise in a country in transition what is the underlying or core rate of inflation and what is not. And a jump to very low inflation, close to zero, could be very costly and even unfriendly to a reform process, especially to economic restructuring. I think that the monetary authorities should partially accommodate the core inflation and introduce policies to combat it over a longer time period. However, estimating the magnitude of the core inflation is a challenging but worthwhile question.

The Czech National Bank naturally makes projections of the expected rate of inflation (together with other basic macroeconomic variables) but does not embark on price level targeting as such. The reason is uncertainty about the transmission mechanism of monetary policy, which divides economists into two camps, Keynesians and monetarists. We can add further uncertainties due to the lack of reliable and swift information or uncertainties arising in the infancy stage of our financial sector.

This is why I am rather unhappy about the concept of the so-called surprise inflation which, according to the rational expectations school, can be created at will by a monetary authority to achieve its goals (as opposed to anticipated inflation, whose effects tend to be undone by the rational private sector). Our experience is that uncertainties in growth of output, velocity of money, selection of the proper monetary aggregate and a number of other factors beyond the central bank's control make price level targeting a very unreliable undertaking. The central bank is often surprised by the actual inflation (particularly on a monthly basis) no less than other economic agents. The backbone of our stabilisation programme has been centred around nominal exchange rate targeting, which has proved to be a comprehensible and credible policy in fighting inflationary expectations and promoting foreign trade.

Longer-term sustainability of the exchange rate anchor depends a great deal on the initial alignment. Sometimes we are blamed for having overshot the 'equilibrium' exchange rate. I would like to stress that it is much easier to brandish the concept of equilibrium rather than to identify convincingly a 'true' equilibrium in practice. We clung to the rule of thumb 'not be caught on the wrong side', on the basis of which we practically closed the gap between the new official and the old black exchange rates.

The policy of a fixed nominal exchange rate co-existed with a more or less independent interest rate policy. This independence, embodied in wide interest rate variability, may contrast with the textbook treatises but is easily explained: the market is not well developed, the economy is not fully opened, the market is not liberalised and is far away from full convertibility. In the process of installing full convertibility of the Czech crown this manoeuvring capability and autonomous interest rate policy will, of course, gradually disappear.

Having mentioned the monetarist hypothesis about a rational and inherently stable private sector let me express my view that behind this proposition, true or false as it may be, there have to be secular processes of learning by doing and natural selection which have brought the developed market economies to the degree of sophistication and entrepreneurial ethos that we can observe today. In a transition economy which undergoes rapid transformation we can see a great deal of incompetence and even fraudulent behaviour on the part of the growing private sector (saying that I do not want to play down examples of incompetence on the part of government agencies). The latest examples are failure of some new small private banks which may undermine the credibility of this particular segment of the economy. Another example is the investment funds which emerged from the voucher privatisation. The message from this is not to curb private initiative or return to greater government involvement but rather to shorten the learning period to a minimum. The programme of external sector liberalisation and external convertibility of the Czech currency, as a result of which our contacts with sophisticated market economies are expected to grow tighter, should contribute a great deal in this direction.

My second block of remarks is addressed to the Phillips curve trade-off. Of course, the basic question for a banker from Central Europe is the relevance of this curve for a country in transition. I would say that transition, i.e. a fundamental change from a centrally planned economy to a market economy, is not easy and there are many problems to be addressed. I would mention especially various disequilibriam existing under the previous system which, after liberalisation, start to be transparent – practically overnight – and which, in combination with devaluation and reductions in subsidies, can make the behaviour of the Phillips Curve appear even paradoxical: specifically, inflation is growing very fast, while output is declining dramatically. In our case this happened in 1991, when inflation jumped by 54 per cent and output measured by GDP went down by 14 per cent. A different paradox can occur in the future as a result of privatisation and changes in ownership structure, when economic activity can go up but unemployment can go up as well. The reason is that the state-owned companies before privatisation are in a kind of agony. It doesn't matter that their output and general performance go down, they still keep their staff and there is a kind of in-house unemployment. But when new private owners come, and when foreign capital starts flowing, in the situation is bound to change: the economy will grow and unemployment will grow as well.

Let me point out that, in the first stage of transition, when the whole radical economic programme is being launched (liberalisation, deregulation, initial systemic changes, the legal framework, privatisation programme), the Phillips curve is probably not valid.

Even in the second stage it may not work perfectly. By the second stage I mean consolidation and adaptation, when the rules of the game are more or less in place but the corporate sector, citizens and government go through some kind of learning and adjusting process, which can take quite along time. During this stage markets are only in an embryonic stage but they are already functioning and it is necessary to cultivate them. Hence, in my opinion, it is not very fruitful to concentrate on casual links between inflation, economic growth and employment development and one should rather treat them as simultaneous variables affected also by other factors.

My third remark concerns the issue of the central bank's independence. I do not want to talk about independence of the Czech National Bank because I think it has no sex appeal for this audience. We have precisely defined legal goals, and the legislation is based on the Bundesbank model. We have a great deal of instrument independence as well, and I think we use our mandate quite properly.

But this is only half of the story. I must say, and this would be my main message, that in the initial stage of economic reform there is a necessity to co-operate with the government.

I am stressing this in view of the fact that the central bank in transition has to assist in many undertakings. It is necessary to establish a two-tier banking system, to handle financial restructuring, to prepare privatisation of large state-owned banks and there are many other activities which exceed the normal activities of a standard central bank. This is why I stress the issue of co-operation. Equally, I would stress another thing: it in indispensable to build up credibility of the central bank right from the outset. Credibility is the main issue for us – we are trying to build it at home among the general public and, of course, abroad, because independence without credibility is not a real independence.

I am afraid that what I have said just now does not sound orthodox enough to the ears of central bank governors, but nevertheless I hope that you will not excommunicate me from your company if I say that the top priority for a country in transition (like the Czech Republic) is political stability, which makes economic transformation irreversible and the central bank can do nothing but to take this fact into account and translate it into its policies.

Open session

Lord Kingsdown   (former Governor, Bank of England)

We have some little time left now for questions and answers or discussion. May I just make one comment – I think what is interesting from this afternoon is the discussion of the element of transition. I suppose all economies are always in a state of transition, but some are more in transition than others; and of the three central bank governors you have heard you will see a difference in where they started from and where they have got to and the sort of problems they met on the way and what they believe to be the right elements in the position of the central bank, the attitude of policy, in order to facilitate that transition.

We had a question this morning about accountability. I think the accountability of the central bank is perhaps in some respects only a formal version of a wider and more important element that I would call acceptability or as Josef Tosovsky used the word just now, credibility. The degree to which the country at large is ready to accept this doctrine, for all its short-term price in terms of employment and wealth. Price stability is a worthy objective and certainly I would be pleased, if I may say this to you, if some of you here who are governors who come from countries in transition would be able to comment on or take up the theme that the three central bank governors presented in response to Stanley Fischer's excellent survey.

Professor Dr Erik Hoffmeyer
(Chairman of the Board of Governors, Danmarks Nationalbank)

It doesn't really matter where you come from. I think it was a very lucid paper by Stanley Fischer but I have some reservations and I will concentrate on one. That is the short-term trade-off on the Phillips Curve: because that is what we are always confronted with, whether you are a developed country or an undeveloped country – the politicians think there is a short-term trade off, and that the central bank should buy it. Now there are two points there. One is that the instruments we have are so uncertain that we couldn't use the short-term trade-off from a monetary policy point of view. Second, the markets are such that when you try to use this new concept of dynamic inconsistency, to use the short-term trade-off, markets will find out and then it becomes shorter and shorter and it ends up by disappearing.

Stanley Fischer

Let me assume I'm not a public official, which I'm not at the moment. I think that that denial of the short-term trade-off is really very misleading and will get central banks into trouble. The trade-off exists – there is always a question of how fast you aim to get somewhere. If I take my own country, the Fed disinflated in a particular way in 1989, 90, 91, 92, very successfully. It did it slowly, it did it by cutting rates slowly and inflation came down in one way. It could have done it very differently. When they got worried they could have raised interest rates to 15 per cent and slammed the economy into reverse and got rid of inflation much more quickly. They did not – and that's the choice that you are faced with all the time and if you say there is no short-term trade-off you're implying that the public is unable to form a judgement on the policy decisions you are making. I think there is such a trade-off and that every one of you faces it all the time. The Bundesbank has faced it, the Banque de France has faced it, everybody faces that choice and they make it in a particular way and you have to argue for it. The Bundesbank argued one way, the Banque de France said that it was worth the slightly longer period of recession to maintain stability, that it would pay off in the longer run and that seems to me a very acceptable political argument which sold well at home. And that's the ultimate test. But I don't think that you'll get by by saying there is no such decision to be made because you do make it.

Miguel Mancera

I think that what may help to explain this issue is that in my view the Phillips curve is not symmetrical whether you go north-west, or south-east. In other words if you go north-west along the curve and the country concerned is one that has experienced much inflation and people have learned about price inflations, I think what Governor Hoffmeyer has said is very true. I think that's our experience. The validity of the Phillips curve going north-west, that's more inflation and less unemployment, is very questionable in countries like mine. But not the other way around. If you go south-east, that's less inflation and more unemployment, then the short-term validity of the curve indeed exists in my view. So in that sense perhaps if you try to reduce inflation without causing much unemployment perhaps you have to go gradually. If you go very fast then you indeed cause unemployment and then the short-term validity of the Phillips curve exists.

Professor Jacob Frenkel (Governor, Bank of Israel)

I would like to come first to this question and then to the former one. I think there is a difference between the statement that monetary policy does affect real economic activity in the short run and the question of whether we have a usable Phillips curve. I think that the fact of the matter is that there may be a Phillips curve but I do side with those who indicated earlier that it is really a non-usable curve. Usable in the sense of being able to manipulate the way we go. The fact of the matter is that as much as the academic evidence will show that in the long run there is no trade-off, and Alan Greenspan indicated this morning that indeed as time passes one sees somehow greater consensus on this, in my judgement most politicians that I meet, especially Finance Ministers, were born with a Phillips curve in their head and it's extremely difficult indeed to show that this phenomenon is not prevailing at the present. This brings me to your second issue of once you are in high inflation how do you get down, how do you get the transition. Well the fact is that when you start from very high inflation there is no way down other than a major leap and the question therefore is how do you solidify the support and the constituency for low inflation – and there is not a great constituency, except the bitter experience from the period of inflation. I think that in this regard the public, knowing very well what the hardship of inflation was, is your greatest ally. At least in Israel this is what we have found – the public, much more than the parliament, was our greatest ally.

Let me also address one remark to indexation. The question was why don't we just index and go ahead and his answer was because inflation typically comes with other distortions in the economy. I think that there are three issues. First, there has never yet been a foolproof indexation scheme and therefore indexation does not remove the cost of inflation. Second it's very hard to sustain high inflation at a given level – it will run away. Third the most important difficulty which we confronted in Israel was that since even with indexation the time will come, then stabilisation becomes inevitable, that the institutions that were created by the indexation schemes themselves will prove to be obstacles. It is very difficult to lower inflation in a very rapid way when there are a lot of indexation clauses within the system and therefore the move to a new nominal system is somewhat difficult.

Josef Tosovsky

I would mention only one thing. We experienced high inflation in 1991 but we experienced for many years in the centrally-planned economy very low inflation. I mean low statistically, because it was hidden. For example, the prices of the goods were the same, unchanged for a decade, but the goods were not available in the shops! Or the price was the same, but the costs were going up so the quality was declining. And this suddenly appeared in full transparency after the liberalisation and cutting subsidies and so on. But in such a case it's good to act in a very radical way because people are not used to inflation because they could see the stable price level for many years. This is why we decided to make a radical cut, and I would say that in our society, and in each society as Michael Bruno wrote quite recently, we can give within the political framework independence to some institutions like courts or central banks. In our case it happened that parliament set a priority by giving a mandate, gave independence to the central bank to reduce inflation – and we used it.

So I would advocate in countries in transition to be very tough from the beginning and to act very very quickly.

Donald Brash

My understanding of the Phillips curve is that you get more output effect if expected inflation is different from actual inflation. So that if you are able to convince people that price stability has arrived and you lock in the wage contracts and so on appropriate to price stability and then if you spring a surprise inflation you get the temporary employment and output gains. The New Zealand structure is designed very explicitly to minimise those gains by saying 'yes Mr Finance Minister you can mandate a higher inflation rate but you have to announce that fact very publicly to get it'. The explicit purpose of that is to minimise the output and employment gains you get in the short-term and thereby to reduce the attractiveness of doing it.

Stanley Fischer

I just wanted to add something to my paper which is mainly about industrialised countries with floating exchange rates and does not at all address the issues that confront many developing countries. I thought I should just add that for countries that have high inflation and that are seeking to stabilise quickly there is almost no alternative, well none that I know of, to using a nominal exchange rate anchor so that a monetary policy that fixes the nominal exchange rate in those conditions is almost certainly best. And similarly, as Mr Tosovsky said, for countries where institutions do not yet exist, a nominal anchor of the exchange rate seems to make most sense. In that connection Courtney Blackman raised a question this morning which I think was asking whether you wanted a currency board if you were a small economy with inflationary history and I would think the answer to that is yes and that as you become stable you can get rid of the currency board feature and move on to a fiduciary currency, eventually.

3 Central banking in transition[1]

Alexandre Lamfalussy

Central banking has never been a static business. Throughout its long history it has performed different tasks in different periods; at the same time, developments have been far from identical in the various national central banks. In a long and broad historical perspective, central banking has always been in transition – just like most of our institutions in modern times.

But there is a sense in which the title of my paper is, I believe, justified. The financial systems of the developed world have been involved during the past twenty years or so in an exceptionally fast process of change, the end of which, moreover, is nowhere in sight. The expression 'acceleration of history' surely applies to the contemporary financial scene. The novelty does not lie only in the pace of change; it has also to do with the fact that change is occurring everywhere in the developed world, and even beyond. We now operate within an internationally integrated, innovative, highly competitive global financial system.

It is in this genuinely new environment that, over the last few years, central banking seems to have acquired enhanced importance – perhaps not in relation to its role at the time of the founding fathers, but surely in comparison with the perception of its role between the end of the Second World War and the early 1970s. Monetary policy has come to be regarded as the dominant element of macroeconomic policy, with the explicit mandate to ensure price stability. Central banks have been granted, or are in the process of being granted, a high degree of independence in the conduct of monetary policy. At the same time, they continue to be called upon to assume responsibilities in securing the integrity of the financial and payment systems. Not surprisingly in such circumstances, quite a few prominent central bankers have acquired a high public profile: regular readers of the economic and financial press will notice the weight attached by journalists to the statements and actual or potential decisions of central bankers.

[1] Text of the 1994 Per Jacobbson Lecture, given on 8 June 1994, reproduced by kind permission of Prof. Alexandre Lamfalussy and the Per Jacobbson Foundation.

Being part of their world I should perhaps feel proud of these developments. My feeling of pride is, however, tinged with some unease. Independence goes hand in hand with accountability, yet achieving price stability and safeguarding the stability of the financial and payment systems is not going to be an easy task in the new financial environment. I nevertheless believe that, with careful policies (by which I do not mean only monetary policies) and with some luck, these are achievable objectives. This is the main point I should like to make in this lecture. My remarks will be grouped around four themes: the macroeconomic policy mix and the quest for price stability; financial innovation and the conduct of monetary policy; systemic stability; and the international dimension.

The macroeconomic policy mix and the quest for price stability

The assumption underlying the proposition that central banks should be given the explicit mandate to ensure price stability is that inflation is a monetary phenomenon. This assumption, I think, is basically true, but it needs to be spelled out. The late Henry Wallich, who cannot be suspected of having been complacent either about inflation or about the role of monetary policy in fighting inflation, used to say that inflation is a monetary phenomenon in the same way as shooting people is a ballistic phenomenon. This may have been, indeed was, an after-dinner *bon mot*, but perhaps not only that.

Inflation is surely a monetary phenomenon in the sense that it cannot last without an accommodating increase in the money supply. Conversely, restrictive monetary policy is always able to put an end to the process of inflation. I would go even further. While, in the short run, monetary and fiscal policies have a joint impact on both activity and the price level, in the long run it is money that exerts a determining effect on prices. Finally, when market participants share these views (and I think that in today's world they actually do) their perception of what the central bank is doing, or will be doing, influences their price and wage setting behaviour. This can shorten the time span elapsing between monetary policy decisions and actual price behaviour. In all these senses inflation is indubitably a monetary phenomenon. There are, however, several qualifications, of which I propose to mention only three. All three relate to the fiscal policy environment in which monetary policy operates.

Firstly, take the case where as a result of a deliberate policy decision the fiscal balance suddenly swings into deficit. Even if monetary policy remains on course there will be an increase in aggregate demand, accompanied by a rise in interest rates. If resources are close to full utilisation there will be an acceleration of price increases. Of course, in the end the fiscal policy move will exhaust its expansionary effects and the influence of higher interest rates will prevail. There will be a recession and inflation will decelerate. Conclusion: the stability-oriented monetary policy has, in fact, stopped the process of inflation, but it could not prevent either an initial inflationary slippage or a deeper recession than would have been warranted without the initial fiscal stimulus. Yet it would be strange to hold monetary policy responsible, first, for the acceleration in price increases and, second, for the depth or duration of the recession.

Secondly, a large and persistent public sector deficit is likely to trigger inflation expectations. Market participants may well be aware that what matters for inflation in the long run is the rate of monetary expansion and not the size of the fiscal deficit in itself. But they also have a long memory and remember how often in the past monetary authorities bowed to political pressure and ended up by financing the public sector's borrowing requirement through monetary expansion. By granting central banks independence from governments and by formally prohibiting central bank financing of the public sector (as is laid down in the Maastricht Treaty) we may help to defuse such expectations. But there is a genuine possibility that market participants will still want to insure themselves against the risk of inflation by adding an inflation premium to long-term interest rates. If central banks want to allay the markets' suspicion, they will have to underpin their credibility by demonstrating their determination to fight inflation. The resulting policy mix will not be optimal for economic growth. But through whose fault?

Finally, let me add to these two rather conventional observations a third which tends to be overlooked. The efficient conduct of a non-inflationary monetary policy can also be hampered by the level of government spending even if it is adequately financed out of fiscal and social security revenues. A high level of transfer payments and the correspondingly higher fiscal or wage cost burden weakens the kind of flexibility in price and wage formation which is essential to the smooth working of the transmission mechanism. In such an environment an anti-inflationary monetary policy will run into a zone of, so to speak, 'diminishing returns'. In other words, a given reduction in the rate of inflation will necessitate a higher degree of monetary restraint, and such restraint will affect not only prices but also output, and perhaps output more than prices. Again, the responsibility would seem to rest with fiscal policy.

My main conclusion is that monetary policy does not operate in a fiscal policy vacuum. The proposition that monetary policy can in the end achieve price stability is true. But it does not tell the whole story and the rest of the story is of quite some importance for economic growth. One cannot circumvent the need for an appropriate policy mix. Granting independence to central banks creates the condition for a balanced dialogue between monetary and fiscal authorities, but an optimum policy mix requires two correct decisions, not simply one.

Financial innovation and the conduct of monetary policy

There are two broad channels through which financial innovation can impede the efficient conduct of monetary policy. In both cases the disturbance arises because elements of uncertainty are introduced either in the monetary authorities' decision-making process or in the transmission mechanism, i.e. the way in which a monetary policy decision affects prices and the real economy.

I shall not dwell much on this second type of disturbance, not that I regard it *a priori* as unimportant but because of ignorance. Little research has been undertaken into the possible influence of financial innovation on the transmission mechanism; and the results have been unimpressive. Take the example of just one, simple, almost 'Stone Age' innovation: the use of floating interest rates. Economists long debated as to whether the wider use of floating interest rates accelerates or slows down the monetary policy impact on the economy. In the end they concluded that a lot depends on the asset/liability balance of households and corporations, on the structure of both assets and liabilities and, naturally, on interest rate expectations as well as on the influence of monetary policy on the rates at the long end of the market. Not a very clear conclusion. It is therefore not surprising that the potential influence of far more complicated devices, such as swaps, interest rate futures or options, is still *terra incognita*. More systematic work is now under way among central banks. I hope that in the not-too-distant future someone will be able to report on this research.

I am, however, ready to stick my neck out on the first topic because we know more about it and also because I know it to be of crucial importance. The main point here is that financial innovation seems to have cast doubt on the usability of an intermediate money supply target. The jury is still out on this issue. On the one hand, the erratic behaviour of the demand-for-money function in the English-speaking countries has led their central banks to downgrade whatever M they have used to the more modest position of an information variable or even to switch explicitly to the final target of price stability. The Bundesbank, on the other hand, has remained faithful to its M3 target on the grounds that the relationship between M3 and prices, when measured over the medium term, has in the past been reasonably stable. The Bundesbank also argues that it has never regarded M3 as the only guide for its monetary policy and that in any event the target has been a range rather than a single figure.

Only time will tell us whether the acceleration of financial innovation which is now under way in Germany will lead to the kind of unpredictable behaviour in the demand-for-money function which occurs elsewhere in the developed world. It is also still too early to say whether the recent behaviour of M3 in Germany foreshadows such a development, or whether it is just a passing aberration.

If Germany were to experience the kind of instability prevailing in the Anglo-American world, the Bundesbank would join the ranks of central banks which are already having a difficult time. Money supply targeting has indeed performed a highly useful role in the conduct of monetary policy, and may have been instrumental in enabling central banks to bring inflation under control.

The main advantage of a money supply target is that the 'stance' of monetary policy is thereby clearly defined, which helps the formation of expectations by market participants. When the targeted rate of growth of M remains unchanged, monetary policy can be said to be on an even course. Whilst central banks still have to take decisions on operational interest rate targets, in a broader sense market interest rates are the outcome of changes in nominal GDP, and therefore of the demand for money, against the background of a steady expansion of the targeted M. The implications of this are substantial. Money supply targeting relieves central banks of some of the pressure which might be exerted on them by governments or parliaments. The decision-making body of the central bank is more easily able to avoid the temptation of 'judgemental' adjustments to monetary policy. Finally – and this is perhaps the most important implication – a money supply target, which is relatively well understood by the public at large, gives a clear signal to market participants as to the range of price adjustments and wage settlements that is compatible with a stability-oriented monetary policy. Beyond this range, they would run the risk of pricing themselves out of the market.

If we were to cast aside money supply targeting altogether, the conduct of monetary policy would clearly become more difficult. For this would not simply mean a return to the judgemental type of monetary policy which had prevailed during the twenty-five years following the Second World War. It would mean carrying out a judgemental type of monetary policy in a new set of circumstances, in which central banks are entrusted with the explicit mandate to secure price stability and have no excuse for failure, because as independent entities they do not have to comply with the whims of their political masters.

While all this signals difficult times ahead, I am nevertheless not unduly pessimistic. Let us assume that it will be impossible to find in the future a specific, well-defined M which can be effectively controlled by the central bank and displays at the same time a sufficiently stable relation to prices to make itself usable as a strictly interpreted intermediate target; and by 'strictly interpreted' I mean that any departure from that target would have to be countered within a predetermined time by a change in monetary policy. I note, to begin with, that targeting of this kind has hardly ever been practised. And central banks have always taken other considerations into account. The main point, however, is that it is a long way from this kind of targeting to decision-making based purely on an ad hoc review of current economic circumstances.

There are a great number of intermediate solutions. One which I could see gradually emerging is that an M would be announced as a target, but the target would be interpreted as an obligation for the central bank to publicly explain, if it wishes to disregard a deviation in the growth of M from the targeted path, why it does not intend to take corrective action. A somewhat looser commitment would consist in the designation of more than one M, which would of course give greater leeway for interpretation. Whether the announced M would still deserve in this case to be called a target or would have to be called just an indicator, is a matter of semantics. The substance is the commitment to explain the reasons why the decision is taken to disregard the signal given by a divergence from the target. Such an obligation would mean that the central bank is not free to undertake *ad hoc* decision-making: the obligation to go public is a constraint. It would also imply that, while we may have trouble in finding the proper money supply figure, the role of money (indeed of money supply) in the inflationary process would remain firmly acknowledged. Finally, it would be very much in line with the doctrine of democratic accountability.

Systemic stability

Preserving the stability of the financial system has been a traditional task of central banks – indeed, historically, very often they were entrusted with this task at the same time as with that of issuing banknotes. While today in many countries the micro-prudential function has been given to institutions distinct from central banks, there is little doubt that even in these countries central banks continue to be held responsible, or at least co-responsible, for securing the stability of the financial and payment systems as a whole. In fact, central banks have played a major role in recent years – and a successful one – in preserving systemic stability, even though they have not been the only players. The new financial environment is not going to make this macro-prudential task easier to carry out. Let me list briefly the main reasons for this.

Firstly, there is the globalisation of financial markets, by which I mean not only international financial integration but also the fading of demarcation lines between financial products as well as between different segments of the financial industry. Add to this the steady progress in information systems and communications technology, and the result is the transmission, with lightning speed, of financial impulses originating in one country or in one market segment to other countries or the rest of the industry.

Secondly, all financial asset prices – the recent behaviour of bond markets is a case in point – display a high degree of variability. This means both short-term volatility and large movements apparently disconnected from underlying fundamentals which, of course, are eventually corrected, but often only after a long time. There is no simple explanation for this price behaviour, at least not one that would be obvious to me. Inappropriate policies or uncertainties surrounding policy decisions may in some cases have been responsible for excessive volatility or for misalignments, but I do not share the view of those who argue on a priori grounds that all erratic price movements are caused by policy mismanagement. Anyone who has operational experience in markets is likely to have come across very strange collective market behaviour which it would be hard to explain by reference to public policy blunders. But I do not claim to know why such market behaviour occurs and still less why it occasionally persists sufficiently long to take on the dimensions of a genuine misalignment. The globalisation of markets may be part of the explanation. Some derivatives may have increased volatility. The very large share of trading in total transactions may have played a role. But I suspect that this is not the whole story.

Thirdly, globalisation, in combination with financial innovation (in particular of the off-balance-sheet type), has significantly increased the opaqueness of the financial markets. This lack of transparency has two facets. One is the difficulty of assessing the creditworthiness of individual market participants on the basis of publicly available information. Imaginative financial structures, spreading across borders, add to the confusion. I suppose that everyone would agree that this does not help the smooth functioning of free markets, which requires adequate information. The other is that it has become exceedingly difficult, and in some cases almost impossible, to evaluate the interconnection between market segments either geographically or functionally. Gone are the happy days when central bankers, by looking at the BIS statistics, could assess, for instance, the country risk exposure of individual banking systems. They can still do this as regards on-balance-sheet claims on individual countries, but no information is available on off-balance-sheet links. This should be a matter for concern. For how could anyone, in this situation, make even an educated guess as to whether an initial major shock originating somewhere could develop into a global systemic problem, requiring immediate action?

Fourthly, central banks have to face up to the dual challenge of the relative decline in the role of banks in the financial system and the fading specificity of banking itself. Some thirty years ago banks, i.e. commercial banks, were the privileged market interlocutors of central banks – because banks were monetary institutions and stood at the centre of the financial system by supplying liquidity, distributing credit and managing the payment flows. By safeguarding the stability of the banking system as a whole, central banks could be reasonably sure that they were protecting, indirectly but effectively, the stability of the financial system as a whole. This still remains true to some extent, but that extent is diminishing.

Finally, we have witnessed a spectacular surge in the volume and average size of financial transactions, resulting in an unprecedented rise in the volume of payments. Intra-day settlement exposures, and with them liquidity and credit risk, have reached a new dimension, putting a premium on the efficiency and soundness of clearing and settlement arrangements.

I should not like to sound alarmist. All this does not necessarily add up to a basically unstable worldwide financial system in the sense that the likelihood of a financial crisis has demonstrably increased. Many of the features of our new system have two facets: while they may be a source of instability, they often contain built-in shock absorbers. Financial innovation has put at the disposal of market participants powerful hedging devices which enable the wise ones to protect themselves precisely against asset price instability. Globalisation itself has increased the depth and liquidity of markets. Securitisation has led to a wider distribution of risks throughout the system. Market efficiency, in a number of senses of this term, has increased. The point, however, is that in the unlikely event of a financial crisis the crisis could take on genuinely global dimensions. Central bankers will have to bear this in mind. In fact, I think they do.

What sort of preventive measures can they take?

The most important one is the conduct of a monetary policy directed, in a medium-term perspective, towards the attainment of price stability. The lack of a credible commitment to that objective could seriously aggravate the risk of market overreaction and therefore that of systemic instability. Or, to put it more bluntly, the best way to avoid asset market 'bubbles' is to stick to a cautious monetary policy. This may not eliminate all misalignments nor significantly reduce short-term volatility, but it would at least mean that monetary policy ceased to be a contributory factor to both types of disturbance. The fact that central banks are now recognising this is good news.

A more difficult task is to ensure that market participants attach full credibility to the central bankers' commitment to ensure price stability. The difficulty arises in connection with the downgrading (and, a fortiori, the phasing out) of intermediate targets. To the extent that the setting of a money supply target no longer provides an unambiguous indicator of the resolve of central banks to pursue a stability-oriented monetary policy, central banks will have to find other ways and means of conveying their message to the markets. This will necessarily entail better and more detailed information on the economic analysis forming the basis for monetary policy decisions. The initiative of the Bank of England to publish its quarterly reviews of the outlook for inflation is surely a step in the right direction.

As a second measure, central banks should do everything in their power to make the financial system more transparent. More complete and comparable disclosure by all market participants – and not only by banks – should be a priority objective. This will require co-operation not only between regulatory agencies but also with the accounting profession and with market participants themselves. We also have to improve the statistical information on market linkages – even if this turns out to be a tedious and costly exercise.

Thirdly, central banks should contribute to enhancing the safety of both domestic and international payment, settlement and clearing systems, since these are the transmission mechanisms which could amplify crisis manifestations and turn a local or sectoral crisis into a genuinely global one. The 'Report on Interbank Netting Schemes', to which I contributed in my previous capacity, was a beginning, but not more than that.

Last but not least, a controversial question. Should central banks be directly involved in supervision? Those who give a negative answer to this question base it on considerations relating to moral hazard: there is the risk that supervision may arouse destabilising expectations of support from the central bank. This, indeed, is a powerful argument. But so is the opposite, which says that it is difficult to draw a practical distinction between systemic and micro-prudential responsibilities. The prevention of systemic risk can hardly be effective without intimate knowledge of the participants in the market and the linkages between them. Given the kind of financial world in which we operate, the second argument would seem to me to outweigh the first. But it is perhaps not inconceivable for a central bank to acquire this intimate knowledge without a 'line responsibility' in supervision.

The international dimension

'Globalisation' means that cross-border capital flows, be they actual or potential, have created a very high degree of interdependence between countries. This has a bearing on all three topics I have discussed so far.

The pursuit of price stability through monetary policy can be helped, or hindered, by exchange rate developments. By saying this I clearly dissociate myself from the orthodox monetarist view according to which freely floating exchange rates would secure individual countries full freedom to pursue their domestic policy objectives, and, first and foremost, the objective of price stability. I have two quarrels with this assumption. Firstly, because it implies that monetary policies directed towards domestic stability will also stabilise the exchange rate. Whilst I would fully agree that diverging stances of policies have a destabilising effect on exchange rates, stable monetary policies by themselves will not secure exchange rate stability. Fiscal policies also matter, either because of their possible influence on inflation expectations, or by creating current-account imbalances and therefore a shift in financial portfolios. Admittedly, monetary policy will always be able to offset the undesirable impact of fiscal policy on exchange rates, but at a cost, i.e. by resorting to changes in short-term interest rates which could be unjustified in terms of domestic balance. Secondly, exchange rate changes, whatever their origin, will affect domestic prices, and will therefore have an impact on price expectations.

The practical conclusion is two-fold. In their quest for price stability, central banks cannot disregard exchange rate developments. But nor are they able to influence exchange rates, in the case of a fiscal imbalance, solely through monetary policy means, or through exchange market intervention, without running the risk of deviating from the pursuit of their domestic policy objective. The need for an appropriate policy mix is even more important in an open economy than in a closed one. However, the problem is compounded by the fact that in a world of rigid fiscal policies international agreement on a correct configuration of policy mixes will be even harder to come by than agreement on the appropriate domestic policy mix.

The international dimension has implications for the use of money supply targeting as well. On the level of definition and measurement there is the intellectually not very exciting but practically quite tricky question of including or not in the targeted M such items as non-residents' holdings of assets denominated in domestic currency or residents' holdings of foreign currency assets. Then there is the associated question of how to deal with assets held in offshore centres. More fundamentally, the combination of changes in interest rate differentials with shifting exchange rate expectations may induce portfolio movements which can significantly destabilise the behaviour of the targeted M. Finally, the large-scale use of derivatives certainly has a major impact on the treasury and liquidity management of corporations and is therefore likely to have an impact on the behaviour of M. I do not claim to know what this impact is going to be.

By definition, systemic stability cannot be preserved without active co-operation between central banks. Measures directed towards fuller disclosure and better statistical information, improvements in the payment, settlement and clearing systems and, naturally, effective banking supervision – all these preventive measures must be taken within the framework of international co-operation. Central banks are keenly aware of the need for such co-operation, and have demonstrated this in the work carried out under the aegis of the BIS.

They have also displayed a clear willingness to fight manifestations of financial crisis by the concerted provision of liquidity to markets whenever they feared that a generalised retrenchment by market participants could lead to a liquidity crisis. With hindsight, some of us might think today that the liquidity creation in the autumn of 1987 was excessive. Maybe. There might in any case have been market developments preventing a tailspin of prices leading to a general financial crisis. Possibly there were such market forces at work. But despite a feeling of dissatisfaction that our intellectual curiosity was not satisfied, I believe it was a good thing that the central banks did not wait to see how effective the built-in brakes of the market mechanism would have been if they had been left to operate on their own.

The story of 1987, just like the more specific fire-fighting activities which were undertaken on several occasions within a co-operative framework, shows that we can count on international co-operation between central banks to preserve systemic stability. What these experiences have also demonstrated is that, to be successful, this co-operation has to embrace on a very wide basis all central banks whose financial systems are part and parcel of our global system. There may be scope for somewhat tighter regional co-operation in this area, but the interconnections between the regions are such that at the end of the day systemic stability can be secured only by co-operative endeavours on a worldwide scale.

When it comes, however, to the pursuit of price stability (the other major task of central banking), which also requires co-operation, I would put the emphasis in the reverse order. Admittedly, situations may arise in which co-operation on, say, the G-10 level is called for with a view to co-ordinating monetary policies and trying to influence the behaviour of exchange rates. But any systematic co-ordination of monetary policies requires an institutional framework which is just not available on a worldwide basis, and I doubt that it could become available in the foreseeable future. A firm institutional framework is needed for ensuring that the endeavours of individual central banks to reach price stability are helped, rather than hindered, by the policies of neighbouring central banks. It is also needed for securing a minimum of fiscal policy co-ordination and for attaining exchange rate stability. Such a framework does exist in Europe: prospectively a very strong one, if and when we reach Stage Three; a more flexible one, within which we operate at present. It was not my remit today to talk to you about the work of the EMI, nor about the prospects for EMU, but I do not want to conclude without reminding you that the European Union does exist, and without conveying to you my conviction that this is a firm framework within which central banking policies (still in the plural today) will evolve in the right direction.

4 The philosophy of central banking: a panel discussion

Lord Richardson

You might think that, after having heard the many distinguished contributions today, we have already got a great deal about the philosophy of central banking – but we are going to have some more. I've been looking at the definition of 'philosophy'. In its original and wider sense according to the Oxford English Dictionary, it is the love, study and pursuit of wisdom – that's how it starts and that seems to me, although perhaps not sufficient for the occasion, a thought or a sentiment which should be allowed to float over the whole discussion, because the central bank which in fact is missing that particular quality is likely, however professionally equipped, not to get very far. But when you add the word 'of' after 'philosophy' – it's the study of the general principles of a particular branch of knowledge, experience or activity. That's a more general description and I'm going to ask Paul Volcker if under that rubric he will say something.

Paul Volcker

We are closely approaching the end of a long and productive programme, at a time when fresh thought is probably not possible and certainly not welcome. Yet, those who arranged this programme have obviously felt it appropriate that a group of retired central bankers, whose principal qualification may be that their combined ages are approaching that of the Bank of England, pronounce the benediction on all the useful and provocative discussion of today.

What is bound to strike anyone of us here is the degree of unanimity on the basic issues: the role of central banking, its purposes, and its proper organisation. I am also sensitive to the fact that this programme consisted largely of central bankers talking to each other. While rightly celebrating this great institutional occasion, we also take the risk of reinforcing our tribal prejudices.

However, it cannot be either parochialism or mere sense of occasion on a

300-year anniversary that accounts for the growing and substantial support from, of all places, the academic community (so well documented today by Stan Fischer) of the central ideas of central bankers. That consensus encompasses the concept that price stability (by some definition or another and they do vary) is to be treasured and enshrined as the prime policy priority; that that objective is inextricably part of a broader concern about the basic stability of the financial and economic system; and, finally, that to improve prospects for achieving the objectives there is need to insulate the monetary authority in its operational decision-making from partisan or transient political pressure – to be, in the jargon 'independent'.

What is still more remarkable and significant than the growing degree of academic support is a broader political consensus – reflected in the decisions of one country after another – supportive of greater priority for stability as an objective of policy and of a greater degree of central bank independence to help achieve it.

Needless to say, I share and rejoice in that consensus. Yet, I can't refrain from some nagging concerns – concerns growing out of my own experience.

The intellectual climate was very different when I entered the world of central banking. Then, academic, and certainly political, thinking tended to denigrate the significance of monetary policy as an operational matter and the sanctity of price stability as an objective. To the extent monetary policy was significant, it was seen as one of several policy instruments that needed to be brought to bear in a co-ordinated way in the interests, above all, of full employment. In economic terms, it was, dare I say it, full-blooded Keynesianism. In political terms, co-ordination plainly meant co-ordination by responsible (and responsive) political officials, not something that might emerge from the vagaries of negotiation with a truly independent central bank.

What we are seeing now is reaction to the perceived (and real) failures of that approach – just as the earlier doctrine was a reaction to the Great Depression. We have learned the hard way that passive tolerance of a little inflation often led to more, and in the long run that was not good for unemployment and it was positively destructive of stability and growth.

At the same time, in absorbing that lesson, we cannot be oblivious to the fact that, after a decade or more of increasing emphasis on price stability, a truly satisfactory measure of success has still eluded us. Inflation is, happily, much more restrained, and a few countries can reasonably claim they are reaching stability in prices. But unemployment has been intolerably high for some time in a number of important countries, and the growth trend slower. The rest of matching progress toward stability with sustained growth at a satisfactory pace has not yet been met.

Charles Goodhart made the analytic point earlier today that if price stability were the only objective of monetary policy, we would do well without having central banks, which, after all, have been given the magic power of creating money – and by corollary the possibility of too much money. I am not about to support the idea of abandoning central banks, but a certain degree of modesty seems to me appropriate, and I would conclude that it is not monetary policy alone that will seize the holy grail at acceptable cost. Instead, I join Alexandre Lamfalussy in emphasising that fiscal policy, labour markets, social policies, and other difficult questions inextricably tied up with the political process remain relevant. To put the point starkly, whatever the formal independence of a central bank, it's a broad mix of policies, ideally a suitable co-ordination of policy, that will count.

What a central bank naturally brings to that mix – what in my view it must bring – is emphasis on the crucial importance of stability, stability in the more specific sense of price stability and in the more general sense of the orderly performance and continuity of financial markets. If it is to be effective in that role, I am convinced that, beyond all the technical argument about how to conduct policy, the central bank will have to be able to defend and sustain its policies and approaches in the public – and inevitably the political – arena.

The central bank is inherently and properly a conservative creature, in the sense of the 'cautious skeptic' that Charles Goodhart described and welcomed this morning.

The lasting qualities – the philosophy if you will – that seem to me the hallmark of central banking are a triumvirate:

> Continuity and all that implies for experience and nurturing a long view;
>
> Competence and all that implies for a high degree of professionalism and careful deliberation and communication; and
>
> Integrity and all that implies for accountability and simple honesty.

Now you may think that I am lost in misty abstractions, and my list is trite. But those are qualities, I would submit, that are regrettably, in short supply in governments today.

That, I would also suggest, is a main reason why central banks have attained their present prestige and influence whatever the particular institutional relationships.

The corollary is that maintenance of that present exalted position is dependent on maintaining these qualities, qualities that have distinguished central banks, sad as that may be, from much of the rest of government. Obviously, those qualities that central banks bring to the table are not the whole of human experience. We need initiative, we need entrepreneurship, we need experimentation – all that is critical to economic progress, critical to the success of countries. But, none the less, there is a counterside to those qualities associated with instability and change.

I think of those critical responsibilities of the central bank emphasised by the Prime Minister this morning.

Defence of the currency

Defence of the nations' credit

Defence of its own position in the political firmament.

Think, too, of the enormous emphasis in modern analysis on an old thought – the relevance of expectations and importance of credibility to the success of policy.

Think, too, of the crucial importance at times of co-operation among central banks internationally at the point of crisis – crisis for a particular country, or a more systemic financial crisis.

Think of the added confidence typically extended by private banks and private markets when a nation's central bank, by name and deed, is attached to a national promissory note or to a national policy.

Continuity, competence, integrity, these are and should be the true and lasting hallmarks of central banking – qualities that in the end lie behind its influence in the political process and the respect in which it is held by the public, its credibility and its success in achieving stability at home and in constructive co-operation with its counter-parts abroad.

To the extent those qualities are lost by one institution or another, the whole community of central banking is weakened, perhaps imperceptibly in particular instances, but weakened none the less. And, at the end of the day, it is only those qualities that can justify responsible sustained independence in a democratic society.

Continuity, competence, integrity – those are the kinds of thing we learn at mother's knee – maybe in simpler words of fewer syllables. But it strikes me appropriate to emphasise them once again at this celebration of the mother of all central banks.

Keynes once spoke of the influence of the theories of defunct economists on living politicians. Let me acknowledge the enormous influence, conscious or not, on every participant in this room of the traditions and sense of responsibility nourished by the Bank of England over these past 300 years.

Let me say Eddie – as your institution enters is fourth century, you have a particularly heavy responsibility. All those 150 or more central banks listed by Charles Goodhart are in some sense the Bank's children. We all share pride in our institutional mother, and look to her and to you for continued leadership.

Karl-Otto Pohl

Under the given circumstances I think I should limit myself to some very brief remarks, in particular since I do not want to repeat what was said this morning and this afternoon in very brilliant exposes. My first remark is that one thing amazed me a little bit and it was the fact that nobody, if I have listened carefully enough, nobody has mentioned the statute for a European Central Bank in this context. This statute was drafted by governors of central banks, most of them – I would guess – are represented here. I want to mention just two of them: Jacques de Larosiere and myself (I was the Chairman of the Group). In my opinion this statute for a European Central Bank could be a model for a modern central bank system due to the fact that it already incorporates all the elements which have been mentioned this morning. It is an excellent document – if I may say this being one of its authors. Almost by definition it is an excellent paper and it states very clearly the independence of the central bank and all of its procedures. The appointment of Governors, their tenure etc., are explicitly specified in this document. The European Central Bank has a clear mandate, something which the Bundesbank lacks by the way. The Bundesbank law fails to clearly define the mandate of the Bundesbank. The law foresees that the Bundesbank should safeguard the currency and this is rather vague. According to the law the Bundesbank is also in charge of preserving the external value of the currency. I will come to this a little later. There can often be a contradiction between these two targets. The statute of the European Central Bank clearly states that its first and foremost priority should be to defend price stability. It is also very clearly provided that the central bank is not allowed to finance the deficit in the public sector.

The only issue where we could not reach a consensus, especially not with our governments, was the role of exchange rates. And so we found a compromise which is very realistic because in most countries it is the government which controls the exchange rate regime ie whether a fixed exchange rate system, a floating system or something in between is maintained. Ultimately – and I am tempted to say unfortunately – the governments have to be blamed for this because they were not willing to give this responsibility to the central bank, to this independent institution. But after long discussions we established that the central bank is responsible for exchange rate policy ie interventions in the market and that this exchange rate policy should not contradict the main objective namely defending price stability – which it very often does in practice and that's my second remark.

I was a little puzzled by the fact that nobody elaborated on the conflict of having to defend fixed exchange rates versus maintaining price stability – as mentioned this morning by Alan Greenspan and by Stanley Fischer. And I think that the reason for this is very simple. For most countries this does not really constitute a problem. Pegging your currency for a bigger currency is a normal procedure. But it is a huge problem, and I am tempted to say an overwhelming problem for a country like Germany, because Germany is a country with a currency which is widely used as a reserve currency as you all know. Over the past twenty years or even longer, this contradiction between the obligation – the old Bretton Woods system and later in the EMS – to defend fixed exchange rates and the main objective in the eyes of the Bundesbank to maintain price stability has always been the main preoccupation of the Bundesbank. The efforts to defend exchange rate stability, or fixed exchange rates, led to enormous inflows of liquidity and money which could be neutralised only to a certain extent, and have been in fact inflationary. There is clear evidence for that in the history of the past twenty years; inflation in Germany was often at least accelerated by inflows of huge amounts of capital into the country. This has therefore been a big problem in the old Bretton Woods system. It was one of the reasons why the Bretton Woods system collapsed in '73 – the occasion when Paul Volcker and myself met for the first time. There were many other reasons but one reason was that the Bundesbank did not want to intervene and buy dollars indefinitely.

As far as the dollar is concerned many other efforts have been made in the meantime. And whenever I met Paul Volcker he was on the other side – e.g. in 1979 in Hamburg, and you were President of the Fed in New York at that time, and then you went back home and did the only thing which helped – instead of intervening you raised interest rates. We had other experiences at that time, for instance the Louvre Accord. All these efforts failed. From the German point of view at least, we have never been able to combine price stability and exchange rate stability. I am only talking about exchange rate stability *vis-à-vis* the dollar.

Then we got the EMS and we had the same problem. At the beginning of the EMS we had about twelve crises – which in the end always led to realignment, at the last moment and under terrible pressure and only because the Bundesbank threatened to stop intervening. Starting two years ago the collapse of the European Exchange Rate Mechanism came about. One of the reasons was of course the fact that the Bundesbank, I think it is fair to say – and my friend Helmut Schlesinger is here so I am very careful with what I am saying, but I was not in charge at that time – he was in charge – but I think it is fair to say that one of the reasons why the exchange rate system finally collapsed was that the Bundesbank was, for very good reasons which I do not criticise, on the contrary, not ready to subordinate exchange rate stability or fixed exchange rates to the main objective namely defending price stability. This I think it is fair to say.

Well, one could argue and say that by definition there will be no exchange rates in a complete European monetary union and therefore this problem will not exist any more provided that this European monetary union will pursue a monetary policy which included floating against other reserve currencies, in particular the dollar of course. Nevertheless, I think that even in such a world of big monetary blocks without exchange rates we would still have the problem of let's say, shock waves which could emerge in one region and could move to the other region as we have seen very recently in Europe with high interest rates in America. It was not possible to isolate Europe from this effect, in spite of the fact that the situation in Europe differs in many respects from the situation in the United States. And I think that this kind of transmission of shock waves is likely to become the major problem for central banks in the future. Thanks to the talks and discussions about the monetary union people in Europe have understood to a certain extent that price stability is a very valuable asset. But besides that we will get other problems. If you have achieved price stability, and we have more or less achieved it for the time being, this does not mean that central banks have no other jobs to do and very different they may be. In countries in transition like the Czech Republic it may be to contribute to political stability, but in the western or the capitalist developed country I think that a central bank has to think more and more about the financial stability in a wider sense not only price stability but stability in the financial system.

Well, I have no suggestions in that context and I am very reluctant to follow those who ask for further regulations. I fully agree with Alan Greenspan that we should leave it in the first place to the markets. Nevertheless it is becoming more and more of a problem and I think almost certain that in future the volatility in financial markets is increasing due to globalisation and the disappearance of capital controls etc., and more often will we see crises. I do not want to go into this but derivatives, which dominated the IMC Meeting the other day, will be a big issue for central banks to discuss.

Whether price stability will be maintained, whether we can declare victory, remains to be seen I think. I am not so sure about that – I would add a little oil to that because it is a very new general agreement as Paul has said, and I could mention a number of examples where it has not always been the case. What we have to aim for, I think, is to develop a culture – the culture of stability. In Europe I am convinced that we have made enormous progress in that respect and one very important contribution to this progress was I think the work of the central bank governors in the context of the preparation of the Maastricht Treaty and the monetary union in Europe.

Jacques de Larosiere

Let me start perhaps with a personal memory.

When I became Governor of the Banque de France seven years ago, I asked to be heard by the Commission des Finances of the French National Assembly. This was at the time a most unusual procedure. I expressed on that occasion, in a rather robust manner, my philosophy of central banking. I stated in short;

that the objective of monetary policy as I saw it was price stability; that this objective had to be pursued steadily in a medium-term framework. Continuity and the fight against inflation was indeed of the essence;

that there was in my opinion a long-term relationship between money growth and price performance;

and that therefore, in addition to the exchange rate stability provided by the European Exchange Rate Mechanism the Banque de France should adhere to a publicly set of intermediate monetary objective.

This statement was underpinned by a strong plea for the notion that inflation was inimical to growth and employment. I don't know whether my statement convinced the MPs of the Commission des Finances. At that time they had little exposure to monetary policy which was still legally determined by the Government. But I was on the record and my views had been made public. Nothing I said on that occasion, if my memory is correct, contradicts Professor Fischer's and Professor Goodhart's remarkable papers.

At the same time I also made a resolution to myself to leave the central bank if I was not in a position to lead a monetary policy which would be consistent with the above principles. This I did not state publicly but confided to each of the four Ministers of Finance with whom I worked. This precaution was helpful to me given the state of high dependency which legally characterised relations between the Banque de France and the government at that time.

A few thoughts derived from my experiences.

Firstly, policy mix. The central banker is often seen as a guardian of price stability. But he has only one key to that temple. And there are other doors such as fiscal policy and public wage policies that are not under his guard. Therefore the correct policy mix is fundamental not so much to the right stance of monetary policy but to the success of non-inflationary growth.

Secondly, the more a central bank is vulnerable to short-term political influences, the more important it is to be able to rely on externally explicable and publicly stated medium-term indicators; exchange rate stability, quantitative monetary objectives. Discretionary policy is always a source of temptation for a government that has legal control of monetary policy. It is also a source of uncertainty for the markets and for the public. Better in that case an imperfect set of rules than pure discretion.

I am well aware that money is becoming an elusive concept and that money aggregates are affected by a host of shifts in portfolio preferences that are amplified by the globalisation of financial markets; I am also conscious that in some cases a multiplicity of objectives may lead to some possible contradictions or over-determination of monetary policy. But the adherence to the exchange rate anchor provided by the Deutschemark has been in the case of my country, a positive factor in the attainment of price stability. I also believe that an intermediate monetary objective had the great advantage of giving flesh to and illustrating the stance of monetary policy. Until Germany's reunification and the subsequent alteration of the German policy mix, this system worked well. The two objectives reinforced themselves mutually. Of course, the over-riding one was the exchange rate which provided the element of discipline that we needed after so many years of chronic inflation. Things, of course, became more difficult when the German anchor drifted because of the policy mix, and when the transmission mechanism compounded recessionary conditions in France. A difficult period 1992/93 was experienced then with massive speculation on exchange markets. But exchange rate stability eventually prevailed essentially because of the strong competitive position that the French franc had gained through years of monetary discipline and disinflation. With some flexibility the system has regained its place again.

Thirdly, preventing systemic risks has become one of the major concerns of any central banker. I strongly believe that the central bank should be in charge of bank supervision and that they should be heavily involved in the conception and monitoring of payment systems. Given the globalisation of financial markets, solutions to systemic risks must involve domestic surveillance and international co-operation. The amount of collaboration that has been developed over the years among central bankers in these fields is, in my view, one of the most important aspects of recent monetary policy developments. The fact that any central banker can rely on the understanding and the assistance of his colleagues is one of the greatest elements of reassurance that I have enjoyed in my years at the Banque de France. And I should like to thank my former colleagues for their unstinting help.

Lastly, as we have all said greater independence has become a common trend in the art of modern central banking. I am happy to have with my European colleagues and foremost with Karl-Otto Pohl to establish a model of independent central banking for the European Union. I believe that the recent changes in the Statutes of the Banque de France would have been practically impossible to achieve without a clear concept and a strong political will on European monetary union; but independence implies accountability. Accountability to parliament, to the executive branch and to the electorate. In the event, the electorate has to be convinced of the advantages of monetary stability. It is the public at large and the markets that are eventually the constituency that will support the continuation of anti-inflationary policies. This is all the more important to communicating clearly the right messages. Say what you do, and do what you say, is the key to credibility.

Lord Richardson

After so many distinguished contributions little remains to be said and little time remains to say it. Given all that has gone before, I will confine myself to some very brief remarks this afternoon, and in keeping with our theme of 'philosophy', I shall attempt to touch only on some very broad principles that seem to be relevant both to the theories we have discussed today and to the practice of central banking.

At the outset I would like to confess myself, as so many of my former colleagues have, as a total anti-inflationist. Even before price stability was put in the mandate of central banks in the form in which it is now often seen, this was of course the purpose and the centre of our activities and the core of our struggles. Obviously, as Jacques de Larosiere has just said, the key is getting electorates into the same frame of mind and making them understand the distortions, the difficulties, the costs of an inflationary system.

Sometimes I think that it is almost possible to go back, far more simply than anybody has today, to the original notion. Central banks are there, and are concerned with money – and what is money about? Money is what has been devised as a measure of value, a medium of exchange and a store of value; and these are the concepts which are actually at the very heart of the money exchange system, which itself is at the root of the functioning of modern society. And yet from the moment that inflation begins to touch money, you have an inefficiency in each of these basic functions and the distortions begin and spread from there and accumulate upon themselves.

As people talk about inflation, and as the discussion becomes more and more sophisticated, as the lists of the costs are made and quantification is attempted, the argument becomes almost in a sense too well-rehearsed. Take for example the expression 'social costs'. We need to see what it means in fact. We are talking about something which includes: broken lives, physical distress, despair. This kind of concreteness, as it seems to me, helps to account for the fervour with which we who have been through the central banking mill feel about inflation. And it is this connection that we need to communicate to others.

Then again, economic costs. Think about the effects on the shortening of time horizons by the effect of inflation. If you are going to discount at the kind of rates of interest you have with high and variable inflation, the value in anything is constantly brought back – and it is brought back to a point where it is impossible to talk about the long-term. We complain about everybody's short-term reactions but we are, between ourselves and govern-ments, the agents of a good deal of that. The essence of central bank thinking, as you have heard again and again today, is looking through time, through the medium-term, into the long-term. It seems to me that we should try to make more vivid how much of the present bias towards the short-term arises from inflation and inflationary expectations. The malign consequences are often only too clear, in any time frame.

I am also anxious about the talk of indexation, because it implies accommodation rather than correction. Of course if you have bad inflation, you are bound to think about the pace of correction. What is the timescale over which you can get it down – because it would be silly, and fly in the face of political reality, to try to bring it to a juddering halt. But that is a very different thing from being in a situation at the other end of the game, with inflation subdued, when, under pressure to get faster growth, you start playing with the inflationary standards which you have set. Of course we shall never come to a nirvana. It has been said: 'the price of freedom is eternal vigilance'. The price of non-inflationary, sustainable growth is precisely that.

It is right that central banks should focus, as has this symposium, on their primary objective of monetary stability, but if one thinks back to one's own life as a central banker it was in that other wing, as we now call it, of financial stability that a great part of one's time was taken up. In particular, the business of dealing with crises, – in my own case a domestic crisis in late 1973 and early 1974, followed by the Herstatt Case in June 1974, a case which immediately called into being the best kind of inter-central bank co-operation. The first agreements on the respective responsibilities for international supervision were reached at the Governor's meeting in Basle in July 1974, and certainly could only have been done with that kind of speed by central banks. The international banking crisis of 1982 which started with Hungary and then quickly passed on to Latin American coun-tries, also involved an enormous amount of time and effort.

These were not, I think, simply some kind of side play. The system, domestically in the first case I mentioned, internationally in the second, was at risk, and if in fact those crises had not been managed, the consequences would have of course been widespread on the monetary side, and more generally economically. So there is something there. It rests on co-operation between central banks which is one of the marked features of this particular profession – marked for example by the presence of all of you here today. It involves complete trust in one's colleagues and a knowledge that to the extent that they can they will work together when common problems arise. And it has something also to do too with the way central bankers treat each other. There is a tradition – and it is a natural way of behaving – that you listen with respect when a case is made to you. It comes partly out of the fact that you know that if a colleague is saying things which are awkward for you, then he is saying them because he cannot avoid saying them, and that of course is the basis for some kind of accommodation between both. I think that this co-operation, trust and mutual respect are distinguishing marks and part of the philosophy of central banking.

Another feature is the unique way in which central banks, by reason of what they have to accomplish, are themselves extraordinarily interesting places; unique in the extent to which practical and theoretical knowledge come together and interact. You have the opportunity of action on the one hand, concern with markets, operating in markets; and at the same time you have to ensure the most rigorous intellectual standards not only in relation to the theoretical underpinning, but also in relation to the expanding professional knowledge involved in practical execution. This duality is a most attractive and stimulating feature of the life.

Mr Justice Holmes, that towering figure in American law, reflecting on the essentially learned subject of the law, observed in relation to its practice that 'the life of the law has not been logic; it has been experience'. If the phrase has a resonance as adapted to central banking – as for me it does – we are back to another aspect of its philosophy.

Courtney Blackman

Here all day we have been extremely concerned about monetary stability and currency stability and still the IMF visitors to our developing countries promote the tremendous instability in those currencies, it never occurs to them to carry out a real currency reform and prevent the effects of currency instability from feeding back into the system. So they will come to a country and say 'leave it to the market' and the currency drops from, say $10 to US$1, to $100 to $10 and they are very happy and comfortable about it and I wonder why this is so.

Jacques de Larosiere

I think the IMF is very conscious of the importance of stability. Some of the most successful recent examples of currency reform and stabilisation have been underpinned by IMF programmes, so I think we should not generalise. Now what I can say is that you can't rush to monetary reform just because it's [nice]. You have to be sure that you've got the underlying conditions right and maybe that in some of the cases you are alluding to the Fund felt that the underlying conditions for the full success of a monetary reform were not there and I'm not going to enter into the details of those preconditions but they are very important. And it's very dangerous to embark on a monetary reform if you do it wrong and if it slips away. We've had some examples recently and that can discredit the whole notion of monetary reform. So you have to be very cautious.

Roque B. Fernandez
(Governor, Banco Central de la Republica Argentina)

Argentina is a case where we undertook a monetary reform and a programme with the IMF. But I must say that we started with a regular standby agreement and after following the steps of accomplishing with targets that were set for the standby then we approached the IMF with the second programme. In that second part we introduced the monetary reform. We were very successful in terms of producing a very important reduction in the rate of inflation. So you can see that in the case of Argentina the rate of inflation in 1989 was 200 per cent per month and then, after fundamental reforms, privatisation and then currency reform, we are at the present time with an annual rate of inflation of 3.4 per cent. This is something is closely related to the previous presentation by Professor Stanley Fischer where he mentioned the problem of the Phillips curve trade off and he was very careful to emphasise that he was talking about developed nations. The case where you are having run away inflation, probably you have to forget about everything including the Phillips curve and go straight ahead to the fundamental reform of the country because we have introduced this monetary reform and the country during the last three years at the rate in the order of 7–8 per cent, so we are not paying any costs in terms of unemployment or recession due to the stabilisation effort. Of course we have unemployment but that is as a consequence of the reform of the public sector. We had that unemployment before, but it was in the form of public sector employees that were employed doing nothing.

So I wouldn't say that the IMF would try to fix a policy of avoiding monetary reform, probably I am in agreement with Mr Larosiere in the sense that the IMF would look at the fundamental problems in the economy. If the situation is there that you can fix exchange rates or introduce monetary reform the IMF would not object to that particular policy. At least that is the experience that we have in Argentina and I think that that is the point of the question.

Richard Erb

I sort of agree with that point. I think also that it is important to remember what Alexandre Lamfalussy said last night and that is the critical role that fiscal policy plays in achieving not only ultimately price stability but also exchange rate stability and also for underpinning the monetary policy. So the two have to go together. A devaluation alone without the monetary reform and without the fiscal adjustment is just a recipe for another big round of inflation.

Dr Chris Stals   (Governor, South African Reserve Bank)

I think like the previous two speakers I don't really want to put a question to the Panel, perhaps make a small contribution to this discussion on the philosophy of central banking and that is the philosophy of central banking from a country that as you all know underwent major social and political reforms – a country in a different kind of transition perhaps than some of the other people talked about today.

I just want to make three basic philosophical statements about the problems of central banking in a country in transition as we experienced. Number one because of the special political setup in our country for about three years the government in transition was not a very effective government. It was extremely difficult to take important decisions. Politicians were really much involved and very busy with the debate and discussion on political changes in the country and therefore had very little time for the central bank and for monetary policy. Without going into the details de facto in terms of the statute the South African Reserve Bank is a very independent institution but never in its seventy-three years of existence had it experienced the kind of independence we had for the last three years. For more than two years I never met with the Cabinet, I never made any presentation to the Cabinet. Sometimes for periods of two months I did not even have any discussions with a Minister of Finance. Now if I can say anything about this experience it certainly tempered me. It can get very lonely! I did at one stage contact a Minister of Finance and I said this independence must really not be applied in isolation. As a governor of a central bank you sometimes need a politician to share the burden with you so I think that the lesson that we have learned is that cooperation, consultation, regular discussion between the governor of a central bank and a Minister of Finance is very important.

Number two is what did we do in the situation of independence. Well we used the opportunity. It was a wonderful period. We realised it would not last for ever but on the institutional arrangements in the country the basic philosophy was reduce the powers of the central bank to make monetary policy more effective and to make the central bank more influential. Reduce the powers of the central bank to increase the power of the central bank and again without burdening you with the details what I mean if I say 'reduce the powers' of the central bank. Number one thinking of the future, thinking ahead. We withdrew all kinds of central bank participation in schemes like export financing, temporary finance for the agriculture sector to meet seasonal demands, we closed the banking accounts for regional governments, for local governments. Indeed we converted the branches of the bank into note distributing centres, closed some of the branches, reduced the total staff of the bank by 16 per cent and now as a very clearly defined small little central bank that we feel can be more effective.

Last point on monetary policy in this period. Well, again our philosophy was we talk about intermediate objectives, eventual or final objectives – our guiding principles through this period was reduce the total assets of the central bank and the foreign assets of the central bank will increase. Reduce the total assets of the central bank and inflation will come down. Now apart from some recent disturbances and so on this worked extremely well. Today the total assets of the central bank is about 2 billion rand less in nominal terms than what it was five years ago and the rate of inflation now is 7 per cent compared to the 21 per cent of five years ago. But these are three basic philosophies that I think we learned during this period.

Dr Chakravarty Rangajaran   (Governor, Reserve Bank of India)

We're all agreed that price stability is very important and all central bankers should concentrate on it but in the context in which some of the developing countries are placed where supply shocks can be very sudden because of the failure of the monsoon and so on and so forth, the achievement of price stability purely through monetary measures alone can become very difficult. While we take on the responsibility for agreeing price stability I think we should be somewhat modest in being able to achieve that with all this. I'm not saying that price stability should not be the objective of the central bank and I think that is the main concern but I think we should also understand at least in these countries the factors that might be operating outside the monetary sphere which may have a bearing upon the price level – so this is one comment.

But the other thing I wanted to raise, we talked about the independence of the central bank and I think that in almost all countries we are moving towards that. Even in our own country we are now putting a limit on the extent of borrowing that the central government can make from the Reserve Bank of India and we intend to phase it out in a matter of three years this kind of borrowing from the Reserve Bank.

But one issue that I would like to raise is that we also think that banking supervision should be part of the central banking function. There are very valid reasons why it should be part of the central bank and how it helps the pursuit of monetary policy. But the moment you bring banking supervision also under the functions of the central bank I feel the ability to secure independence is somewhat reduced. In the light of the recent events in our own country when there were very serious problems in the banking system, the Parliamentary Committee went into it and we had a basket of bricks thrown on our heads and we're trying to get out of it. Therefore I feel that the responsibility of banking supervision being carried on to the central bank might make it more difficult in my opinion to gain the kind of independence that we are talking about.

Paul Volcker

Well I have a very short word. I think there is ambivalence here. I am very strongly in favour of the central bank having important supervisory responsibilities and don't think it can do its job without it and I guess Jacques de Larosiere made that comment earlier. At the same time it can involve the central bank in very difficult political issues at times of trivial importance to central banking and I haven't found any way to get rid of the trivial issues and maintain control over the important issues. The trivial issues from a central banking point of view are not trivial from a political point of view or from the point of view of particular institutions that may be affected and sometimes they devote a lot of time and sometimes they do get you into a political question. I think you just have to absorb the punishment in the interest of the greater good and it comes down to the importance of conducting those responsibilities too as independently as you can. I am not a great disbeliever in what is obviously a complicated situation in the US where you have several supervisors – at least some of this complication can be pushed off on others and it minimises the degree. You have to get into all the details if you maintain control and leverage over the main decision making points about the structure of the banking system and the liquidity of the banking system and the capital of the banking system – that's an ideal situation that you can't obviously easily reach but to the extent you can do that, you can do it.

Karl-Otto Pohl

Well, only a brief remark in that context. You know in Germany the central bank is not responsible for banking supervision for very good reasons I think. I myself was almost more on the side of Jacques and Paul, we discussed that over and over again. For convenience sake it is better to have everything concentrated in the central bank which gives the central bank simply more power. But one has to admit that a conflict of interest could easily arise. So I am a little undecided.

I think in practice if there is a crisis in the banking system, a big bankruptcy or something like this people always come to the central bank as a last resort for help and even in Germany the central bank is of course involved. They do not have ultimate responsibility but they are involved. They perhaps provide liquidity etc and they do the field service for the government agency in this area.

So what I want to emphasise is what Jacques said on the Basle Committee on Banking Supervision which became very well known as the Cooke Committee first and we agreed on the capital adequacy rules, tier 1, tier 2 etc and then later Gerry Corrigan was the Chairman. That committee I think has done an incredibly good job and that is a very strong case to put banking supervision also in the hands of the central bank because they have a very good framework as you have said. I think in many respects their framework is better than the one of the government. On top of that central banks have money, which is also sometimes quite useful.

I want to give my view on the independence issue which was mentioned here very often. As you know the Bundesbank is very independent and it may be the only central bank which is not at all accountable neither to the government nor to parliament. The members of the Central Bank Council of the Bundesbank, the decision making body of the Bundesbank, are appointed by the Federal Government or the State Government. But after having been appointed for a tenure of eight years, they are completely independent. I myself have doubts whether that is a good system. I must say I am very much in favour of course of an independent central bank. And there are many many reasons why a European central bank in particular has to be absolutely independent. It is inconceivable that four, five, six or more countries participating in such a system can ever agree on a monetary policy. So you have to have an independent, efficient organisation to take decisions. That is for sure but I think along with this independence goes a lot of power, political power, and that needs accountability. The statute of the European Central Bank stipulates that this institution should be accountable to the European Parliament and to the Council of Ministers. I think the best way is maybe the American way. Our colleague Greenspan has to testify in front of Congress, in Europe we would say to Parliamentary Commissions. This gives the central bank governor also the opportunity to explain the policy of the central bank, something which is very very important for the independence of the central bank. The central bank needs to explain its policy in order for people to understand the reasons why the central bank has taken action in a certain way, e.g. why they have decided on higher interest rates etc.

In Germany, I have to say we have always been in a very happy situation because people like the Bundesbank much more than the government or any other institution in their country and they are absolutely right of course. Jacques Delors once said not all Germans believe in God but all Germans believe in the Bundesbank. So this was a rather comfortable position. Nevertheless we, that is myself, my successors and our predecessors have always tried to explain the policy of the Bundesbank to the public-admittedly in a rather unstructured way and not always under full control of what was received at the other end of the spectrum. So I myself am very much in favour of a clear accountability of a central bank and a clear definition of the independence of the central bank which should be limited to monetary policy. I am saying this because in the case of Germany and other countries as well, there can be situations where the government takes a political decision which the central bank has to respect. In the case of Germany the most important political decision which the Bundesbank at the beginning did not like very much was the offering of monetary union to another country. I am saying another country, it was the German Democratic Republic. It was an independent country with a seat in the United Nations and the government decided to offer them a monetary union. Well finally that has contributed to the process of German reunification which in the beginning was not very secure and could not be taken for granted. The Bundesbank, therefore, was a little nervous about this aspect but we made it very clear that this was a political decision which had to be respected by the central bank. The same would go for let's say a decision to establish economic and monetary union in Europe which would by definition mean the end of the independence of the existence of the Bundesbank as a monetary policy agent. The President of the Bundesbank would just be a member of a Council and have one vote amongst others. But it would be a political decision which has to be taken by Parliament, Government and not by a central bank. The central bank can decide on interest rates, money supply, liquidity etc., maybe even on banking supervision but not on political issues. The members of the central bank would be overburdened by this and this would lead to a kind of parliament and not a central bank.

Lord Richardson

Well I'm afraid those words, in which Karl-Otto vouchsafed to all of us the sort of vision of what we can look forward to as central bank heaven, where all the inhabitants of the country believe in a central bank rather than anything else, must be the concluding note for this afternoon. I'd like to thank all my colleagues at the table here for their contributions.

Remarks by Prime Minister John Major on the opening of the symposium

I am delighted to be able to welcome you all to London for this very special occasion. Eddie George has told me that a gathering of central bankers of this kind is almost unprecedented. All the great names in central banking are here, with distinguished current and former central bank governors from right around the world. I would not really be surprised if Montagu Norman were to make a guest appearance. It is, I am told, the largest gathering of central bankers ever to meet completely free of the restraining influence of finance ministers.

'Completely free' – as a former finance minister, I view that with some concern. The old Punch joke: 'See what they're doing. And tell them they mustn't't', springs unbidden to my mind.

But that would scarcely be fair. Because you, in turn, might reflect that, this morning, there are 110 finance ministers, scattered around the world, completely free of the restraining influence of their central bank governors. Only heaven above knows what they are up to.

This meeting, as you know, is to celebrate the tercentenary of the Bank of England. The Bank is not quite the oldest central bank in the world – that honour is held by the Swedish Riksbank. But even by Brian Lara's standards, 300 not out is a good innings.

Those of you who have no idea who Brian Lara is should seek out a colleague from a cricket-playing country. Explaining the rules of cricket is an excellent test for high-powered brains. It should take up your lunch break quite comfortably.

Before it had reached its first century, the Bank of England was being described by one of my predecessors as a part of the constitution, 'from long habit and usage of many years'. Both as a private bank before 1946, and as a public corporation afterwards, it has played a major part in guiding the financial affairs of the nation.

The Bank's founding Charter, given by King William and Queen Mary in 1694, speaks of the 'publick good and benefit of our people' as the purpose for which the Bank was 'chiefly designed and intended'. To begin with, the 'publick good and benefit' generally meant the provision of finance to government. But over time, the maintenance of stability – monetary and financial – has come increasingly to predominate.

It was in the Bank of England that the modern concept of a central bank evolved – according to some views, as early as 1802. But most notably, it came about in the latter part of the nineteenth century, under the influence of Walter Bagehot, the distinguished political commentator and sometime editor of *The Economist*. Today I am glad to see another former editor of *The Economist* helping guide the Bank's destiny. Whether this makes *The Economist* part of either the 'dignified' or the 'efficient' parts of our constitution I must leave to others to judge! Perhaps it can be both.

It was from the Bank of England that the impetus for co-operation between central banks came – most notably during the 1920s and 1930s. Many central banks were encouraged into existence by the Bank's example or active help. Then, after the Second World War, the Bank provided technical assistance on a large scale to central banks in the Commonwealth. Now, with its Centre for Central Banking Studies, the Bank is again helping the development of central banks in the former centrally-planned economies, notably the former Soviet Union.

So it is fitting that so many central bankers should gather here to mark the Bank of England's birthday. I know that you have many distinguished contributors to listen to today.

I don't doubt that once this sole representative of the world of politics has left the room, the question of central bank relations with government will arise. All I would say is that this is far from being a new question. It was in 1797, at the time of the suspension of the convertibility of bank notes into gold, that the dramatist Sheridan rose in the House of Commons to give the Bank the image that has survived to this day. 'There is', he said, 'an elderly lady in the City, of great credit and long standing, who has unfortunately fallen into bad company.'

The 'bad company' was one of my revered predecessors, William Pitt the Younger, already struggling with the costs of defending Britain's freedom during the Napoleonic wars. It was from this speech that the picture of the 'Old Lady of Threadneedle Street', jealously guarding the nation's credit, has come down to us, to the joy of generations of political cartoonists.

The relationship between central bank and government is one in which some tensions are bound to arise, whether or not the Bank has some measure of independence in the discharge of its functions. What central bankers are for is to work for stable money – for a sound financial system – in whatever constitutional and political framework they find themselves. That the Bank has done, with distinction, for many years, as I know it will continue to do under Eddie George. I know from personal experience, first as Chancellor and latterly in my present job, how strongly he feels about the control of inflation, and I share that feeling with him.

The Government now has an explicit low-inflation target. I know the Bank is firmly committed to this. The Governor has a responsibility to advise the Chancellor how to achieve his objective – and the published minutes of their meetings now reveal to the public, after a few weeks, the advice that has been given.

I have never been in any doubt about the benefits of price stability. Since I first became Chancellor, I have put the battle against inflation at the top of my economic priorities. It is a matter of great personal satisfaction to me that in my three and a half years in No. 10, the underlying rate of inflation in Britain has fallen from over 9 per cent to under 2½ per cent. Our inflation has been below the European Union average since 1991. Today it is at its lowest level for a generation.

I believe that honest money, which holds its value in terms of what it will buy, is a social good in itself. Indeed the alternative, high and variable inflation, is a form of theft practised by government on the people. Unexpected and unpredictable variations in inflation involve an arbitrary redistribution of wealth from savers to borrowers – a brutal transfer from the weak to the strong.

Inflation is like a hard drug; you may feel good for a while, but in time its evil effects become apparent. That is why I have been so determined to bring it under control.

Inflation, and the expectation of inflation, also create a climate in which business is discouraged from investing. Money ceases to perform its economic purpose. In the long run, therefore, inflation causes us to have less output, less employment, less wealth.

Today's low inflation gives us the firmest basis for sustainable growth and job creation that we have known since the 1960s. We are already seeing its results. We are leading Europe's recovery: our industrial production has risen 5.6 per cent over the past year, the fastest growth in the European Union. And our unemployment has fallen much earlier in this recovery than in the previous cycle – down already by nearly 300,000 from its peak. This week's message from OECD – that deregulated, flexible labour markets mean more jobs – is being clearly demonstrated in Britain.

I know, of course, that I don't need to persuade this audience – much of what I have said amounts to the articles of faith of the central banking community. The question I would leave with you is how that consensus for stability – which underlies the papers prepared for today's symposium – can be reinforced and deepened, so that it is shared by all: Not only by those who take monetary decisions, but by those who are affected by them.

I wish you well in your deliberations today.